READING FOR REAL

D0077479

Alex Crittenden
Minneapolis Community and Technical College

PEARSON
Prentice Hall

Upper Saddle River, New Jersey 07458

Library of Congress Cataloging-in-Publication Data

Crittenden, Alex.
  Reading for real / Alex Crittenden.
    p. cm.
  Includes index.
  ISBN-13: 978-0-13-150034-1
  ISBN-10: 0-13-150034-1
  1. Reading (Higher education) 2. Study skills. I. Title.
  LB2395.3.C75 2008
  428.4071'1—dc22

2007014455

Editorial Director: Leah Jewell
Editor in Chief: Craig Campanella
Acquisitions Editor: Vivian Garcia
Editorial Assistant: Deborah Doyle
Operations Specialist: Benjamin Smith
Production Liaison: Shelly Kupperman
Production Editor: Shelley Creager/
  Aptara, Inc.
Director of Marketing: Brandy Dawson
Marketing Manager: Lindsey Prudhomme
Interior Designer: Aptara, Inc.
Cover Designer: Bruce Kenselaar
Permissions Specialist: Michael Farmer

Director, Image Resource Center:
  Melinda Patelli
Manager, Rights and Permissions:
  Zina Arabia
Manager, Visual Research: Beth Brenzel
Manager, Cover Visual Research
  and Permissions: Karen Sanatar
Image Permission Coordinator:
  Kathy Gavilanes
Composition/Full-Service Project
  Management: Aptara, Inc.
Cover Photo: Photos.com

This book was set in 10.5/12 Goudy by Aptara, Inc. and was printed and bound by Edwards Brothers. The cover was printed by Phoenix Color Corp.

Copyright © 2008 by Pearson Education, Inc., Upper Saddle River, New Jersey 07458.

Pearson Prentice Hall. All rights reserved. Printed in the United States of America. This publication is protected by Copyright and permission should be obtained from the publisher prior to any prohibited reproduction, storage in a retrieval system, or transmission in any form or by any means, electronic, mechanical, photocopying, recording, or likewise. For information regarding permission(s), write to: Rights and Permissions Department.

Pearson Prentice Hall™ is a trademark of Pearson Education, Inc.
Pearson® is a registered trademark of Pearson plc
Prentice Hall® is a registered trademark of Pearson Education, Inc.

Pearson Education LTD.
Pearson Education Singapore, Pte. Ltd
Pearson Education, Canada, Ltd
Pearson Education–Japan
Pearson Education Australia PTY, Limited

Pearson Education North Asia Ltd
Pearson Educación de Mexico, S.A. de C.V.
Pearson Education Malaysia, Pte. Ltd
Pearson Education, Upper Saddle River, NJ

10 9 8 7 6 5 4 3 2 1

ISBN-13: 978-0-13-150034-1

ISBN-10:   0-13-150034-1

I would like to dedicate this
book to my husband, David Crittenden.

CONTENTS

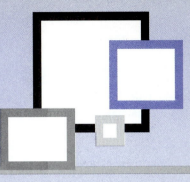

CHAPTER 2   Seeing the Organization of Ideas: Part One   35

CHAPTER 3   Seeing the Organization of Ideas: Part Two   67

CHAPTER 4 Interpreting Charts and Graphs   99

CHAPTER 7   Reading to Write Research Papers   205

CHAPTER 8 Memorizing Ideas from Textbooks 253

CHAPTER 9   Preparing to Take Standardized Reading Tests 293

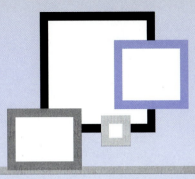

PREFACE

To the Student

Challenges of College Reading

You may wonder what you would learn in a college reading course. After all, by this point, you have been reading fluently for years. However, college reading poses some special challenges even for skilled readers.

VOCABULARY. College readings use a wider vocabulary and a more formal style than any other kind of text. Here is a sample paragraph from a psychology text:

> Younger children can think logically, but only in terms of concrete things. Adolescents can understand and manipulate abstract concepts. With this ability, adolescents can formulate general rules about the world and then test them against the available facts. Thought is no longer dependent on direct experience. Adolescents can—if they wish—speculate about alternative possibilities, reason in hypothetical terms, and understand analogies and metaphors.
>
> (From Charles G. Morris, *Psychology: An Introduction*, 8th ed., p. 394.)

To understand the author's point, you need to be able to translate the ideas into plainer speech in your mind. Look at the word "concrete." Here, it does not mean "a mix of cement, sand, and water." It means "existing in reality, not just as an idea." The word "abstract" means the opposite—something that exists only as an idea and isn't tied to reality. The author is saying in this paragraph that teens are more capable than young children of thinking about ideas they haven't personally experienced.

Your vocabulary will expand rapidly as you are exposed to new words. It is also helpful to systematically memorize the meanings of words that are used over and over in college texts. However, as your vocabulary is growing, you need some strategies to make sense of unknown words in passages like this one. The first chapter in this book explains some techniques you can use to troubleshoot unfamiliar words.

SEEING THE ORGANIZATION OF IDEAS IN TEXTS. College reading assignments can be quite heavy. Typically, you would be asked to read about forty pages per week for each class. If you took three classes, that works out to 120 pages of reading per week. Students often lose concentration and feel overwhelmed by the volume of the reading. The second chapter of this book covers how to notice and mark the flow of topics in a text so that you maintain a sense of focus and control.

PARAGRAPH STRUCTURE. Authors typically have a number of important points that they put forward and support in a paragraph or a longer section. You need to be able to spot these key ideas, notice the supporting detail used to elaborate them, and see how one idea relates to another. The third chapter of this book discusses how to find central points and supporting detail.

INTERPRETING CHARTS AND GRAPHS. College texts often include charts, graphs, and tables that you are expected to study. Many key ideas are actually communicated through charts and graphs rather than by the text itself. Additionally, you would often be expected to combine information across several charts and graphs. The fourth chapter of your book explains how to interpret the point of a chart or graph, how to identify data of special importance, and how to combine information from several graphic sources.

READING OPINIONS: TONE, PURPOSE, BIAS, AND INFERENCES. Every field has its controversial topics. For example, in chemical dependency counseling, there is a long-standing debate over whether alcoholism is a disease or whether it should be regarded as a failure of self-discipline. In reading about controversial topics, students should be able to tell when an author leans to one side or the other of an issue, to outline the points a writer makes in support of an opinion, and to infer the point of stories or research studies used to back up a point. The fifth chapter of this book will help you develop these skills.

EVALUATING EVIDENCE. When reading opinions on controversial issues, students are expected to examine whether the points made in support of a position are justified by factual evidence. The sixth chapter of this book covers how to evaluate the strength of the evidence for an opinion.

READING TO WRITE RESEARCH PAPERS. Many college courses require that students write research papers. To prepare to write a paper, you must narrow your topic and develop a research question, collect articles and books on your subject, mark relevant information in the readings you collected, and organize the ideas from across many sources. These reading tasks must be done properly before you begin to write if the paper is to be any good. Managing the preparatory reading for a research paper is the focus of Chapter 7.

MEMORIZING IDEAS FROM TEXTBOOKS. Material from certain kinds of readings—especially textbooks—must be memorized and retained over a long period of time. Final exams are often cumulative (covering the whole semester). The eighth chapter of this book explains how to create useful review notes and memorize ideas in a systematic way.

PREPARING TO TAKE STANDARDIZED READING TESTS. Many college students have to take a standardized reading test of great importance at least once during their college careers. For instance, to start your college program, you may need to earn an acceptable score on a reading skills exam. Chapter 9 of this book covers the common types of questions on these standardized reading tests and explains how to use the skills you have developed to earn a good score.

How College Reading Is Taught

Teaching college reading is a lot like coaching a sport. For example, take basketball. Coaches will strengthen team members on the subskills that go into being a good player: having them run laps to strengthen their endurance, practicing blocking techniques, and running drills of various sorts. Then the coach will organize practice games so that players can put all these skills together in a low-pressure way. Finally, the team members test their skills in a real game.

College reading skills are taught in much the same way. Your instructor will strengthen your skills in areas like troubleshooting difficult vocabulary, finding the point of a paragraph, or identifying the central idea of a chart or graph. Typically, you practice these skills in shorter, easier practice sets before being asked to tackle full-length college texts.

The way that college reading is taught and learned makes it difficult for students to catch up if they miss too much class. A reading skills textbook can provide a description of the skills to learn followed by some practice passages. However, students learn by being coached by their instructors as they move first through practice sets and then to texts used in college courses.

How You Will Be Tested

College reading instructors use a number of methods to judge how well you understand and can respond to what you read. For example, you may be asked to do any of the following:

- answer comprehension questions
- write a summary or personal reflection on a reading

- describe what you read to others, either in a small group or a formal presentation
- apply information from readings to solve a practical problem or make a decision

These tests of understanding should be familiar, because they are used in all kinds of classes. However, many college reading instructors will also collect samples of your reading notes to score. Your instructors may give you a difficult text and ask you to create some kind of notes—an outline, a concept map, or annotations on the text. Reading notes are collected because they show a lot about how well students understand a text and whether they can apply reading techniques taught in class. This type of assessment—scoring note samples—is unique to reading courses.

SCORING THE QUALITY OF NOTES. Reading notes are often scored using a rubric. A rubric is something like a scorecard with categories that assign points to different parts of a person's performance. Rubrics are useful in scoring when there is more than one thing to look for in assessing overall quality.

For example, suppose that an instructor wants to know if a student can figure out what unfamiliar words mean. Students may be given a passage containing words that would likely be unknown to them and told to mark in the meanings of any words they don't understand using a dictionary. Here is a sample paragraph from a longer passage that one student turned in. Look at the underlined words and the meanings that the student wrote in above them.

The Difference Between Majors and Careers

Students often confuse choosing a major with selecting a career. Knowing

little of the job market, many college students assume that if they earn a

(to obtain with effort)
degree in a major they find interesting, they will <u>secure</u> enjoyable work

(thinking)
upon graduation. However, <u>the assumption</u> that an <u>intellectually</u>

(interesting)   (that matches)
<u>stimulating</u> major will automatically lead to a job <u>compatible with</u> one's

(containing something that is incorrect)
personality is <u>erroneous</u>.

In scoring the quality of the student's markings, suppose the instructor is looking for two things that were emphasized during the lessons. First, many words have more than one meaning. The student should have selected the dictionary meaning that is correct for the way the word is used here. Second, the definitions should have been simplified and shortened, if possible. Copying long, formal definitions straight from the dictionary shows a lack of real understanding. Here is a rubric that the instructor might use to score each student's work:

ACCURACY OF ANNOTATED DEFINITIONS (5 points possible)				
1	2	3	4	5
all or almost all wrong	more than half wrong	over half right	almost all right	all correct

SIMPLIFYING DEFINITIONS (5 points possible)				
1	2	3	4	5
all copied straight from dictionary	almost all copied from dictionary	over half simplified	almost all simplified	all simplified

Notice that in the previous student sample, the penciled-in definitions of the words the student didn't know were correct. This student would get 5 points in the "Accuracy of Annotated Definitions" section. However, two of the definitions were copied straight from the dictionary with no attempt to simplify them. For instance, a simpler way to express the meaning of "erroneous" would be to say it means "wrong." The student would get 3 points in the "Simplifying Definitions" section. The student's total score would be 8 out of 10, or 80 percent.

Trying Out New Reading Techniques

One of the greatest difficulties students have in developing college reading skills is that it requires them to change their habits. People can be quite stubborn about clinging to familiar ways of doing things even if they don't work all that well. College reading instructors will teach you some ways of working with readings that are quite different from what you may be used to. You need to keep an open mind and try out the new techniques. You will be surprised at how big an impact some of the new methods will have on your ability to understand difficult readings.

To illustrate this point, let me tell you about an experience I had learning to draw. I have always wanted to be able to sketch portraits of people in my family. However, whenever I tried to draw them, I was disappointed at the results, and concluded that I had no artistic talent. Nevertheless, I signed up for a drawing

FIGURE 1 ■ *Sketch of author's grandmother.*

course. The first day, the art instructor talked to us about how we go about drawing what we see. He said our drawings would be much better if we followed a certain procedure used by professional artists. The drawing instructor gave us a list of steps to follow to produce better drawings. He said he would circulate through the room to give us feedback as we tried creating portraits using this method. Inwardly, I didn't have much confidence that following his method would make any difference, but I was willing to give it a try. To my astonishment, it worked. Following the steps he described, I made this drawing of my grandmother from an old family photo (Figure 1). It turned out much better than anything I had been able to do before.

After that experience, I changed my way of thinking about drawing. I used to believe that if people had "artistic gifts," then they would produce great drawings. Now I think that making good drawings is a matter of knowing the steps to take. The same is true of being able to read difficult college texts. If you follow certain steps in working with college texts, you will be able to figure out unfamiliar words, see the important points, analyze the quality of evidence, and remember the ideas over a long period of time. Don't worry about being "not naturally good at reading." Try the new strategies your instructor teaches you with an open mind, and you will see that being a competent college reader is mostly a matter of using the right techniques and practicing them until they feel natural and familiar.

To the Instructor

Content and Organization

The first half of the book covers reading skills that are foundational for any college reading task in order to achieve basic understanding:

Chapter 1: Managing unfamiliar words

Chapter 2: Identifying topics and academic thought patterns

Chapter 3: Finding main ideas, supporting details, and thesis statements

Chapter 4: Interpreting charts and graphs

The two middle chapters of the book focus on skills related to critical reading. The lessons in these chapters are tied to two common college reading tasks: (1) outlining an author's argument, noting strong and weak points, and (2) selecting high-quality source materials for one's own writing. The section on inferences centers on helping students understand the implications of research study findings, because studies are the primary type of justification offered for opinions in college texts.

Chapter 5: Tone, purpose, bias, and inferences

Chapter 6: Facts versus opinions and logical flaws

The next chapters address the reading skills that underpin two reading tasks that new college students find especially difficult: reading in preparation to write a research paper and memorizing ideas from textbooks.

Chapter 7: Reading to write: narrowing the topic and combining ideas across texts

Chapter 8: Textbook chapters: deciding what to memorize and creating useful notes

The final chapter of the book focuses on teaching students how to use the skills learned in previous chapters to perform well on standardized reading tests. Many students must pass a state-mandated exam before being allowed to enter their college programs or be awarded their diplomas. The last chapter serves as a review of skills taught throughout the book and gives students opportunities to practice answering questions similar to those found on standardized tests.

Chapter 9: Preparing to take standardized reading tests

At the end of the book, there is also a full-length sample textbook chapter taken from a family social science textbook. It is included so that students can practice their skills on a reading that is typical in length of the material they will be given in college.

Special Features

FULL-LENGTH PRACTICE TESTS.   Each chapter ends with a full-length practice test that asks students to first prepare a reading several pages in length using the skills they learned. Next, the students use the reading they prepared to answer test questions.

PERSONAL FINANCE READINGS.   The readings used for the test found at the end of each chapter are focused on personal finance issues of special interest to students, such as economic issues in career decision making, establishing good credit, balancing work and school, and avoiding graduating with excessive debt.

READINGS DRAWN FROM POPULAR CAREER PROGRAMS. The longer practice readings found in each lesson are selected from textbooks used in career programs that are popular with many students, such as nursing, marketing, law enforcement, counseling, and child development.

APPLICATION OF IDEAS FROM READINGS TO REAL-LIFE SITUATIONS. To encourage students to apply ideas they learn through reading, many passages are followed with a "Reading for Real Life" box that presents them with a practical application of the information they read. For instance, after students read a passage about the similarities and differences between migraine, tension, and cluster headaches, they are asked to diagnose the type of headache that a patient is suffering from, given the symptoms he reports.

Acknowledgments

I would like to thank the many people who contributed ideas, inspiration, and support for this book. I am especially grateful for the thoughtful advice of the reviewers: Joel L. Bailey III, Mountain Empire Community College; Christina Chapman, Lewis and Clark Community College; Linda Edwards, Chattanooga State Technical Community College; John Grether, St. Cloud State University; Sue Hightower, Tallahassee Community College; Danica Hubbard, College of DuPage; Joyce Kevetos, Palm Beach Community College; Debbie Naquin, Northern Virginia Community College; Rick Richards, St. Petersburg College; Melinda Schomaker, Georgia Perimeter College; Heather Severson, Pima Community College; Deborah O'Brien-Smith, Nassau Community College; Sharon M. Taylor, Western Wyoming Community College; Margaret Triplett, Central Oregon Community College; and Lynda Wolverton, Polk Community College. I hope they will be pleased to see how many of their suggestions I incorporated into the book.

The editorial staff at Prentice Hall was wonderful. Editor in Chief, Craig Campanella, provided invaluable guidance in shaping the manuscript, and Deborah Doyle, Editorial Assistant, was particularly helpful in selecting photos for the cover. I am also grateful for the work of Shelley Creager in coordinating the design and production of the book. Sheryl Rose took immense care in polishing the manuscript and checking it for errors. Michael Farmer did a fine job of obtaining permissions.

Finally, I am deeply appreciative of the encouragement of my colleagues in the Reading and Study Skills department at Minneapolis Community and Technical College: Kim Zernechel, Sherry Dilley, Peggy MacRae, Ann Ludlow, Melissa O'Connor, Nancy Patton, Rita Schweiss, and Sara Clowes.

CHAPTER 1

Managing Unfamiliar Words

OVERVIEW

LEARNING GOALS

After completing this chapter, you should be able to

- Make a skillful guess as to the meaning of a word using its context.
- Annotate the meaning of an unfamiliar word.
- Use context to identify the relevant dictionary definition of a word.
- Simplify and shorten the dictionary definition when annotating words.
- Put the ideas of an annotated text in your own words without changing the meaning.

One of the things you will notice when you open your college textbooks is that the pages are filled with words you may never have seen before. You may wonder why the authors of college textbooks use so many unusual words. Are their ideas so advanced that they can't be communicated in plain English? If not, why don't they express their ideas more simply? ∎

Why There Are So Many Unfamiliar Words in College Texts

Perceived Need for Formal Tone. Although the culture of college can be relaxed—for example, professors may wear blue jeans and allow you to call them by their first names—it is one in which respect for ideas is often expressed through the use of formal language. If the everyday word for an idea sounds too plain, is slightly vulgar, or is too much like slang, it may be upgraded to a fancier equivalent. For example, even if textbook authors describe a person who flatters his boss to get promotions as a "kiss up" when speaking with friends, in print such a person might be referred to as a "sycophant" or a "toady."

A slangy, overly informal style is inappropriate for college texts. However, some college textbook authors get carried away and use unnecessarily complex phrasing for simple ideas. My mother used to call this wrapping a 5¢ thought in $25 language. The humor columnist Dave Barry makes fun of such excesses in his "advice" to would-be professors:

> For example, suppose that you have observed that children cry when they fall down. You should write: "Methodological observation of the sociometrical behavior tendencies of prematurated isolates indicates that a causal relationship exists between downward tropism and lachrymatory, or 'crying,' behavior forms."

You will occasionally have to read textbooks or articles written in this style. Translate the ideas back into plain English for your notes.

Avoidance of Repetition. Sometimes writers employ a fancier term for an ordinary idea to avoid using the same word over and over. For instance, suppose that a specialist in animal behavior is writing on the issue of whether or not primates such as chimpanzees and gorillas are capable of lying. For the first draft, he writes this:

> Lucy, one of the first chimpanzees to be taught to communicate through sign language, was known to lie occasionally. When Dr. Fouts, her trainer, arrived for a visit one day, he noticed a pile of excrement on the floor of her living space. When he asked Lucy what it was, she signed "dirty, dirty." When Fouts asked Lucy whose "dirty, dirty" it was, she signed "Sue" (Fouts's colleague). When Fouts expressed doubt that Sue would do such a thing, Lucy accused Fouts himself! In another instance, Koko, a gorilla who communicated through sign language, was caught eating a crayon when she was supposed to be drawing a picture (Figure 1.1). When her trainer asked her "You're not eating that, are you?", Koko signed "Lip" and quickly took the crayon out of her mouth and moved it across her lips as if applying lipstick. Apparently primates are as capable of lying as humans are.

FIGURE 1.1 ■ *Koko.*
Source: Courtesy of Ron Cohn/The Gorilla Foundation/Koko.org.

After reading over what he has written, the writer is dissatisfied with using "lie" and "lying" within the same paragraph. To eliminate the repetition, he revises his last sentence to read as follows:

Apparently, primates are as capable of mendacity as humans are.

"Mendacity" means the same thing as "lying." Substituting "mendacity" for "lying" solves the problem of using the same word too many times.

Precision. Another reason textbook writers select uncommon words is to express their meanings more exactly. For example, suppose a professor of education is writing about how the schooling of young children should be reformed. She wants to criticize the practice of forcing everyone to learn at the same pace. This is what she writes:

The American educational system is a procrustean bed in which those quick to learn are held back while those needing more time are left behind.

The term "procrustean bed" comes from Greek mythology. Procrustes offered travelers a bed for the night. He required that all guests fit his bed exactly. If a guest was too tall, Procrustes cut off his feet so they wouldn't poke over the end of the bed. If the guest was too short, Procrustes stretched him until he was the precise length of the bed. Using the phrase "procrustean bed" allows the professor to communicate how damaging she thinks a one-size-fits-all educational policy is to young children.

Technical Vocabulary. All fields of study have a discipline-specific vocabulary that enables people with that training to communicate with efficiency and precision. For example, students in crime investigation programs are given readings describing how to handle fire scenes in which arson is suspected. When several small fires merge to become one enormous fire, this is referred to as a "conflagration." Part of understanding a discipline is learning its vocabulary.

The Impact of Too Many Unknown Words on Understanding

Some of the texts you must read for college courses will be full of words you don't know. If a text has only a word or two on each page that you don't understand, you will most likely be able to follow the author's line of thought without much trouble. However, if many more words are unfamiliar, your understanding will fall apart.

Level at Which Understanding Breaks Down. Suppose that you understand seven out of every ten words in a text. After you finished reading it, would you understand about 70 percent of the ideas? If you knew eight out of ten words, would you have a grasp of 80 percent of the concepts?

No. Studies have shown that in order to make sense of a text, readers must understand the meanings of more than 95 percent of the words. If more than five words in every hundred are unfamiliar, readers have a great deal of difficulty in understanding the meaning of the passage at all. They can identify the topic but miss many of the points being made about it. The following excerpt from a medical technology textbook is missing fewer than 10 percent of the words. See if you can figure out what the author meant to say.

Since the 1950s, glass eyes, also called ocular prostheses, are no longer made of glass. Today, they are _____ of a medical-grade acrylic plastic (Figure 1.2). The acrylic is more _____ than glass, and enhances _____, where that is feasible.

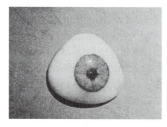

FIGURE 1.2 ■ *Ocular prosthesis made of acrylic plastic.*
Source: Courtesy of Alex Crittenden.

Notice that is possible to gather that glass eyes are now made of plastic, but it is impossible to figure out what the advantages of plastic are over glass. Here is the original passage with the missing words reinserted. The words that were removed are not common in everyday conversation.

> Since the 1950s, glass eyes, also called ocular prostheses, are no longer made of glass. Today, they are <u>fabricated</u> of a medical-grade acrylic plastic. The acrylic is more <u>resilient</u> than glass, and enhances <u>motility</u>, where that is feasible.

Readers who don't know the meanings of "fabricated," "resilient," and "motility" experience them as blanks, and consequently, their understanding of the passage will be shallow.

Annotating the Meanings of Unfamiliar Words

As a short-term solution, you need to annotate the meanings of unfamiliar words you find in your texts. Here is the text on ocular prostheses with the unknown words annotated:

> Since the 1950s, glass eyes, also called ocular prostheses, are no longer
> (made)
> made of glass. Today, they are <u>fabricated</u> of a medical-grade acrylic plastic.
> (flexible)   (movement)
> The acrylic is more <u>resilient</u> than glass, and enhances <u>motility</u>, where that
> is feasible.

Writing in the meanings of unfamiliar words makes it possible to read through a text with understanding. Much of the time you will need to look up words in your dictionary in order to annotate word meanings, but it is also possible to figure out word meanings from context in some cases. After you have annotated the unfamiliar words, you should read back through the passage to make sure you understand the author's meaning.

Figuring Out Word Meanings from Context

In a surprisingly large number of cases, you can make a correct guess as to the meaning of a word from its context. *Context* refers to the words around the unknown term. The words around the unfamiliar expression give clues to the meaning that is required in that spot. For example, suppose you are preparing for a career in law enforcement, and you are reading a textbook chapter on the investigation of arson cases. See if you can guess the meaning of the underlined word.

> The U.S. has one of the highest rates of fire-related <u>mortality</u> of any industrialized nation. Nearly 5,000 people die in fires each year.

Could you guess that "mortality" means "death"? Notice that to guess a meaning correctly, you can't just look at one or two words to the left and right of an unknown word. You must look at the entire sentence. In fact, often you need the ideas in the whole paragraph to figure out the meaning of an unfamiliar word.

Sometimes an author will define a new word right after it is introduced, as in this example:

> Arson, the burning of a building or other property for a criminal or harmful reason, is estimated to be responsible for one in seven fires.

However, even if the author doesn't define the word for you, you may be able to make an accurate guess as to what the word means using the surrounding ideas. Here are three types of reasoning skilled college readers use to figure out an unfamiliar word.

SKILLS PRACTICE 1

Use the examples provided for each method of figuring out an unknown word to make a guess as to the meaning of the underlined word.

Possibility #1: The word must mean the same kind of thing as the idea coming before or following it. Suppose that you are reading this sentence: "He was mean, vicious, _____, and everyone hated him." What kind of idea must go in the blank for the sentence to make sense? Did you say something like "evil" or "nasty"? Using the same line of reasoning, make a guess as to the meaning of "inadvertent":

> Law enforcement officers should not assume that fires start through mistakes, bad luck and other such <u>inadvertent</u> causes.

Inadvertent means _____.

Possibility #2: The word must mean the opposite of the idea coming before or following it. For example, look at this sentence: "We expected her to be tall. To our surprise, she was _____." What idea do you need to logically complete the thought? Did you say "short"? Now use this strategy to figure out the meaning of "incendiary":

> Fires that appear accidental may actually be <u>incendiary</u>.

Incendiary means _____.

Possibility #3: The meaning of a word can be guessed by looking at the examples and elaborating details that come before or follow it. For instance, read these sentences: " _____ is a common problem in late spring when many plants are pollinating. Those who suffer from it sneeze often, their eyes itch and water, and they may break out in skin rashes." What kind of thing must the author be discussing? Did you figure out it must be some sort of allergy? Now figure out the meaning of "accelerant" using the same strategy.

<u>Accelerants</u> such as gasoline and turpentine are often used to start incendiary fires.

Accelerant means _____.

Notice that in order to use these strategies, you must be sensitive to connecting and transition words. For example, the term "similarly" will lead you to expect that one idea will be like another. "By contrast" lets you know that the next idea will be different. "Such as" or "for instance" signals that you might be able to use examples to figure out the meaning of an unfamiliar word.

SKILLS PRACTICE 2

Figure out the meaning of the underlined word. Try covering up the target word so you must focus on the ideas around it. Write your guess as to the meaning of the word in the space provided.

1. Arsonists set fires for many reasons. Some set fires by <u>mischance</u>. For example, a nine-year-old burned down a barn. The child was sneaking a cigarette and dropped the match on a bale of hay by accident when he thought someone was coming.

    Mischance means _____.

2. Thrill-seeker arsonists consider fire setting a game they play with police. Commonly, thrill-seeker arsonists leave clues to see if investigators will be able to trace the fire to them. They have a <u>callous</u> attitude toward the danger their activities pose to others.

    Callous means _____.

3. In other cases, fire setting is motivated by mental illness. An individual may hear voices telling him he must set a fire to kill the devil or stop an evil plan. After the arsonist is treated for <u>psychosis</u>, the fire-setting behavior stops.

    Psychosis means _____.

4. Some arsonists engage in fire setting to get rid of tension and <u>alleviate</u> stress. One arsonist was seventy years old, had never been caught, and had set hundreds of fires of all different sizes. Any time he felt uncomfortable, he set a fire to feel better.

    Alleviate means _____.

5. Some arsonists set fires to destroy evidence or conceal a murder. For example, a murderer may put the body of a victim inside a car and set the car on fire. Fire causes bones to break. It can be difficult for <u>pathologists</u> to determine whether a skull fracture occurred before a body was burned or whether it was caused by the heat of the fire.

    Pathologists means _____.

SKILLS PRACTICE 3

Read the passage entitled "Difficulties in Conducting Arson Investigations." Above each underlined word or phrase, write down your guess as to what it means.

Difficulties in Conducting Arson Investigations

Arson is one of the most difficult crimes to investigate. One arson specialist commented: "It's a clandestine crime. It's rarely done with witnesses to observe what goes on." However, the greatest difficulty in investigating arson cases is that the destructive power of the fire eradicates evidence from the beginning. One investigator of thirty years' experience describes his first fire scene (Figure 1.3):

> The site was a woolen mill. I stood on the ground floor of the ruined building, surrounded by carbonized debris and asked myself, "How can anyone extract useful information from this situation?"

FIGURE 1.3 ■ *An investigator examines the charred remains of a building after a fire.*
Source: Courtesy of Pearson Education/PH College.

Even if the investigator searches diligently, it may be impossible to determine how a fire started or why it burned in a particular way. For example, in one fatal fire, an elderly woman was found burned to death in her bed. The bed itself was completely charred, and it had burned a perfectly rectangular hole in the bedroom floor. Although there were many combustible objects in her bedroom, nothing burned except the bed.

The problem of finding and preserving evidence is exacerbated by the presence of the large numbers of police, firefighters, reporters and interested observers at most fires. The movements of so many people increase the chances that evidence of how a fire started will be contaminated, moved, or destroyed.

Spoliation of evidence may result in a case against an arsonist being dismissed. The U.S. Department of Justice has published guidelines for fire and arson investigators to prevent contamination of evidence. For example, investigators should use clean disposable gloves for collecting items of evidence. To avoid cross-contamination, gloves should be changed between collection of unrelated items, and each item should be placed in its own container. Evidence should be placed in clean, unused containers and sealed immediately.

READING FOR REAL LIFE

Investigating Arson Cases

Suppose you are a police detective called to the scene of a house fire. The body of a man has been found in the bedroom. A firefighter mentions that the fire may have been caused by a space heater. You are expected to direct the actions of officers at the site after the fire is extinguished. How would you respond to these requests? Base your answers on what you learned in the reading.

Neighbor: The man who lived here had two dogs that he was crazy about. Would it be all right for me to poke around in the rubble to look for them in case they are hurt?

Patrol Officer: The photographer is done taking pictures of the bedroom. The space heater and burned bedding should probably be saved as evidence. Should I put them and other objects in a large box to take back to the station?

PRACTICE PASSAGE 1.1: LAW ENFORCEMENT

In the practice passage that follows, read through the selection, underlining the words you don't know. Then go back and see if you can guess what they mean using the ideas around them. You won't be able to figure out every word, but you will probably be able to guess the correct meaning of many of them.

Profit-Motivated Arson

Arsonists in this category expect to profit from their fire setting, either directly for monetary gain or more indirectly to profit from a goal other than money. Examples of direct monetary gain include insurance fraud and to gain employment. The latter is exemplified by the case of a construction worker wanting to rebuild an apartment complex he destroyed or of an unemployed laborer seeking employment as a forest firefighter or as a logger to salvage burned timber.

Arson-for-profit may have interesting twists where the offender benefits directly or indirectly. Arsonists have set fire to western forests in order to have their equipment rented out to support part of the suppression effort. Other nonmonetary reasons from which arsonists may profit range from setting brush fires to enhance the availability of animals for hunting to burning adjacent properties to improve the view. Also, fires have been set to escape an undesirable environment, such as in the case of seamen who do not wish to set sail.

CASE EXAMPLE: PIZZA SHOP EXPLOSION AND FIRE

An early-morning explosion and fire did considerable damage to a pizza shop (Figure 1.4). A large quantity of gasoline had been poured inside the premises. The remains of a plastic oil can were found melted on the floor, with residues of gasoline still inside the container. The gas stove in the kitchen (with pilot light) was identified as the ignition source. The rear door appeared to have been broken by the explosion and then exposed to a sooty fire. The remains of a toilet paper roll trailer were found adjacent to the rear door (the roll bearing gasoline

FIGURE 1.4 ■ *Broken glass forced outward from the explosion within the shop. Note the toilet paper roll inside the door with paper extending up the stair to the right.*
Source: Courtesy of Ross Brogan, New South Wales Fire Brigade, Fire Investigation & Research Unit, Greenacre, NSW, Australia. Used by permission.

residues). Near the rear stairs was a badly scorched athletic shoe with surface scorching and melting consistent with brief exposure to flames.

Farther away were blood droplets and the remains of burned clothing in the alleyway leading to the apparent location of the "getaway car." Two individuals arrived at a local hospital at about the same time as the fire report, each reporting a different address as the location where his burns and other injuries were obtained. The fire service responded to both addresses and found no fires at either. One suspect was apparently inside the structure pouring the gasoline while the other was outside preparing the trailer. Bloodstains from the step and parking area were matched to one of the suspects. The individual inside succumbed to his burn injuries some three months after the fire. The surviving suspect eventually implicated the pizza shop owner in a "hired torch" scheme.

Source: Adapted from David Icove and John D. DeHann, *Forensic Fire Scene Reconstruction,* 182–84 and 319–23. Reprinted with permission.

Using College Dictionaries

Although you can often figure out the meanings of words you don't know from context, sometimes there isn't enough information in the surrounding words for you to feel 100 percent confident of your guess. In such situations, you should pull out your dictionary and look up the word. Here are two important points to keep in mind when using college dictionaries:

First, be careful not to automatically grab the first definition that appears in the list of meanings. It may not be the one you need. Use the context in which the unfamiliar word appears to decide which definition makes most sense. Make a guess before you look up the word. For example, suppose you are studying a chapter on trash disposal. You read this sentence:

> The deposition of trash in landfills has become an issue of great concern (Figure 1.5).

Suppose you weren't sure of the exact meaning of "deposition" and decided to look it up. Here are the definitions you would see:

1. Testimony that is given under oath, especially a statement given by a witness that is read out in court in the witness's absence

2. The act of removing somebody from high office or power

3. Something that has been placed somewhere

4. The accumulation of natural materials by a gradual process

FIGURE 1.5 ■ *Landfills attract enormous numbers of seagulls that pick at the trash.*
Source: Courtesy of AT&T Archives and History Center.

Which definition makes the most sense in the sentence you are reading? Notice it is the third one ("something that has been placed somewhere"), not the first.

You need to be aware that many everyday words have second and third meanings, which are less well known. For example, suppose that you read this sentence:

> The refuse created by each American citizen is estimated to be
> about four pounds per day.

Here the word "refuse" is used to mean garbage. It is not being used in the more common sense of "unwillingness to give, allow, or agree to something." If you think you know what a word means, but the meaning you have in mind doesn't make sense in the sentence you see, it is likely that the word has a second or third meaning you don't know. Pencil in your guess based on the context, and then check to see if you were right by looking up the word in the dictionary. Notice that a word that has one meaning when used as a noun may have a very different meaning when used as an adjective or a verb.

SKILLS PRACTICE 4

First, pencil in a guess as to the meaning of each underlined word. Next, look at the dictionary definitions. Circle or highlight the correct dictionary definition of the underlined word. Make sure that meaning fits the context here.

1. Waste disposal is not a <u>novel</u> problem. For example, in the 1800s, when horses were used for transportation instead of cars, thousands of dead horses were piled outside the limits of large cities.

   > Novel (noun) 1. A fictional prose narrative of considerable length, typically having a plot that is unfolded by the actions, speech, and thoughts of the characters. 2. The literary genre represented by novels.

   > Novel (adjective) strikingly new, unusual, or different

2. In ancient cities, people often simply left trash where it fell on the floor of their homes, covering over it with a fresh <u>stratum</u> of clay or hard-packed dirt.

   > Stratum (noun) 1. A horizontal layer of material, especially one of several parallel layers arranged one on top of another. 2. A bed or layer of sedimentary rock having approximately the same composition throughout. 3. A level of society composed of people with similar social, cultural or economic status. 4. One of a number of layers, levels, or divisions in an organized system: *a complex poem with many strata of meaning.*

3. In the capital cities of Europe, people threw their garbage into the streets. In the U.S., the idea that streets should be kept clear of household trash did not gain <u>currency</u> until the early 1900s.

   > Currency (noun) 1. Money in any form when in actual use as a medium of exchange, especially circulating paper money. 2. Transmission from person to person as a medium of exchange; circulation; *coins now in currency.* 3. General acceptance or use; prevalence.

Second, your annotations of word meanings should be as short and sim-ple as possible. If you have to correct your original annotation because it wasn't quite right, write in a simple, short phrase. Look at the dictionary definition to shape your understanding of what the word means, but shorten and simplify the definition for your annotation. For example, here is how you might annotate the meaning of "deposition." The full dictionary definition read "something that has been placed somewhere."

(placing)
The deposition of trash in landfills has become an environmental issue of

great concern.

You could also write in "dumping," "leaving," "dropping," "storage," or any other word that gets the idea across.

SKILLS PRACTICE 5

First, pencil in a guess as to the meaning of each underlined word. Next, look at the dictionary definitions. Make sure that your annotation of each word's meaning is both correct and simple. The first item has been done for you as an example.

(things that used to be alive)
1. About three-fourths of the contents of trash are organic materials such as paper, wood, leaves and grass clippings, and food wastes.

> **Organic** (adjective) 1. Of, relating to, or affecting organs or an organ of the body: *an organic disease.* 2. Of, relating to, or derived from living organisms: *organic matter.* 3. Using or produced with fertilizers of ani-mal or vegetable matter, using no synthetic fertilizers or pesticides: *organic gardening.* 4. Having properties associated with living organ-isms. 5. Constituting an integral part of a whole; fundamental. 6. *Law.* Denoting or relating to the fundamental or constitutional laws and precepts of a government or an organization. 7. *Chemistry.* Of or des-ignating carbon compounds.

2. There are three possible ways to dispose of trash: burying it in landfills,

recycling, and combustion.

> **Combustion** (noun) 1. The process of burning. 2. A chemical change, especially oxidation, accompanied by the production of heat and light. 3. Violent anger or agitation.

3. In the 1970s, the dumps in many municipalities were converted to landfills.

> **Municipality** (noun) 1. A political unit, such as a city or town, incor-porated for local self-government. 2. A body of officials appointed to manage the affairs of a local political unit.

4. In a landfill, waste is covered with dirt, keeping <u>vermin</u> populations down.

> **Vermin** (noun, plural). 1. Various small animals or insects, such as rats or cockroaches, that are destructive, annoying, or injurious to health. 2. Animals that prey on game, such as foxes or weasels. 3a. A person considered loathsome or highly offensive. b. Such people considered as a group.

5. Over time, the material in a landfill <u>decomposes</u>.

> **Decompose** (verb) 1. To separate into components or basic elements. 2a. To cause to rot; to become broken down into components; disintegrate. b. To decay; putrefy.

PRACTICE PASSAGE 1.2: WASTE MANAGEMENT

In the practice passage that follows, mark unfamiliar words, pencil in your guess as to what they mean, and check your guess against the dictionary definitions, making corrections as needed.

Problems of Landfills

LEACHATE GENERATION AND GROUNDWATER CONTAMINATION

The most serious problem by far is groundwater contamination. Recall that as water percolates through any material, various chemicals in the material may dissolve in the water and get carried along in a process called *leaching*. The water with various pollutants in it is called *leachate*. As the water percolates through municipal solid waste (MSW), a noxious leachate is generated that consists of residues of decomposing organic matter combined with iron, mercury, lead, zinc, and other metals from rusting cans, discarded batteries, and appliances—generously "spiced" with paints, pesticides, cleaning fluids, newspaper inks, and other chemicals. The nature of the landfill site and the absence of precautionary measures funnel this "witches' brew" directly into underground aquifers.

METHANE PRODUCTION

Because it is about two-thirds organic material, MSW is potentially subject to natural decomposition. However, buried wastes do not have access to oxygen.

Therefore, their decomposition is anaerobic, and a major byproduct of this process is biogas, which is about two-thirds methane and the rest hydrogen and carbon dioxide, a highly flammable mixture. Produced deep in a landfill, biogas may seep horizontally through the soil and rock, enter basements, and even cause explosions if it accumulates and is ignited. Over 20 homes at distances up to 1000 feet from landfills have been destroyed, and some deaths have occurred as a result of such explosions. Also, gases seeping to the surface kill vegetation by poisoning the roots. Without vegetation, erosion occurs, exposing the unsightly waste. A number of cities have exploited the problem by installing "gas wells" in old and existing landfills. The wells tap the biogas, and the methane is purified and used as fuel.

INCOMPLETE DECOMPOSITION

The commonly used plastics in MSW are resistant to natural decomposition because of their molecular structure. Chemically, they are polymers of petroleum-based compounds that microbes are unable to digest. Biodegradable plastic polymers have been developed from such sources as cornstarch, cellulose, lactic acid, soybean protein, amides, and others. So far, however, none of the biodegradable plastics has seen common usage in consumer products.

A team of "archeologists" from the University of Arizona, led by William Rathje, has been carrying out research on old landfills. Their research has shown that even materials formerly assumed to be biodegradable—newspapers, wood, and so on—are degraded only slowly, if at all, in landfills. In one landfill, 30-year-old newspapers were recovered in a readable state; layers of telephone directories, practically intact, were found marking each year. Since paper materials are 38% of MSW, this is a serious matter. The reason paper and other organic materials decompose so slowly is the lack of suitable amounts of moisture; the more water percolating through a landfill, the better the biodegradation of paper materials. However, the more percolation there is, the more toxic leachate is produced!

SETTLING

Finally, waste settles as it compacts and decomposes. Luckily, this eventuality was recognized from the beginning, so buildings have never been put on landfills. Settling presents a problem where landfills have been converted to playgrounds and golf courses, though, because it creates shallow depressions (and sometimes deep holes) that collect and hold water. This process can be addressed by continual monitoring of the facility and the use of fill to restore a level surface.

Source: Adapted from Bernard J. Nebel and Richard T. Wright, *Environmental Science,* 459–60. Reprinted with permission.

READING FOR REAL LIFE

Problems of Landfills

The most serious problem with landfills is the contamination of underground aquifers with rainwater that has run through buried trash and picked up dangerous chemicals and bacteria (leachate).

If a landfill is made by simply digging a hole in the ground, filling it with trash, and piling dirt over the top, leachate is not prevented from reaching the aquifers. Can you think of a way to prevent the contaminated water from reaching an underground aquifer? Make a simple sketch of your idea. Then compare your plan with those of your classmates.

Note: This is exactly the kind of design task given to people in civil and environmental engineering programs.

Paraphrasing

After you have marked in the meanings of unfamiliar words, you should read back over the passage to see if you understand what the author is saying. Skilled college readers paraphrase an author's ideas to themselves to make sure they are following the train of thought and to improve concentration and understanding.

This is what it means to paraphrase. In conversation, people sometimes stop a speaker with "Let me see if I understand what you are saying." Then the listener will repeat the speaker's ideas back in different words. For example, suppose your instructor says, "The first section of the test is mandatory for all students; the second section is optional—for extra credit." You say, "So you are saying that everyone has to do the first section, but we only do the second section if we want extra credit." What you did was paraphrase your instructor's words. *Paraphrasing* means saying or writing the same ideas in different words without changing the meaning. Notice that in paraphrasing you are *not* responding to the speaker or writer's ideas. You are simply repeating back his or her idea in different words.

Skilled college readers treat reading as a kind of conversation between themselves and the author of a text. Just as listeners will stop and paraphrase a speaker's words to make sure they are following the train of thought, college readers pause after a sentence or a paragraph to paraphrase the ideas to themselves before going on. Paraphrasing is especially important when you are reading a text that is written in a more formal manner. You paraphrase in your mind to express the ideas in plainer speech.

However, when you paraphrase, it is important not to shift the meaning. People are especially likely to change the meaning if the topic is controversial. In describing what someone else said, they tend to insert their own reaction to it. Although there is nothing wrong with responding to what you read, make sure you separate what the author said from your reaction.

SKILLS PRACTICE 6

Look at the following sentences. Chose the sentence that is the best way to paraphrase the original and does not shift the meaning.

1. Cigarettes are the only legally available product that is harmful when used as intended.

   a. Cigarettes are the only product that is legal to make and sell even though they are dangerous when used properly.

   b. Because cigarettes hurt people, it should not be legal to sell them.

   c. It is legal to sell products that are known to be hazardous.

2. Tobacco companies have claimed that cigarettes are not addictive and that they do not cause cancer.

   a. Cigarette companies lied in saying their product is safe.

   b. Cigarette companies said their product is not dangerous.

   c. There is no evidence that cigarettes are addictive or cause cancer.

3. Some people have brought suit against cigarette companies, holding them responsible for the deaths of family members due to smoking.

   a. Although it is sad when people die from smoking-related diseases, cigarette companies should not be blamed.

b. Cigarette companies have been sued by the families of people who died of smoking-related diseases.

c. Cigarette companies should have to pay the families of people who died because of use of their products.

After you finish annotating unfamiliar words in a text, you should be able to read through it and put the author's ideas in plainer speech. Sometimes college students write short paraphrasings of an author's point to the side of a text.

SKILLS PRACTICE 7

Read the passage entitled "Product Liability." The meanings of difficult words in the passage have already been annotated. Jot down some notes in the side margin of the text that paraphrase the ideas of each paragraph. The first paragraph has been done for you.

■ PRODUCT LIABILITY

Products must be safe when used normally.

If not, maker can be sued—must pay.

Manufacturers have a duty to ensure that the products they
   (make)
fabricate are safe for ordinary use. A manufacturer will
     (responsible)   (gets)
typically be liable for injuries a user of the product sustains

while using the product. For example, suppose a woman

purchased a blow dryer. The protective plastic shield covering
   (inside)   (fell off)
the interior fan became detached. The woman's finger came into
                      (cuts)
contact with the fan blades, resulting in severe lacerations. The

manufacturer would be liable for the injuries.
                (responsible)
    However, a manufacturer will not be held liable for a user's
         (changed a lot)
injuries if the product was altered substantially after its

manufacture. For example, suppose a man purchased a chain

saw in order to cut down some trees on his property. The chain

saw was designed such that a metal protective guard prevented
         (touching)
the chain saw blade from coming into contact with the user's

hand. The buyer of the chain saw believed he could work more

(faster)
efficiently if the metal hand guard were removed, and therefore

(Later)
he used a blowtorch to remove it. Subsequently, the purchaser

of the chain saw injured his hand while using the saw to cut

down trees. He sued the manufacturer. The manufacturer will

(win) _(big)_
likely prevail because the purchaser made a substantial change to

the product after it left the manufacturer's control, and it was

this change that caused the purchaser's injury.

(say or argue)
A manufacturer may allege lack of responsibility because the

(wrong use)
injury was due to misuse of the product. For the manufacturer to

(win) _(wrong use)_
prevail in this argument, the misuse of the product must be

(not expected) _(expected beforehand)_
unforeseeable. If the misuse of the product is foreseeable, the

(responsible)
manufacturer will still be liable. For instance, the manufacturer

of an oven was sued when a child used the open oven door as a

step stool to reach an object on a high shelf. The oven door

(broke)
collapsed, and the child was injured. In this case, the court ruled

(responsible)
that the manufacturer was liable for the child's injuries because

(wrong use) _(expected)_
the misuse of the product should have been foreseen. The oven

(built) _(be stronger than)_
manufacturer should have constructed the product to withstand

(expected wrong use)
anticipated misuse.

(say or argue)
A manufacturer may allege as a defense that the user's

(helped cause)
own actions contributed in some way to his or her injury.

(Mistakes) _(make not guilty)_
Error on the part of a user does not typically exculpate a

manufacturer. However, an injured person who is also

(less money)
responsible for an accident may receive diminished compensation,

but only depending on the degree to which he or she was at fault.

READING FOR REAL LIFE

Product Liability

Using the concepts in the passage you just read, see if you can predict the outcome of this lawsuit. It is a real case.

A man bought a lawn mower. One afternoon, he was mowing his grass when he noticed that his bushes were looking a bit overgrown. It struck him that a lawn mower would probably cut bushes also. He dropped the handle of the mower, picked it up by the sides, and lifted it to trim the bushes. The mower did a fine job of cutting off overgrown branches. Suddenly, however, the man lost his grip on the mower, and his hand came into contact with the blades, resulting in the loss of two fingers. The man sued the manufacturer of the lawn mower. Do you think the court required the lawn mower manufacturer to pay the man for his injuries or not?

PRACTICE PASSAGE 1.3: BUSINESS

Texts used in business and law programs are often written in a very formal style. After you have written in the meanings of unfamiliar words, you should paraphrase the ideas to yourself to make sure you understand what the author is saying. Try paraphrasing the ideas in the following practice passage.

Landlord's Duties

The duties a landlord owes a tenant are either expressly provided in the lease, set forth in statute, or implied by law. The landlord's duties are discussed in the following paragraphs.

LANDLORD'S DUTY TO DELIVER POSSESSION OF THE LEASED PREMISES

A lease grants the tenant *exclusive possession* of the leased premises until (1) the term of the lease expires or (2) the tenant defaults on the obligations under the lease. The landlord is obligated to deliver possession of the leased premises to the tenant on the date the lease term begins. A landlord may not enter leased premises unless the right is specifically reserved in the lease.

DUTY NOT TO INTERFERE WITH THE TENANT'S RIGHT TO QUIET ENJOYMENT

The law implies a *covenant of quiet enjoyment* in all leases. Under this covenant, the landlord may not interfere with the tenant's quiet and peaceful possession, use, and enjoyment of the leased premises. The covenant is breached if the landlord, or anyone acting with the landlord's consent, interferes with the tenant's use and enjoyment of the property. This is called *wrongful* or *unlawful eviction*. It may occur if the landlord actually evicts the tenant by physically preventing him or her from possessing or using the leased premises or if the landlord *constructively evicts* the tenant by causing the leased premises to become unfit for its intended use (e.g., by failing to provide electricity). If the landlord refuses to cure the defect after a reasonable time, a tenant who has been constructively evicted may (1) sue for damages and possession of the premises or (2) treat the lease as terminated, vacate the premises, and cease paying rent. The landlord is not responsible for wrongful acts of third persons that were done without his or her authorization.

LANDLORD'S DUTY TO MAINTAIN THE LEASED PREMISES

At common law, the doctrine of "caveat lessee"—"lessee beware"—applied to leases. The landlord made no warranties about the quality of leased property and had no duty to repair it. The tenant took the property "as is." Modern real estate law, however, imposes certain statutory and judicially implied duties on landlords to repair and maintain leased premises. States and local municipalities have enacted statutes called building or housing codes that impose specific standards on property owners to repair and maintain leased premises. They often provide certain minimum standards regarding heat, water, lights, and other services. Depending on the statute, violators may be subject to fines by the government, loss of their claim for rent, and imprisonment for serious violations.

The courts of many jurisdictions maintain that an *implied warranty of habitability* applies to residential leases for their duration. This warranty provides that the leased premises must be fit, safe, and suitable for ordinary residential use. For example, unchecked rodent infestation, leaking roofs, and unworkable bathroom facilities have been held to breach the implied warranty of habitability. On the other hand, a small crack in the wall or some paint peeling from a door does not breach this warranty. If the landlord's failure to maintain or repair the leased premises affects the tenant's use or enjoyment of the premises, state statutes and judicial decisions provide various remedies. Generally, the tenant may (1) withhold from his or her rent the amount by which the defect reduced the value of the premises to him or her, (2) repair the defect and deduct the cost of repairs from the rent due for the leased premises, (3) cancel the lease if the failure to repair constitutes constructive eviction, or (4) sue for damages for the amount the landlord's failure to repair the defect reduced the value of the leasehold.

Source: Adapted from Henry R. Cheeseman, *Business Law,* 5th edition (Upper Saddle River, NJ: Prentice Hall, 2003), 992–93. Reprinted by permission of Prentice Hall, Inc.

READING FOR REAL LIFE

Landlord's Duties

Sharon Love entered into a written lease agreement with Monarch Apartments for apartment #4 at 441 Winfield in Topeka, Kansas. Shortly after moving in, she experienced serious problems with termites. Her walls swelled, clouds of dirt came out, and when she checked on her children one night, she saw termites flying around the room. She complained to Monarch, who arranged for the apartment to be fumigated. When the termite problem persisted, Monarch moved Love and her children to apartment #2. Upon moving in, Love noticed that roaches crawled over the walls, ceilings, and floors of the apartment. She complained, and Monarch called an exterminator, who sprayed the apartment. When the problem continued, Love vacated the apartment. Is Love lawfully terminating the lease?

Note: You should be able to point to the sentences in the reading that support your answer.

Putting It All Together

■ ANNOTATING UNFAMILIAR WORDS IN TEXTS

When you are given a text containing words that are unfamiliar to you, do these three things:

1. Mark any unfamiliar words and pencil in a guess as to what each word means right next to the word. Don't list the definitions on a separate sheet of paper. Annotate the text itself.
2. Check your guess against the dictionary to see if you were right. If not, correct the meaning, but keep your annotated definition simple.
3. Read through the entire passage to make sure you understand it well enough now to explain the author's ideas in your own words (paraphrase it).

Here is an example of text that has been annotated:

TREATING PHOBIAS

The most frequently used method of treating a phobia *(fear)* is called systematic

desensitization. Systematic desensitization is a method for gradually

reducing irrational *(not reasonable)* fear. For instance, suppose a girl is brought to a

therapist because of a snake phobia. The first thing the therapist will do is

amass *(gather)* more details about the child's fear. The therapist will ask questions

to elicit *(get)* information about situations the child feels to be upsetting. Then

the therapist will arrange the information in a hierarchy *(list by ranking)* from most

threatening to least threatening.

Next, the therapist will teach the child techniques of deep relaxation.

Once the child has learned to calm herself, the therapist will ask her to

imagine the least threatening situation, such as looking at a picture of a

snake. The child will be asked to signal if she begins to feel tense. At the

signal, the therapist will instruct the child to stop imagining the snake

picture and focus on relaxing. The child and therapist work their way

(step-by-step)

incrementally up the hierarchy until the child can visualize the most

(situation)

threatening scenario without anxiety—holding a snake. When the child

can imagine the most upsetting situation while still staying relaxed, then

she will work on staying calm while handling a rubber snake, viewing a

live snake through a window, and finally holding a live snake.

PRACTICE PASSAGE 1.4: COUNSELING

When you are done annotating the unfamiliar words in a text, you should be able to read through the passage with good understanding and put the ideas of the text in your own words. For instance, after reading the following practice passage, you should be able to describe the steps a therapist follows to cure people of phobias.

Notice that you could understand much of the meaning of this passage without annotating unfamiliar words. However, suppose you didn't know the meanings of "hierarchy" or "incrementally." Your understanding of the passage would be fuzzy, and you would be missing some key ideas on how phobias are treated. Do not be satisfied with just a rough idea of what a passage means—its gist. Sharpen your understanding by annotating the unfamiliar words so that the ideas are perfectly clear.

Social Phobia

> "In any social situation, I felt fear. I would be anxious before I even left the house, and it would escalate as I got closer to a college class, a party, or whatever. I would feel sick at my stomach—it almost felt like I had the flu. My heart would pound, my palms would get sweaty, and I would get this feeling of being removed from myself and from everybody else."

> "When I would walk into a room full of people, I'd turn red and it would feel like everybody's eyes were on me. I was embarrassed to stand off in a corner by myself, but I couldn't think of anything to say to anybody. It was humiliating. I felt so clumsy, I couldn't wait to get out."

> "I couldn't go on dates, and for a while I couldn't even go to class. My sophomore year of college I had to come home for a semester. I felt like such a failure."

Social phobia, also called social anxiety disorder, involves overwhelming anxiety and excessive self-consciousness in everyday social situations. People with social phobia have a persistent, intense, and chronic fear of being watched and judged by others and being embarrassed or humiliated by their own actions. Their fear may be so acute that it interferes with work or school, and other ordinary activities. While many people with social phobia recognize that their fear of being around people may be excessive or unreasonable, they are unable to surmount it. They often worry for days or weeks in advance of a dreaded situation.

Social phobia can be limited to only one type of situation—such as a fear of speaking in formal or informal situations, or eating, drinking, or writing in front of others—or, in its most severe form, may be so pervasive that a person experiences symptoms almost any time they are around other people. Social phobia can be very debilitating—it may even keep people from going to work or school on some days. Many people with this illness have a hard time making or keeping friends.

Physical symptoms often accompany the intense anxiety of social phobia and include blushing, profuse sweating, trembling, nausea, and difficulty talking. If you suffer from social phobia, you may be mortified by these symptoms and feel as though all eyes are focused on you. You may be afraid of being with people external to your family.

People with social phobia are aware that their feelings are irrational. Even if they manage to confront what they fear, they usually feel very anxious beforehand and are intensely uncomfortable throughout. Afterward, the unpleasant feelings may linger, as they worry about how they may have been judged or what others may have thought or observed about them.

Social phobia affects about 5.3 million adult Americans. Women and men are equally susceptible to social phobia. The disorder usually commences in childhood or early adolescence, and there is some evidence that genetic factors are involved. Social phobia often co-occurs with other anxiety disorders or depression. Substance abuse or dependence may develop in individuals who attempt to "self-medicate" their social phobia by drinking or using drugs. Social phobia can be treated successfully with carefully targeted psychotherapy or medications.

Source: Adapted from the National Institute of Mental Health, *Anxiety Disorders* (2000).

PRACTICE TEST
Managing Unfamiliar Words

PART I: READING TO PREPARE

Directions: Read through the passage entitled "Economic Issues in Career Decision Making." As you read, underline any unfamiliar words. When you have finished, go back and annotate the meanings of the words you marked, using the context and your dictionary. You should be able to explain any of the sentences using your own words.

ECONOMIC ISSUES IN CAREER DECISION MAKING

THE DIFFERENCE BETWEEN MAJORS AND CAREERS

1   Students often confuse choosing a major with selecting a career. Knowing little of the job market, many college students assume that if they earn a degree in a major they find interesting, they will secure enjoyable work upon graduation. However, the assumption that an intellectually stimulating major will automatically lead to a job compatible with one's personality is erroneous.

2   First, graduates of many programs find work in occupations unrelated to their studies. This is particularly true in the liberal arts. Liberal arts majors are those in which studies are not closely tied to a particular profession. Psychology, biology, history, political science, English literature, and art history are examples of liberal arts majors. One might think that most psychology majors find work as counselors, journalism majors become reporters, English literature majors work for book publishers, and art history majors work for museums. However, this is not true. The primary type of employment that liberal arts majors find is in financial services, sales, and office management.

3   The chief reason why so many liberal arts graduates end up in sales and office-related professions is the relative size of job pools. For instance, think how many art museums there are in your town. Only a minute number of art history graduates are needed to select new paintings and arrange exhibits. By contrast, there are thousands of stores and offices that need managers.

4 Second, even if a major is closely tied to a profession and there is a huge demand for new graduates, people who enjoy learning about a subject may not be suited for the occupations that use such knowledge. For example, a nursing major who takes pleasure in learning about the human body may find that he or she does not relish day-to-day contact with sick people.

MATCHING INTERESTS TO CAREERS: THE HOLLAND CODE SYSTEM

5 To ensure that one's major will lead to satisfying employment, it makes sense to first identify the occupations compatible with one's interests, skills, and aptitudes, and then select a major that leads to such work. The Holland code system was devised to help people match their temperaments to career fields. Individuals are assessed to identify their strongest areas, and this information is used to match them with appropriate occupations. The Holland code system assesses individuals' strengths in six areas: realistic, investigative, artistic, social, enterprising, and conventional.

6 **Realistic.** This personality type excels at tasks that are practical and concrete. Realistic people are often good with tools and machines and enjoy working with their hands. Career fields compatible with realistic individuals are engineering, agriculture, and technical jobs.

7 **Investigative.** Investigative people enjoy analyzing information to find the sources of problems. They often prefer solitary, independent work, and tend to be good at math and science. They flourish in research-related occupations.

8 **Artistic.** Artistic personalities like to work in environments where they can use their creativity and produce aesthetically pleasing products. They are often introspective, but also enjoy performing. Careers in music, dance, visual arts, and drama are attractive to artistic individuals.

9 **Social.** Social people prefer work situations involving substantial interaction with other people. They enjoy counseling, teaching, or helping others, and have empathetic personalities. Social personalities often gravitate toward occupations in education, social work, and religion.

10   **Enterprising.**   Enterprising individuals thrive in work environments which require them to influence others. They enjoy attention, like to lead, and tend to be persuasive, gregarious, and extroverted. Examples of careers in which this personality type excels are sales, business management, law, and politics.

11   **Conventional.**   Conventional people are organized, systematic, and meticulous in handling tasks involving detail. They appreciate order, and enjoy structured work environments. They are excellent at managing records and data.

12   After people are assessed to identify which three Holland groups are most dominant in their personalities, they can identify occupations which are a good match. Many career databases assign Holland codes to each job. For instance, nursing is coded SIR (social, investigative and realistic). People who know their own Holland codes can search the database for compatible jobs.

PAY ISSUES

13   Although students may give careful thought to what program of study they might enjoy, they are prone to ignore the work, pay, and opportunities available to graduates with the degree they are considering. Let's first consider the issue of pay. Having a college degree has a much greater impact on lifelong earnings than in the past. In the 1970s, college graduates made twelve dollars for every ten earned by people with only a high school diploma. However, over the past thirty years, the divergence in pay has increased. Now college graduates make sixteen dollars for every ten earned by those without a college degree. According to the Bureau of Labor Statistics, in 2005, the average annual earnings of a person without a high school diploma was $23,612. Those with only a high school diploma had average annual pay of $31,664, while the average pay for a person with a bachelor's degree was $56,740.

14   However, students, particularly those who are the first in their families to attend college, often assume that any job requiring a college degree must pay well. Such is not the case. There are huge pay disparities between jobs requiring equivalent amounts of education. Those with bachelor's degrees in business, health care,

computers, and engineering tend to earn more than those in other professions. For instance, in 2005, child and family social workers had average annual earnings of $38,780, while computer systems analysts earned an average of $70,430. As you can see from the Department of Labor data, some people with bachelor's degrees earn much more than others, even though they spent comparable amounts of time and money on degrees.

15 Another mistake commonly made by students is confusing typical starting pay with the average pay of experienced workers . For example, even though the average pay for an elementary school teacher in 2005 was $46,990, starting pay is likely to be closer to $29,000. The average pay of a stockbroker in 2005 was $87,990, but the starting pay is around $30,000. Although people choose majors for reasons other than pay, it is important to be conversant with both starting pay rates and average pay for experienced workers when setting a career goal.

DIFFICULTY OF FINDING A JOB AFTER GRADUATION

16 An important issue to consider is the size of the job pool. The job pool refers to the number of people that work at a particular kind of job. The bigger the job pool, the easier it tends to be to find a job after graduation. Many job openings are created for new graduates when current workers retire or leave the field. If the job pool is large, more people are likely to be retiring. For example, in Minnesota, there were 49,390 people employed as registered nurses but only 190 people working as film and video editors in 2005. It is easier for nursing graduates to find a job than it is for people with a degree in videography.

17 Related to the size of the job pool is the issue of whether it is growing or shrinking. There are a number of reasons why a field would gain or lose jobs. First, changes in the population create or diminish demand for workers. For example, the aging of the population is increasing the demand for geriatric specialists, and so that field is growing. Second, jobs may be lost to competition overseas. Certain kinds of computer programming jobs have been moved to foreign countries, notably India. Third, the demand for workers may contract because small companies are bought up by larger ones. For instance, the total number of farm management

positions has been shrinking because family farms are being bought up by huge agriculture corporations. Last, automation has resulted in the loss of some jobs.

18 Competition for jobs after graduation is also an important consideration. In some countries, the government limits the number of students that can study for a particular profession so that there is not an oversupply of graduates. However, in the United States, colleges may accept as many qualified students as they like into their programs, whether or not there are enough openings for new graduates. For example, in some years, there are twice as many graduates from law school as there are openings for new lawyers.

19 Before you decide on a major, you should know what jobs graduates of that program routinely find, what these jobs pay, and how difficult it is to find a position. While a student could certainly choose a major that had a problematic career outlook, such a decision should be made with all the facts laid bare, particularly since earning a degree often requires going into debt.

READING FOR REAL LIFE

Economic Issues in Career Decision Making

If you are interested in having your career aptitudes tested, you can make an appointment at the career counseling center of your school. If you want to look up pay and job outlook information for a particular profession, go to the Bureau of Labor Statistics Web site (www.bls.gov) and click on Occupational Outlook Handbook. You will find reports on hundreds of different jobs.

PART II: TEST QUESTIONS

Directions: Choose the best definition or paraphrasing of the underlined section of the following sentences. You should refer back to any annotations you made on the article "Economic Issues in Career Decision Making." Do not use a dictionary or any other notes.

_____1. **Paragraph 1:** The assumption that an intellectually stimulating major will automatically lead to a job compatible with one's personality is erroneous.

    a. It is not true that just because you find your major program interesting you will like the job it leads to.

      b. Choosing an interesting major will lead to a job you like.

      c. College studies are always more interesting than jobs.

      d. It is hard to find a job that matches your personality.

_____2. **Paragraph 1:** The assumption that an intellectually stimulating major will automatically lead to a job <u>compatible</u> with one's personality is erroneous.

      a. fitting together well, matching well

      b. going against

      c. interesting

      d. wrong

_____3. **Paragraph 2:** <u>Liberal arts majors are those in which studies are not closely tied to a particular profession.</u>

      a. Liberal arts programs are connected to jobs.

      b. People in liberal arts programs do not get jobs after graduation.

      c. Liberal arts programs do not prepare people for a particular job.

      d. Liberal arts programs are not practical.

_____4. **Paragraph 2:** The <u>primary</u> type of employment that liberal arts majors find is in financial services, sales, and office management.

      a. main   **c.** least desirable, hateful

      b. best, most desirable   **d.** least important, smallest

_____5. **Paragraph 3:** The chief reason why so many liberal arts graduates end up in sales and office-related professions is the <u>relative</u> size of job pools.

      a. having to do with family   **c.** changing

      b. considered in comparison   **d.** small

_____6. **Paragraph 4:** For example, a nursing major who takes pleasure in learning about the human body may find that he or she does not <u>relish</u> day-to-day contact with sick people.

      a. enjoy, like   **c.** take good care of

      b. excel, do well at   **d.** understand

_____7. **Paragraph 6:** This personality type excels at tasks which are practical and <u>concrete</u>.

      a. mixture of cement, sand, and water

      b. able to be seen or touched

      c. hard, difficult

      d. having to do with words and ideas rather than action

_____8. **Paragraph 8:** Artistic personalities like to work in environments where they can use their creativity and produce <u>aesthetically pleasing</u> products.

    a. unusual, surprising

    b. profitable, can be sold at a high price

    c. beautiful; attractive

    d. an expression of the artist's personality

_____9. **Paragraph 10:** Enterprising individuals enjoy attention, like to lead, and tend to be persuasive, <u>gregarious</u>, and extroverted.

    a. bossy   **c.** selfish

    b. friendly   **d.** good at selling

_____10. **Paragraph 11:** Conventional people are organized, systematic, and <u>meticulous</u> in handling tasks involving detail.

    a. careful and precise   **c.** fast and efficient

    b. not artistic   **d.** traditional

_____11. **Paragraph 13:** Although students may give careful thought to what program of study they might enjoy, they are <u>prone</u> to ignore the work, pay, and opportunities available to graduates with the degree they are considering.

    a. lying face down   **c.** reluctant

    b. likely to, inclined to do   **d.** knowledgeable, well-informed

_____12. **Paragraph 14:** There are huge pay <u>disparities</u> between jobs requiring equivalent amounts of education.

    a. similarities   **c.** differences

    b. equalities   **d.** amounts

_____13. **Paragraph 14:** Some people with bachelor's degrees earn twice as much as others, even though they spent <u>comparable</u> amounts of time and money on degrees.

    a. a lot   **c.** different

    b. very little   **d.** similar, nearly the same

_____14. **Paragraph 17:** It's important to be <u>conversant</u> with both starting and average pay rates.

    a. familiar, knowledgeable

    b. being able to communicate well

    c. on the other hand; by contrast

    d. well paid

_____15. **Paragraph 17:** Changes in the population create or <u>diminish</u> demand for workers.

    a. increase   **c.** change

    b. reduce; make less   **d.** keep in balance

_____16. **Paragraph 17:** For example, the aging of the population is increasing the demand for <u>geriatric</u> specialists, and so that field is growing.

    a. having to do with insurance

    b. having to do with health care

    c. having to do with old people

    d. having to do with housing problems

_____17. **Paragraph 17:** Last, <u>automation</u> has resulted in the loss of some jobs.

    a. work done by machines, especially computers

    b. work done without thought

    c. work done using many workers

    d. work done by cheaper workers from overseas

_____18. **Paragraph 18:** In some countries, the government limits the number of students that can study for a particular profession so that there is not an <u>oversupply</u> of graduates.

    a. too few   **c.** setting high standards

    b. too many   **d.** setting low standards

_____19. **Paragraph 19:** Before you decide on a major, you should know what jobs graduates of that program <u>routinely</u> find.

    a. rarely   **c.** thoughtfully, carefully

    b. commonly, usually   **d.** after much effort

_____20. **Paragraph 19:** <u>While a student could certainly choose a major that had a problematic career outlook, such a decision should be made with all the facts laid bare.</u>

    a. Students should only choose careers without problems.

    b. Knowing the facts will help students avoid problem careers.

    c. Students can choose any career field they like, but should be well informed about their choice.

    d. It is hard to find facts about careers with problems.

CHAPTER 2

Seeing the Organization of Ideas: Part One

OVERVIEW

LEARNING GOALS

After completing this chapter, you should be able to

- Identify the topic of a paragraph.
- Recognize academic thought patterns and use them to create useful annotations.
- Use annotations on paragraph topics and academic thought patterns to find information quickly.

The Problem of Staying Oriented in Longer Readings

The reading load in a typical college course is quite heavy—commonly at least forty pages per week for each class. Students often read late at night when they are tired after a long day of classes, a fatiguing shift at work, and household chores. When they sit down to read, here is what commonly happens:

The student starts in on the first paragraph of the assigned chapter. Let's suppose it is for a psychology course. Here is an excerpt from a psychology textbook. The topic is the way abnormal behavior has been viewed throughout history.

> *No one knows for sure what was considered abnormal behavior thousands of years ago. On the basis of studies of contemporary primitive tribes, however, we can hazard a general description: In such cultures, nearly everything was attributed to supernatural powers. Madness was a sign that spirits had possessed a person. Sometimes people who were "possessed" were seen as sacred, and their visions were considered messages from the gods. At other times, the tribal wise men diagnosed the presence of evil spirits. Presumably, this supernatural view of abnormal behavior dominated early societies.*
>
> *The ancient Greeks viewed strange behavior differently. Hippocrates (c. 450–377 B.C.), for example, maintained that madness was like any other sickness—a natural event arising from natural causes. Epilepsy, he reasoned, was caused by the brain melting . . .*

A short way into the text, the student realizes that she has lost her concentration and is thinking about her to-do list for the next day. After looping back to re-read from the beginning, she manages to get through six pages, marking up spots here and there with a yellow highlighting pen. However, the ideas don't hang together very well in her head. One reading specialist compared this problem to a person walking a mile down a forest path at night holding a flashlight. At the end of the path, she sees only the part that is currently in the small beam of light. Very little remains in her memory of the journey.

This sort of reading experience would not be a problem if by saying "read the chapter by Tuesday" an instructor meant only for students to give the book a quick look as a warm-up before these same ideas would be discussed in class. However, "read the chapter" in college usually means that students are expected to read and memorize key points. After reading the chapter, the students in the psychology class would be expected to be able to write essay answers to questions like "Describe the changes in the historical views of abnormal behavior from earliest times through the late 1800s."

Annotating the Focus of a Paragraph

To keep your mind from wandering or getting lost in a long reading assignment, it helps enormously to annotate the topics you see after you read each paragraph or section. Marking the text will enable you to see the order of ideas and the relationship between the topic of one paragraph and another. For instance, here is the section from the psychology text on historical views of abnormal behavior. Look at the annotations to the left.

HISTORICAL VIEWS OF ABNORMAL BEHAVIOR

Tribes—madness caused by spirits

No one knows for sure what was considered abnormal behavior thousands of years ago. On the basis of studies of contemporary primitive tribes, however, we can hazard a general description: In such cultures, nearly everything was attributed to supernatural powers. Madness was a sign that spirits had possessed a person. Sometimes people who were "possessed" were seen as sacred, and their visions were considered messages from the gods. At other times, the tribal wise men diagnosed the presence of evil spirits. Presumably, this supernatural view of abnormal behavior dominated early societies.

Ancient Greeks —madness came from natural causes

The ancient Greeks viewed strange behavior differently. Hippocrates (c. 450–377 B.C.), for example, maintained that madness was like any other sickness—a natural event arising from natural causes. Epilepsy, he reasoned, was caused by the brain melting down into the body, resulting in fits and foaming at the mouth. Melancholia, an imbalance in the body fluids, was cured with abstinence and quiet. Although Hippocrates' ideas may seem fanciful to us, they had a positive influence on the treatment of disturbed people, who as a result received care and sympathy like that offered to people suffering from physical ailments.

Middle Ages— disturbed people thought demon possessed

In the Middle Ages, disturbed behavior, like almost every aspect of life, was seen in a spiritual context. The people of the time sought supernatural explanations for melancholy, incoherence, self-abusive or violent behavior, or mere eccentricity. Abnormal behavior was often considered the work of demons; the disturbed person was often believed to be a witch or possessed by the devil. Exorcisms, from mild to hair-raising, were performed, and a number of unfortunate people endured horrifying torture. Some were burned at the stake.

Late Middle Ages—terrible conditions in asylums

Not all disturbed people were persecuted or tortured. Beginning in the late Middle Ages and continuing through the fifteenth and sixteenth centuries, public and private asylums where mentally ill people could be confined (if not well cared for) were established. Although some of these institutions were founded with good intentions, most were little more than prisons. In the worst cases, inmates might be chained down and given little food, light, or air. Although the idea of offering disturbed people some kind of "asylum" was an advance over treating them as witches, until the late eighteenth century, little was done to make sure that humane standards prevailed in these institutions.

Philippe Pinel (France)— humane reforms in asylums (1793)

The year 1793 was a turning point in the history of the treatment of the mentally ill. In that year, Philippe Pinel became director of the Bicetre Hospital in Paris. Under his direction, the hospital was drastically reorganized: Patients were released from their chains and allowed to move about the hospital grounds, rooms were made more comfortable and sanitary, and dubious and violent medical treatments, such as bleeding, were abandoned. Pinel's reforms were soon followed by similar efforts in England, and somewhat later, in America.

Reform in America— Dorothea Dix (mid-1800s)

The most notable American reformer was Dorothea Dix (1802–1887), a schoolteacher from Boston, who led a nationwide campaign for humane treatment of mentally ill people. The very concept of mental illness dates back to Dix; under her influence, the country's asylums were gradually turned into hospitals staffed by doctors, nurses, and attendants.

Use of hypnotism to treat mental illness— Mesmer's influence on Charcot and Freud (late 1800s)

At about the same time that institutional reforms were beginning, Franz Anton Mesmer was achieving considerable fame in Europe for his success in curing everything from melancholy to blindness through hypnosis. Although Mesmer was something of a showman, a number of doctors took him seriously, among them the neurologist Jean-Martin Charcot. Charcot sought connections between the workings of the brain and the miraculous effects of hypnosis. Sigmund Freud, who studied under Charcot, based much of his early psychoanalytic work on the effects of hypnosis on disturbed people. Thus, Mesmer's experiments had a lasting indirect influence on our understanding of abnormal behavior.

Fournier— connection to medical causes (1894)

Although the idea that disturbed behavior might have an organic or physiological basis dates back to Hippocrates, this notion had little experimental support until 1894. In that year, Fournier published an explanation of paresis—an overall breakdown of the mind and the body that was common among nineteenth-century merchants and soldiers. He found that most of them had at some point contracted syphilis. Fournier concluded that syphilis caused the massive mental deterioration that characterized paresis. Thus began the search for medical cures for all forms of madness.

Source: Adapted from Charles G. Morris, *Psychology,* 8th edition (Upper Saddle River, NJ: Prentice Hall, 1993), 548–50. Reprinted by permission of Prentice Hall, Inc.

Notice the difference that awareness of the sequence of topics makes. Can you now see the points that a good answer to the essay question "Describe the changes in the historical views of abnormal behavior from earliest times through the late 1800s" should include? What are they?

Although you will not always choose to mark up texts in this way, you can see that being aware of the organization of ideas makes a huge difference in your grasp of the material and your ability to do well in your college courses.

Identifying the Topic of a Paragraph

The trick to staying oriented in long readings is to see the text as a series of blocks of information on various topics, rather than thinking of it as a string of words. *Pay attention to the focus of each paragraph; don't get lost in individual words.*

For example, let's say you are reading a textbook chapter on entrepreneurship. Entrepreneurs are people who come up with an idea for a business, create a business plan, put together the resources needed, and do whatever it takes to make the new company successful. When you read the text, you should notice the topic of each paragraph. This is the kind of thing that should be going on in your head after reading a two-page section:

> I see we start out with a paragraph on the definition of entrepreneurship, then there are six paragraphs on the personality traits of successful entrepreneurs—each focused on a different trait.

Viewing the text in this way directs your attention to the information you are supposed to learn, and it will keep you from feeling overwhelmed and lost. To identify the topic of each paragraph, ask yourself, "What is this part about? What is it focused on?"

A common problem students have in correctly identifying the topic of a paragraph is that they tend to be distracted by words and phrases that are interesting (like examples) even if these ideas are not really the focus of the paragraph. To test whether you have accurately identified the topic, ask yourself whether the *whole* paragraph is about that idea. If so, then you have found the topic.

SKILLS PRACTICE 1

Read the section entitled "Finding the Right Idea." It is about how people who would like to run their own businesses could come up with an idea for a product or service. After you read each paragraph, circle the phrase that more accurately expresses the topic of the paragraph. Remember that the whole paragraph must be about that idea.

■ FINDING THE RIGHT IDEA

1. The most potent of the idea-generating tactics is to identify a compelling unserved need. It can be a two-step process: the first step is to create a list of people you know who have a great understanding about some field. Find as many people as you can who know much about a subject or industry you might be interested in pursuing. When you have put together a list, here is the question to ask the people on it: "What compelling unserved (or underserved) need do you perceive in your specialty?" Let them think it over—often it can take a few days. Don't be embarrassed to inquire about others who might be able to help, particularly if your contact has no answer for you.

    a. putting together a list of people you know
    b. finding an unserved need

2. Another tactic is to accumulate a list of the things that really annoy you or your friends. Poor service at the cable company, egg cartons that hold a dozen eggs instead of four, five-day bank holds on out-of-town checks, a confrontation with someone at the airline ticket counter, pop-up advertisements in your Web browser, and so on. List all of these irritations. It is not yet time to discard any idea. Believe it or not, there are remarkable new business venture potentials in each of these possibilities. I suggest you try this for one week, taking notes. You should come away with some serious candidates for further examination.

    a. listing irritating things
    b. poor service at the cable company

3. Next, consider the businesses you know that have refuse or by-products that are already manufactured or built and are being discarded. There is an old proverb about figuring out how to sell the "sleeves off the vests." It refers to the fact that the clothing manufacturer was able to use the cloth saved to make some other product. The image of the sleeves lying around on the cutting room floor is the source of the wisdom. Do you know of any waste that might have a use? Nothing is too insignificant for consideration. Natural gas being burned off the oil fields in Siberia was the inspiration to build a compact yet powerful electricity generation plant powered by that same natural gas. The same logic might apply to the events, people, and equipment that accumulate around a great ski lodge. What could you do with them in the summer?

    a. making something out of sleeves
    b. finding uses for wasted materials

4. Another idea is to find a new technology or a new use for an existing technology. Within the past twenty years, we have witnessed the advent of PCs, Macs, cellular phones, direct broadcast satellites, 500 channels of video on cable and satellite, the Internet, e-mail, and much more. What is coming next? My guess is that the next twenty years will see things we can hardly

imagine now. Is there a new technology out there that can be tapped? For example, an entrepreneur with the right technical skills could create video stringing software for cell phones.

a. new technologies and new uses of existing technologies

b. cell phones

    A useful way to apply your skills in correctly identifying the topic of a paragraph is to annotate the topic of each paragraph as you finish reading it. It takes just a few seconds, but the benefits of annotating are great. You will see that annotating the topics will give you a wonderful overview of what ideas you should notice.

    The following passage is from a business textbook. Individuals that want to own their own businesses are not the only ones looking for new product ideas. Established companies are also always looking for ideas for new products. For example, Apple Computer came up with the iPod, and that product has become so successful that it now makes up a major part of the company's business.

Source: Adapted from Thomas K. McKnight, *Will It Fly?* (Upper Saddle River, NJ: Prentice Hall, 2003), 3–6. Used with permission of Prentice Hall, Inc.

PRACTICE PASSAGE 2.1: MARKETING

Try annotating the topic of each paragraph at the side to get an overview of the ideas in the passage. Don't be distracted by examples.

Why New Products Succeed or Fail

We all know giant product successes—such as Microsoft Windows, Swatch watches, or CNN. Yet the thousands of failures every year that slide quietly into oblivion cost American businesses billions of dollars. Recent research suggests that it takes about 3,000 raw unwritten ideas to produce a single commercially successful new product. To learn marketing lessons and convert potential failures to successes, we analyze why new products fail and then study several failures in detail. As we go through the new-product process later in the chapter, we can identify ways such failures might have been avoided—admitting that hindsight is clearer than foresight.

MARKETING REASONS FOR NEW-PRODUCT FAILURES

Both marketing and nonmarketing factors contribute to new-product failures. Using the research results from several studies on new-product success and failure, we can identify critical marketing factors that often spell failure for new-product launches.

    The first problem is an insignificant point of difference. A distinctive point of difference is essential for a new product to defeat competitive ones—through having superior characteristics that deliver unique benefits to the user. In the mid-1990s, General Mills introduced Fingos, a sweetened cereal flake about the size of a corn chip. Consumers were supposed to snack on them dry, but they didn't. The point of difference was not important enough to get consumers to give up eating competing snacks such as popcorn, potato chips, or Cheerios from the box late at night.

Incomplete planning is another common problem. Ideally, a new product needs a precise protocol, a statement that, before product development begins, identifies (1) a well-defined target market; (2) specific customers' needs, wants, and preferences; and (3) what the product will be and do. Without this protocol, loads of money disappear as research and development (R & D) tries to design a vague product for a phantom market. Apple Computer's hand-sized Newton MessagePad personal digital assistant (PDA) that intended to help keep the user organized fizzled badly because no clear protocol existed and users found it too complicated to use. Sometimes large markets can be served better by taking features out of a product and actually making it simpler.

The market was too small. The ideal situation every new-product manager looks for is a large target market with high growth and real buyer need. But often, when looking for ideal market niches, the target market was too small and competitive to warrant the R & D, production, and marketing expenses necessary to reach it. In the early 1990s, Kodak discontinued its Ultralife lithium battery with a 10-year shelf life, although the battery was designed to last twice as long as an alkaline battery. The problem was the product was only available in the 9-volt size, which accounted for less than 10 percent of the U.S. battery market.

The product failed because of poor execution of the marketing mix. The marketing mix is made up of the name and package (product), price, promotion, and distribution (place). Coca-Cola thought its Minute Maid Squeeze-Fresh frozen orange juice concentrate in a squeeze bottle was going to be a hit. The idea was that consumers could make one glass at a time, and the concentrate stayed fresh in the refrigerator for over a month. After two test markets, the product was finished. Consumers loved the idea, but the product was messy to use, and the advertising and packaging didn't educate them effectively on how much concentrate to mix.

Another problem is that the product is of poor quality or is insensitive to customer needs. This factor stresses that problems on one or two critical factors can kill a product, even though the general quality is high. For example, the Japanese, like the British, drive on the left side of the road. Until 1996, U.S. carmakers sent Japan few right-drive cars—unlike German carmakers who exported right-drive models in a number of their brands.

Bad timing can also cause product failure. The product is introduced too soon, too late, or at a time when consumer tastes are shifting dramatically. Bad timing gives new-product managers nightmares. In March 2001, Boeing announced it would start multibillion-dollar development of its Sonic Cruiser, designed to cross oceans at almost the speed of sound and seat over 400 passengers. But the tragic attacks of September 11, 2001, caused such declines in air travel that airlines were no longer able to afford new, expensive aircraft. By late 2002, the Sonic Cruiser was shelved, unlikely to emerge for years to come.

The product lacks economic access to buyers. Grocery products provide an example. Today's mega-supermarkets carry over 30,000 products. With about 34 new food products introduced each day in the United States, the fight for exposure is tremendous in terms of costs for advertising, distribution, and shelf space. Because shelf space is judged in terms of sales per square foot, Thirsty Dog (a zesty beef-flavored mineral-loaded, lightly carbonated bottled water for your dog) must displace an existing product on the supermarket shelves, a difficult task with the exact measures of sales per square foot these stores use.

Source: Adapted from Roger A. Kerin, Steven W. Hartley, and William Rudelius, *Marketing: The Core* (2004), 222–23.

READING FOR REAL LIFE

Why New Products Succeed or Fail

As explained in the text, new products often fail for one or more of seven reasons. See if you can identify the reasons that a tissue made by the Kimberley Clark Corporation failed.

The product—named Avert Virucidal tissues—contained vitamin C derivatives scientifically designed to kill cold and flu germs when users sneezed, coughed, or blew their noses into them.

After ten months in test markets in upstate New York, the product was taken off the shelves because it was selling so poorly. Can you guess which of the seven reasons were responsible for the failure of this product? (There was more than one reason.)

Academic Thought Patterns

The topics of many paragraphs follow certain academic thought patterns. Knowing these patterns will make it easier for you to quickly recognize what a paragraph is about.

The term *academic thought pattern* refers to a type of information given about a topic. For instance, suppose you are the world's foremost expert on diabetes.

You have been asked to write a chapter on the disease for a health sciences textbook. You would certainly want to include this information:

Definition	what is diabetes
Types/Classification	what are the types of diabetes
History/Chronology (also called Time Order)	medical advances and discoveries that have changed how we treat diabetes
Causes	causes of diabetes
Effects	effect of diabetes on the circulatory system
Parts (also called Spatial Order)	diagram—pancreas and other parts of the digestive system
Process	how the body produces insulin and controls sugar levels
Listing	racial and ethnic groups at high risk for diabetes
Comparison/Contrast	diabetes in children versus adults—similarities and differences
Problem-Solution	prevention and treatment of diabetes

Every paragraph you read in college texts does not necessarily follow an academic thought pattern, but many do. Here is an example of a passage on an eating disorder called pica with the topic of each paragraph annotated:

Definition of pica	Pica is the Latin term for magpie, a bird known for the diversity of objects that it eats. Pica is characterized by the habitual eating of substances usually considered inedible, such as paint, dirt, paper, fabric, hair, and bugs.
Diagnosing pica	During the first year of life, most infants put a variety of objects into their mouths, partly as a way of exploring the environment. Within the next year, they typically learn to explore in other ways and come to discriminate between edible and inedible materials. The diagnosis of pica is therefore usually made when there is a persistent eating of inedibles beyond this age, and pica is most common in 2- and 3-year olds. Information regarding prevalence is limited, but pica is reported to be particularly high among individuals with developmental disabilities.
Effects/Dangers of pica	Pica can lead to a variety of damage, including parasitic infection and intestinal obstruction due to the accumulation of hair and other materials. The disorder also appears to be related to accidental poisoning.

Source: Adapted from *Behavior Disorders of Childhood,* 6th edition.

Notice that two out of the three paragraph topics—"definition of pica" and "effects of pica"—are examples of academic thought patterns. Much of the information you read in college will be organized around one or more academic thought patterns. There are at least two benefits in becoming familiar with them:

- You will be able to follow the author's train of thought and see paragraph topics and key points more easily.

- You will be able to spot likely test questions faster. Many test questions are drawn from information organized around academic thought patterns. Look back to the diabetes examples. Wouldn't any of them make excellent test questions?

Sometimes it will seem to you that a paragraph or a longer section falls into two or more patterns. Often people think a paragraph falls into more than one pattern because they aren't very skilled at recognizing academic thought patterns yet. However, many things you read *will* follow more than one pattern. For example, suppose you read this: "Ketosis is the process by which the body breaks down fat to use as fuel." Is this an example of a definition or a process? It is both. When you run across situations like this, choose the pattern that you think fits best and use it to make your notes. You could write down "definition of ketosis" or " process—how body breaks down fat for fuel." Either way will cover the same ideas and lead to useful notes.

SKILLS PRACTICE 2

Read the section entitled "The Growth of Portion Size." Circle the letter a, b, or c after you decide which academic thought pattern the paragraph follows.

■ THE GROWTH OF PORTION SIZE

a. definition
b. causes
c. effects

A portion is the amount of food one person is served. The recommended standard portion size for foods is defined by the U.S. Department of Agriculture. The USDA standards are also used by the Food and Drug Administration in creating the Nutrition Facts panels that shoppers can use when they are choosing foods in grocery stores.

a. process
b. comparison/ contrast
c. problem- solution

The amount of food people are actually served either at home or in restaurants is commonly much greater than the government standards. For example, the cookies people buy in coffee shops are seven times bigger than the government standard. The typical portion of pasta is almost five times bigger.

a. types
b. history
c. parts

The amount of food people eat has not always been different from the recommended portion size. Over the last forty years, the serving size of foods at home and in restaurants has increased greatly. Serving sizes began to grow in the 1970s, rose sharply in the 1980s, and are continuing to increase. For example, fast-food hamburgers, French fries, and sodas are two to five times larger than they were in the 1950s. Restaurants that serve meals on plates have increased their plate sizes from 10 inches to 12 inches in diameter so they can hold more food.

a. comparison/
   contrast
b. definition
c. effects

People differ in how aware they are of the portion size issue. Most do not realize that the amounts of food they are given to eat have grown. Six out of ten people surveyed guessed that the portions of food served in restaurants were the same or smaller than they were ten years ago. However, Americans under 35 were more likely to realize that their portions have grown compared to people over 35.

a. causes
b. history
c. problem-solution

Nutritionists recommend that Americans be better educated about the importance of portion size in controlling weight. Restaurants should also reduce the size of portions.

Many skilled college readers annotate their texts. For example, they may jot down the topic of a paragraph or section off to the side. If experienced readers see an academic thought pattern, they will often include it in their text annotations. Doing this helps them see the organization of ideas.

SKILLS PRACTICE 3

The first two paragraphs have been annotated with the academic thought pattern and topic of the paragraph. Do the last three yourself or with a partner.

■ OBESITY IN AMERICAN CHILDREN

Definitions—
overweight
and obese

In discussing weight problems in children, it is important to define terms. A child will be described as "overweight" if he or she has a body mass index (BMI) over the 85th percentile. Obesity refers to a body mass index over the 95th percentile.

History—rise in
numbers of kids
who are
overweight

Over the past forty years, the percentage of children ages 6 to 11 who are seriously overweight has been rising at an alarming rate. According to the Centers for Disease Control, up until the early 1970s, only 4% of American children were overweight. During the mid-1970s, the rate began to increase. By 1980, 7 percent of American children were overweight. By the early 1990's, the rate had risen to 11 percent, and the most recent figures show that 15 percent of children are overweight.

The rise in childhood obesity has been linked to a number of other trends. First, the amount of time schools allocate for

FIGURE 2.1 ■ *As portion size has risen, so has the number of overweight children and teens.*
Source: Photograph by Dennis MacDonald. Courtesy of PhotoEdit Inc.

physical education and recess has dropped. Children spend less time in exercise and free play during the school day. Second, the amount of television children watch has risen. Obesity is associated with a greater amount of television watching. Third, portion sizes have increased (Figure 2.1).

Obesity in children is of great concern because overweight children are more likely to suffer from health problems both in childhood and in adulthood. Excessive body fat is associated with diabetes, heart attacks, cancer, gall bladder disease, osteoarthritis, and stroke.

To prevent children from becoming overweight, experts suggest increasing the amount of time children engage in free play, reducing the time they spend watching television, and limiting their access to "junk food."

One of the advantages of learning academic thought patterns is that it helps you anticipate test questions. For example, if you notice that a paragraph follows the "causes" pattern and is about the reasons for obesity in children, you could predict that you would be asked "What are the causes of obesity?" or "What are the reasons for obesity?" How you phrase the question doesn't matter, as long as the meaning is the same.

SKILLS PRACTICE 4

After you have identified the pattern each paragraph follows, see if you can predict a test question that an instructor might ask based on that pattern. The first paragraph has been done for you.

■ PROTEIN-ENERGY MALNUTRITION

Definition

What is protein-energy malnutrition?

Protein-energy malnutrition (PEM), also called protein-calorie malnutrition (PCM), is the world's most widespread malnutrition problem. The body needs both an adequate number of calories and certain nutrients. When children's diets do not include enough calories to supply them with energy or are lacking in important nutrients, protein-energy malnutrition is the result.

There are three forms of protein-energy malnutrition. Kwashiorkor is the name given to the disease that results from a diet lacking protein. The most striking signs of kwashiorkor are a swollen abdomen and changes in hair and skin pigment. The hair of black African children with kwashiorkor becomes reddish. The second type of protein-energy malnutrition is marasmus, the condition resulting from too few calories in the diet. The bodies of marasmic children are skeletal and their faces resemble those of elderly people. The third form is marasmic kwashiorkor. The types of PEM overlap, and why a child develops one form rather than another cannot be solely explained by what is lacking in the diet (Figure 2.2).

Kwashiorkor occurs most frequently in developing countries where the diet consists mainly of starchy vegetables or cereals. Although such a diet may contain enough calories, it lacks the constituents of protein found in milk or meat. Children who have been recently weaned from breast milk and given watery cereal to eat instead frequently develop protein-energy malnutrition.

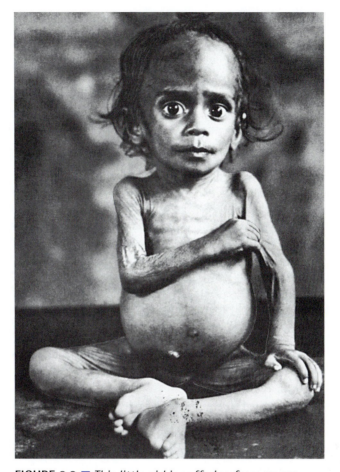

FIGURE 2.2 ■ *This little girl is suffering from severe malnutrition.*
Source: Copyright WHO/Photographer. Courtesy of World Health Organization.

Kwashiorkor also occurs in high-income countries among poor children, children with chronic disease, those who are institutionalized, and adolescents suffering from anorexia nervosa.

When the body receives insufficient nutrition, it first responds by reducing activity. Children suffering from kwashiorkor are apathetic and do not play. As their bodies weaken, they will not even cry for food. Growth stops. Sores fail to heal. The digestive tract breaks down, and the child is unable to benefit from what little food is eaten. Proteins and hormones that previously kept fluids correctly distributed are reduced. Fluid leaks out of the blood and settles in the belly and legs, causing the child to look almost fat. Other symptoms include enlarged fatty liver, atrophy of muscles, anemia, and severe diarrhea. Diarrhea depletes the body of nutrients, especially minerals. Diseases not normally fatal, such as measles, will kill a child with kwashiorkor in a few days.

Unlike children with kwashiorkor, marasmic children are not receiving any food at all. Marasmus is associated with famine and severe neglect. The symptoms of marasmus are similar to kwashiorkor; however, there are some important differences between the two conditions. Children with marasmus convert body fat to fuel (ketosis) to conserve body protein, while children with kwashiorkor do not, since they are still receiving some food. Consequently, kwashiorkor is actually a less balanced state and more fatal disease than marasmus.

Marasmic children need to be wrapped and kept warm because they have lost their insulating layer of fat and their body temperatures are subnormal. They also need love and attention because the condition often results from neglect. Both marasmic children and those with kwashiorkor need nutrition therapy. However, the order in which foods are given is critical to saving the child's life. First, the body's potassium stores and other salt balances need to be rebuilt. Afterward, nonfat milk can be introduced, followed by fat when body protein is sufficient to provide carriers.

PRACTICE PASSAGE 2.2: NURSING

In the practice passage that follows, try annotating the topic of each paragraph. You will see that many of the paragraphs follow academic thought patterns. If you see that the topic follows an academic thought pattern, work the name of that pattern into your annotations. For example, you could write "Diabetes—definition" for the first paragraph.

Diabetes

Diabetes is a disease in which the body does not produce or properly use insulin, a hormone that is needed to convert sugar, starches, and other food into energy necessary for daily life. It is estimated that approximately 6.6 percent of the population has diabetes, with about one-third of that number unaware of their serious medical condition.

There are four major types of diabetes. Type 1 diabetes results from the body's failure to produce insulin. It is estimated that 5–10 percent of Americans who are diagnosed with diabetes have type 1 diabetes. Type 2 diabetes results from insulin resistance (a condition in which the body fails to properly use insulin) combined with relative insulin deficiency. Most Americans who are diagnosed with diabetes have type 2 diabetes. Type 2 diabetes may be delayed, or even prevented from ever developing, through diet and exercise. Gestational diabetes affects about 4 percent of all pregnant women in the United States each year. Pre-diabetes is a condition that occurs when a person's blood glucose levels are higher than normal, but not high enough for a diagnosis of type 2 diabetes.

Many people remain undiagnosed because many of the diabetes symptoms seem harmless. Studies indicate that the early detection of diabetes symptoms and treatment can decrease the chance of developing the complications of diabetes. Diabetes symptoms include the following: frequent urination, excessive thirst, extreme hunger, unusual weight loss, increased fatigue, irritability, and blurry vision.

Most people with diabetes have high risk factors that impact other conditions, such as high blood pressure and cholesterol, which increases one's risk for heart disease and stroke. It is estimated that more than 65 percent of people with diabetes die from heart disease or stroke. With diabetes, heart attacks occur earlier in life and often result in death.

Diabetes is not something that should be taken lightly, and anyone can assess their risk through pre-diabetes screening. Diabetes is a major chronic disease that causes significant morbidity and mortality due to heart and circulatory problems, renal failure, and blindness. By managing diabetes, high blood pressure, and cholesterol, people with diabetes can greatly reduce their risk. Treatment may include proper diet and exercise, oral hypoglycemics, insulin, or a combination of therapies.

Source: Adapted from Mike Johnston, *Pharmacology* (Upper Saddle River, NJ: Prentice Hall, 2005), 192–99. Used with permission of Prentice Hall, Inc.

Using Annotations to Find Information Quickly

One of the great advantages of annotating the topics of paragraphs is that doing so allows you to check back on facts quickly. Imagine that you are a student in culinary arts and you have just finished a twenty-five-page chapter on cultural differences in eating patterns. Your instructor has given you a sheet listing the questions you should be able to answer after reading the chapter. Annotating the paragraphs would help you to find the information fast. If you hadn't annotated, you would find yourself pawing through pages and pages of material trying to find the paragraphs in which key facts were discussed.

To see how useful annotations are in helping you complete follow-up assignments for course readings, first annotate the topics in the following passage, and then try answering the questions that follow.

PRACTICE PASSAGE 2.3: CULINARY ARTS

Food Patterns in Central America and Mexico

The foods commonly eaten in Mexico and Central America are a flavorful blend of the native plants and fish eaten by the Indians mingled with pork, spices, and other European ingredients brought by the Spanish invaders. Although there are some differences in various regions of Mexico and its neighbors to the south, most people today eat a diet that strongly reflects the heritage of the Indian ancestors. Corn, the hardy cereal crop that formed the foundation of the diet prior to the arrival of the Spanish, still is the dominant staple, augmented by wheat and rice brought by the Spaniards. Beans of various types, chilies, and tomatoes were eaten by early Indians, while today they are likely to be flavored with lard, onions, and garlic, the contributions of the Spanish.

Corn is featured on the menu all day long throughout this entire region. Tortillas appear at all meals. Their preparation often is done at factories today; they frequently are made at home too. Preparation of tortillas requires *masa harina*, the flour made in earlier days by grinding hull-less, lye-soaked corn (*nixtamal*) with a hand-shaped stone (*mano*) on a flat stone quern (*metate*). After masa harina is worked into a dough with added water, balls of dough are patted or pressed into flat circles about one-eighth inch thick and usually 6 to 8 inches in diameter. These flat disks of dough are baked on a flat, cast-iron griddle (*comal*) and served immediately, or the baked tortillas may be reheated (often by frying) when used later.

Wheat is used to make flour tortillas, particularly in the northern part of Mexico. The gluten in the wheat flour makes the tortilla dough easier to manipulate than the dough made with corn. This characteristic is evident in the much larger disks commonly made when preparing flour tortillas. The malleable texture of flour tortillas is illustrated effectively in burritos, the Mexican dish featuring a hearty filling such as beans or meat (or both) and other ingredients wrapped in a large flour tortilla and often garnished with salsa (sauce of chopped tomatoes and other ingredients and seasoned with chilies and various spices).

Several recipes use corn tortillas as their base. Tacos are made with tortillas (either fried to make a crisp shell or soft) folded in half to hold the desired filling made with any combination of beans, slivered meats, chopped tomatoes and lettuce, salsa, grated cheese, and sour cream. Enchiladas are another dish made with corn tortillas, but these are rolled with a filling and covered with a sauce and grated cheese, then baked. *Quesadillas* are made by placing a rather thin layer of grated cheese or other filling over half of a tortilla and then folding the other half over to make a turnover that is heated in the oven or sometimes fried. A tostada is made by frying a tortilla (either corn or flour) in a bowl shape to make it crisp, then generously filling it with layers of refried beans, slivered meats, chopped tomatoes, onions, cilantro, grated cheese, guacamole, and salsa. *Flautas* are made by putting a small amount of filling very tightly into a corn tortilla and rolling it into a pencil shape, then frying it until crisp. Guacamole, a favorite salsa of pureed avocado flavored with chilies and other seasonings, is often an accompaniment to flautas as well as many other dishes. Other dishes featuring corn tortillas are *chalapas* (fried tortillas topped with ingredients similar to those used in a tostada), *chilaquiles* (shredded tortillas, fried before baking with chili sauce), and *gorditas* (thick, small tortillas fried with meats or vegetables, or both, and cheese).

Tamales with a variety of fillings are popular throughout this region. Their place in the menu may be as the main part of a meal, while sweet tamales are a dessert item. Basically, tamales are a cornmeal dough with a filling; the filled tamale is wrapped in cornhusks (or banana leaves, in tropical regions) and steamed until the dough is done and the filling is cooked. The wrapping is then discarded, and the tamales are devoured with enthusiasm.

Many different types of chilies are grown in Mexico and Central America, and are used as flavoring or even as a main ingredient, as in *chiles rellenos*. Anaheim (or California) long green chilies are used in making chiles rellenos, and various other dishes utilize these or other chilies. Considerable care is required when working with chilies to avoid burning hands, mouth, and eyes with the juices and fumes that come from them while removing the seeds and interior veins—the extremely hot parts of the chilies. Chilies for chiles rellenos are singed over a gas flame or in the oven to blacken and crisp the skin for easy removal; the cleaned chile is filled with grated cheese and dipped in a frothy egg batter, then deepfried, usually in lard (Figure 2.3).

Beans are a staple item in diets throughout Mexico and Central America. Frequently, they are fried with lard and sometimes cheese, a dish called *frijoles refritos* (refried beans). Sometimes, beans are served after they have been simmered until soft, but without adding lard or other fat. The protein content of beans is augmented with rice, often served as Spanish rice seasoned with tomatoes and chilies. These two protein sources complement each other to provide the equivalent of a complete protein. This is of particular importance for people who may not be able to afford meat on a daily basis.

Lard is the preferred and commonly used fat in this cuisine. Before the Spaniards brought pigs, the fat content of the diet was very low because of lack of sources. The cuisine now has evolved to one encompassing many fried foods and generous use of lard in recipes. Butter is available, but has not replaced lard in cooking.

Milk and dairy products are somewhat limited, although fresh cheeses are available. Canned and sweetened condensed milk are the preferred sources of milk, a pattern that developed because these products do not require refrigeration until opened, and refrigeration is of limited availability to many. Milk may be used in cooking, but is not generally used as a beverage in this region.

Some unique items in the Mexican and Central American diets are *nopales* (leaves of prickly pear cactus, usually pickled or fried), *tajaditas* (fried banana chips), *jicama* (root vegetable with a crisp texture, often sprinkled with chili powder and eaten raw), and fruit of the prickly pear cactus.

FIGURE 2.3 ■ *Chiles rellenos, rice, beans, guacamole, and albondigas soup are the main course of this meal, which also includes tortilla chips and salsa.*
Source: Courtesy of Margaret McWilliams.

Beverages include *atole* (a thick, cornmeal-based drink), hot chocolate (often flavored with cinnamon and beaten with a carved wooden beater), tequila (twice-distilled alcoholic beverage prepared from sap of the agave or century plant, often served with salt and lime), and *pulque* (mildly alcoholic beverage from agave sap). Coffee, usually served *con leche* (with milk), is very popular.

Meal patterns are influenced by economic factors and rural or urban locations of families. Breakfast (*desayuno*) may be as simple as café con leche and a bread, pastry, or tamale before people leave for work, while rural workers may do some chores before eating a more substantial breakfast that includes beans and tortillas as well. To help hungry workers survive until the typically late lunch (*almuerzo*), usually a tortilla-based dish and a beverage is served shortly before noon. The main meal is *comida*, which is eaten in mid-afternoon and followed by a siesta. The menu for this meal is large, often beginning with soup and continuing with beans, rice, and tortillas or a hearty main dish, a dessert (flan is a favorite), and a beverage. A very late afternoon refreshment is the *merienda*, a time for enjoying a sweet pastry or roll, such as *bunuelos*, and a beverage (perhaps atole, hot chocolate, or coffee). Finally, supper (*cena*) may be served sometime between 8:00 p.m. and midnight in the city. This may be as simple as leftovers from comida. Snacking often also adds to the food intake of most people.

Questions

1. List the main meal of the day and note the time of day it is served and the foods it would typically include.

    _____

    _____

2. Which ingredients common in Mexican and Central American cuisine come from Indian peoples and which were introduced by the Spanish invaders?

    _____

    _____

3. In Mexican and Central American cuisine, beans are often served with rice. What is the nutritional advantage in pairing those two foods?

    _____

    _____

4. Chilies are an important ingredient in a number of dishes. Which parts of the chilies need to be removed during preparation?

    _____

    _____

5. Flour made from corn is used to make tortillas. What is the name of the flour made from corn?

    _____

    _____

6. What recipes use corn tortillas as their base?

    _____

    _____

7. What is the advantage of using wheat flour to make tortillas rather than corn?

    _____

    _____

8. There are two alcoholic beverages made from the sap of the agave plant. What are their names and which one is stronger?

    _____

    _____

Source: Adapted from Margaret McWilliams and Holly Heller, *Food Around the World: A Cultural Perspective* (Upper Saddle River, NJ: Prentice Hall, 2002), 314–17. Reprinted by permission of Prentice Hall, Inc.

Putting It All Together

Now that you have practiced annotating topics and are sensitized to the common academic thought patterns, try working a bit on your speed. You want to be able to spend just a few seconds per paragraph jotting down the topic to the side. See how quickly you can annotate paragraph topics while maintaining the quality of your markings.

PRACTICE PASSAGE 2.4: AUTOMOTIVE TECHNOLOGY

How Brakes Stop Vehicles

Brakes are an energy-absorbing mechanism that converts vehicle movement into heat while stopping the rotation of the wheels. All braking systems are designed to reduce the speed of and stop a moving vehicle and to keep it from moving if the vehicle is stationary. **Service brakes** are the main driver-operated brakes of the vehicle. Service brakes are also called **base brakes** or **foundation brakes.**

Most vehicles use a brake on each wheel. To stop a wheel, the driver exerts force on a brake pedal. The force on the brake pedal pressurizes brake fluid in a master cylinder. This hydraulic force (liquid under pressure) is transferred through steel lines to a wheel cylinder or caliper at each wheel. Hydraulic pressure to each wheel cylinder or caliper is used to force friction materials against the brake drum or rotor. The friction between the stationary friction material and the rotating drum or rotor (disc) causes the rotating part to slow and eventually stop. Since the wheels are attached to the drums or rotors, the wheels of the vehicle also stop.

The heavier the vehicle and the higher the speed, the more heat the brakes have to be able to absorb. Long, steep hills can cause the brakes to overheat, reducing brake efficiency.

Drum brakes are used on the rear of many rear-wheel-drive, front-wheel-drive, and four-wheel-drive vehicles. Since the early 1970s, few vehicles have used drum brakes on the front wheels. When drum brakes are applied, brake shoes are moved outward against a rotating brake drum. The wheel studs for the wheels are attached to the drum. When the drum slows and stops, the wheels also slow and stop. Drum brakes are economical to manufacture, service, and repair. Parts for drum brakes are generally readily available and reasonably priced. On some vehicles, an additional drum brake is used as a parking brake on vehicles equipped with rear disc brakes.

Disc brakes are used on the front of most vehicles built since the early 1970s and on the rear wheels of many vehicles. A disc brake operates by squeezing brake pads on both sides of a rotor or disc that is attached to the wheel. In contrast to drum brakes, the rotating part of a disc brake is the rotor or disc, and the friction part is the brake "pad." In drum brakes, the rotating part is the brake drum, and the friction part is the brake "shoe."

To summarize, the events necessary to stop a vehicle are as follows: first, the driver presses on the brake pedal. Second, the brake pedal force is transferred hydraulically to a wheel cylinder or caliper at each wheel. Third, hydraulic pressure inside the wheel cylinder or caliper presses friction materials (brake shoes or pads) against rotating brake drums or rotors. Fourth, the friction slows and stops the drum or rotor. Since the drum or rotor is bolted to the wheel of the vehicle, the vehicle also stops. Finally, when the wheels of the vehicle slow and stop, the tires must have friction (traction) with the road surface to stop the vehicle.

BRAKE FLUID

Brake fluid is made from a combination of various types of glycol, a nonpetroleum-based fluid. Brake fluid is a polyalkylene-glycol-ether mixture called **polyglycol** for short. All polyglycol brake fluid is clear to amber in color. Brake fluid has to have the following characteristics: a high boiling point, a low freezing point, and the ability to not damage rubber parts in the brake system.

Automotive technicians should be familiar with the Department of Transportation (DOT) brake fluid specifications. All automotive brake fluid must meet Federal Motor Vehicle Safety Standard 116. The Society of Automotive Engineers (SAE) and the Department of Transportation (DOT) have established brake fluid specification standards for various kinds of brake fluid. For instance, the standard for DOT 3 brake fluid is a dry boiling point of 401 degrees Fahrenheit and a wet boiling point of 284 degrees Fahrenheit. For DOT 4 brake fluid, the dry boiling point is 446 degrees Fahrenheit and the wet boiling point is 311 degrees Fahrenheit. DOT 5 brake fluid has a dry boiling point of 500 degrees Fahrenheit and a wet boiling point of 356 degrees Fahrenheit. The wet boiling point is often referred to as "ERBP," meaning equilibrium reflex boiling point. ERBP refers to the method in the specification for how the fluid is exposed to moisture and tested.

DOT 3 is the type of brake fluid most often used. It absorbs moisture. According to the Society of Automotive Engineers, DOT 3 can absorb 2% of its volume in water per year. Moisture is absorbed by the brake fluid through microscopic seams in the brake system and around seals. Over time, the water will corrode the system and thicken the brake fluid. The moisture also can cause a spongy brake pedal due to reduced vapor-lock temperature. DOT 3 must be used from a sealed (capped) container. If allowed to remain open for any length of time, DOT 3 will absorb moisture from the surrounding air.

DOT 4 is formulated for use by all vehicles, imported or domestic. It is commonly called LMA (low moisture absorption). DOT 4 does not absorb water as fast as DOT 3 but is still affected by moisture and should be used only from a sealed container. DOT 4 is approximately double the cost of DOT 3. DOT 4 can be used wherever DOT 3 is specified.

DOT 5 is commonly called **silicone brake fluid** and is made from polydimethylsiloxanes. It does not absorb any water. DOT 5 brake fluid is purple (violet) in color to distinguish it from DOT 3 or DOT 4 brake fluid. DOT 5 brake fluid should not be mixed with any other type of brake fluid. Therefore, the entire braking system must be completely flushed and refilled with DOT 5. DOT 5 is approximately four times the cost of DOT 3 brake fluid. It is important to note that DOT 5 brake fluid is not recommended for use with antilock braking systems because it absorbs air. In antilock braking systems, valves and pumps are used that can aerate the brake fluid. Brake fluid filled with air bubbles cannot properly lubricate the antilock braking system components and will cause a low and soft brake pedal.

DOT 5.1 is a non-silicone-based polyglycol fluid and is clear to amber in color. This severe duty fluid has a boiling point of over 500 degrees Fahrenheit equal to the boiling point of silicone-based DOT 5 fluid. Unlike DOT 5, Dot 5.1 can be mixed with either DOT 3 or DOT 4 according to the brake fluid manufacturer's recommendations.

Most import brand vehicles specify a brake fluid replacement service interval. This recommendation is usually every 2 years or every 30,000 miles. Always check for the exact recommended brake fluid change interval. Most domestic vehicle manufacturers do not specify a brake fluid change interval. There are several ways to test or inspect the brake fluid. First, the brake fluid should look clear or amber. If the brake fluid looks like black coffee or coffee with cream, it would be wise to replace the fluid. Second, test strips may be dipped into the brake fluid. They change color when the brake fluid is contaminated. Third, a brake fluid tester can be used to test the boiling point of the brake fluid.

It is important to change brake fluid when it becomes old. Old brake fluid often has a boiling point under 300 degrees Fahrenheit. When the air temperature is over 100 degrees, it does not take much more heat to start boiling the brake fluid. If the brake fluid boils, the brake pedal will feel soft and the brakes will not work normally.

Source: Adapted from James D. Halderman and Chase D. Mitchell Jr., *Automotive Technology*, 2nd edition (Upper Saddle River, NJ: Prentice Hall, 2002), 734–39. Used with permission of Prentice Hall, Inc.

Reading For Real Life

How Brakes Stop Vehicles

While on a long road trip, a person is driving a four-year-old car in very hot weather through mountainous country. Suddenly, the brake pedal starts sinking to the floor. When the vehicle was cold, the brakes worked fine. However, as soon as the car was in motion a short time and the brakes had been used several times, the pedal became soft and spongy. What do you think is causing the problem? What needs to be done to fix it?

PRACTICE TEST
Seeing the Organization of Ideas

PART I: PASSAGE TO PREPARE

Directions: Read the following article entitled "Sending Money Home." Mark in the meanings of any unfamiliar words. Then annotate the topic of each paragraph. You will notice that many paragraphs follow academic thought patterns.

SENDING MONEY HOME

1 The practice of immigrants to the United States sending part of their earnings back to family members in their native countries has received an increasing amount of attention. The funds sent back to native countries are called international remittances. Many immigrants send as much money as they possibly can in remittances, even though it puts them under enormous financial stress. For instance, many college students send money to family members in their home countries, even though they are themselves struggling to cover their tuition and living expenses. According to a study conducted by the Pew Hispanic Center and Multilateral Investment Fund, "Remittances are the expression of profound emotional bonds between relatives separated by geography and borders, and they are a manifestation of a profound and constant interaction among these relatives regardless of the distances between them."

2 The amounts sent back to family members are commonly wired through a money transfer company such as Western Union or MoneyGram. After the worker in the United States has arranged for the money to be sent, he or she calls the family in the home country to notify them of the remittance. Then a family member goes to the local branch of the money transfer company to pick up the funds.

3 A problem in sending money back home is that there are a number of fees to pay all along the process. For instance, most immigrant workers do not have a bank account so they must use a check-cashing service. Check-cashing companies charge between 1 and 3 percent of the paycheck amount, with 2.5 percent being

a typical charge. For example, if the amount of the check to be cashed is $300, then the fee to cash it will be $7.50. After the paycheck is cashed, another fee will be charged by the money transfer company (such as Western Union or MoneyGram) to wire the funds. For instance, it may cost anywhere from $15 to $25 to wire $200. When the family goes to pick up the funds, they will likely have to pay more fees to access the cash or convert it to the local currency. Fortunately, banks and credit unions anxious to attract new customers are offering remittance services at lower prices than Western Union and MoneyGram. For instance, World Council of Credit Unions formed the International Remittance Network in 1999. The remittance fee is usually $10.

4   The practice of international remittances from immigrants in the United States is not a new phenomenon. The earliest known money transmittal business was created in California in the early 1900s to serve immigrants that wanted to send a portion of their earnings back home. However, over the last decade, the total amount of money sent in international remittances has grown tremendously. For instance, within one year—2001 to 2002—the amount of money sent to El Salvador and the Dominican Republic grew 17 percent.

5   Until recently, India received the greatest share of remittances from immigrant workers in the United States. However, the total amount of money sent to Mexico has recently surpassed that sent to India. The countries receiving the largest remittances as of 2002 (in order) were Mexico, India, the Philippines, Morocco, Egypt, Turkey, and Lebanon. Latin America and the Caribbean receive about 31 percent of total remittances, South Asia receives 20 percent, the Middle East and North Africa receive 13 percent, and Southern Africa receives 5 percent.

6   Immigrants in the United States typically send money to their native countries at least seven times per year, and the average amount sent each time is $260. However, the average amounts sent vary by country. For example, the average amount sent to families in Mexico is $378 each time, while the average amount sent to Haiti is $142. The funds are used by the families to pay for their rent, food, clothing, and health care expenses.

7   The amount of money that immigrants send to family members in their home countries is influenced by how long they have been in the United States. Remittances tend to be lower during the first five years because workers often have low-paying jobs at first. After five years, the amount that immigrants send back tends to rise and also become more steady as their employment situation improves and their incomes increase. After ten years in the United States, the amount that immigrants send home tends to drop off. Sometimes the immigrants' expenses are going up as they improve their own standard of living; for instance, they may buy a house. Additionally, other family members may become more able to share financial responsibility for the support of the family. It is also possible that after so many years apart, family ties weaken.

8   Sending money to family members is not the only kind of contribution that immigrant workers make to the well-being of their home communities. They also work to alleviate poverty. Immigrants send money back to their native countries for economic and community development projects. The funding of these projects is organized through hometown associations. Immigrants from the same region form clubs. For example, Mexican immigrants have formed approximately 600 hometown associations in 30 different U.S. cities. The groups raise money to build health clinics, roads, schools, and wells in their home communities. One Salvadoran hometown association in the Washington, D.C. area raised $10,000 to fund a farm cooperative. The idea behind these projects is to raise the standard of living for all members of the communities in their home regions and relieve poverty by attacking it at the roots.

PART II: TEST QUESTIONS

Directions: The following questions ask you to identify the topic or academic thought pattern of a paragraph. There are also some detail questions that assess your ability to use the annotations of topics you made in Part I to find the relevant section quickly. You may refer back to any annotations you made on the article "Sending Money Home." Do not use a dictionary or any other notes.

▪ STATING PARAGRAPH TOPICS

_____1. The best way to state the topic of paragraph 1 is

   a. stress faced by immigrants to the United States

   b. the Pew Hispanic Center and Multilateral Investment Fund

   c. the meaning of international remittances

   d. emotional bonds between family members

_____2. The best way to state the topic of paragraph 2 is

   a. how money is sent to immigrants' families

   b. Western Union and MoneyGram

   c. international remittances

   d. notifying family members

_____3. The topic of paragraph 3 can be best described as

   a. check-cashing companies

   b. fees involved in wiring money

   c. credit unions

   d. converting wired funds to the local currency

_____4. The best way to state the topic of paragraph 4 is

   a. how the amount of international remittances has grown over time

   b. El Salvador and the Dominican Republic

   c. the first money transmittal company

   d. why immigrants send money to their home countries

_____5. The best way to state the topic of paragraph 5 is

   a. immigrant workers in the United States

   b. India

   c. Mexico

   d. countries that receive money from workers in the United States

_____6. The best way to state the topic of paragraph 6 is

   a. how families use the money sent by immigrants from the United States

   b. average amount sent to Mexico

    c. average amount sent to Haiti

    d. how much money immigrants send to their families on average

_____7. The best way to state the topic of paragraph 7 is

    a. why the amounts sent by immigrants change

    b. increasing earnings

    c. buying a house

    d. working for low pay

_____8. The best way to state the topic of paragraph 8 is

    a. building health clinics

    b. the Salvadoran hometown association in Washington, D.C.

    c. sending money for economic and community development projects

    d. severe poverty in other countries

■ IDENTIFYING ACADEMIC THOUGHT PATTERNS

_____9. The academic thought pattern that paragraph 1 follows is

    a. parts

    b. listing

    c. definition

    d. comparison

_____10. The academic thought pattern that paragraph 2 follows is

    a. comparison

    b. parts

    c. listing

    d. process

_____11. The academic thought pattern that paragraph 3 follows is

    a. problem-solution

    b. definition

    c. types/classification

    d. parts

_____12. The academic thought pattern that paragraph 4 follows is

    a. causes

    b. history/chronology

    c. comparison

    d. process

_____13. The academic thought patterns that paragraph 5 follows are

    a. parts and process

    b. listing and comparison

    c. definition and example

    d. history and causes

_____14. In paragraph 6, we see this statement: "The average amounts sent vary by country. For example, the average amount sent to families in Mexico is $378 each time, while the average amount sent to Haiti is $142." The academic thought pattern the statement follows is

    a. effects

    b. history/chronology

    c. comparison

    d. process

_____15. The academic thought pattern that paragraph 7 follows is

    a. causes

    b. definition

    c. types/classification

    d. parts

_____16. The academic thought pattern that paragraph 8 follows is

    a. definition

    b. history/chronology

    c. problem-solution

    d. types/classification

■ USING ANNOTATIONS TO CHECK INFORMATION RAPIDLY

_____17. The average amount of each international remittance that immigrants send to Mexico each year is

    a. $300   c. $200

    b. $260   d. $378

_____18. The country that receives the second largest amount of international remittances is

    a. India

    b. Mexico

    c. the Philippines

    d. Egypt

_____19. How much does it typically cost to wire money overseas?

    a. about $7.50

    b. between $15 and $25

    c. $260

    d. It's free.

_____20. In general, what has been found to be true of immigrants in the United States that have lived here for more than ten years?

    a. They send more money than they did previously.

    b. They send less money than they did previously.

    c. They send the same amount of money, but more regularly.

    d. Their pattern of sending money doesn't change over time.

3

Seeing the Organization of Ideas: Part Two

OVERVIEW

LEARNING GOALS

After completing this chapter, you should be able to

- Identify or infer the main idea of a paragraph.
- Find the major supporting details of a main idea.
- State the thesis of a section.

In the last chapter, you strengthened your skills in identifying paragraph topics and common academic thought patterns. In this chapter, we will look more closely at the relationship of ideas within and between paragraphs. ■

Highlighting Main Ideas and Supporting Details

In addition to annotating topics and academic thought patterns, you should also mark main ideas and their major supporting details. For instance, take a look at the following paragraph. The topic is marked to the side of the text. Notice that the topic follows an academic thought pattern. The main idea and its major supporting details have been underlined.

Early childhood in Nordic countries compared to the United States

There are some interesting differences between the early experiences of children in Nordic countries and those of children in the United States. Many child development experts consider the policies of Nordic nations a model for the world. First, Nordic countries typically provide free day care of excellent quality to all families. The day care centers are specially designed by architects to stimulate the children's intellectual and physical development and provide them with a sense of community. Second, by law parents are entitled to a period of paid parental leave upon the birth of a child. Parents that take advantage of this policy are guaranteed to get their jobs back; they do not risk losing their positions. Third, children do not typically start their formal education until the age of seven. Waiting until the age of seven to begin academic instruction has resulted in a much lower rate of academic failure in elementary school than is found in the United States.

Highlighting or underlining the main idea and major supporting details will enable you to see the most important information at a glance.

Identifying Thesis Statements

If you have ever taken a college preparatory writing course, you will have heard about the importance of having a thesis. The *thesis* is the central organizing idea of an essay, a passage in a textbook, or a research paper. Being able to identify thesis statements in longer texts is an important skill for college readers. A thesis is to a written piece what the spine is to the body. All the other parts connect to it. Together, the thesis and the main ideas of paragraphs make up the basic framework of ideas in a longer section. If you can spot the thesis and see how the main ideas of paragraphs relate to it, your understanding of what the author is trying to communicate will be much sharper.

Main Ideas

■ WHAT IS A MAIN IDEA?

If you have ever taken a writing course, you probably learned that each paragraph is supposed to have a main idea. The main idea is not quite the same thing as the topic. Let's look at topics first. The *topic* of a paragraph refers to who or what it is about. Take a look at this paragraph:

When he was nine months old, Dan crawled under the kitchen table and unscrewed the wing nuts that held it together. At eighteen months, he dragged the mixer around by its cord, studied how the beaters popped in and out, and insisted on sleeping with it at night. When he was two, he took the phone apart to see why it made noise. At five, he fixed a broken chain on his grandmother's bicycle.

Now, if I asked you for the topic of this paragraph—who or what this paragraph is about—you would say "Dan." Dan is the topic of the paragraph.

The *main idea* refers to the *point* the author wants to make about the topic— in this case, Dan. What point do you think the writer is making about Dan? Would you say something like: "He liked machines from a young age" or "From the time he was little, he liked to know how things worked"? If so, you are right. Either sentence expresses the main idea of the paragraph. Notice that the main idea is just that—an idea, not necessarily a particular sentence.

■ HOW TO KNOW IF YOU HAVE CORRECTLY IDENTIFIED THE MAIN IDEA

Every sentence in the paragraph should tell more about the main idea in some way. If this is not true of the idea you have in mind, then your idea is not the main idea. For instance, in the example about Dan, the whole paragraph is *not* about how he unscrewed the wing nuts that held the kitchen table together. Therefore, the first sentence can't be the main idea.

On the other hand, if you see that all the sentences in the paragraph either introduce or develop the idea you have in mind, then you have found the main idea. Suppose you see the sample paragraph and think, "The point seems to be that Dan showed interest in how things worked at an early age." Do all the sentences in the paragraph fit under that idea? Yes. Therefore, it would be one good way to express the main idea.

■ WHY IT CAN BE CONFUSING TO FIND THE MAIN IDEA

Many people become horribly lost when asked to find the main idea of a paragraph. This is not their fault. Here are some reasons it can be confusing to spot the main idea.

Main ideas may not actually appear anywhere in the paragraph. Notice that there is no sentence in our example that says "From babyhood, Dan loved machines," and yet people still understand the idea. The paragraph has a main idea, but it is not directly stated.

There are two special terms that are used when discussing a main idea that doesn't actually appear in the paragraph: imply and infer. We say that the author has *implied* the main idea. You have to pull the idea out of your own mind (*infer* it) based on the information you read in the paragraph.

Main ideas can be stated more than once in the same paragraph. The same idea could show up in two different places. Read the following paragraph, noticing the two spots where the main idea has been underlined.

> From an early age, Dan enjoyed taking things apart. When he was nine months old, Dan crawled under the kitchen table and unscrewed the wing nuts that held the table together. At eighteen months, he dragged the mixer around by its cord, studied how the beaters popped in and out, and insisted on sleeping with it at night. When he was two, he took the phone apart to see why it made noise. At five, he fixed a broken chain on his grandmother's bicycle. Even when Dan was a baby, he loved to tinker with machines to see how they worked.

We would not say that this paragraph has two main ideas. It has one main idea that is expressed twice in different words.

A main idea may be found anywhere in the paragraph. It is not necessarily the first sentence. It is true that main ideas are usually found at the beginning of a paragraph. Writers in the United States are taught to start with their point and then elaborate on it. (People in many other countries have the opposite way of presenting ideas; they end with their point.) However, many times authors choose to express their point later on in a paragraph. Look at this example:

> At five, Katrina runs faster than any other child in her neighborhood. She throws a ball with greater accuracy than children twice her age, both boys and girls. She shows unusual strength, balance, and control in doing gymnastics. Katrina has uncommon athletic skills.

In this case, the main idea came at the end.

Pieces of the main idea may be located across more than one sentence. Look at this example. The two parts of the main idea have been underlined.

> Preschool boys tend to be better at gross motor skills than preschool girls. Gross motor skills refer to control over movements involving the whole body. Running, throwing, jumping, and climbing are examples of gross motor skills. Preschool boys develop gross motor skills earlier than girls do. On average, they are better at throwing a ball or going up and down a ladder, for instance. However, as a group, preschool girls are superior to boys at fine motor skills. Fine motor skills refer to the precise control of small groups of muscles. As a group, girls develop fine motor skills earlier than do boys. Girls tend to be better at balancing on one foot, for example, or controlling a pencil.

SKILLS PRACTICE 1

Read the following paragraphs. Decide whether sentence a or b is the main idea. Test your choice—every sentence in the paragraph should either introduce or develop the main idea.

_____ 1. When kindergarten teachers were surveyed, they identified six areas as crucial to children's readiness for school. The most important area was language richness. Children should know the alphabet and enjoy reading and telling stories. Emotional maturity was ranked second, followed by general knowledge, social confidence, and moral awareness. Physical well-being was also mentioned, because poor health interferes with learning.

> **a.** Kindergarten teachers listed six areas that are especially important to children's readiness for school.
>
> **b.** The most important area was language richness.

_____ 2. In previous generations, kindergartners painted, listened to stories, played with toys, and took naps. Today's five-year-olds are expected to know the alphabet when they arrive at kindergarten. Time that used to be spent in free play is now taken up with learning the foundational concepts of mathematics. Kindergarten has changed from being centered on play to preparation for schoolwork, so the readiness requirements are higher.

> **a.** In previous years, kindergartners painted, listened to stories, played with toys, and took naps.
>
> **b.** Kindergarten has changed from being focused on play to preparation for schoolwork, so the readiness requirements are higher.

_____ 3. Singing songs is one way parents can nurture a preschool child's language skills. Second, reading stories together every night builds young children's vocabularies and teaches them to enjoy reading. Third, enrolling children in preschool can be helpful in developing the language skills needed for school readiness. A number of research studies show that young children who have attended preschool tend to be better prepared for kindergarten than those who did not. Fourth, parents should engage their children in conversation, encouraging them to describe their friends, activities and observations. One study found that the better educated the parent, the more time they spent in conversation with their preschoolers.

> **a.** Singing songs is one way parents can nurture a preschool child's language skills.
>
> **b.** There are many things parents can do to develop their child's language skills.

SKILLS PRACTICE 2

The topic of each of the following three paragraphs has been annotated. Highlight the main idea. Remember that all the other sentences in a paragraph should either introduce or develop the main idea.

Intellectual development of young children

[1]Intellectual development refers to the ability of a child to learn and remember. The range of normal intellectual development for young children is very wide, particularly from preschool to age eight. For instance, although most children learn to read around age six, it is normal for children to learn as young as four or as old as seven. The same is true for other school-related skills such as writing, counting, and following complex directions. A child that is not ready to learn to read at an early age should not be viewed as inferior. Albert Einstein, the brilliant physicist, had a great deal of trouble his first year of school because he was a "late bloomer."

Holding children back from kindergarden

[2]By law, any child that reaches the age of five by the cutoff date may start kindergarten. However, about 9 percent of parents, especially those of high socioeconomic status, choose to hold their five-year-olds back for an additional year of development. The typical child starting at age six is male, white, born a few months before the cutoff, and has parents who are wealthier and better educated than average. Affluent parents are far more likely to choose to give their children the benefit of an extra year of development before starting kindergarten than are low-income parents.

Research on keeping children back from kindergarten one year

[3]There is some evidence that it may be wise for a parent to hold an immature five-year-old back from kindergarten for a year. On the one hand, studies show that children who are less mature than their peers can benefit from kindergarten. They will still make one year's progress. However, more mature children starting from an advanced point also make one year's progress. Even if he or she is passing, the less mature child may feel bad to be always at the tail of the class. Studies show that children who started school at age six are less likely to fail kindergarten or first grade, and some had higher achievement scores later than children who started school at age five.

PRACTICE PASSAGE 3.1: COUNSELING

Now try annotating topics and highlighting main ideas yourself. Following is a practice passage on psychologists' advice on the proper way to break up with an unsatisfactory partner. Give it a first read-through and annotate the topic of each paragraph to the side. Then go back and highlight the main idea of each paragraph. In this passage, all the paragraphs have a directly stated main idea.

Breaking Up

Partners who are initiating a breakup should be sure that this is what they want. If they have doubts or start seesawing, they should write down the negative aspects of the relationship. This helps clarify the situation and can reinforce the decision to end the relationship, especially later on, when they may not remember some of the more destructive things that were going on during the relationship.

They also advise making a clean break. It isn't wise to taper off a relationship that the other person doesn't want to end. Later, especially if both partners have gone on to other relationships, it may be possible (though not likely) to be friends, but not when one partner wants to continue the relationship and the other does not. The reluctant partner's on-and-off again availability will simply intensify feelings of loss, loneliness, and deprivation in the other partner.

One should not simply disappear without notice or explanation, or announce an intention to break up by a letter or a telephone call. Explanations should be made face-to-face in a neutral public place such as a quiet, unfamiliar restaurant (not one that they frequented as a couple). In this kind of public setting, the situation is less likely to get loud and out of hand, and the partner who wants to break up can leave promptly and alone after saying what has to be said. And this should be said honestly and in terms of his or her own needs, values, and goals, without criticizing or blaming the other partner.

It is also important to choose the right time to make a break. Avoid major holidays and times in which either partner is going through a major change or crisis, such as a death in the family, a job loss, or a health problem. This will intensify feelings of abandonment and isolation.

How does one recover from the loss of a partner? Psychologists point to emotional stages, similar to those of mourning, that most people go through: numbness and trouble eating, sleeping and concentrating; then denial (the partner didn't mean it and will return); anger at the partner; self-blame (for provoking the breakup or being unlovable); and then, after six months or so, recovery—which is inevitable for most losses. Psychologists advise keeping busy with work, hobbies, and new or old interests, joining clubs, taking classes, and going to museums, parks, resorts, supermarkets, bookstores—whatever people are interested in and can afford to do that will distract them from obsessional thinking about reconciliation or revenge.

Finally, there are a number of issues to consider in finding a new partner. Finding a new partner depends not only on motivation, but also on social location: age, class, and ethnic origin, especially, and the availability of eligible new partners. Intense new involvements (in less than three months) may be rebound relationships formed to compensate for the loss, not because of feelings

READING FOR REAL LIFE

Breaking Up

Suppose you are a therapist that has been counseling a woman involved with a controlling and verbally abusive boyfriend. He has been pressuring her to move in to his apartment. She has been increasingly dissatisfied with the relationship. When your client arrives for her session, she announces that she has decided to break up with her boyfriend. She asks for some coaching on how to manage the breakup so that it goes as smoothly as possible and she doesn't lose her resolve. Based on the ideas in the passage, what advice will you give her?

of love, or even liking, for the new partner. These relationships are likely to break up also.

Source: Adapted from Betty Yorburg, *Family Realities: A Global View* (Upper Saddle River, NJ: Prentice Hall, 2001), 117–18. Used with permission of Prentice Hall, Inc.

Supporting Details

■ MAJOR AND MINOR SUPPORTING DETAILS

Supporting details tell more about the main idea of a paragraph. In addition to marking the main idea (where it is directly stated), you should pay special attention to any major supporting details. To better understand the relationship of major and minor details, put yourself in the position of an author. Let's say you are writing a paragraph on the artistic development of children. Here is your main idea—the point you want to develop:

> According to researcher Rhoda Kellogg, the artistic development of children goes through four stages.

Obviously, to elaborate on this idea, you will want to mention what the four stages are.

> According to researcher Rhoda Kellogg, the artistic development of children goes through four stages. The first stage is scribbling. Around age three, children move from scribbling to the shape stage. Next comes the design stage. Finally, children enter the pictorial stage.

The sentences that follow the main idea are all major details. They are called *major details* because they tell more about the main idea directly.

However, notice that the information in the paragraph feels a little thin. Readers will want to know a bit more about each stage. This is where minor details come in. *Minor details* give further information about a major detail. Here is the same paragraph with minor details added. The major details are underlined.

According to researcher Rhoda Kellogg, the artistic development of children goes through four stages. <u>The first stage is scribbling.</u> The two-year-old focuses on controlling the movement of the crayon or other drawing tool over the paper. <u>Around age three, children move from scribbling to the shape stage.</u> They produce simple geometric shapes such as rectangles, ovals, or intersecting lines. Drawings are not necessarily intended to represent anything. <u>Next comes the design stage.</u> In the design stage, children mix shapes to make more complex combinations. Most children have transitioned to the design stage by age four. Design stage art is abstract rather than representational; a child in the design stage is still principally interested in form and color. Their shapes are not poor attempts to draw what they see. <u>Finally, children enter the pictorial stage.</u> The pictorial stage, which usually occurs around age five, represents a major shift in a child's artistic development (Figure 3.1). For the first time, children become

FIGURE 3.1 ■ *Drawing that a 5-year-old Chinese girl made of herself, her mother, and her grandmother.*
Source: Copyright Ellen Senisi.

interested in drawing the world around them. Their initial attempts at drawing a person often consist of a circle with two stick legs sprouting directly from the head. More advanced drawings will include details like eyelashes, fingernails, shoes, and socks. The more detail, the more advanced the child.

It is important to note that labeling a statement as a "major detail" or a "minor detail" has nothing to do with whether or not it is interesting or important enough to memorize. It simply refers to whether the statement is giving more information about the main idea of the paragraph or tells more about one of the major details.

Some paragraphs have more clear-cut major and minor details than others. For example, look at this paragraph. The main idea has been underlined.

While it would be a mistake to use children's drawings as the sole measure of development, the stage of a child's artwork provides parents and educators with useful information about whether a child is developing faster or more slowly than other children. Changes in artistic development mirror changes in language, reasoning, and social skills. For example, a three-year-old child that has started drawing people would be advanced in artistic development. Such a child is also likely to be ahead of other five-year-olds in terms of reading readiness and social skills. Kellogg notes that adults should resist the temptation to interfere with a child's artistic development. Children's artwork evolves as their thinking processes mature.

The second paragraph also has supporting details, but they are not so easy to divide into major and minor details. However, in paragraphs that *do* have clear-cut major and minor details, it is useful to mark both the main idea and major details.

Main ideas that follow certain academic thought patterns tend to have clear-cut major and minor details. Look at the following examples:

Types	There are three types of blood vessels.
Causes	Asthma has several possible causes.
Effects	Poor nutrition has a number of bad effects on infant growth and development.
Listing	There are many good sources of calcium.
Comparison/Contrast	Children's immune systems differ from those of adults in several ways.
Process	Language skills in infants and toddlers move through distinct developmental stages.

SKILLS PRACTICE 3

Here is a passage typical of what you would find in health sciences textbooks. The topic of each paragraph has been annotated already. Highlight the main idea and major details.

Functions of bones   Bones serve five important functions in the body. First, they protect vital organs. For example, the ribs protect the heart and lungs. Second, they provide the body with structure and support. For instance, the bones of the vertebral column provide a framework for the trunk. Third, bones provide the mechanical basis for movement. The bones of the limbs act as levers, pushing and pulling with the help of muscles. Fourth, the marrow in bones produces red blood cells. Finally, bones serve as a storehouse for minerals, particularly calcium. Approximately 97 percent of the body's calcium is stored in the bones.

Types of skeletal systems   There are three types of skeletal systems. A hydrostatic skeleton is composed of a compartment within the body that holds pressurized fluid. Animals with a hydrostatic skeleton, such as jellyfish or worms, use muscles surrounding these compartments to change their shape and produce movement. An exoskeleton is a hard covering in which the skeleton is located outside the body and the muscles are within. An example of an exoskeleton would be the shell of a lobster or a crab. Ants also have an exoskeleton. An important advantage of an exoskeleton is that it provides protection from predators. The last type of skeletal system is the endoskeleton, in which the skeleton is located inside the body with the muscles exterior to it. Human beings have an endoskeleton. The advantages of the endoskeleton are that it is lighter and permits greater speed.

Endoskeleton of human beings   The endoskeleton of human beings is composed of two main parts. The first is the axial skeleton. The axial skeleton consists of the skull, the vertebral column, the sternum, and the ribs. The second is the appendicular skeleton. The appendicular skeleton is made up of the bones of the pectoral (shoulder) and pelvic (hip) girdles and the limbs.

Skeletons of women versus men   The skeletons of women differ from those of men in several respects. First, the shape of the forehead is different in men and women. The forehead of women is more rounded than that of men. Also, the width of the pelvic bones is greater in women. This change takes place in puberty and is designed to prepare the body for childbirth; however, it reduces women's ability to run fast. Women also have proportionally longer legs in comparison with men. The thigh takes up a greater percentage of leg length. Finally, women's feet are commonly smaller in proportion to the rest of the skeleton.

PRACTICE PASSAGE 3.2: MEDICAL TECHNOLOGY

In the following practice passage, first annotate the topic of each paragraph. Then go back and highlight or underline the main ideas and major supporting details you see in each paragraph.

Microbe Identification

When a wound appears to be infected, a swab culture should be performed in order to identify the microbe responsible for the infection. Offending microbes are most commonly bacteria, but may also be viruses or fungi. In the laboratory, several methods are used to identify the microbes from the wound culture: shape, means of reproduction, response to staining, and the environment in which they grow best.

Bacteria may be identified by shape. They are named by their genus (e.g., *Pseudomonas*) and species (e.g., *aeruginosa*). The genus name may describe the shape of the bacteria. Spherical bacteria are called cocci. Helical bacteria are called spirilla. Rod-shaped bacteria are called bacilli.

All bacteria reproduce by cellular division. Bacteria that divide in chains are identified by the prefix *strept-*, and bacteria that divide in clusters are identified by the prefix *staphyl-*. Some bacteria, such as *Bacillus anthracis* (anthrax), form spores when faced with harsh environmental conditions. Spores represent a stasis-like condition which enables bacteria to exist indefinitely. When favorable conditions arise, the spores germinate and then metabolize and reproduce as before.

Staining is another way of identifying microbes. Organisms that are stained by crystal violet are called gram-positive bacteria. Bacteria that are not stained by crystal violet, but are stained by safranin, are called gram-negative.

Last, bacteria are identified by the environment most conducive to their growth: oxygen-rich or oxygen-free. Bacteria that require an oxygen-rich environment to survive are called aerobes; those that cannot survive in an oxygenated environment are called anaerobes. Some bacteria have the ability to adapt their metabolism to either oxygen-rich or oxygen-free environments. For example, *Staphylococcus aureus* is a spherical-shaped, gram-positive bacteria that divides in cluster. Staphylococci are aerobic bacteria; that is, they prefer an oxygenated environment. However, they are facultative anaerobes, meaning that they are also able to survive in an oxygen-depleted environment, if necessary.

Source: Adapted from Betsy A. Myers, *Wound Management: Principles and Practices* (Upper Saddle River, NJ: Prentice Hall, 2003), 96. Used with permission of Prentice Hall, Inc.

READING FOR REAL LIFE

Microbe Identification

Staphylococcus aureus is a spherical-shaped, gram-positive bacteria that divides in cluster. Suppose you were suspicious that a wound was infected with *Staphyloccus aureus* bacteria. Would you test by staining the bacteria taken from the wound with crystal violet or with safranin?

Beyond the Paragraph: Thesis Statements

So far, we have focused on the topic, main idea, and supporting details of a single paragraph. It's also important to notice the overall organization of a section. A section is composed of more than one paragraph on the same general topic and is usually introduced by a heading. The overall point of a section is called its *thesis*. The thesis is to a section what a main idea is to a paragraph.

Everything that is true of paragraphs—that they have topics, can be organized according to an academic thought pattern, are supposed to have an overall point that may be directly stated or implied—is true of a section as well. Sections are organized in much the same way that paragraphs are. Whether information is condensed into a single paragraph or expands into a longer section depends on how much information the author decides to include. However, the basic organization doesn't change.

For example, look at the following paragraph. Its main idea and major supporting details have been underlined.

> The interactions between bones occur at joints, the sites at which one bone meets another. There are three kinds of joints: fibrous, cartilaginous, and synovial. Fibrous joints permit the least movement. The cranial bones are connected through fibrous joints. Cartilaginous joints allow for slightly more movement. The vertebrae are articulated by cartilaginous joints. The third type, synovial joints, also called freely movable joints, permit the widest range of motion. The knee would be an example of bones connected by synovial joints.

Now suppose that the author of the anatomy textbook wants to tell a bit more about each of the types of joints. There will be too much information to stuff in a single paragraph. The paragraph will be broken up and expanded into a section. Look at what happened to the main idea and major supporting details of the paragraph.

THREE TYPES OF JOINTS

Bones allow the body to move. The interactions between bones occur at joints, the sites at which one bone meets another. There are three kinds of joints: fibrous, cartilaginous, and synovial.

Fibrous joints permit the least movement. A fibrous joint is almost completely immobile. The bones are joined by a thin layer of connective tissue. The cranial bones of the skull are articulated by a type of fibrous joint. In a fetus, the cranial bones are not fully formed in order to permit some flexibility as the head travels down the birth canal. There are spaces of connective tissue which are later replaced with bone.

Cartilaginous joints allow for slightly more movement. The vertebrae of the spine are connected by cartilaginous joints. Cartilage pads called intervertebral disks allow for limited motion while absorbing shocks that could otherwise damage the spine.

The third type, synovial joints, also called freely movable joints, permit the widest range of motion. They are swinging hinge and ball-and-socket joints bridged by pads of cartilage and secured by bands of connective tissue called ligaments. Friction in this type of joint is reduced by the presence of synovial fluid contained in membranes. The bones of the knee are connected by synovial joints.

Notice that the main idea became the thesis. Each major supporting detail turned into the main idea of a paragraph.

■ FINDING THE THESIS OF A SECTION

The first paragraph in a section often has a special function—to introduce the thesis. If it is directly stated, the thesis of a section frequently will be found at the very end of an introductory paragraph. Don't worry about finding the main idea of an introductory paragraph. Its only purpose is to lead up to the thesis.

SKILLS PRACTICE 4

First, read the introductory paragraph and highlight the thesis. Then mark the main ideas of the three paragraphs that follow the thesis paragraph. Notice how the main ideas of each paragraph develop the thesis.

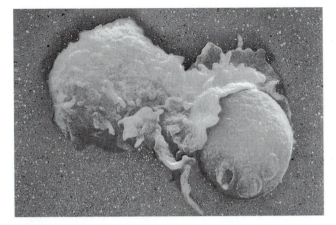

FIGURE 3.2 ■ *The War Within White blood cells, shown here, attacking and engulfing a pathogen, form a major part of the body's system of defense against bacteria, viruses, and other invading organisms.*
Source: Photograph by Biology Media/Science Source. Courtesy of Photo Researchers, Inc.

Cells That Kill Invading Microbes

The most important counterattack to infection is mounted by white cells that kill invading microbes. These cells patrol the bloodstream and await invaders within the tissues. The three basic kinds of white cells are macrophages, neutrophils, and killer cells, and each has a unique method of destroying the microbes that cause disease (Figure 3.2).

Patrolling white blood cells called macrophages ("big eaters") kill bacteria one at a time by ingesting them, much as an amoeba surrounds and engulfs a food particle. Although some macrophages are anchored within certain organs, particularly the spleen, most of them patrol the byways of the body, circulating in the blood, lymph, and interstitial fluid. They are among the most actively mobile cells of the human body.

Other white cells, called neutrophils, act like terrorist bombers. They release chemicals that are identical to household bleach to "neutralize" the entire area, killing any bacteria in the neighborhood—and themselves—in the process. Neutrophils kill everything in the vicinity, while macrophages kill only one invading cell at a time, but live to keep on doing it.

A third kind of white blood cell, called killer cells, do not attack invading microbes, but rather the cells infected by them. They are particularly effective at detecting and attacking body cells infected with viruses. Killer cells destroy "sick" cells by secreting granules loaded with perforin molecules, a special chemical that punctures the membrane of the target cell. This allows water to rush into the infected cell, which then swells and bursts.

SKILLS PRACTICE 5

Now try this one. Again, read the introductory paragraph and highlight the thesis. Then mark the main ideas of the paragraphs that follow the thesis paragraph. Notice how the main ideas of each paragraph develop the thesis.

Stages of Change

Before seeing an addiction counselor, many clients will have tried and failed to quit the habits that are ruining their lives. Clinical psychologists James Prochaska, John Norcross, and Carlo DiClemente investigated why some people are able to break addictions successfully while others fail. They learned that the great majority of persons who succeed in stopping a bad habit move through six stages.

The first stage is precontemplation. People in the precontemplation stage do not think that they have a problem, and they have no desire to change. Counselors see addicts in the precontemplation stage only because they have been forced into counseling, often by concerned family members. A person in this stage is likely to ask the counselor, "How can I get my family to leave me alone? They are the ones with the problem, not me."

The contemplation stage represents a shift from not acknowledging that a problem exists to considering the possibility of change. A person in the second stage of change will admit that there is a problem, but feels stuck. The average time in this stage is two years.

In the third stage, preparation, the person is making a plan to change. A start date of the change is set, and friends and family members are told of it. If this stage is skipped, success at changing the unwanted habit is much less likely. Only about one in five of the clients addiction counselors see are at this point; most are in the earlier stages of change.

The fourth stage, action, is the most visible stage of change to others. It is at this point that the person activates the plan. When others think of "changing a bad habit" it is the action stage that springs to mind. However, the earlier, less visible stages of change are just as important as action to long-term success.

The fifth stage is maintenance. During this stage, the person uses strategies to keep from sliding back into an old habit; this stage usually lasts six months, but for some addictions will last a lifetime. If the person regresses into the old habit from this point, it is common to move all the way back into the precontemplation stage.

The final stage is termination. At this point, there is no temptation or threat of falling back into the old habit; the desire to go back is gone, and the change has become permanent. Some addiction specialists argue that this stage does not exist, and that clients will always be mildly tempted to return to their old habits.

Researchers have found that the same stages of change hold for all addictions whether the problem is smoking, drugs, overeating, or gambling. Counselors should assess new clients to see which stage they are at and seek to move them to the next stage, but not jump prematurely to action. If a counselor forces a client to take action too early, the likelihood of failure is very great. Research shows a much higher success rate at breaking addictive behaviors when the counselor helps the client move through the six stages of change in order.

PRACTICE PASSAGE 3.3: ADDICTION STUDY 1

Now try these two sections on gambling addiction. Mark the main ideas of each paragraph as well as the thesis of each section.

Identifying Gambling Addiction

Unlike other addictions, compulsive gambling has no obvious physical manifestations—no needle marks or bloodshot eyes. How, then, are gambling addicts distinguished from those that simply enjoy betting as recreation and don't mind losing a little money? According to the *Diagnostic and Statistical Manual of Mental Disorders (DSM)*, a tool to guide psychotherapists in their diagnoses, gambling addicts may be identified and classified according to the number of problem behaviors they exhibit.

The DSM lists ten behaviors associated with gambling addiction. The first group is associatied with difficulty in stopping: the person is unable to stop, has tried to control or stop gambling, and becomes restless and irritable when attempting to stop. The next set of behaviors deals with mood: the gambler is preoccupied, needs to gamble with increasing amounts of money to feel excited, and gambles to escape from problems or improve mood. Financial problems related to gambling are also listed as indicators that an addiction may have taken hold: after losing money, the gambler returns another day to get even and has relied on others to provide money to relieve a desperate financial situation caused by gambling. Finally, damage to relationships and opportunities are also signs of gambling addiction: the person lies to conceal the extent of gambling, has committed illegal acts to finance gambling, or has jeopardized or lost a significant relationship, job, or educational or career opportunity because of gambling.

Addiction specialists recognize three categories of problem gambling. Gambling addicts are classified according to the number of problem behaviors they display. The most serious type is the compulsive gambler. Compulsive gamblers are also called pathological gamblers. A compulsive gambler will exhibit at least five out of the ten behaviors. The next type, the problem gambler, will show at least three or four of the behaviors. The final type, the person designated "at risk," will meet one or two of the criteria.

Ideally, a person showing just one or two of the behaviors associated with a gambling problem could take steps to prevent a full-blown addiction. However, Dr. John M. Eades, a therapist in gambling addiction and a recovered gambling addict himself, notes that the addiction can develop with shocking speed. "By the time you know you've got a problem, you're hooked." Addiction counselors report that they see instances of people going from never having gambled to having the entire house mortgaged and the insurance policies cashed out within a month.

PRACTICE PASSAGE 3.4: ADDICTION STUDY 2

Treating Gambling Addiction

In spite of the speed with which a gambling addiction develops, its hold on the psyche of an addict is strong. Gambling addiction often occurs in tandem with drug or alcohol addiction, and many addicts say that gambling is a harder addiction to break than either drinking or drug use. The most effective way to break gambling addiction appears to be a combination of individual counseling with a therapist familiar with gambling addiction, some form of group therapy, and spiritual renewal.

Support groups are helpful, but they are not typically effective enough to bring about a cure on their own. Perhaps the most well-known support group for gamblers is Gamblers Anonymous, an association of gambling addicts that meet together to help each other overcome addiction. While joining a support group such as Gamblers Anonymous can be an important step in recovering from gambling addiction, it is not sufficient for most addicts. One study showed that only 8 percent of Gamblers Anonymous members were still abstinent after a year in the group.

One-to-one counseling appears to be crucial. The first step in treating gambling addiction is to connect the addict with an addiction counselor familiar with gambling issues. Support groups like Gamblers Anonymous are helpful add-ons to professional one-to-one help, but a gambling addict is unlikely to recover without personal, individualized counseling by an addiction specialist.

Therapist skilled in counseling gambling addicts also often encourage them to draw strength from their religious traditions. Dr. John M. Eades commented, "I don't think people recover without a spiritual transformation. I don't care how great the psychiatrist or psychologist is."

Although it is difficult, it is possible to prevail over a gambling addiction and restore order to one's life and finances. Admitting that there is a problem, finding a skilled counselor, joining a support group, and seeking spiritual renewal can help people succeed in breaking even the most severe kinds of gambling addictions.

READING FOR REAL LIFE

Stages of Change and Gambling Addiction

This is a true case. Shortly after Beth got married to a man she met in college, she noticed that things they received for wedding presents—a bread machine, a toaster oven—started disappearing. Next, her husband told her that their apartment had been robbed while she was out and the stereo, TV, and computer had been taken. Soon afterward, she returned home to find that the furniture was gone and there was a voicemail message from her husband. He was in jail for stealing money from his employer. Beth learned that her husband had developed a gambling addiction since they married and had run up over $80,000 in debt on credit cards. Her husband said if Beth could just borrow a little money from her parents, he could go back to the casino and win enough money to put back all the money he had stolen and pay off the creditors.

- What stage of change is Beth's husband at?
- Of the three types of gambling addict, which kind is he and why?
- What would you recommend he do to overcome his addiction? Base your answer on the information in the reading.

Putting It All Together

Combine the skills you learned in this chapter with those you learned previously.

1. Annotate the topic of each paragraph. You will notice that many follow academic thought patterns.

2. Look for the thesis in the introductory paragraph. Mark any clearly stated main ideas and major details you see in the paragraphs following the thesis.

Here is an example of what the text would look like:

RUMINATION DISORDER

First described in 1687, rumination (or mercyism) is a syndrome

with a long history (Kanner, 1972). It is characterized by the

(vomiting)

voluntary and repeated regurgitation of food or liquid in the

(natural)
absence of an organic cause. When infants ruminate, they appear
(start)
deliberately to initiate regurgitation. The child's head is thrown

back, and chewing and swallowing movements are made until

food is brought up. In many instances, the child initiates

rumination by placing his or her fingers down the throat or by
(shows)
chewing on objects. The child exhibits little distress; rather,

**Thesis—
rumination is
dangerous,
must identify
and treat**

pleasure appears to result from the activity. If rumination

continues, serious medical complications can result, with death

being the outcome in extreme cases; therefore, it is important to

be alert to its presence in groups at higher risk and understand its

causes and treatment.

**Groups most
likely to develop
rumination
disorder**

Rumination is most often observed in two groups, in infants and in

persons with developmental disabilities. Among children who are

developmentally normal, rumination usually appears during the

first year of life. In individuals with mental retardation, later
(start)
onset is often observed, and the incidence of the disorder seems

to increase with greater degrees of mental retardation. In both
(common)
groups, rumination appears to be more prevalent in males

(Kerwin & Berkowitz, 1996; Mayes, 1992).

**Causes of
rumination**

Rumination in infants is often attributed to a disturbance in the

mother–infant relationship (Mayes, 1992). The mother is

described either as having psychological difficulties that prevent

her from providing the infant with a nurturant relationship or as

experiencing significant life stress that interferes with her ability

to attend to the infant. Rumination is sometimes seen as the

(interest)
infant's attempt to provide this missing stimulation.

Alternatively, others view the act as habitual in nature. The pattern

may start, for example, with the normal occurrence of spitting up by

the infant. The behaviors may then be reinforced by a combination

of pleasurable self-stimulation and the increased attention from

adults that follows (e.g., Kanner, 1972; Linscheid & Rasnake, 2001).

Treatment   Management of the problem will probably involve a
of rumination

multidisciplinary team. Treatments emphasizing use of social
(connected to)
attention contingent on appropriate behavior have been

successful, and there is some suggestion that with infant

ruminators, improving mothers' ability to provide a nurturing and

responsive environment is effective (Mayes, 1992; Nichols, 2004).

These procedures have the advantage of being easily
(put into action)
implemented by the parents in the home and of being acceptable

to them. However, controlled evaluations of interventions

are needed.

Source: Adapted from Rita Wicks-Nelson and Allen C. Israel, *Behavior Disorders of Childhood*, 6th edition (Upper Saddle River, NJ: Prentice Hall, 2005), 380–81. Reprinted by permission of Prentice Hall, Inc.

■ MANAGING CONFUSING PARAGRAPHS

The following practice passage has a thesis statement and main ideas that are directly stated. Many paragraphs do have nice, clean, directly stated main ideas and obvious major details. However, others don't. When you come across a paragraph that doesn't seem to have a directly stated main idea or major details that pop right out, just settle for annotating the paragraph topic. Remember that your goal in annotating is to maintain concentration and sharpen your awareness of the organization of ideas. However, when you are working with long readings, speed is also important. Don't allow yourself to spend too long on any one paragraph. Mark the topic to the side and keep going.

PRACTICE PASSAGE 3.5: INFORMATION TECHNOLOGY

Computer Viruses

A computer virus is a computer program that attaches itself to another computer program (known as the host program) and attempts to spread itself to other computers when files are exchanged. A computer virus's main purpose is to replicate itself and copy its code into as many other files as possible. The majority of viruses have secondary objectives or side effects, ranging from displaying annoying messages on the computer screen to the destruction of files or the contents of entire hard drives. Because computer viruses do cause disruption to computer systems, including data destruction and information theft, virus creation is a form of cybercrime. Although thousands of computer viruses and variants exist, they can be grouped into five broad categories based on their behavior and method of transmission.

Boot-sector viruses replicate themselves into the Master Boot Record of a hard drive. The Master Boot Record is a program that executes whenever a computer boots up, ensuring that the virus will be loaded into memory immediately, even before some virus protection programs. Boot-sector viruses are often transmitted by a floppy disk left in a floppy drive. When the computer boots up with the disk in the drive, it tries to launch a Master Boot Record from the floppy, which is usually the trigger for the virus to infect the hard drive. Boot-sector viruses can be very destructive: they can erase your entire hard drive.

Logic bombs are viruses that execute when a certain set of conditions are met. The conditions are often specific dates keyed off the computer's internal clock. The Michelangelo virus, first launched in 1992, is a famous logic bomb that is set to trigger every year on March 6, Michelangelo's birthday. The effects of logic bombs range from annoying messages being displayed on the screen to reformatting of the hard drive, causing complete data loss.

Worms are slightly different from viruses in that they attempt to travel between systems through network connections to spread their infections. Viruses infect a host file and wait for that file to be executed on another computer to replicate. Worms can run independently of host file execution and are much more active in spreading themselves. The Sasser worm broke out in April 2004, infecting millions of individual computers and servers. This worm exploits a weakness in the Windows operating system and therefore antivirus software doesn't protect against it. However, having a firewall installed and applying software patches as they are issued can protect you from most worms.

Some viruses are hidden on Web sites in the form of scripts. Scripts are lists of commands, actually mini programs, that are executed without your knowledge. Scripts are often used to perform useful, legitimate functions on Web sites, such as collecting name and address information from customers. However, some scripts are malicious. For example, say you receive an e-mail encouraging you to visit a Web site full of useful programs and information. Unbeknownst to you, clicking a link to display a video runs a script that infects your computer with a virus.

Macro viruses are attached to documents (such as Word and Excel documents) that use macros. A macro is a short series of commands that usually automates repetitive tasks. However, macro languages are now so sophisticated that viruses can be written with them. In March 1999, the Melissa virus became the first major macro virus to cause problems worldwide. It attached itself to a Word document. Anyone opening an infected document triggered the virus, which infected other Word documents on the victim's computer.

The Melissa virus was also the first practical example of an e-mail virus. E-mail viruses use the address book in the victim's e-mail system to distribute the virus. When executed, the Melissa virus sent itself to the first 50 people in the address book on the infected computer. This helped ensure that Melissa became one of the most widely distributed viruses ever released.

Source: Adapted from Alan Evans, Kendall Martin, and Mary Anne Poatsy, *Technology in Action,* 2nd edition (Upper Saddle River, NJ: Prentice Hall, 2005), 287–99. Used with permission of Prentice Hall, Inc.

PRACTICE TEST
Seeing the Organization of Ideas

PART I: PASSAGE TO PREPARE

Directions: Read the following article entitled "Credit Scores." Mark in the meanings of any unfamiliar words. Then do these two things for each paragraph:

1. Annotate the topic of the paragraph. You will notice that many follow academic thought patterns.

2. Highlight or underline the main idea and any major details.

CREDIT SCORES

1   A credit score is a number that lenders use to assess the likelihood that a borrower will pay back a loan on time. Lenders use credit scores to decide, first, whether they will lend money to an individual, and second, at what interest rate. A person with a low credit score will either be refused a loan or will have to pay higher rates of interest. Use of credit scores is pervasive, and if people apply for a car loan, auto insurance, a credit card, or a loan to buy a home, the lender will look at their credit scores before agreeing to extend credit.

TABLE 3.1 ▪ Effect of Credit Score on Interest Rates and Monthly Mortgage Payments

If Credit Score Is	Interest Rate Would Be	Monthly Payment Would Be
720–850	5.540%	$855
700–719	5.665%	$867
655–699	6.203%	$919
620–654	7.353%	$1,034
560–619	8.531%	$1,157
500–559	9.289%	$1,238

Source: Adapted from Fair Isaac Corporation (Upper Saddle River, NJ: Prentice Hall, 2005). Reprinted by permission.

2   There are two types of credit scores: generic scores and custom scores. Custom scores are developed by some individual lenders for use in their own companies. For example, a department store might develop its own custom credit scoring system to decide which customers will be approved for a store credit card. By contrast, generic scores are used by more than one company and are based on statistical models of the risk that a given person will not pay back a loan on time. Many stores and other businesses rely on generic credit scores in deciding to whom to offer credit.

3   Generic credit scores range from 300 to 850. Most people have scores between 600 and 800, with the median score around 721. An individual with a score of 720 or higher will typically get the most favorable rates on loans. For example, suppose a person wanted to get a mortgage to buy a home costing $150,000. Depending on the individual's credit score, the interest rate charged by the lender and the monthly payment for a 30-year mortgage would change as shown in Table 3.1.

4   An analogous situation holds for other types of credit, such as car loans and credit cards. Additionally, insurance companies and utility companies use credit scores to set rates for their customers. Those with low credit scores are charged more.

OVERVIEW OF CREDIT SCORES

5   Through most of the last century, loan officers used their own judgment in deciding which applicants would receive credit and which would be refused a

loan. This system was subject to human error. Many creditworthy applicants were turned away, while others were approved for loans simply because of superficial attributes such as personal charm and a persuasive manner.

6   Many lenders next moved to a point system in which variables on a loan applicant's credit record were scored. The point system represented an improvement over a loan officer's opinion of an applicant's creditworthiness. However, the number of points given to each variable was based on guesses as to which were the most important factors in whether or not a person would repay a loan on time.

7   Credit scores based on statistical models drawn from the activities of thousands of borrowers were first developed by the Fair Isaac Corporation, and came into wide use in the 1980s. The scores generated by these models, called FICO scores after the company that developed them, were much better predictors of which borrowers would repay loans and which would not. The use of FICO scores to determine who should be granted credit meant that loan decisions would not be based on loan officers' personal opinions. Credit scores have made it easier for many people to have loan requests approved, especially those who suffered discrimination in the past.

8   Until very recently, many people did not know that they had a FICO score, and that it would be used to determine whether or not they could get a loan. Lenders were prohibited from telling borrowers their credit score or how it was calculated. The Fair Isaac Corporation worried that if people knew their credit score and how it was determined, they would try to change their behavior to affect their rating, thus making the score less reliable.

9   However, complaints about erroneous information in credit reports and demands by consumers to know how their scores were calculated resulted in changes in policy. Now consumers can buy a copy of their credit scores from numerous sources. Additionally, as of the end of 2005, everyone is entitled to one free credit report each year.

CALCULATION OF CREDIT SCORES

10   A few years ago, the algorithm by which credit scores are determined became public. When an individual takes out a loan, information about the repayment of the debt is reported to a credit bureau. Credit bureaus have a record of the debt levels and repayment history of every person that has ever taken out a loan. The record contains notes on things like previous and existing auto loans, how many credit cards a person has, the balance on each card, and whether or not payments were made on time. The Fair Isaac Corporation and companies that provide similar services use information gathered by credit bureaus to compute a credit score. Credit scores are calculated according to a formula that assigns weight to a number of different factors.

11   The most important element in credit scoring is how reliably an individual pays his or her bills. This factor is weighted at 35 percent. Chronic late payments bring down a credit score. Paying on time consistently raises a credit score. Having an account sent to collections is particularly damaging, but the most detrimental event in this category is declaring bankruptcy.

12   The second area, worth 30 percent of the total score, is a person's existing debt—how much he or she owes on school loans, credit cards, auto loans, and so on. Also included in this category is the total amount of credit a person has available. For instance, if an individual has eight credit cards, each with a limit of $5,000, that represents $40,000 of available credit. Researchers have learned that those with large amounts of credit available are likely to use it, which makes lending money to them a riskier proposition. Similarly, people who "max out" their credit cards are perceived to be at higher risk of defaulting on a loan. Those with the highest credit scores keep their balances low and use credit in moderation.

13   The length of a person's credit history is the third factor, weighted at 15 percent. The longer an individual has used credit, the higher the credit score will be. For instance, a person that has a track record of borrowing money and paying back loans for 10 years will have a higher credit score than a person that has a one-year history of loan repayment, all other factors being equal.

14   The mix of credit is worth 10 percent of a credit score. People that have experience repaying both revolving credit, such as credit cards, and installment credit such as mortgages and car loans will have higher credit scores. Studies of borrowing and repayment patterns have shown that people with a greater variety of experience with different types of loans pay back their loans more reliably.

15   The final category in a credit score is the individual's interest in new credit—how many loan applications he or she is filling out. This area is weighted at 10 percent of the credit score. While shopping for a good rate on a car loan or home mortgage will not hurt a credit score, applying for new credit after a series of late payments is viewed as a sign that a borrower is in financial trouble.

16   Credit scores do not consider age, marital status, education, income or length of employment at a job, how long people have lived at an address, or whether they own a home or rent. A lender may consider some of these factors when people apply for a loan. However, they are not weighted in calculating a credit score.

HOW TO ESTABLISH OR IMPROVE A CREDIT SCORE

17   People that have never taken out a loan may not have a credit score. Credit reports contain information about an individual's past history of paying off loans on time. A person that always pays with cash or a check is not creating a track record of loan repayment and is sometimes referred to in the financial services industry as a credit "ghost." There are currently discussions underway as to whether timely payments of rent and phone bills should be included in credit reports so as to generate a credit score for people that have never taken out a loan. At present, rent, phone and utility payments are only included in credit reports if the person *fails* to pay, and the debt is subsequently turned over to a collection agency.

18   To establish a credit history, many people begin by applying for a credit card with a retailer, a gas card, or a secured bankcard. Secured cards are offered by banks to help people with no credit history demonstrate the ability to repay loans on time. The individual agrees to keep, for example, $500 in a savings account and the bank then approves a credit card with a limit of $500. The money in the savings

account functions as security for the card. After the individual has a track record of prompt payments, the bank no longer requires the $500 to be left in the savings account, and it may be withdrawn from the account.

[19] People with low credit scores due to heavy debt or a poor repayment history can improve their scores over time. Credit scores are always in flux; they change as the information in an individual's credit report is updated. Damaging information, such as the recording of a bankruptcy, stays on a credit report for up to ten years. However, recent information in each category of interest is weighted more heavily than older information. Reducing debt levels, using credit sparingly, and always making payments on time will result in an excellent credit score over time. Consumers should know that companies that promise to "repair" bad credit cannot remove accurate but detrimental information from a credit report. They can only help individuals correct errors on their reports, and they offer no services that people cannot manage without their help.

CHECKING CREDIT SCORES

[20] A major drawback to credit scores is that they are calculated based on information on credit reports that is frequently inaccurate. Therefore, it is vital that consumers check the veracity of the information in their reports at least once a year. It is also recommended that consumers pull a copy of their credit reports several months before planning to buy a house or a car, so that there is time to rectify any errors in the report before approaching a lender.

READING FOR REAL LIFE

Credit Scores

If you would like to see a copy of your credit report for free, you can go to www.annualcreditreport.com. Seeing your credit score costs about $15 and can be requested through one of the three main credit bureaus:

TransUnion (www.transunion.com)

Equifax (www.equifax.com)

Experian (www.experian.com)

PART II: TEST QUESTIONS

Directions: The following questions ask you to identify the topic, main idea, academic thought pattern, or thesis of part of the text. There are also some detail questions that assess your ability to use awareness of topics and main ideas to find the relevant section quickly. You may refer back to any annotations you made on the article "Credit Scores." Do not use a dictionary or any other notes.

■ IDENTIFYING TOPICS AND MAIN IDEAS

_____1. The main idea of paragraph 2 is that

    a. there are two types of credit scores: generic scores and custom scores.

    b. custom scores are developed by some individual lenders for use in their own companies.

    c. generic scores are used by more than one company.

    d. many department stores have their own custom credit scoring systems.

_____2. The best way to describe the topic of paragraph 6 is

    a. an applicant's creditworthiness.

    b. point systems.

    c. loan officers' opinions.

    d. variables on credit histories.

_____3. The main idea of paragraph 8 is that

    a. it is important that credit scores be reliable.

    b. the Fair Isaac Corporation did not want people to know their credit scores.

    c. until recently, many people didn't know they had a FICO score or how it was used.

    d. in the past, lenders were not allowed to tell people their credit scores.

_____4. The topic of paragraph 11 is

    a. how reliably an individual pays his or her bills.

    b. having accounts sent to collections.

    c. declaring bankruptcy.

    d. several ways to raise a credit score.

_____5. The best way to express the topic of paragraph 15 is

   a. the final category.

   b. an individual's interest in new credit.

   c. car loans and home mortgages.

   d. late payments.

_____6. The main idea of paragraph 17 is that

   a. people that have never taken out a loan may not have a credit score.

   b. credit reports contain info about an individual's past history of paying loans.

   c. people that always pay with cash or checks are called credit "ghosts."

   d. rent, phone, and utility payments are not used in credit scoring.

_____7. The best way to express the topic of paragraph 18 is

   a. credit cards with retailers.

   b. bank savings accounts.

   c. gas cards.

   d. how to establish a credit history.

_____8. The main idea of paragraph 19 is that

   a. credit scores are always changing as credit information is updated.

   b. people with low credit scores can improve them over time.

   c. damaging information stays on a credit report for up to ten years.

   d. companies that promise to repair bad credit can't remove true information.

■ ACADEMIC THOUGHT PATTERNS

_____9. The academic thought patterns that paragraph 2 follows are

   a. definition and causes.

   b. effects and process.

   c. types and comparison/contrast.

   d. problem–solution and causes.

_____10. The academic thought pattern that the "Overview of Credit Scores" section (paragraphs 5–9) follows is

    a. history.   c. effects.

    b. definition.   d. parts.

_____11. The academic thought pattern that the ideas in paragraph 4 follow is

    a. effects.   c. definition.

    b. history.   d. process.

_____12. The academic thought pattern that the section "How to Establish or Improve a Credit Score" (paragraphs 17–19) follows is

    a. comparison/contrast.

    b. definition.

    c. types.

    d. problem–solution.

■ THESIS STATEMENTS

_____13. The thesis of the section entitled "Calculation of Credit Scores" (paragraphs 10–16) is

    a. the most important element in credit scoring is how reliably an individual pays his or her bills.

    b. credit scores are calculated according to a formula that assigns weight to a number of different factors.

    c. credit bureaus have a record of every person who has ever taken out a loan.

    d. it is important to know your credit score.

_____14. The thesis of the section entitled "How to Establish or Improve a Credit Score" (paragraphs 17–19) is

    a. people with no credit history or a low credit score can improve their credit scores over time.

    b. people that have never taken out a loan may not have a credit score.

    c. rent, phone, and utility payments are only included in credit reports if the person fails to pay and the debt is turned over to a collection agency.

    d. secured cards help people establish credit and build a good credit score.

■ USING ANNOTATIONS TO FIND DETAILS QUICKLY

_____15. Credit scores do *not* weight information about an individual's

    a. income and length of employment at a job.

    b. interest in new credit.

    c. existing debt.

    d. length of credit history.

_____16. Custom credit scores are

    a. the same thing as generic scores.

    b. created for the use of more than one company.

    c. developed by some individual lenders for their own use.

    d. based on statistical models of risk.

_____17. According to the article, how often should people check their credit reports for erroneous information?

    a. every week

    b. once a month

    c. only before a major purchase, such as a car or a house

    d. once a year

_____18. What percentage of a person's credit score is related to the mix of credit experiences he or she has had?

    a. 10 percent   **c.** 30 percent

    b. 15 percent   **d.** 35 percent

_____19. Which of the following is true of trying to improve a low credit score?

    a. Bankruptcies stay on credit reports up to twenty years.

    b. Credit repair companies can remove true information from a report.

    c. New information is weighted more heavily than old information.

    d. Once a person has a low credit score, it cannot be changed.

_____20. During what historical period did FICO scores come into wide use?

    a. 1970s   **c.** 1990s

    b. 1980s   **d.** after 2000

4

Interpreting Charts and Graphs

OVERVIEW

LEARNING GOALS

After studying this lesson, you should be able to

- Troubleshoot any unfamiliar words on a chart or graph.
- See the question that a chart or graph answers.
- Identify and annotate information of special interest.
- Combine information from more than one graphical source.

In reading materials for college courses, you will see many charts, tables, and graphs. Don't skip them—graphics often contain important information you will need to succeed in your courses and, later, in your profession. Charts, graphs, and tables are especially likely to be found in discussions of problems and how to solve them. ∎

Graphs on the Scope of Problems

One of the most common places to see charts and graphs is in sections on the scope of a problem—how many people are affected, the types of people at especially high risk, and so on. Suppose that students in a dental health program are studying tooth decay. To be effective in reducing the number of people with tooth decay, dental public health workers need answers to the following questions:

- How many people in the United States have decayed teeth?
- Are some groups at higher risk for tooth decay?
- Are we progressing at reducing the incidence of tooth decay?

The answers to these questions are likely to be expressed in the form of a chart or graph. For instance, dental public health workers have a goal of providing water containing fluoride (to reduce tooth decay) to every person in the United States. Figure 4.1 is the graphic that shows how many people in each state have access to fluoridated water. Students would be expected to notice and remember that, in general, lack of fluoridated water is a bigger problem in the West and South than in the North and East.

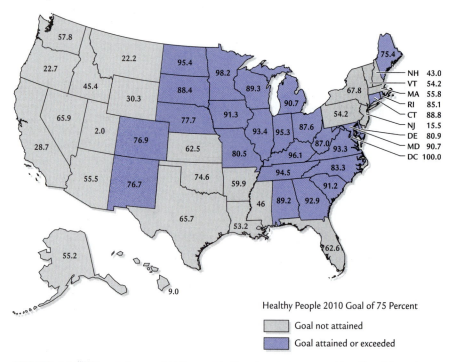

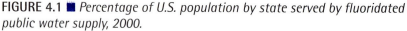

FIGURE 4.1 ■ *Percentage of U.S. population by state served by fluoridated public water supply, 2000.*
Source: Adapted from the Centers for Disease Control, 2000; U.S. Census Bureau; MMWR 2002, 51(07); 144–47.

TABLE 4.1   Classic Fluoridation Studies: Demonstration Phase

Fluoridated Cities	Year	Percentage Decrease in Decayed, Missing, or Filled Teeth per Child Since Implementing Water Fluoridation
Grand Rapids, Michigan	1959	55.5%
Newburgh, New York	1960	70.1%
Evanston, Illinois	1959	48.4%
Brantford, Ontario	1959	56.7%

Note: All four communities began fluoridating in 1945–1946.
Source: Adapted from Norman O. Harris and Franklin Garcia-Godoy, Primary Preventive Dentistry, 6th edition (Upper Saddle River, NJ: Prentice Hall, 2004), 186.

Graphs of Study Results

You will also see graphs of study results. Many of these studies explore solutions to problems. For example, suppose dental health researchers want to know how much fluoridated water reduces cavities in children's teeth. They measure the average number of cavities in children's teeth *before* the city water was fluoridated. Then they measure again a number of years *after* the water was fluoridated. Table 4.1 contains the study results.

Notice that children's dental health problems dropped by about half after the water in their cities was fluoridated. In one city, the improvement was even more dramatic.

Key Skills in Reading Charts and Graphs

You will see many kinds of charts, graphs, and diagrams in your textbooks. This chapter focuses on graphics that communicate numerical data. These charts and graphs can be especially perplexing for students because they are uncertain of how to manage them. "Surely," they think, "the instructor doesn't expect us to memorize all those numbers!" Rarely will you have to commit an entire table of numbers to memory. However, you *are* expected to understand the general point that the chart or graph is making, to be aware of which data are worthy of special attention, and to combine information from several charts or graphs. These skills are the focus of the next chapter.

Seeing the Question That a Chart or Graph Answers

In order to see the point of a chart or graph, you first need to troubleshoot any vocabulary problems. One of the issues that may come up when you study a chart or graph is that you may not understand all the words used in the titles and labels.

Charts and graphs often use formal language in their titles and labels. For instance, here are some titles of charts and graphs taken from a dental public health textbook. Across from each title, I have written a simpler way to say the same thing.

Varieties of Odontalgia   Kinds of Toothache

Prevalence of Odontalgia   The Percentage of People That Suffered
in the U.S. in 2005   from Toothache in the U.S. in 2005

Incidence of Odontalgia   Number of New Cases of Toothache
in the U.S. in 2005   in the U.S. in 2005—How Many
by Gender   Among Men versus Women

Notice that the more formal terms often save space, which is why they are used. However, if you are not yet familiar with words used in the charts and graphs you study, you will need to look them up in your dictionary. You don't want any gaps in your understanding.

SKILLS PRACTICE 1

The following paragraphs and tables were taken from a dental hygiene textbook. After you have read the paragraph, mark any unfamiliar words on the table, and see if you can figure out their meanings using the context and your dictionary. Write in a simpler word or phrase for each unfamiliar word.

Sugar in plaque is a contributory factor in dental caries. Two animal studies and three human clinical studies have contributed to the understanding of the importance of sugar in the development of caries. In a rodent study led by Kite (1950), one group of rats was fed a caries-producing diet containing large amounts of sugar by means of a stomach tube, with no food coming in contact with the teeth. No caries resulted. When the same diet was fed orally and allowed to come in contact with the teeth, caries did occur (Table 4.2).

TABLE 4.2   Caries in Rats Fed a Decay-Producing Diet
via Normal and Stomach Tube Routes

Group	Methods of Feeding	Number of Rats	Average Number of Carious Molars	Average Number of Carious Lesions
A	normal	13	5.0	6.7
B	stomach tube	13	0	0

Source: Adapted from Norman O. Harris and Franklin Garcia-Godoy, *Primary Preventive Dentistry*, 6th edition (Upper Saddle River, NJ: Prentice Hall, 2004), 405.

Toothpastes contain several or all of the ingredients listed in Table 4.3. Gels contain the same components as toothpastes, except that gels have a higher

TABLE 4.3   Toothpaste Constituents

Ingredient	Percentage
Abrasives	20–40%
Water	20–40%
Humectants	20–40%
Foaming agents (soap or detergent)	1–2%
Binding agent, up to	2%
Flavoring agent, up to	2%
Sweetening agent, up to	2%
Therapeutic agent, up to	5%
Coloring or preservative, less than	1%

Source: Adapted from Norman O. Harris and Franklin Garcia-Godoy, *Primary Preventive Dentistry,* 6th edition (Upper Saddle River, NJ: Prentice Hall, 2004), 124.

proportion of the thickening agents. Both tooth gels and toothpastes are equally effective in plaque removal and in delivering active ingredients.

After you have annotated any unfamiliar words, the next step is simply to familiarize yourself with the question that each chart or graph answers. Pay special attention to titles. Turn each title into a question, and see how the information in the graph answers the question. Write the question next to the chart or graph.

For example, look back to the tables you just annotated. Working from the title and the kind of information you have in the table itself, you can see these questions:

Table 4.2 Caries in Rats Fed a Decay-Producing Diet via Normal and Stomach Tube Routes	Which group had more cavities in their teeth—the ones that ate sugary food normally or the ones that were fed with a stomach tube?
Table 4.3 Toothpaste Constituents	What are the main ingredients of toothpaste?

Now try marking in the question that each chart or graph answers for the following practice passage. You can also note the answers.

PRACTICE PASSAGE 4.1: DENTAL HYGIENE

The Epidemiology of Oral Diseases

TOOTH LOSS

By the age of 50, most individuals in the United States have lost an average of 12.1 teeth, including third molars. Overall, a higher percentage of individuals living below the poverty level are edentulous than those who are living above

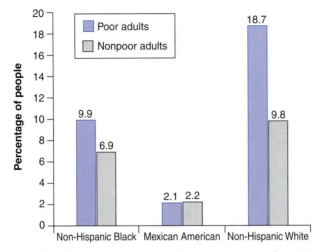

FIGURE 4.2 ■ *Complete tooth loss varies by race/ethnicity and poverty status.*
Source: Adapted from Christine N. Nathe, *Dental Public Health,* 2nd edition (Upper Saddle River, NJ: Prentice Hall, 2004), 206.

(see Figure 4.2). Tooth loss is related to race and ethnicity as well. Of all population groups, Mexican Americans are the least likely to lose their teeth.

Although the overall rate of edentulism for adults 18 and older is approximately 10 percent, the rate increases with age, so that about a third of those 65 years and older are edentulous (see Figure 4.3).

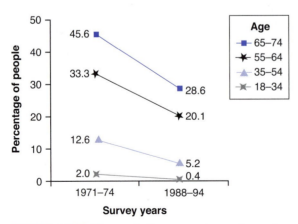

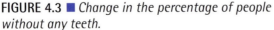

FIGURE 4.3 ■ *Change in the percentage of people without any teeth.*
Source: Adapted from the National Center for Health Statistics (NCHS), Department of Health and Human Services, 1975, 1996.

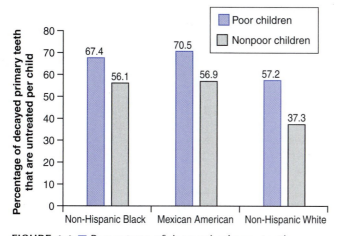

FIGURE 4.4 ■ *Percentage of decayed primary teeth that are untreated in poor and nonpoor children.*
Source: Adapted from the National Center for Health Statistics (NCHS), Department of Health and Human Services, 1996.

CARIES

Dental caries is one of the most common childhood diseases. Among 5–17-year-olds, dental caries is more than five times as common as a reported history of asthma and 7 times as common as hay fever. The majority of children aged 5 to 9 years had at least one carious lesion or filling in the coronal portion of either a primary or a permanent tooth. Despite progress in reducing dental caries, individuals in families living below the poverty level experience more decay than those who are economically better off. Furthermore, the caries seen in these individuals are more likely to be untreated than caries in those living above the poverty level (see Figure 4.4).

Improvements have been noted over the past 30 years with regard to dental caries. Younger adults have experienced a decline in dental caries during this time period, as measured by the average number of teeth without decay or fillings (see Figure 4.5). The number of untreated decayed teeth per person has also declined among all age groups.

ORAL AND PHARYNGEAL CANCER

Approximately 30,200 individuals develop oral and pharyngeal cancers every year in the United States, and sadly, of these cases, about 7,800 Americans die every year. The overall five-year survival rate for people with oral and pharyngeal cancer is about 52 percent. Tobacco use has been estimated to account for over 90 percent of cancers of the oral cavity and pharynx. Thus this represents the greatest single preventable risk factor for oral cancer (see Figure 4.6).

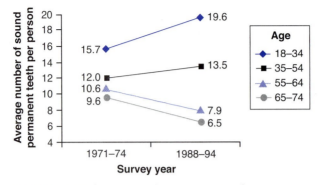

FIGURE 4.5 ■ *Change in the average number of permanent teeth without decay or fillings.*
Source: Adapted from the National Center for Health Statistics (NCHS), Department of Health and Human Services, 1975, 1996.

Incidence rates for oral and pharyngeal cancers vary by race and ethnicity. In the United States, Asians and Pacific Islanders, American Indians and Alaska Natives, and Hispanics have lower incidence rates than whites and blacks (see Figure 4.7).

TOOTHACHES

Oral facial pain can greatly reduce quality of life. Toothache pain can be caused by dental caries infections, periodontal infections, trauma, mucosal sores, and temporo-mandibular joint (TMJ) disorder. Twenty-two percent of adults experience

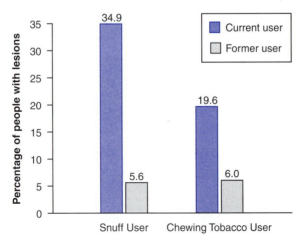

FIGURE 4.6 ■ *Tobacco-related oral lesions by type of tobacco use.*
Source: Adapted from Tomar et al., 1997.

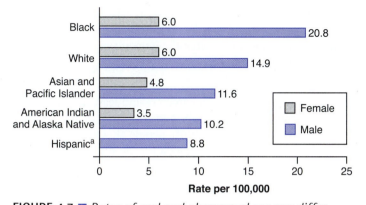

FIGURE 4.7 ▪ *Rates of oral and pharyngeal cancers differ by gender as well as race/ethnicity.*
Note: Age adjusted to the 1970 U.S. standard.
[a]Data are unavailable for Hispanic females.
Source: Adapted from the U.S. Bureau of the Census. *Intercensal Population Estimates by Race, Sex, and Age, 1980–1909.* U.S. Department of Commerce. Bureau of the Census. Washington, DC.

at least one type of oral facial pain per six-month period. In fact, adults living in poverty were more likely to report toothaches than adults living above the poverty level.

SUMMARY

Many oral health disparities exist between gender, race/ethnicity and SES. Periodontal diseases and dental caries are major issues in the nation's health and are widespread in the United States. These findings reflect the overall minor value society places on oral health care. Moreover, there are a variety of oral diseases and conditions that individuals in the United States experience. The dental hygienist must be aware of the epidemiology of all oral diseases, conditions, and manifestations.

Source: Adapted from Christine N. Nathe, *Dental Public Health,* 2nd edition (Upper Saddle River, NJ: Prentice Hall, 2004), 202-11. Used with permission of Prentice Hall, Inc.

Annotating Information of Special Importance

You may have noticed that the graphs from the dental hygiene textbook passage tended to focus on certain kinds of information, such as whether one group or another was more likely to lose their teeth or whether people had more or fewer cavities than in the past. When you look at charts and graphs, you should watch for some special types of information:

Changes over time. Some charts and graphs give data on changes over time. Look for the trend—is whatever is being measured rising, falling, or staying about the same? Also take note of what the rates are for the most current year.

Comparisons. If there is data for more than one group, check for similarities and differences.

Greatest/least. Pay attention to the greatest and least. For instance, if you see a pie chart of the types of snacks Americans eat, look for the three most common and three least common things people choose. If you see a map of the rates of tuberculosis in each state, look for the states in which it was the highest and the states in which it was lowest.

Notice that each of these types of information leads to questions that would be particularly likely to appear on a test. For example, if your textbook contains a bar chart on how often men versus women suffer from migraine headaches, you might be asked this question:

Are migraine headaches more common in women or men?

When you mark in questions and answers next to graphs, be especially careful to notice things like changes over time, comparisons between groups, or the greatest/least. For instance, take a look at this graph taken from a marriage and family textbook (Figure 4.8).

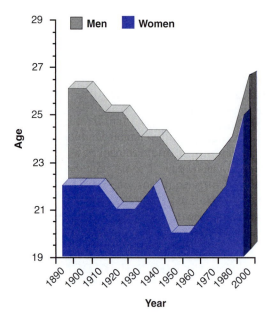

FIGURE 4.8 ■ *At what age do men and women first marry?*
Source: Adapted from the U.S. Bureau of the Census. *Marital Status and Living Arrangements.* Bureau of the Census. Washington, DC, 2002.

The title of the graph reads "At what age do men and women first marry?" When you look at the graph itself, you see that it shows changes over time. So the question this graph answers is, "How has the age at which men and women first marry changed over time?" You should annotate both how it has changed (risen, fallen, or stayed about the same) and also the age at which men and women commonly marry now.

SKILLS PRACTICE 2

1. Write the central question for each of the following charts' or graphs' answers off to the side (Figures 4.9 through 4.13). Pay attention both to the title and to what you actually see presented in the chart or graph. Phrase your questions in terms of changes over time, how groups are different, or most/least.

2. Note down the answer as well.

Next, try annotating the charts and graphs in the following passage. Notice how the information in the charts or graphs reinforces the points made in the text.

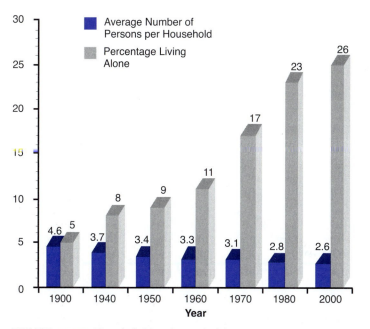

FIGURE 4.9 ■ *The shrinking household.*
Source: Adapted from the U.S. Bureau of the Census. *Household and Family Characteristics.* Bureau of the Census. Washington, DC, 2002.

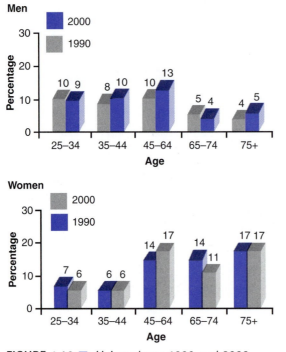

FIGURE 4.10 ■ *Living alone: 1990 and 2000.*
Source: Adapted from the U.S. Bureau of the Census.
Household and Family Characteristics. Bureau of the
Census. Washington, DC, 2002.

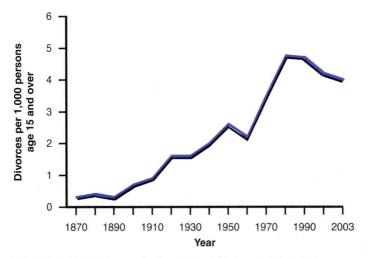

FIGURE 4.11 ■ *Divorce in the United States, 1870–2003.*
Source: Adapted from the U.S. Bureau of the Census. *Marital Status and
Living Arrangements.* Bureau of the Census. Washington, DC, 2002.

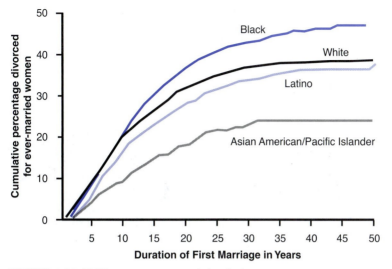

FIGURE 4.12 ■ *Divorce among racial-ethnic groups.*
Source: Adapted from the U.S. Bureau of the Census. *Marital Status and Living Arrangements.* Bureau of the Census. Washington, DC, 2002.

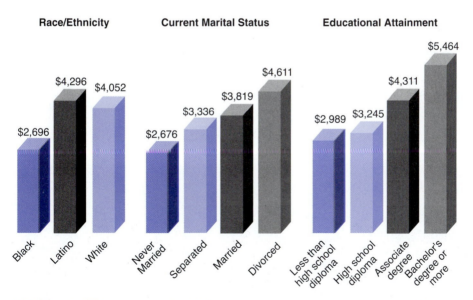

FIGURE 4.13 ■ *Average yearly child support payments received by custodial mothers: 1999.*
Source: Adapted from the U.S. Bureau of the Census. *Marital Status and Living Arrangements.* Bureau of the Census. Washington, DC, 2002.

PRACTICE PASSAGE 4.2: FAMILY COUNSELING

⌸ Juggling Family and Work Roles

The widespread employment of mothers is often cited as one of the most dramatic changes in family roles in the twentieth century. Except for a brief period after the end of World War II, the numbers of working women have been increasing steadily since the turn of the century (see Table 4.4).

Women's labor force rates are expected to grow more rapidly than those of men in the future. By 2005, for example, the Bureau of Labor Statistics predicts that about 63 percent of women will be in the labor force, compared with 74 percent of men. One reason is that female baby boomers are far more likely than their predecessors to have gone to college and to have more and better-paying work opportunities.

An even more dramatic change has been the increase of mothers in the labor force who have an infant at home. Historically, African American mothers with infants are more likely than any other group to be employed, but the gap has narrowed. As Figure 4.14 shows, except for Latinas, the majority of women with babies are going back to work within the child's first year of life.

TABLE 4.4   Women and Men in the Labor Force in the Twentieth Century

Year	Percentage of All Men and Women in the Labor Force		Women as a Percentage of All Workers
	Men	Women	
1890	84	18	17%
1900	86	20	18%
1920	85	23	20%
1930	82	24	22%
1940	83	28	25%
1945	88	36	29%
1947	87	32	27%
1950	87	34	29%
1960	84	38	33%
1970	80	43	37%
1980	78	52	42%
1990	76	58	45%
2001	74	60	47%

Source: Adapted from the U.S. Bureau of the Census. Washington, DC, 1997, 2002.

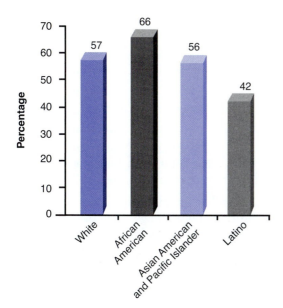

FIGURE 4.14 ■ *Percentage of mothers with infants in the labor force, 2000.* Source: Adapted from the U.S. Bureau of the Census. *Fertility of American Women.* Bureau of the Census. Washington, DC, 2002.

Labor force participation rates are appreciably higher for women with graduate or professional degrees (65 percent) and for women with college degrees (63 percent) than for women who are high school graduates (55 percent) or who are not high school graduates (39 percent). Women who have invested more time in their education return to work more rapidly because they have a greater career commitment, can command higher salaries, and have more work experience than do women with fewer years of schooling. In addition, they have the resources to purchase child care services, especially if a husband is also employed (Bachu and O'Connell, 2001).

Source: Adapted from Nijole V. Benokraitis, *Marriage and Families: Changes, Choices, and Constraints,* 5th edition (Upper Saddle River, NJ: Prentice Hall, 2004), 371–72. Reprinted by permission of Prentice Hall, Inc.

Combining Information Across Charts and Graphs

Charts and graphs are often used to analyze problems or to devise a strategy of some kind. To fully understand the scope of an issue, you usually need to compare and combine information across charts and graphs. This is particularly true in planning programs to address a problem.

For instance, suppose you are preparing for a career as an educator specializing in teaching children with mental retardation. One of the classes you are taking is focused on program management, and you are given some readings that relate to planning educational services for children.

Based on the readings, your assignment is to design teaching spaces and create a budget for a program that would serve a big-city school district of about 100,000 students. You know that approximately 1 out of every 100 people is affected by mental retardation. So, in a region with 100,000 students, you could expect approximately 1,000 children to be in need of special services for this problem.

However, in order to plan a program for 1,000 children, you would need to know these things:

- What are the different levels of mental retardation?
- How many children would you expect to find at each level?
- What sort of education and training would children at each level need? (This would help you decide what kinds of teaching spaces you need and also how many students each teacher could manage.)

Much of this information would be found in tables and graphs; however, it's not likely that a single chart or graph would give you the information you would need to answer these questions. You would find the answers across several tables and graphs, and you might need to combine information or do a simple calculation.

PRACTICE PASSAGE 4.3: EDUCATION

Read the following passage and study each of the charts. Annotate the questions they address and the information of special importance (trends, comparisons between groups, greatest/least). Then see if you can combine information from them to answer the program planning questions that follow in the Reading for Real Life box.

Educating Children with Mental Retardation

About 1% of the general population is affected by mental retardation, a broad-ranging impairment in the development of cognitive and social functioning (APA, 2000). The course of mental retardation is variable. Many children with mental retardation improve over time, especially if they receive support, guidance, and enriched educational opportunities. Those who are reared in impoverished environments may fail to improve or may deteriorate further.

Mental retardation is diagnosed by a combination of three criteria: (a) low scores on formal intelligence tests (an IQ score of approximately 70 or below); (b) impaired functioning in performing life tasks expected of someone the same age in a given cultural setting; and (c) development of the disorder before the age of 18 (APA, 2000; Kanaya, Scullin, & Ceci, 2003; Robinson, Zigler, & Gallagher, 2001).

The DSM classifies mental retardation according to level of severity, as shown in Table 4.5.

Most children with mental retardation fall into the mildly retarded range. These children are generally capable of meeting basic academic demands, such as learning to read simple passages. As adults they are capable of independent

TABLE 4.5   Levels of Mental Retardation

Degree of Severity	Approximate IQ Range	Percentage of People with Mental Retardation within the Range
Mild mental retardation	50–55 to approximately 70	Approximately 85%
Moderate mental retardation	35–40 to 50–55	10%
Severe mental retardation	20–25 to 35–40	3–4%
Profound mental retardation	Below 20 or 25	1–2%

Source: Adapted from the *Diagnostic and Statistical Manual of Mental Disorders,* 4th edition (Washington, DC: American Psychological Association, 2000).

functioning, although they may require some guidance and support. Table 4.6 provides a description of the deficits and abilities associated with various degrees of mental retardation.

READING FOR REAL LIFE

Suppose you are responsible for planning a public school program for children with mental retardation that will serve a school district of about 100,000 students. Since 1% of the population is affected by mental retardation, you expect to have about 1,000 students referred to your program.

- How many children would you expect find at each level of mental retardation?
- What sort of education and training would children at each level need?
- How many students could each teacher manage, given the kinds of skills that would need to be taught?
- What kind of teaching facilities would be needed? Do you need any special equipment?

Putting It All Together

You know that when you read text, you may choose to annotate unfamiliar words and the topics or main ideas of paragraphs. When you come across a chart or graph, you simply do the same thing. Jot down the question that is addressed by the graphic and include the information of special importance that answers that question. Your annotated text would look something like Figure 4.15.

TABLE 4.6   **Levels of Retardation and Types of Adaptive Behaviors Shown**

Approximate IQ Score Range	Preschool Age 0–5 Maturation and Development	School Age 6–21 Training and Education	Adult 21 and Over Social and Vocational Adequacy
Mild 50–70	Often not noticed as retarded by casual observer, but is slower to walk, feed self, and talk than most children.	Can acquire practical skills and useful reading and arithmetic to a 3rd- to 6th-grade level with special education. Can be guided toward social conformity.	Can usually achieve social and vocational skills adequate to self-maintenance; may need occasional guidance and support when under unusual social or economic stress.
Moderate 35-49	Noticeable delays in motor development, especially in speech; responds to training in various self-help activities.	Can learn simple communication, elementary health and safety habits, and simple manual skills; does not progress in functional reading or arithmetic.	Can perform simple tasks under sheltered conditions; participates in simple recreation; travels alone in familiar places; usually incapable of self-maintenance.
Severe 20–34	Marked delay in motor development; little or no communication skill, may respond to training in elementary self-help—e.g., self-feeding.	Usually walks, barring specific disability; has some understanding of speech and some response; can profit from systematic habit training.	Can conform to daily routines and repetitive activities; needs continuing direction and supervision in protective environment.
Profound Below 20	Gross retardation; minimal capacity for functioning in sensorimotor areas; needs nursing care.	Obvious delays in all areas of development; shows basic emotional responses; may respond to skillful training in use of legs, hands, and jaws; needs close supervision.	May walk, may need nursing care, may have primitive speech; will usually benefit from regular physical activity; incapable of self-maintenance.

Source: Adapted from S. A. Rathus, *Essential of Psychology,* 5th edition (1996). Copyright © 2001. Reprinted with permission of Wadsworth, a division of Thomson Learning: www.thomsonrights.com. Fax 800-730-2215.

Trend
in violent
crime?
-dropping all
groups
Most
victimized
groups?
1. men more
   than women
2. Blacks,
   followed by
   Hispanics

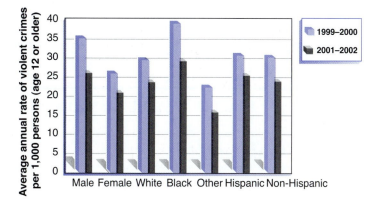

What
self-report
studies
are

Self-Report Studies

The third major technique for collecting data on delinquency and criminal behavior is the use of self-report studies. In self-report studies, individuals are asked to identify the types of crimes they have committed over the study period. Although there are some sig- *(important)* nificant concerns about truthfulness when individuals are asked to admit to criminal behavior, there are also reasons to believe that these data provide a different and important picture of crime that is not supplied in studies done by government officials.[33]

Self-report studies are important because they are not filtered through criminal justice system agencies. The UCR provides better measures of what the police do than what *(view)* the picture of crime actually looks like. Victimization surveys provide the perspective of

advantages
of self-report
studies

those who have suffered some loss, but they fail to record crimes that have no direct victim. Self-report studies provide an accurate picture of crime without having to view delinquency and criminal behavior through the lens of law enforcement agencies or victims, both of whom may introduce bias.

(ul first)
Researchers were initially concerned about the willingness of respondents to admit to delinquent or criminal behavior in self-report studies.[34] Surprisingly, people were forthcoming in these studies about many behaviors that they would not admit to publicly. Questions about the underreporting of criminal behavior were eventually.

FIGURE 4.15 ■ *Sample of three kinds of annotating—unfamiliar words, paragraph topics, and key points from a graph.*
Source: Adapted from Callie Marie Rennison and Michael R. Rand, *Criminal Victimization, 2002* (Washington, DC: Bureau of Justice Statistics, 2003), 4, Online at http://www.ojp.usdoj.gov/bjs/pub/pdf/cv02.pdf

Marking up the charts and graphs in this way will ensure that you understand them as well as you know the ideas in the surrounding text. Try annotating both the text and the charts and graphs in the following passage on "Age and Health."

PRACTICE PASSAGE 4.4: SOCIAL WORK

Age and Health

While popular images of poverty often feature older people, persons over age 65 are less likely to be poor than are younger adults. Older individuals are also much less likely to be poor than are children. The lower incidence of poverty among the aged is a relatively new phenomenon. When the war on poverty began in the mid-1960s, poverty rates among the aged were triple those of younger adults and far above those of children. As Figure 4.16 illustrates, that disparity has been reversed.

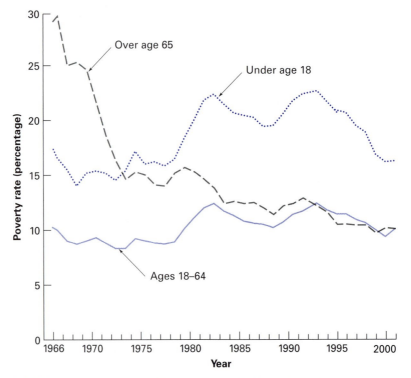

FIGURE 4.16 ■ *Changes in Poverty Rates by Age, 1966–2001.*
Source: Adapted from the U.S. Bureau of the Census. *Consumer Income.* Bureau of the Census. Washington, DC, 2002.

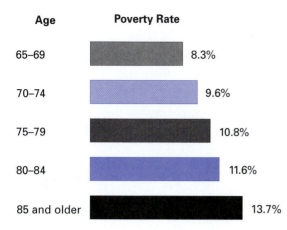

Age	Poverty Rate
65–69	8.3%
70–74	9.6%
75–79	10.8%
80–84	11.6%
85 and older	13.7%

FIGURE 4.17 ■ *Poverty rates by age.*
Source: Adapted from the U.S. Bureau of the Census. *Consumer Income.* Bureau of the Census. Washington, DC, 2002.

Before looking closer at the economic situation of the aged, it is important to recognize the diversity among the aged. Young people tend to regard all people over 65 as "old." But people in their sixties often feel quite youthful and look at their parents or similarly aged persons when asked about the "old people." With so many Americans living long past age 65, it has become increasingly necessary to distinguish the *old old* from those who are merely old. The distinction between the old and the old old is not simply a matter of age. The old old tend to have more health problems and to live alone. As a consequence, they are also more likely to be poor (Figure 4.17).

The largest subgroup of people over 85 are widows living alone (shown as "nonmarried" in Table 4.7). For people aged 65–84, married couples comprise the largest group. Whereas only 12 percent of the married couples aged 65–84 are poor, one out of five widows over age 85 is poor. What makes the latter statistic particularly frightening is that the fastest growing subgroup among the aged are the widows over 85.

Everyone realizes that the aged are likely to experience high rates of sickness and disability. Over half of the people over age 65 have arthritis. Aged individuals also have a high incidence of high blood pressure, hearing impairments, heart disease, cataracts, and bone deterioration. As a result of these and other ailments, only one out of six older persons rates their own health as "excellent." As people age, they not only incur more illness, but also lose the ability to perform everyday tasks. The Activities of Daily Living include eating, bathing, dressing, toileting, and simply getting in and out of a bed or a chair. As people age, they need more and more assistance with these activities. As Figure 4.18 shows, the old old are particularly dependent on ADL assistance.

Figure 4.19 illustrates the income dimension of the health problem. The probability of having a low income is highly correlated with physical and mental disability. Illness and disability not only reduce incomes, but also increase household expenses.

TABLE 4.7   **Age, Sex, and Marital Status of Individuals over 65**

Characteristic of Person	Age of Person	
	85 or Older	65–84
Total (percent)	100	100
Female	65	56
Married	8	25
Nonmarried	57	31
Living alone	39	22
Living with family	18	9
Male	35	44
Married	18	33
Nonmarried	17	11
Living aline	13	8
Living with family	4	3
Number of persons (in millions)	3.3	29.7

Source: Adapted from Susan Grad, *Income of the Population 55 or Older, 2000* (Washington, DC: Government Printing Office, 2002).

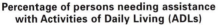

Percentage of persons needing assistance with Activities of Daily Living (ADLs)

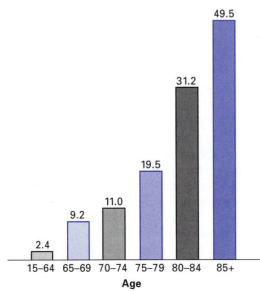

FIGURE 4.18 ■ *Functional disability of the aged.*
Source: Adapted from the U.S. Bureau of the Census, *65+ in the United States* (Washington, DC: U.S. Government Printing Office, 1996), Figure 3-13.

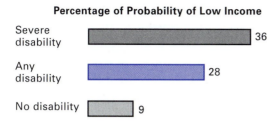

Percentage of Probability of Low Income

Severe disability — 36

Any disability — 28

No disability — 9

FIGURE 4.19 ■ *Disability and poverty.*
Source: Adapted from the U.S. Bureau of the Census. *Current Population Survey.* Bureau of the Census. Washington, DC, 1998.

Poverty among the aged is not a natural product of biological development. Rather, it emerges from a diminution of income sources, a lack of accumulated resources, and frequently rising expenses. Maintaining income sources or providing financial relief from taxation and illness will prevent many aged individuals from falling into poverty. For others, however, poverty does not emerge in old age but is, instead, a continuing condition. The causes of poverty for these people must be sought elsewhere and earlier. Identifying and eliminating the causes of poverty for the nonaged is a critical step in minimizing later poverty among the aged.

Source: Adapted from Bradley R. Schiller, *The Economics of Poverty and Discrimination,* 9th edition (Upper Saddle River, NJ: Prentice Hall, 2003), 107–23. Reprinted by permission of Prentice Hall, Inc.

PRACTICE TEST
Interpreting Charts and Graphs

PART I: READING TO PREPARE

Directions: Read the following article entitled "Charting an Affordable Path to a Quality Education." Next to each chart or graph, write in the question that it answers and any points of special importance (trends over time, comparisons, or greatest/smallest).

You may also choose to annotate unfamiliar words and the topics of paragraphs if you decide that marking them will build your overall understanding of the text.

CHARTING AN AFFORDABLE PATH TO A QUALITY EDUCATION

Everyone knows that earning a college degree can result in more interesting and better-paid work. However, as the cost of college has risen, some students are facing a new dilemma: whether to pay their tuition bills by going too deeply into debt or keep loan totals down by working imprudently long hours while in school.

RISE IN COLLEGE COSTS

While college has always been expensive, costs have risen dramatically over the last twenty years, particularly at private colleges (see Figure 4.20).

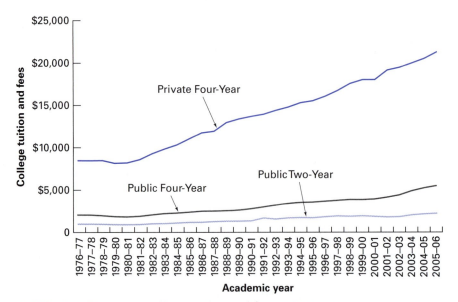

FIGURE 4.20 ■ *Average college tuition and fees: 1976–2006 (in constant 2005 dollars).*

Source: Adapted from the College Board, Annual Survey of Colleges.

However, federal grants for college students have not kept pace over the same period. For example, many college students rely on Pell Grants to help pay for their tuition and fees. Although the Pell Grant program has helped more students every year, the average grant does not cover the full cost of college tuition and fees (Figures 4.21 and 4.22).

UNREASONABLE WORK SCHEDULES

Some students have responded to the rise in college costs by taking on heavy work schedules. Twenty-one-year-old Mark Williams (not his real name) was determined to work his way through college. He would be the first in his family to earn a college degree. Mark unloaded trucks at Wal-Mart, tended bar, and found early-morning employment in construction. He worked up to fifty hours per week while taking a full load of college courses. However, as his work hours increased, his grades dropped. Mark had inadequate time for study or trips to the library. His low grades mandated a change in career plans. Williams had hoped to become a teacher, but the education department would not admit him because his grade point average was too low. After being rejected by his first choice, Williams decided to major in political science, but he is not certain of what he will do with the degree, especially since his grades are so bad. Reflecting on why he earned a D in a political science course, Williams commented, "I knew I needed a tutor, but

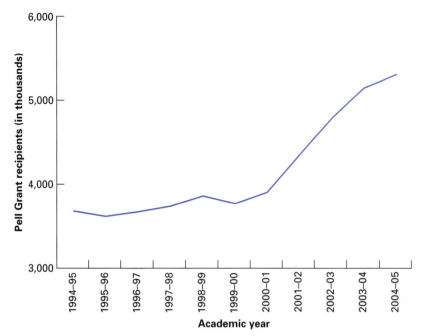

FIGURE 4.21 ■ *Number of Pell Grant recipients.*
Source: Adapted from the College Board.

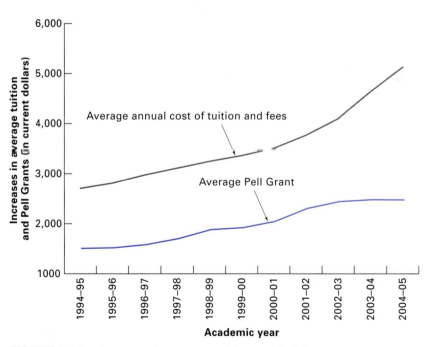

FIGURE 4.22 ■ *Increases in average tuition and Pell Grants: 1994–2005.*
Source: Adapted from the College Board.

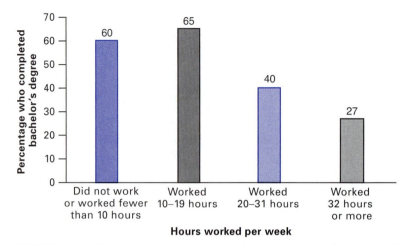

FIGURE 4.23 ■ *Bachelor's degree completion by number of hours worked per week.*
Source: Adapted from the Department of Education—GAO analysis of Education's EPS 1995–1996 data.

I didn't have time for that." Due to graduate soon, Williams worries what his degree will be worth, given his grades.

Although Williams worked too many hours, studies show that college students that work a light schedule (up to 20 hours a week) actually have higher grades than students that don't work at all. However, working beyond 20 hours results in lower grades and higher dropout rates (Figure 4.23).

Unfortunately, in order to bridge the gap between high tuition bills and meager financial aid packages, students are increasing their work hours far beyond reasonable levels. Three-fourths of all full-time undergraduate students work; the average number of hours is 25.5 hours per week. One out of five students works more than 35 hours per week, nearly twice as many as was the case ten years ago.

EFFECTS OF CONSTANT STRESS ON LEARNING

Combining heavy work schedules with full-time study is often a recipe for disaster. Students try to get by with fewer hours of sleep than they need, and they are under chronic stress, never feeling relaxed or in control. They get behind in their reading and try to do course assignments at work or on the bus. The perpetual stress impairs their immune systems, causing them to be more susceptible to illnesses. Additionally, tension and worry trigger the release of the stress hormone cortisol. Cortisol helps people respond quickly to an emergency. However, when the brain of a chronically stressed person is constantly bathed in cortisol, it diminishes the ability to think. In particular, it impedes the ability to analyze complex ideas or link one idea with another—the very skills that college study demands.

If the stress of juggling heavy school and work schedules becomes too much, some students simply drop out. Although roughly two-thirds of high school students enter college, attrition is high—at many schools, half drop out after the first year. In a recent survey at Montana State University, the number one reason students gave for dropping out of school was financial problems.

UNMANAGEABLE LEVELS OF DEBT

Elizabeth Wilson (not her real name) made heavy use of student loans to pay for her four-year degree in social work at a private college. She graduated with $60,000 in student loan debt. The monthly payments take about a third of what she earns as a fledgling social worker, making it hard for her to support her three young children. Although Wilson's case is extreme, more college students are finding it necessary to take out school loans to finance their college educations and they are borrowing larger amounts (see Table 4.8).

Financial counselors advise students to borrow as little money for college as possible, and to make sure that the monthly student loan payments will not exceed 8% of their gross monthly income after graduation. Therefore, students entering career fields with unusually high pay and many open positions can safely take on more student loan debt than those entering fields with lower pay or uncertain job opportunities. However, often students entering less well-paying fields take on more school loan debt to finance their educations than those entering fields associated with higher pay. Over half of all students are graduating with unmanageable amounts of student loan debt (see Tables 4.9 and 4.10).

TABLE 4.8 ■ Percentages of Students Earning a Bachelor's Degree Who Borrowed to Finance Their Undergraduate Education, by Gender and Race/Ethnicity

	Percentage Who Borrowed		Average Amount Borrowed	
	1992–1993	1999–2000	1992–1993	1999–2000
Males	49.7	64.7	$12,400	$19,100
Females	48.9	65.9	$11,800	$19,500
Asian/Pacific Islander	42.7	60.5	$13,500	$17,900
Black	64.1	79.8	$11,400	$19,800
White	47.8	63.7	$12,300	$19,700
Hispanic	60.7	70.6	$ 9,500	$17,000

Source: Adapted from the National Center for Education Statistics, U.S. Department of Education.

TABLE 4.9 ■ Debt Burden First Year After Graduation by Type of Baccalaureate Degree Major

Baccalaureate Degree Major	Average Amount Borrowed	Average Monthly Salary	Average Monthly Loan Payment	Median Debt Burden (Percentage of Gross Pay)
Business	$17,200	$3,300	200	5.6%
Education	$18,100	$2,300	210	7.7%
Engineering, math and science	$19,500	$3,500	220	5.8%
Humanities and social sciences	$20,500	$2,500	200	7.6%
Other	$20,000	$2,700	210	7.4%

Source: Adapted from the National Center for Education Statistics (2001). U.S. Department of Education.

KEEPING BOTH WORK HOURS AND STUDENT LOAN TOTALS MANAGEABLE

There are two key strategies that can help students get through college without incurring unreasonable amounts of debt. First, attending state colleges and universities rather than private schools can make an enormous difference in reducing college costs (see Table 4.11 and Figure 4.24). The quality of the instruction offered is not necessarily better at a private college. For instance, two of the best three accounting programs in the United States, according to *U.S. News and World Report*, are found at public universities. There are top-ranked and well-respected programs of nursing, social work, education, criminal justice, child

TABLE 4.10 ■ Debt Burden First Year After Graduation of Students Earning a Bachelor's Degree by Monthly Income

Monthly Salary in 2001	Average Amount Borrowed	Average Monthly Salary	Average Monthly Loan Payment	Median Debt Burden (Percentage of Gross Pay)
Lowest quarter	$20,500	$1,000	$180	15.4%
Lower middle quarter	$18,700	$2,000	$190	8.6%
Upper middle quarter	$18,800	$2,700	$210	7.0%
Highest quarter	$20,200	$4,300	$230	5.0%

Source: Adapted from the National Center for Education Statistics (2001). U.S. Department of Education.

TABLE 4.11 ■ Percentage Distribution of Annual College Tuition and Fees Paid by Undergraduate Students at 4-Year Colleges

Annual Tuition and Fees Paid	Students Attending Public 4-Year Colleges and Universities	Students Attending Private Not-for-Profit 4-Year Colleges and Universities
Less than $2,000	10%	0%
$2,000 to $3,999	53%	6%
$4,000 to $5,999	21%	2%
$6,000 to $7,999	6%	4%
$8,000 to $9,999	4%	6%
$10,000 to $11,999	3%	7%
$12,000 to $13,999	2%	9%
$14,000 to $15,999	1%	15%
$16,000 to $17,999	1%	14%
$18,000 to $19,999	0%	7%
$20,000 to $21,999	0%	5%
$22,000 to $23,999	0%	10%
$24,000 or more	0%	14%

Source: Adapted from the National Center for Education Statistics, 1999–2000 Postsecondary Student Aid Study. U.S. Department of Education.

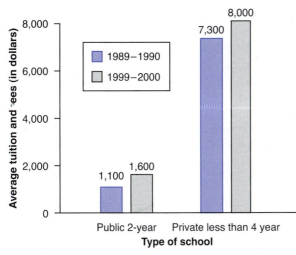

FIGURE 4.24 ■ *Average tuition and fees at college programs of less than 4 years.*
Source: Adapted from C. C. Wei, X. Li, and L. Berkner, *A Decade of Undergraduate Student Aid: 1989–1990 to 1999–2000* (National Center for Education Statistics, 2004). U.S. Department of Education.

development, business, and engineering at public colleges and universities that cost a fraction of what private schools charge.

   Second, students that must work more than 15 hours a week should consider signing up for a reduced course load. For example, Nate Madison (not his real name) wants to be a math and physics teacher. He has a two-year-old daughter to support and he works full-time as a teaching assistant in the public schools. Madison is taking no more than two classes per semester, but he signs up for courses during both summer sessions as well. It will take him a little under six years to complete his bachelor's degree instead of four, but he will finish with a high grade point average and a low student loan total. To Madison, the most important point is that, unlike many of his classmates that dropped out, he *will* graduate and go on to the career of his dreams.

PART II: TEST QUESTIONS

Directions: Refer to the charts and graphs in the article and the annotations you made to answer the following questions.

_____1. According to Figure 4.20 on page 122, what was the average annual cost of tuition and fees at a public two-year college in 2004–2005?

   a. $20,485

   b. $5,239

   c. $2,124

   d. $4,140

_____2. What trend does Figure 4.20 on page 122 illustrate?

   a. College costs have been rising, particularly at private schools.

   b. Costs have been falling at public colleges and universities.

   c. Costs have been rising at private colleges, but have remained flat at public colleges and universities.

   d. Costs at public colleges and universities have risen, but have remained stable at private colleges.

_____3. According to Figure 4.21 on page 123, in 1998–1999, how many people received a Pell Grant to help pay for college expenses?

   a. 3,855

   b. 3,264

   c. 3,264,000

   d. 3,855,000

_____ **4.** The best way to express the question that Figure 4.21 on page 123 answers is:

  a. How much money does the federal government put toward Pell Grants?

  b. Do Pell Grants cover the cost of tuition and fees?

  c. How many people received Pell Grants each year?

  d. How much money did people receiving Pell Grants get?

_____ **5.** According to Figure 4.22 on page 123, approximately how great was the Gap between the average cost of tuition and fees and the average Pell Grant in 2004–2005?

  a. $800

  b. $1,500

  c. $2,700

  d. $4,000

_____ **6.** What point does Figure 4.22 on page 123 illustrate?

  a. Pell Grants cover the full cost of tuition and fees at public universities.

  b. Increases in Pell Grants have not kept up with increases in average tuition.

  c. Both tuition costs and Pell Grants have remained stable over the last decade.

  d. Students do not need Pell Grants to finance their college educations.

_____ **7.** According to Figure 4.23 on page 124, which group is *most* likely to complete a bachelor's degree?

  a. Students that are not working at all.

  b. Students that work between 10 and 19 hours.

  c. Students that work between 20 and 31 hours.

  d. Students that work 32 hours or more.

_____ **8.** What point does Figure 4.23 on page 124 illustrate?

  a. Working heavy schedules helps people succeed in college.

  b. College students should not work at all if they hope to finish a degree.

  c. Students' success is endangered by working too many hours.

  d. Work hours and the likelihood of graduation are not connected.

_____9. According to Table 4.8 on page 125, which group borrowed the smallest amount in 1999–2000?

   a. Males
   b. Females
   c. Asian/Pacific Islanders
   d. Hispanics

_____10. According to Table 4.8 on page 125, on average how much school loan debt did males graduate with, in 1999-2000?

   a. $12,400
   b. $19,100
   c. $11,800
   d. $19,500

_____11. Table 4.8 on page 125 illustrates the point that

   a. a greater percentage of college students are borrowing to finance their educations and they are graduating with more debt.
   b. fewer college students borrow than previously, and their loan totals are lower.
   c. there were essentially no changes in borrowing patterns during the 1990s.
   d. male college students are borrowing more than in the past, but female college students are borrowing less.

_____12. According to Table 4.9 on page 126, graduates with which kinds of baccalaureate degree majors have the highest average monthly salary?

   a. Business
   b. Education
   c. Engineering, math, and science
   d. Humanities and social sciences

_____13. The article states that financial counselors say that school loan payments should not be more than 8 percent of gross pay. Using this guideline, the payments are considered unmanageable. According to Table 4.9 on page 126, which group has an average debt burden closest to that amount?

   a. Business majors
   b. Education majors
   c. Engineering, math, and science majors
   d. Humanities and social science majors

_____14. According to Table 4.10 on page 126, what was the average monthly salary of the lowest fourth of new college graduates in 2001?

    a. $1,000

    b. $2,000

    c. $2,700

    d. $4,300

_____15. According to Table 4.10 on page 126, what is true of the recent graduates in the lowest fourth for monthly salary in 2001?

    a. They graduated with less total debt than those with higher earnings.

    b. They graduated with higher total debt than those with higher earnings.

    c. Their school loan payments were manageable.

    d. Their monthly loan payments were higher than those of other groups.

_____16. According to Table 4.11 on page 127, what percentage of students attending public colleges and universities paid annual tuition and fees between $2,000 and $3,999?

    a. 6%

    b. 10%

    c. 21%

    d. 53%

_____17. According to Table 4.11 on page 127, what percentage of students attending private colleges pay between $14,000 and $15,999 in annual college tuition and fees?

    a. 1%

    b. 2%

    c. 9%

    d. 15%

_____18. Table 4.11 on page 127 illustrates the point that

    a. the tuition and fees at private colleges are typically much higher than those at public colleges.

    b. no one should attend a private college.

    c. the tuition and fees at public colleges are always lower than those at private colleges.

    d. students graduating from private colleges will graduate with more debt.

_____**19.** According to Figure 4.24 on page 127, what was the difference between the tuition and fees at a public two-year college and a private less-than-four-year college in 1999–2000?

    a. about $6,400 per year

    b. about $4,700 per year

    c. about $3,200 per year

    d. about $1,600 per year

_____**20.** Figure 4.24 on page 127 illustrates the point that

    a. tuition costs at both public and private colleges that offer programs of less than four years have been falling.

    b. private colleges of less than four years are no more expensive than public two-year colleges.

    c. the tuition costs at both private and public colleges that offer programs of less than four years have been rising.

    d. the quality of education at a private college that offers programs of less than four years will be better.

5

Reading Opinions: Tone, Purpose, Bias, and Inferences

OVERVIEW

LEARNING GOALS

After completing this chapter, you should be able to:

- Identify an author's tone from the wording he or she uses to express ideas.
- Notice when an author switches from a neutral to a biased position.
- Outline an author's opinion and major supporting points.
- Correctly infer the meaning of stories or research studies used to make a point.

Reading About Controversial Issues

Every field has its controversies. For example, in education, there are arguments among experts over the best way to teach mathematics, the reasons for the poor performance of American students in science compared to other industrialized countries, and the most effective method of introducing children to reading. In the health sciences, there are discussions of the pros and cons of various ways of treating cancer, debates over the causes of eating disorders, and disagreements over the use of non-Western methods of treating disease. You will see discussions of controversial issues in your textbooks, and if the issue is a particularly important one, you will probably get extra readings on it.

Skills Needed to Understand the Arguments of Each Side

You should be able to follow the arguments of each side when you read opinions on a controversial topic. To do this, you need a number of skills.

Awareness of Tone. When people have strong feelings about an issue, their tone of voice often changes from neutrality to something that expresses emotion: anger, sadness, enthusiasm, or admiration, for example. In reading controversies, you should be aware when authors' word choices show their feelings about the topic.

Seeing Shift from Neutral to Biased Position. We say an author is "biased" when he or she is taking a clear position for or against something. For instance, if the topic is whether or not the death penalty is an appropriate punishment for some crimes, the author is likely to lean one way or the other.

The concept of "bias" does not come up when we are discussing facts of a noncontroversial nature. For instance, let's suppose an author is writing a chapter on alcoholism. The section on the effects of too much alcohol on the body (liver damage and so on) will likely be written from an unbiased point of view. No one disagrees that excessive amounts of alcohol are harmful to health. However, suppose the next section of the chapter is about the *causes* of alcoholism—whether it is a disease like diabetes or whether it reflects poor self-discipline on the part of the person who drinks too much. This *is* hotly debated, and the writer of the textbook may have a biased view. When you are reading, you should be aware of places where the writer has switched from a neutral to a biased position.

Outlining an Author's Supporting Arguments. When authors have a biased position, they typically seek to persuade you to agree with them. In everyday life, when people seek to persuade you, they offer some reasons why you should see things their way. Reading opinions is no different. When you read an opinion, you need to look for the reasons that authors use to back up their position. It is very helpful to list the major supporting points offered by each side when you are reading about controversial issues.

Inferring the Meaning of Stories or Research Studies. When you read through the supporting points of someone's argument, you will see that the writer will often back up points with stories or research studies. You need to be able to infer the meaning of these stories or studies and see how they support the writer's point.

Developing an Awareness of Tone

It is interesting to listen to people holding a conversation in a language you don't understand. Although you don't know the topic, the speakers' tone of voice tells you how they feel about what they are discussing—angry, approving, discouraged, and so on.

The word "tone" is also used to refer to the attitude an author has to the subject he or she is writing about. Although we can't actually hear writers' voices, their feelings come across in the words they choose to express their ideas. For instance, suppose two writers are discussing a plan to upgrade the conditions in prisons. Can you tell something about the feelings of each writer from their word choices?

Writer #1   The appalling conditions of the cells in our state prisons are a disgrace. Fortunately, money has been allocated for their improvement. At long last, inmates will be treated as human beings.

Writer #2   Rather than increasing the budgets of police departments so they can better protect the public, taxpayers' dollars will be going to create more luxurious accommodations for dangerous criminals.

In most college texts, the writer has no strong feelings about the topic under discussion. The tone in college texts is usually neutral. For instance, you could probably describe the three types of blood vessels or explain the steps involved in correcting a malfunction in a computer without getting your emotions stirred up. However, when the topic is controversial, writers *do* often have strong feelings. Although we can't hear their tone of voice because they aren't speaking, their feelings about the topic show through in their word choices.

SKILLS PRACTICE 1

Read each of the introductions to articles about problems with our justice system and see if you can tell which way the writer leans from the word choices.

_____1. Capital punishment refers to the execution of a person convicted of a horrendous crime. It is used in situations in which the crime in question was cold, brutal, and an affront to human decency.

   a. The writer is in favor of capital punishment.

   b. The writer is against capital punishment.

_____2. Sadly, young people sometimes commit serious crimes in a moment of poor judgment. In their desire to "get tough on crime," the prosecution may request that the child's case be transferred from the juvenile justice system to the criminal court so that the child can receive the harshest possible punishment normally reserved for hardened adult criminals.

   a. The writer is in favor of transferring juvenile cases to criminal court.

   b. The writer is against transferring juvenile cases to criminal court.

_____3. The tendency of police officers to act like cowboys who think they are above the law has been termed the "Dirty Harry" problem by criminologist Carl B. Klockars. The name "Dirty Harry" refers to a character named Harry Callahan played by Clint Eastwood. Eastwood's character thinks nothing of breaking rules in his quest to bring the "bad guys" to justice. Although the *Dirty Harry* movies are entertaining, the issue of police misconduct is no joke.

    a. The writer thinks that police misconduct is rare.

    b. The writer thinks that police misconduct is common.

■ DENOTATIVE VERSUS CONNOTATIVE MEANINGS OF WORDS

Some words have a strong negative or positive feeling to them. For instance, suppose that you are a person with very little body fat. Which word would you rather have applied to your looks—slender or bony? If you look up the dictionary definition for each word, you will see that both words mean something like "to be thin." The dictionary definition of words is called their *denotative* meaning.

However, if you ask native speakers of English about these two words, they will tell you that anyone would prefer to be called "slender" rather than "bony." The word "slender" is associated with beauty and gracefulness, whereas "bony" gives the idea that the person described is not attractive. The associations people have with a word is called its *connotative* meaning.

When you are first learning to identify tone, you may only notice that an author appears to be in favor of or against something. However, you should try to become sensitive to shadings of feeling. For example, here are some words to describe different negative attitudes to an event:

    harsh; sarcastic

    sorrowful

    disappointed

    skeptical

    despairing

    disrespectful; contemptuous

    regretful

    frustrated

Notice that a skeptical attitude is not the same as a regretful one, although both are negative. In the same way, there are lots of different positive emotions and attitudes:

    admiring

    sentimental; nostalgic

    enthusiastic

    calm; tranquil

    playful

    sympathetic

It is useful to know many words that describe others' attitudes. It is worth your while to expand your vocabulary so that you can express the attitudes you see with precision.

When you read a passage about a controversial issue, see if you can find a word that describes the author's tone. One hotly debated topic in criminal justice is the use of the insanity plea. The insanity plea is occasionally used by lawyers defending clients charged with serious crimes. For instance, a man charged with murder might claim that he was insane at the time the crime took place and therefore did not understand that the action was wrong. When defendants enter an insanity plea, the court will ask psychologists to interview them and give an opinion as to whether they were able to distinguish right from wrong at the time of the crime. If the jury believes that the defendant was insane, he or she will be sent to a mental institution for treatment instead of to prison. Also, a defendant found insane would escape the death penalty in states where it is still used. Although the insanity plea is used in less than 1 percent of cases involving serious crimes, it is controversial.

SKILLS PRACTICE 2

Look at the following statements about the insanity plea. Decide which words best describe the author's tone. Mark the words or phrases that show the writer's feelings.

1. The psychologists who testify that dangerous criminals were "insane" at the time of their horrible crimes are hired guns. They are selected by the defense attorneys for their willingness to say whatever would support the insanity plea, and they receive obscenely large fees for their services.

   a. regretful; apologetic
   b. angry; outraged
   c. disappointed

2. When news of a horrifying murder is brought to the attention of the public, it is natural for people to feel outrage. Often the public reaction to such crimes is to say "a person would have to be crazy to do that." Indeed, many of the perpetrators of such crimes are mentally ill. If the person who has committed a crime is indeed "crazy," is it fair to hold him or her responsible for criminal acts? Mental illness has been doubly disastrous for such defendants, first by undermining the health of their minds and second by causing them to commit violent crimes.

   a. gentle; sympathetic
   b. playful; humorous
   c. admiring; enthusiastic

Now try applying the same skills to the following passage on shamans. A shaman is a person who performs certain rituals in order to heal someone who is sick. Shamans act as go-betweens in the physical and spiritual worlds. Shamans are commonly consulted in many native cultures in matters of spiritual and physical health. They often wear special clothing, which indicates their status as healers (see Figure 5.1).

FIGURE 5.1 ■ *Headdress used by Tibetan shaman.*
Source: Photograph by Alex Wilson
© Dorling Kindersley. Courtesy of the Cecil Williamson Collection.

Here is a passage about shamanism written with a fairly neutral tone:

> Among aboriginal Canadians such as the Eskimos, Cree, Ojibwa, and the Tlingit a variety of factors were said to cause disturbance. Most frequently, disorder was attributed to supernatural causes. Disease was related to the violation of taboos, to witchcraft malevolence, to demon possession or intervention by harmful demons or spirits, and to soul loss (Margetts, 1975). Treatments also varied depending on the specific causal explanation. Thus people sometimes used magic, herbal preparations, physical devices and regimens designed to recapture the soul, and strategies to drive out spirits.
>
> (From Mark Tausig, Janet Michello, and Sree Subedi, *A Sociology of Mental Illness*, 2nd ed., p. 170.)

PRACTICE PASSAGE 5.1: MENTAL HEALTH

Now read the following passage. It is not written from a neutral point of view. Is the author positive or negative about the activities of shamans? What words tipped you off to the author's attitude? What words would you choose to most precisely describe the author's tone?

Shamans

If evil spirits and black magic are believed to cause death and illness, then it is perfectly permissible to employ white magic to counter the work of the evil person or supernatural entity causing the suffering. This belief created the need for healers, known as witch doctors or shamans, who work at producing a cure by applying magical arts grounded in folk medicine and prevailing religious beliefs. The mostly commonly held image of a shaman is that of a medicine man who is susceptible to possession by spirits and through whom the spirits are able to communicate. Shamans can be either men or women, although men apparently are more likely to be extraordinarily successful. This is probably because men can "act" more violently during rituals and thereby appear more powerful. Advanced age, high intellect, and sometimes sexual deviance, such as transvestitism and homosexuality, are characteristics of shamans. Also, being an orphan, being physically disabled, or even being mentally ill is not uncommon.

The most important equipment for a shaman is a strong imagination, for the shaman theoretically gains his strength by mentally drawing upon power that he or she believes exists outside him- or herself in nature or in the cosmos. Shamans try to accomplish this through deep concentration while engaging in a mind-set stimulated by chants, prayers, drugs, drinking, ritual dancing, or perhaps sex. Shamans work themselves into a frenzy until they sense they have become the very force they seek; when this happens, they project their supposedly powerful thoughts out of their mind toward the intended target. The extent of their influence depends upon the belief that other people have in their ability to conjure up and control supernatural forces for either good or evil.

Although witch doctors have often had considerable power and prestige among the group they serve, they by no means have always occupied a desirable role in society. They may be viewed as deviant and odd, a condition perhaps reinforced by the need to work with undesirable people and matter (e.g., snakes, insects, human organs, and excretion). Kiev (1972) notes that primitive shamans were often recruited from the ranks of the mentally disturbed. Skill in performance is apparently the most significant criterion in shamanism, rather than heredity or special experience, although the latter can be particularly important. In this occupation, a degree of craziness can be an advantage for the performer.

Typically, the shaman's performance reflects certain principles of magic, such as similarity or "sympathetic magic" and solidarity or "contagious magic." Sympathetic magic is based upon the idea that two things at a distance can produce an effect upon each other through a secret relationship. That is, two things that look alike affect each other through their similarity because the shared likeness places them in "sympathy" with each other. Thus, "like" is believed to produce "like." A well-known example of this notion comes from voodoo and is the sticking of pins into a doll made in the image of a certain person to inflict pain on that individual. In healing, a shaman might act out a sick person's symptoms and recovery, supposedly to "orient" the illness toward recovery. An example of sympathetic magic in relatively recent times comes from the Shona tribe living in southern Zimbabwe in Africa. Here, a common practice of witch doctors is to administer the shell of a tortoise in some form to a patient to promote a feeling of strength and security; or a portion of bone removed from a python's back may be used to try to restore strength in a patient's back by having the patient eat the bone fragments.

Contagious magic is based on the idea that things that have once been in contact continue to be related to each other. Hence, a shaman might use a fingernail, a tooth, or hair as the object of a magical act to affect the source of the part in some way. Among the Shona, all shamans practice contagion. A member of the Shona group might, for example, obtain some article of clothing that an enemy has worn close to his or her body, take it to the shaman who can produce a spell on it, and supposedly cause the enemy to become ill.

Source: Adapted from William C. Cockerham, *Sociology of Mental Disorder,* 7th edition (Upper Saddle River, NJ: Prentice Hall, 2005), 6–7. Reprinted by permission of Prentice Hall, Inc.

Identifying Purpose and Bias

When you read texts for your college courses, you should be aware of the author's purpose—what he or she wants to accomplish in a given section. You are already expert at identifying purpose in conversation. What you need to do is transfer these listening skills to your reading. In particular, you need to be aware of when an author is seeking to persuade you to a particular point of view.

People talk to each other for different purposes. For example, sometimes they want to explain how something works. At other times, they want to tell an interesting story or convince others of their point of view. Here are five purposes a person might have in speaking to someone else:

Inform: explain facts and discuss ideas

Narrate: tell a story or explain something that happened

Describe: paint a picture in words so others can visualize it themselves

Entertain: tell something that others will find amusing

Persuade: convince others of a particular point of view

It usually doesn't take many words before you pick up on a speaker's purpose. For instance, if someone says to you, "Yesterday I went to the zoo with my little brother. We were passing the tiger cage when . . ." then right away you can tell the speaker is going to tell a story. If the speaker says, "Our state government should not be raising money through the lottery. For one thing, it increases the numbers of people addicted to gambling . . ." When you hear that, you know that the speaker wants to persuade you. Bring the same kind of awareness to your reading.

In thinking about reading for college courses, you could argue that because the author is always discussing ideas in some way, his or her purpose is always to inform. However, "informing" gives the idea that the author is just presenting facts in a neutral way. Even in textbooks, authors will develop your understanding of a topic through stories, descriptions, opinions, and (occasionally) jokes.

SKILLS PRACTICE 3

Read each of the following paragraphs and identify the author's purpose. Find the point at which the author's purpose moves to persuasion.

1. When Robert was a child, he was known for his outgoing personality. His friends nicknamed him "The Mouth" because he talked all the time. Shortly after Robert turned 21, his friends and family noticed a change in his personality. He became increasingly silent and withdrawn. Robert's concerned parents took him to a mental health clinic, and he was diagnosed with schizophrenia.

   a. to inform

   b. to narrate

   c. to describe

   d. to entertain

   e. to persuade

2. The brain of a person with schizophrenia contains less tissue than that of a person in good mental health because the cavities and spaces in the folds of the brain are larger. Picture two sponges of the same size. Both sponges have holes throughout their structure. However, the holes in one sponge are the size of a nickel, while the holes in the other are the size of a pea. The sponge with the larger holes will contain less material even if it appears to be the same size on the outside.

   a. to inform

   b. to narrate

   c. to describe

   d. to entertain

   e. to persuade

3. It is a mistake to believe that the differences between the brains of schizophrenics and those in good mental health are caused by the medication used to treat schizophrenia. For one reason, we see the larger cavities and spaces between folds in schizophrenics that have not received any medication. Second, the amount of medication a person treated for schizophrenia receives seems to be unrelated to the size of the cavities and spaces between folds of the brain.

   a. to inform   d. to entertain

   b. to narrate   e. to persuade

   c. to describe

4. Experts in schizophrenia have noted a "rule of thirds." Approximately one-third of those with schizophrenia are increasingly disabled by the disease over time. Another third decline to a certain extent but then grow no worse. The final third regains mental health and shows no further symptoms of schizophrenia.

    a. to inform

    b. to narrate

    c. to describe

    d. to entertain

    e. to persuade

■ IDENTIFYING BIAS

In every field, there are some topics so controversial that experts disagree strongly and argue among themselves. For instance, in breast cancer treatment, specialists might argue whether it is sufficient just to cut out a cancerous lump or whether it is necessary to remove the entire breast. In elementary education, experts disagree on the best way to teach early reading—by emphasizing phonics or by using interesting stories. These arguments can grow quite hot, and specialists may divide into camps.

When you are reading a text on one of these controversial issues, the author may feel so strongly that he or she does not try to present both sides equally. Instead, the author will take one side and present the evidence for that position. In such a case, we say the author is *biased*. A biased author's purpose is to persuade you to agree with his or her point of view by presenting you with evidence for the rightness of his or her side.

■ OUTLINING THE AUTHOR'S MAJOR POINTS IN SUPPORT OF AN ARGUMENT

When you see that an author is taking a position on a controversial topic, look for the major points that he or she brings forward in support of the argument. For instance, suppose that I am an educator arguing in favor of including personal finance education as a required subject for all high school students. Here are my reasons:

■ Teens will soon have access to credit cards and need to know how to use them wisely.

■ Young people need to go to college or a technical program after high school in order to qualify for the better-paying jobs. Earning a degree often requires taking out loans.

- Responsibility for saving for old age has shifted from the employer to the worker. Students need to begin managing their 401(k) and individual retirement accounts as soon as they begin full-time work.

If I were writing up this opinion, I would introduce the topic and give my opinion that personal finance should be a required subject in high school. Then, in the paragraphs that followed, I would bring forward my three reasons in an attempt to persuade others to agree with me.

When you read an opinion, look for the writer's overall position and the major points that support that position.

■ SKILLS PRACTICE—THE CONTROVERSY OVER MULTIPLE PERSONALITY DISORDER

One controversial issue within psychology is the diagnosis of dissociative identity disorder, more commonly known as "multiple personality disorder" or MPD for short. MPD refers to the existence, within one person, of two or more different identities. Each identity has its own name, preferences, handwriting, and even medical problems. The person with MPD is usually unaware that his or her personality has divided into separate identities. Typically, the personalities of an individual with MPD contrast sharply with each other. For instance, consider the case of Maud and Sara K.:

> In general demeanor, Maud was quite different from Sara. She walked with a swinging, bouncing gait contrasted to Sara's sedate one. While Sara was depressed, Maud was ebullient and happy . . . Insofar as she could, Maud dressed differently from Sara . . . Sara used no make-up. Maud used a lot of rouge and lipstick, and painted her fingernails and toenails deep red . . . Sara was a mature, intelligent individual. Her mental age was 19.2 years, IQ 128. A psychometric done on Maud showed a mental age of 6.6, IQ, 43.
>
> (Carson, Butcher, & Coleman, 1988, p. 206)

Experts in mental illness do not agree on how common this disorder is or whether it can be accurately identified. One side says MPD is common but often goes unrecognized by therapists. The other side argues that MPD is rare if it even exists at all, and that most of the so-called cases of MPD result from a therapist planting the idea in the mind of a mentally ill patient. The patient then rearranges his or her memories to fit the therapist's suggestion.

SKILLS PRACTICE 4

The following passage expresses a biased view of MPD. After you have read the passage, briefly list the three points the author gives in support of the opinion. Notice that the first paragraph introduces the topic and author's position (thesis), and the supporting points are discussed in the paragraphs that follow.

Diagnosing Multiple Personality Disorder

Multiple personality disorder refers to a condition in which an individual has several different personalities that emerge at different times. Each personality has its own name, memories, habits, and speaking voice. In some instances, the personalities are not aware of the existence of other "people" within the same body. MPD is a more common disorder than is often supposed; however, it is frequently overlooked by therapists.

Psychologists should be particularly alert to the possibility of multiple personality disorder in cases where the patient has suffered prolonged and severe abuse during childhood. A child unable to escape a hellish environment may cope by assigning the abuse to a separate personality who emerges only during traumatic incidents such as torture (Gleaves, 1996; Kluft, 1993; Ross, 1995). The development of MPD is a survival strategy in which one personality is free to handle everyday experiences and the other copes with traumatic incidents. In cases of multiple personality disorder, therapists will discover that in almost all instances, one of the personalities will be a child even if the patient is now fully grown.

Revealing the existence of multiple personality disorder requires careful exploration and persistence. Patients are frequently unaware that their personalities have split into separate identities. To expose the condition, clinicians must employ hypnosis and other techniques that will cause the dissociated personalities to emerge.

A diagnosis of MPD can be confirmed by examining the patient's brain wave patterns and other physiological changes. Clients suffering from multiple personality disorder show different EEG patterns for each of their separate personalities. Putnam (1984) also found that for many MPD patients, their separate personalities have varying blood pressure readings, dissimilar allergies, and different responses to medications.

Thesis (opinion): MPD is a common disorder, but it is often overlooked by therapists.

Point 1: _____

Point 2: _____

Point 3: _____

SKILLS PRACTICE 5

Now read the passage entitled "Problems in Diagnosing Multiple Personality Disorder" written by a psychologist with the opposite bias. After you have read the passage, outline the points this author brings forward in support of his opinion. Notice that the author's position (thesis) is introduced in the first paragraph, and the subtitles of the sections help you identify supporting points.

Problems in Diagnosing Multiple Personality Disorder

A diagnosis of multiple personality disorder has legal implications. A woman charges a man with rape, claiming that only one of her personalities consented to having sex with him while another objected; a man commits murder and claims his "other personality" did it. Among mental health professionals, however, two completely different views of MPD currently exist. Some think it is a real disorder, common but often overlooked by therapists working with mentally ill patients. However, there is strong evidence that most cases of MPD are false, and that if it exists at all it is extremely rare.

Problems with EEG Studies. Those who are skeptical about MPD have shown that most of the research used to support the diagnosis is not reliable (Merskey, 1995; Piper, 1997). A review of the claims that MPD patients have different EEG measurements of brain waves associated with each personality concluded that most of the studies were not convincing because they looked at only a single patient and were not set up correctly. Additionally, when other researchers ran the same study with new MPD patients, they did not get the same results (Brown, 1994). Most important, research in this area has been spoiled by that familiar research mistake, the missing control group. When one research team corrected this problem by comparing the EEG activity of two MPD patients with that of a normal person who merely role-played different personalities, they found the EEG differences between "personalities" to be *greater* in the normal person (Coons, Milstein, & Marley, 1982). Other studies comparing MPD with control subjects who were merely role-playing have not found any reliable differences (Miller & Triggiano, 1992). Because normal people can create EEG changes by shifting their moods, energy levels, and concentration, brain-wave activity cannot be used to prove the existence of MPD.

Planting Suggestions. Clinicians and researchers who are doubtful about this diagnosis also point out that cases of MPD seem to turn up only in people who go to therapists who believe in it and are looking for it (McHugh, 1993; Merskey, 1992, 1995; Piper, 1997; Spanos, 1996). Critics fear that clinicians who are convinced of the widespread existence of MPD may actually be creating the disorder in their clients through the power of suggestions. For example, here is the way one psychologist questioned the Hillside Strangler, Kenneth Bianchi, a man who killed more than a dozen young women:

> I've talked a bit to Ken, but I think that perhaps there might be another part of Ken that I haven't talked to, another part that maybe feels somewhat differently from the part that I've talked to . . . And I would like that other part to come to talk to me . . . Part, would you please come to communicate with me?
>
> (Quoted in Holmes, 1994)

Notice that the psychologist repeatedly asked Bianchi to produce another "part" of himself and even addressed the "part" directly. Before long, Bianchi was maintaining that the murders were really committed by another personality called Steve Walker. Did the psychologist in this case *permit* another personality to reveal itself, or did he actively *create* such a personality by planting the suggestion that one existed? Proponents of the view that MPD is real and widespread often seem unaware of the difference.

High-Pressure Interviews. Persons thought to suffer from MPD are subjected to tremendous pressure in an attempt to force the other personalities to reveal themselves. One of the best-known advocates of the MPD diagnosis, Richard Kluft (1987), maintains that efforts designed to determine the presence of MPD—that is, to get the person to reveal a dissociated personality—may require "between 2 and 4 hours of continuous interviewing. Interviewees must be prevented from taking breaks to regain composure, averting their faces to avoid self-revelation, etc. In one recent case of singular difficulty, the first sign of dissociation was noted in the 6th hour, and a definitive spontaneous switching of personalities occurred in the 8th hour." After eight hours of "continuous interviewing" without a single break, how many of us *wouldn't* do what the interviewer wanted?

Alternative Explanation. An alternative, sociocognitive explanation of multiple personality disorder is that it is an extreme form of the ability we all have to present different aspects of our personalities to others (Merskey, 1995; Spanos, 1996). In this view, the diagnosis of multiple personality disorder provides a way for some troubled people to understand and legitimize their problems—or to account for embarrassing, regretted, or even criminal behavior that they commit ("My other personality did it"). In turn, therapists who believe in MPD reward such patients by paying attention to their symptoms and "personalities," thus further influencing the patients to reorganize their memories and make them consistent with the diagnosis (Ofshe & Watters, 1994).

In conclusion, the fact that MPD is a controversial diagnosis with little solid evidence to support it does not mean that no real cases exist. It does mean that caution is needed, especially because diagnoses of MPD have implications regarding responsibility for criminal acts. In the case of the Hillside Strangler, a determined and skeptical prosecutor discovered that Bianchi had read numerous psychology textbooks on multiple personality and had modeled "Steve" on a student he knew! When another psychologist purposely misled Bianchi by telling him that "real" multiple personalities come in packages of at least three, Bianchi suddenly produced a third personality. Bianchi was convicted of murder and sentenced to life in prison. But Paul Miskamen, who battered his wife to death, convinced psychiatrists and a jury that the man who killed his wife was a separate personality named Jack Kelly. Judged insane, Miskamen was committed to a mental hospital and released after 14 months.

Thesis (opinion): Most cases of MPD are false, and if it exists at all it is extremely rare.

Point 1: _____

Point 2: _____

Point 3: _____

Point 4: _____

Source: Adapted from Carole Wade and Carol Tavris, *Psychology,* 6th edition (Boston, MA: Addison Wesley Longman, 1998), 179–83. Reprinted by permission of Addison Wesley Longman.

PRACTICE PASSAGE 5.2: CRIMINAL JUSTICE

Now try outlining the major points of an author's argument on a longer passage. Some specialists in criminal justice have argued that the United States should stop spending so much time and money in the war on drugs. They believe there would be a number of benefits to legalizing many drugs that are currently illegal to use. The first paragraph of the following argument introduces the author's opinion— that the war on drugs causes harm. Outline the major points he brings forward in defense of his opinion. Pay special attention to the main idea of each paragraph.

Harms Caused by the Drug War

The drug war has been aimed at disrupting, dismantling, and destroying the illegal market for drugs. Of course, a war can be conducted only against people, not against an abstract target such as "drugs." The war on drugs not only fails to meet its own goals, but also creates or exacerbates significant harms.

The drug war leads to overburdened criminal justice agencies. Our police, courts, and corrections spend a significant portion of their time and resources dealing with drug offenses. Every minute and every dollar spent fighting the war on drugs are a minute and a dollar not spent fighting those acts that most threaten us, including violent crime and white-collar deviance. Since many drug offenders are sentenced through mandatory sentences, when correctional facilities are overburdened, drug offenders cannot be released early. Instead, more serious offenders are released early, including violent criminals.

The drug war leads to crime and violence. Since drugs are illegal, crimes such as theft, prostitution, and other secondary crimes are committed to support drug habits. Drug offenders are also involved in gangs, drive-by shootings, and murders for the right to sell drugs. Internationally, we see that the drug war creates money laundering, funds revolutionary groups, and provides money for the training of terrorists (Grah, 2001).

In addition to creating crime, the drug war erodes our freedoms. Wisotsky (1991) has enumerated some of these erosions. For example, the police are authorized to stop, detain, and question people who fit the "profile" of drug couriers in airports, even without probable cause. They make searches of automobiles without a warrant. The authority of the police to stop motorists on the road without probable cause has been enlarged. Warrantless searches of public high school students' purses have been allowed. Also, police can seize a person's property through asset forfeiture programs based on suspicion of drug activity. The burden of proof falls on the accused to prove that he or she is not involved in the drug trade; even when this is accomplished, the government can keep up to 30% of the property for administrative purposes. This is inconsistent with the presumption of innocence and due process.

Related to increased powers of police and prosecutors, the war on drugs is a significant source of corruption in agencies of criminal justice. The amount of money involved in the drug trade is a source of unbelievable temptation, leading to numerous highly publicized cases of corruption in law enforcement (Gray, 2001). Recent cases include the Dallas Police Department (Texas) and the Tulia Police Department (Texas), where minorities were arrested after officers planted evidence and invented cases against innocent individuals.

Additionally, the drug war ends up causing death and illness among uses. Addicts are less likely to seek medical attention and treatment because of fear of criminal sanctions. (MacCoun and Reuter, 2001). Since the Food and Drug Administration (FDA) has no power to regulate illicit drugs, the levels of active ingredients in drugs are typically not known and certainly not intentionally managed as is alcohol content. "Imagine that Americans could not tell whether a bottle of wine contained 6%, 30%, or 90% alcohol, or whether an aspirin contained 5 grams or 500 grams of aspirin" (Nadelmann, 1991, p. 33). Also, imagine that manufacturers of legal drugs like alcohol were permitted to add far more dangerous substances to their products, as in the case of cocaine and heroin. The drug war makes even relatively harmless recreational drug use much more dangerous than it would be if drugs were legal and regulated for quality control.

The drug war leads to financial cutbacks to other social services. Every dollar we spend fighting the war on drugs is a dollar not spent on other social services. This ultimately harms Americans. For example, since the 1970s, spending on the war on drugs has increased tremendously. Now that state budgets are in crisis, it is nearly impossible to cut back funding for operations of police, courts, and corrections as they fight the war on drugs. Yet funding for social service functions has been cut, including education, mental health treatment, and welfare assistance, as have basic investments in vital infrastructures needed to run communities effectively.

The drug war also heightens racial disparities. Minorities disproportionately suffer criminal justice processing when it comes to the war on drugs. According to Hamid (1998, p. 122), "Minority persons who have been arrested for drug offenses and other crimes far outnumber European Americans." The penalties they receive are frequently harsh and unfair. Even though Caucasians account for a higher percentage of drug users and people arrested for drugs, minorities account for the majority of inmates convicted of drug offenses and sentenced to the nation's prisons.

The drug war causes environmental damage. Many harms associated with the war on drugs are rarely considered because they tend to be felt most by those who live in producer countries such as Colombia and Afghanistan and transporter countries (e.g., Mexico) rather than consumer countries such as the United States. One of the harms is the destruction of crops, the soil in which it is grown, and the drinking water that surrounds it, by the use of pesticides and other means by the United States government and foreign governments in cooperation with the U.S. government.

The drug war threatens the sovereignty of other countries. Another harm of our drug war is that we threaten the sovereignty of other nations. Countries such as Mexico and Colombia have had numerous disagreements with the U.S. government over our threats to decertify them if they do not cooperate with our war on drugs. This causes resentment among the people of these countries because it interferes with their ability to govern themselves as they see fit.

Source: Adapted from Matthew B. Robinson, *Justice Blind?* 2nd edition (Upper Saddle River, NJ: Prentice Hall, 2004), 338–41. Used with permission of Prentice Hall, Inc.

Making Inferences

You have probably noticed that when writers want to inform or persuade you, they often describe research studies that back up their points. Understanding how a study supports a point requires good inferencing skills. An *inference* is a conclusion drawn from evidence. When you read a description of a research study—the question it is supposed to answer, how the researchers set up their experiment, and what they found—you must make an inference as to what the research findings mean.

College texts across many fields contain discussions of research study findings. For example, preventing wolves and coyotes from eating sheep is a problem for ranchers. Researchers in animal husbandry (the care of farm animals) have argued that it is not necessary to shoot predators to prevent them from attacking sheep. They cite a study conducted by Gustafson and others in 1974. Wolves and coyotes were given pieces of mutton (meat from sheep) containing small amounts of lithium chloride, a chemical that makes animals sick. When the wolves and coyotes ate the meat, they became dizzy and suffered severe fits of vomiting. After they recovered, these same wolves and coyotes were placed in a pen with live sheep. The predators moved in to attack the sheep, but as soon as they smelled their prey, they stopped immediately and moved as far away from the sheep as possible. When the gate to the pen was opened, the wolves and coyotes ran away as fast as they could. Hearing the findings of this study, would you conclude that it is not necessary to shoot wolves and coyotes to protect sheep?

Read the following descriptions of research studies and then select the inference that can be made from the evidence.

1. **Health care—delivery of babies.** The stress levels of infants can be measured by the amount of cortisol present in their saliva. More cortisol is found in stressed infants. When an infant appears to be stuck in the birth canal, doctors may choose to perform a Caesarean section or they may pull gently on the infant's head using forceps. When researchers tested the saliva of infants following difficult deliveries, they found that the infants delivered with the use of forceps had higher levels of cortisol than infants delivered through Caesarean section.

   According to the study, what could be inferred to be more stressful for infants?

   a. use of forceps

   b. use of Caesarean section

2. **Mental health—importance of dreams.** Researcher William Dement (1960) investigated whether or not interrupting people's sleep during dreaming would have any impact on their behavior during the day. He recruited eight men who were willing to sleep in the laboratory attached to brain wave monitors for a period of several nights in a row. Dement woke them up whenever the monitors showed they had begun to dream, but then the men were allowed to go back to sleep. After many nights of dreamless sleep, the men complained of anxiety, irritability, and difficulty concentrating. Five of the eight also reported an increase in appetite, and several gained weight.

   To compare whether these symptoms would also appear if the men were awakened when they were *not* dreaming, Dement let the men dream, but woke them up repeatedly during the night at other points in their sleep cycles. Even when they were awakened numerous times, the men did not report feelings of anxiety or irritability. Neither did they report any increase in appetite.

   According to the study, what could be inferred about the importance of dreaming?

   a. The time people spend dreaming doesn't matter as long as people get enough sleep.

   b. If people don't get enough time dreaming when they sleep, they will feel anxious and irritable. Lack of dreaming may also lead to weight gain.

3. **Public safety—likelihood bystanders will help in emergencies.** Researchers Darley and Latane (1968) were interested to know what influences bystanders to step forward and help in emergencies. They wondered to what extent it depended on the behavior of those around them. The researchers decided to set up a fake "emergency" to see what people would do if they were alone compared with experiencing the "emergency" in the presence of others who

did nothing. The researchers asked college students willing to participate in a study to make an appointment to be interviewed. The students were not told the real purpose of the study. When the students arrived at their appointed time, they were seated in a room and asked to fill out a questionnaire. After a few minutes, smoke started pouring out of a vent in the waiting room. (The smoke was a special mix of chemicals that are not dangerous to breathe.) After a few minutes, the smoke became so thick in the room that it became hard to see. The researchers timed how long each student would wait to report the smoke. Some of the students were alone in the room. In other cases, they were in the company of several others (assistants of the researcher) who had been told to do nothing when the smoke appeared. Darley and Latane found that 55 percent of the students who were sitting alone reported the smoke within two minutes, and 75 percent of them reported it within four minutes. However, the students that waited with a group that did nothing were slower to take action. Only 12 percent of these students ever reported the smoke.

Based on the research findings, what could you infer about people taking responsibility if something is wrong?

a. They are more likely to act if they are the only one to see the problem.

b. They are more likely to act if they are in a group and no one else is doing anything to help.

SKILLS PRACTICE 7

Now see if you can state the logical inference yourself.

1. **Counseling—catching incorrect diagnosis of mental illness.** Rosenhan (1973) was interested in knowing whether patients incorrectly diagnosed as mentally ill and committed to an institution would be quickly discovered to be normal. He recruited eight people, including himself, to be pseudopatients (fake patients). Each person followed the same procedure. They called the hospital, made an appointment under a false name, and complained to the doctors they saw that they heard voices that said the words "empty," "hollow," or "thud." Other than this lie, all patients told the truth about their life histories. All the patients were admitted to mental hospitals, typically with a diagnosis of schizophrenia. Once inside, the patients behaved normally and took notes on their experiences. Not one of the pseudopatients was seen as anything other than mentally ill by the hospital staff. The length of their stays in the mental institution ranged from 7 days to 52 days. When they were released, their mental health status was recorded in their files as "schizophrenia in remission."

What can you infer about the likelihood that mentally healthy people will quickly be discovered to be normal if sent to a mental hospital in error?

_____

_____

TABLE 5.1   Cholesterol Levels and Heart Disease in Men with Type A and Type B Personalities

Group	Average Serum Cholesterol	Percentage with Coronary Heart Disease
Type A	253	28%
Type B	215	4%

Source: Adapted from Roger R. Hock, *Forty Studies That Changed Psychology,* 5th edition (Upper Saddle River, NJ: Prentice Hall, 2004), 213. Used with permission of Prentice Hall, Inc.

2. **Health care—personality type and cholesterol levels.** In 1959, Friedman and Rosenman, two heart specialists, were interested in knowing whether personality type has anything to do with a person's risk for heart disease. Dr. Friedman had noticed that the upholstery on the chairs in his waiting room were worn only on the front edge. Apparently, his patients were not relaxed; they were sitting forward in an impatient posture. Friedman wondered if people with impatient personalities were more likely to suffer from heart disease. To test the idea, he and his colleague Rosenman asked managers of corporations to send them employees that were ambitious, extremely competitive, and impatient (labeled Type A personalities), as well as people who were relaxed and noncompetitive (labeled Type B personalities). There were 83 men in each group, with an average age in the early 40s. The researchers tested the cholesterol levels of the men in each group and also recorded the number that had heart disease. The results are noted in Table 5.1.

According to the findings of this study, what can you infer about the connection between personality type and heart disease?_____

_____

_____

3. **Communication—reading facial expression across cultures.** People are quite good at reading the expressions on others' faces to see whether they are happy, angry, surprised, and so on. However, it was not known whether people can read the facial expressions only of those in their own culture or whether facial expressions are the same all over the world. To see whether people can accurately interpret facial expressions across cultures, Ekman and Friesen (1971) traveled to the Southeast Highlands of New Guinea to find subjects for their study from among the Fore people, an isolated group that had no contact with modern society. Therefore, they had never before seen the expressions of people outside their own tribe. Ekman and Friesen chose 189 adults and 130 children to participate in their study. Each person was presented with three pictures, each picture showing a face with a different emotion. Then the researchers would give a one-line story such as "Her friends have come and she is happy" or "He is angry and about to fight."

TABLE 5.2 Correct Identification of Emotions in Ekman and Friesen's Study

Emotion	Percentage Choosing Correct Photograph
Happiness	92.3%
Anger	85.3%
Sadness	79.0%
Disgust	83.0%
Surprise	68.0%
Fear	80.0%

Source: Adapted from Roger R. Hock, *Forty Studies That Changed Psychology,* 5th edition (Upper Saddle River, NJ: Prentice Hall, 2004), 171. Used with permission of Prentice Hall, Inc.

Then they asked the member of the Fore tribe to point to the picture of the foreign face that showed that emotion. There were no significant differences between the abilities of men, women, or children to correctly identify facial expressions. The results of the study are shown in Table 5.2.

Based on the evidence from this study, what would you infer about people's ability to correctly read facial expressions across cultures? For the most part, are they able to do so accurately?_____

_____

_____

4. Education—brain size and stimulation. Researchers Rosenzweig, Bennett, and Diamond were interested in knowing whether providing a more interesting environment would cause the brain to grow larger—in effect, making its owner more intelligent. To find out, they selected 36 rats and divided them into three groups, each with a different environment. The first group had a wonderful playground containing many toys, which were changed each day so the rats constantly had something new and interesting to explore. The second group had no toys, but had the company of their fellow rats and adequate food and water. The rats in the third group had an impoverished environment; they were put in a smaller cage and had no company—each one was all alone. After a period of some weeks, the rats were humanely killed and their brains were examined. The researchers ran this same experiment sixteen times with fresh groups of rats so as to make sure that any results they found were reliable.

The researchers were mainly interested in the differences between the rats in the best environment and those in the worst. They looked at the cerebral cortex of each rat. The cerebral cortex is the part of the brain that responds to experience and is responsible for movement, memory, learning, and interpreting information from the senses (vision, hearing, touch, taste, and smell). For each rat, they compared the size of the cortex with the overall size of the rat (see Table 5.3).

TABLE 5.3   **Brain Growth and Richness of Environment in Rats**

Experiment Number	Percentage Difference Between Cortex of Rats in Enriched versus Impoverished Environments
1	6.0%
2	8.0%
3	6.5%
4	6.5%
5	6.5%
6	4.0%
7	8.0%
8	4.0%
9	5.2%
10	4.0%
11	6.0%
12	4.0%
13	3.2%
14	4.0%
15	5.0%
16	5.0%

Source: Adapted from Roger R. Hock, *Forty Studies That Changed Psychology,* 5th edition (Upper Saddle River, NJ: Prentice Hall, 2004), 14. Used with permission of Prentice Hall, Inc.

Based on the findings of this study, what inference can you draw about enriched environments and brain growth? Does a more stimulating environment seem to result in a more developed brain?_____

_____

_____

PRACTICE PASSAGE 5.3: CHILD DEVELOPMENT

Now try reading this longer description of a research study. After you read the passage, "Parental Attachment as a Basic Need," reflect on what the study findings show about children's needs and their response to a neglectful parent.

Parental Attachment as a Basic Need

In Harlow's previous studies, infant monkeys to be used in experiments were raised carefully by humans in the laboratory so that they could be bottle-fed, receive well-balanced nutritional diets, and be protected from disease more effectively than if they were raised by their monkey mothers. Harlow noticed that these infant monkeys became very attached to the cloth pads (cotton diapers) that were used to cover the bottoms of their cages. They would cling to these pads and would become extremely angry and agitated when the pads were removed for cleaning. This attachment was seen in the baby monkeys as early as one day old and was even stronger over the monkeys' first months of life. If a baby monkey was in a cage without this soft covering, it would thrive very poorly even though it received complete nutritional and medical care. When the cloth was introduced, the infant would become healthier and seemingly content. Therefore, Harlow theorized that there must be some basic need in these infant monkeys for close contact with something soft and comforting in addition to primary biological needs such as hunger and thirst. In order to test this theory, Harlow and his associates decided to "build" different kinds of experimental monkey mothers (Figure 5.2).

METHOD

The first surrogate mother they build consisted of a smooth wooden body covered in sponge rubber and terry cloth. It was equipped with a breast in the chest area that delivered milk and contained a lightbulb inside for warmth. They then constructed a different kind of surrogate mother that was less able to provide soft comfort. This mother was made of a wire mesh shaped about the same as the wooden frame, so that an infant monkey could cling to it in a similar way as to the cloth mother. This wire mother also came equipped with a working nursing breast and also was able to

FIGURE 5.2 ■ *A newborn Celebes macaque clings to its mother.*
Source: Courtesy of Peter Anderson © Dorling Kindersley.

provide heat. In other words, the wire mother was identical to the cloth mother in every way except for the ability to offer what Harlow called *contact comfort.*

These manufactured mothers were then placed in separate cubicles that were attached to the infant monkeys' living cage. Eight infant monkeys were randomly assigned to two groups. For one group, the cloth mother was equipped with the feeder (a nursing bottle) to provide milk, and for the other group, the wire mother was the milk provider. I'm sure you can already see what Harlow was testing here. He was attempting to separate the influence of nursing from the influence of contact comfort on the monkeys' behavior toward the mother. The monkeys were then placed in their cages and the amount of time they spent in direct contact with each mother was recorded for the first five months of their lives.

RESULTS

You have probably guessed that the monkeys preferred the cloth mother (wouldn't you?), but what was so surprising was the extreme strength of this preference even among those monkeys who received their milk from the wire mother. Contrary to the popular theories at the time of this research, the fulfilling of biological needs such as hunger and thirst was of almost no importance in the monkeys' choice of a mother. The huge influence of contact comfort in producing an attachment between infant and mother monkey was clearly demonstrated (Figure 5.3).

After the first few days of adjustment, all the monkeys, regardless of which mother had the milk, were spending nearly all their time each day on the cloth mother. Even those monkeys who were fed by the wire mother would only leave the comfort of the cloth mother to nurse briefly and then return to the cloth-covered surrogate immediately.

DISCUSSION

Harlow believed that his results could be applied to humans. He contended that as socioeconomic demands on the family increase, women would be entering the workplace with increasing frequency. This was of concern to many at the time of Harlow's research, since it was widely believed that the mother's presence for nursing was necessary for proper attachment and proper child rearing. He went on to state that, since the key to successful parenting is contact comfort and not the *mammalian capabilities* of women, the American male is able to participate on equal terms in the rearing of infants. This view may be widely accepted today, but when Harlow wrote this in 1958, it was revolutionary.

SIGNIFICANCE OF THE FINDINGS

It has been shown that greater skin-to-skin contact between a mother and her very young infant enhances attachment (Klaus & Kennell, 1976). However, the attachment process develops much more slowly in humans: over the first six months compared with the first few days for monkeys. In addition, only approximately 70% of children appear to be securely attached to an adult at one year old (Sroufe, 1985).

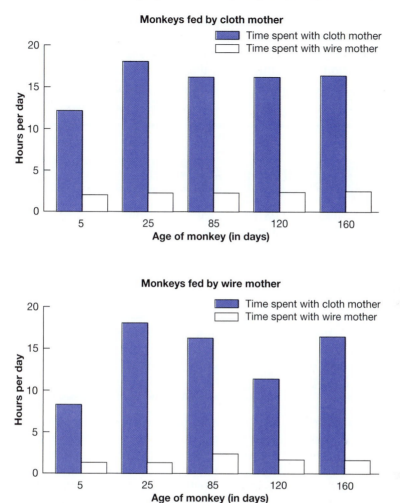

FIGURE 5.3 ■ *Amount of time spent each day on the cloth and wire mothers.*

Source: Adapted from Roger R. Hock, *Forty Studies That Changed Psychology,* 5th edition (Upper Saddle River, NJ: Prentice Hall, 2004), 129. Used with permission of Prentice Hall, Inc.

Harlow's early studies shed light on the terrible problem of child abuse and neglect. One surprising aspect of such abusive relationships is that in nearly all cases, the abused child seems to love and to be firmly attached to the abusive parent. According to a strict behaviorist interpretation, this is difficult to understand. But if attachment is the strongest basic need, as Harlow suggested, then this would far outweigh the effects of the abusive punishment. Harlow actually tested this in later studies. He designed surrogate mother monkeys that were able to reject their infants. Some emitted strong jets of air, while others had blunt spikes that would pop out and force the baby monkeys away. The way the monkeys would respond to this treatment would be to move a small distance away until the rejection ended. They would then return and cling to the mother as tightly as ever (Rosenblum & Harlow, 1963).

Source: Adapted from Roger R. Hock, *Forty Studies That Changed Psychology*, 5th edition (Upper Saddle River, NJ: Prentice Hall, 2004), 127–33. Used with permission of Prentice Hall, Inc.

Putting It All Together

The first paragraph of the passage entitled "Tolerating Poverty" sets forth the author's opinion that the reasons for the higher rates of poverty in the United States than Europe have to do with the degree to which we are willing to tolerate poverty, not economics. Outline the supporting points, paying special attention to the studies used to back them.

PRACTICE PASSAGE 5.4: ECONOMICS

Tolerating Poverty

Americans who live in or even just visit European countries are surprised to see so few signs of poor people. After giving relatives a tour of Germany, for example, I have even had them ask, "So where do the poor people live?" It is hard for many Americans to believe that poverty is so much less common in most of Europe than it is here. Poverty rates in the United States are far higher than in any other industrial nation. Why should this be true when America is so rich? The answer is not that the European economies are stronger; the reason that we have more poor people is that we tolerate poverty.

It is important to note that unemployment is not responsible for the higher rates of poverty in the United States. The U.S. has had an unemployment rate around 5 percent. Germany has a poverty rate that is less than half that of the United States, while the German unemployment rate was over 10 percent throughout the 1990s. Other major industrialized countries in Europe, such as France and Italy, were in the same situation.

While there are many economic differences between the nations on the two sides of the Atlantic, the main reason the Europeans have less poverty is that they have more effective social welfare programs. For example, estimates suggest that Germany would have 22 percent of its population living in poverty without various types of welfare and unemployment benefits. Thus, the German welfare system has been able to reduce poverty by more than 65 percent. France, Italy, Belgium, Denmark, the Netherlands, and Sweden all have similarly low poverty levels because of their welfare programs. The same studies show that the U.S. government reduces poverty by only 28 percent through its welfare benefits, and this was before the major cuts in welfare programs in 1996.

Public opinion polls show that Europeans are far more likely to demand that their government do something to pull its citizens up from poverty. Unlike Americans, Europeans still support expensive welfare and unemployment benefits even if they result in higher taxes and higher unemployment. In other words, Europeans generally recognize that there is some trade-off between extensive welfare benefits and slightly higher unemployment rates, but their value preferences allow them to accept the trade-off.

Another important factor that helps keep welfare benefits low and poverty high in the United States is political. Only around 35 percent of lower-income Americans vote in most major elections, compared to a voter turnout of over 70 percent of higher-income Americans. Because lower-income Americans are less likely to vote, politicians favoring more welfare and unemployment benefits are less likely to be elected. The differences in voting by economic class are much lower in Europe, and therefore, politicians are more concerned with fighting poverty.

Source: Adapted from James William Coleman and Harold Kerbo, *Social Problems,* 9th edition. (Upper Saddle River, NJ: Prentice Hall, 2005), 204. Used with permission of Prentice Hall.

READING FOR REAL LIFE

Tolerating Poverty

Should the United States follow the example of Europe in reducing poverty? Would you be willing to accept much higher tax rates in exchange for things like free day care for everyone, more subsidized housing, health care coverage for all, and generous welfare checks for people who are unable to find a job?

PRACTICE TEST
Reading Opinions, Tone, Purpose, Bias, and Inferences

PART I: PASSAGE TO PREPARE

Directions: The first paragraph of the following passage introduces the author's position that there are a number of reasons why the cost of health care in the United States is unreasonably high. The paragraphs that follow set forth the reasons. Read the passage carefully and create a list of the reasons that the author mentions. Pay attention to the main idea of each paragraph.

WHY HEALTH CARE IN THE UNITED STATES IS SO EXPENSIVE

1   One poll found that almost one-fourth of Americans had put off some medical treatment in the last year because they could not afford it. This situation is not only unjust—it is also foolishly shortsighted. When people delay medical treatment until their problems are so severe that they have no choice but to seek help, the total cost is likely to be far greater than that of timely preventive care. The cost of prenatal care denied to many poor women, for example, is far less than the hundreds of thousands of dollars often necessary to help their gravely ill infants. Not only is the American health care system the most expensive in the world, but its cost continues to go up year by year. Why is health care so much more expensive in the United States than in most other countries?

2   The most fundamental cause is the way the health care industry is organized and financed. Unlike most other countries, medicine in the United States is largely a private business organized for individual profit. The inefficient system of competing private health insurance companies that duplicate each other's services wastes billions of dollars in unnecessary overhead costs. Although estimates vary, private health insurers spend somewhere between 26 to 33 cents of every dollar they take in on administration, marketing, and commissions. In sharp contrast, the Canadian system of national health care spends only 2 or 3 cents on overhead.

3   The lack of centralized buying power has also led to much higher prices on prescription drugs. All the countries in the European Union, for example, have some kind of national health care, and as a whole they spend 60 percent less per person on prescription drugs.

4   Another reason America's health care costs are so high is the staggering salaries paid to many of the people who work in the medical field. Although we would like to think that the primary motivation for someone to become a physician is to help patients, physicians have kept their salaries so high that it severely restricts the access many people have to medical care. Most physicians choose to work in the affluent areas that offer them the best pay, while the inner cities and poverty-stricken rural areas have a desperate shortage of all kinds of medical personnel.

5   However, the physicians look like paupers compared to the executives who run the big medical corporations and pharmaceutical companies. One study that looked at the annual compensation of top executives in 17 health maintenance organizations in the United States found that they were paid an average of $42 million in cash and another $87 million in stock options in 1999! The salaries of the top executives in pharmaceutical companies earn even more. In 1998, the heads of the ten largest drug companies earned an average compensation of $290 million each!

6   Another factor driving the rise in health care costs is that patients have discovered that they can sue doctors for malpractice and win. As a result, the number of those suits has quadrupled since the late 1970s. According to Jury Verdict Research, after three years of median medical malpractice jury awards of $1,000,000, the median award rose to $1,200,000 in 2003. Out-of-court settlements have gone from a median of $400,000 in 1997 to $700,000 in 2003. All doctors—competent or not—must now pay high malpractice insurance premiums. CBS News reported the situation of Dr. Paul Tudder, an obstetrician who figures he has delivered about 4,000 babies in 21 years of medical practice. Dr. Tudder has never been sued, but his malpractice insurance costs have gone through the roof. His annual premium was $23,000 in 2002. Then it jumped to $47,000. In 2004, he got a quote for $84,000.

7   The fear of being charged with malpractice has also forced many doctors to practice "defensive medicine." That is, they may order costly tests or procedures because they do not want to be accused in court of having forgotten something important. For instance, the incidence of Caesarean births has risen sharply over the past twenty years—from 15% to 25% of all births—in large part because doctors want to protect themselves against claims by patients that they did not take strong enough action in situations involving difficult births.

8   Another reason for runaway medical costs is that there are greater numbers of elderly people now than previously. According to the U.S. Bureau of the Census, in 1970, 9.8% of the population was 65 or older. In 2000, 12.7% of the population

was age 65 or older. By 2030, 20% of the population will be age 65 or older. Part of the increase in the numbers of elderly people has to do with life expectancy. According to the Centers for Disease Control, in 1900, only 39% of boys and 43% of girls lived to age 65. A century later, 77% of boys and 86% of girls are expected to live to age 65. Older people require more medical attention. Most Americans over age 65 have at least one chronic illness such as arthritis, heart disease, cancer, diabetes, or Alzheimer's disease.

9   The development of expensive new medical techniques has also contributed to a rise in health care costs. Procedures such as organ transplants are extremely expensive and tend to drive up the overall price tag for health care. For instance, according to O.H. Frazier, a heart surgeon that has performed over 700 transplants, the cost of a heart transplant is enormous, and there's no way of lessening the cost. A heart transplant requires a team of people in the operating room and a large team of people to take care of the patients after their transplant. The Battelle Institute/Seattle Research Center notes that the cost range of a heart transplant is between $50,000 and $287,000, depending on complications, with an average cost of $148,000.

10 Some of the biggest increases have been in the costs of prescription drugs. A steady stream of powerful new drugs has come on the market in recent years, and the costs for their research and development can be staggering. However, pharmaceutical companies raise prices far beyond what is needed to cover development costs. Even though people can't buy their products without the approval of their physician, the pharmaceutical companies have discovered that public advertising provides a big boost to sales both by increasing public interest and by discouraging physicians from prescribing less expensive generic drugs. The big pharmaceutical corporations have consistently been at or near the top of the list of companies with the highest return on their investment.

11 Finally, the fact that there are huge profits to be made in developing new drugs and medical procedures has diverted attention from less expensive, and often more effective, techniques of preventive medicine. As Jeffrey Klein and Michael

Castleman put it, "The processes that drive medical research toward expensive treatments can also turn it away from preventive measures that do not hold the promise of corporate profit." For instance, stress is associated with heart disease. A study of lawyers, dentists, and physicians found a strong relationship between the amount of stress associated with their specialty and their rates of heart disease; thus, general-practice lawyers had less heart trouble than trial lawyers. Interestingly, a study conducted by Columbia University found that workers such as waiters and telephone operators, who face heavy demands but have little decision-making control, are the most likely to have heart and circulatory problems. Decreasing job stress will prevent serious illness, but this "treatment" does not bring in money to medical companies.

Source: Adapted from James William Coleman and Harold R. Kerbo, *Social Problems,* 9th edition (Upper Saddle River, NJ: Prentice Hall, 2005), 175–76. Used with permission of Prentice Hall, Inc.

PART II: TEST QUESTIONS

OUTLINING THE AUTHOR'S MAJOR POINTS (10 POINTS)

In the following spaces, outline the reasons the authors cite for the rising cost of health care. There are ten mentioned in the passage. List only the main points; don't include any supporting detail.

What are some causes of the rise in health care costs?

1. _____

2. _____

3. _____

4. _____

5. _____

6. _____

7. _____

8. _____

9. _____

10. _____

IDENTIFYING TONE (5 POINTS)

Directions: For each excerpt, choose the most accurate way to describe the author's tone.

_____11. **Paragraph 1:** One poll found that almost one-fourth of Americans had put off some medical treatment in the last year because they could not afford it. This situation is not only unjust—it is also foolishly shortsighted. When people delay medical treatment until their problems are so severe that they have no choice but to seek help, the total cost is likely to be far greater than that of timely preventive care.

The authors' attitude to the unaffordable cost of health care is

a. neutral; dispassionate

b. indignant; disapproving

c. enthusiastic; admiring

d. nostalgic; longing for the past

_____12. **Paragraph 2:** Unlike most other countries, medicine in the United States is largely a private business organized for individual profit. The inefficient system of competing private health insurance companies that duplicate each other's services wastes billions of dollars in unnecessary overhead costs.

The authors' attitude to health care overhead costs in the United States is

a. critical   c. neutral

b. approving   d. humorous

_____13. **Paragraph 4:** Another reason America's health care costs are so high is the staggering salaries paid to many of the people who work in the medical field. Although we would like to think that the primary motivation for someone to become a physician is to help patients, physicians have kept their salaries so high that it severely restricts the access many people have to medical care.

The author's attitude to doctors' salaries is

a. neutral; unemotional   c. appalled; judgmental

b. sympathetic; approving   d. playful

_____14. **Paragraph 6:** Another factor driving the rise in health care costs is that patients have discovered that they can sue doctors for malpractice and win. As a result, the number of those suits has quadrupled since the late 1970s. According to

Jury Verdict Research, after three years of median medical malpractice jury awards of $1,000,000, the median award rose to $1,200,000 in 2003. Out-of-court settlements have gone from a median of $400,000 in 1997 to $700,000 in 2003. All doctors—competent or not—must now pay high malpractice insurance premiums.

The authors' attitude to the *doctors* who worry about malpractice suits is

a. sympathetic   c. neutral

b. unconcerned; callous   d. angry; bitter

_____15. **Paragraph 6:** Another factor driving the rise in health care costs is that patients have discovered that they can sue doctors for malpractice and win. As a result, the number of those suits has quadrupled since the late 1970s. According to Jury Verdict Research, after three years of median medical malpractice jury awards of $1,000,000, the median award rose to $1,200,000 in 2003. Out-of-court settlements have gone from a median of $400,000 in 1997 to $700,000 in 2003. All doctors—competent or not—must now pay high malpractice insurance premiums.

The authors' attitude to the *people who sue doctors for malpractice* is

a. gentle; understanding   c. humorous; playful

b. neutral   d. disapproving

MAKING INFERENCES (5 POINTS)

Directions: After you read each study result, choose the point that could be inferred.

_____16. **Paragraph 2:** Although estimates vary, private health insurers spend somewhere between 26 to 33 cents of every dollar they take in on administration, marketing, and commissions. In sharp contrast, the Canadian system of national health care spends only 2 or 3 cents on overhead.

a. Health insurers in the United States spend far more on overhead costs such as marketing, administration, and commissions than Canada does.

b. Canada needs to spend more on overhead costs.

_____17. **Paragraph 5:** One study that looked at the annual compensation of top executives in 17 health maintenance organizations in the United States found that they were paid an average of $42 million in cash and another $87 million in stock options in 1999! The salaries of the top executives in pharmaceutical companies earn even more. In 1998, the heads of the ten largest drug companies earned an average compensation of $290 million each!

a. Executives of health maintenance and pharmaceutical companies are paid too much.

b. Executives in health maintenance and pharmaceutical companies are much more valuable than workers that are paid less.

____18. **Paragraph 6:** According to Jury Verdict Research, after three years of median medical malpractice jury awards of $1,000,000, the median award rose to $1,200,000 in 2003. Out-of-court settlements have gone from a median of $400,000 in 1997 to $700,000 in 2003.

a. Doctors are making more serious types of errors than in the past.

b. The amounts people who sue doctors are awarded have been rising.

____19. **Paragraph 8:** Part of the increase in the numbers of elderly people has to do with life expectancy. According to the Centers for Disease Control, in 1900, only 39% of boys and 43% of girls lived to age 65. A century later, 77% of boys and 86% of girls are expected to live to age 65.

a. It is better to be born a girl than a boy.

b. More people are living longer than in the past.

____20. **Paragraph 11:** For instance, stress is associated with heart disease. A study of lawyers, dentists, and physicians found a strong relationship between the amount of stress associated with their specialty and their rates of heart disease; thus, general-practice lawyers had less heart trouble than trial lawyers. Interestingly, a study conducted by Columbia University found that workers such as waiters and telephone operators, who face heavy demands but have little decision-making control, are the most likely to have heart and circulatory problems.

a. All jobs are equally stressful.

b. Waiters, waitresses, and telephone operators are under greater job stress than other types of workers.

CHAPTER 6

Evaluating the Evidence for Opinions

OVERVIEW

LEARNING GOALS

After completing this chapter, you should be able to

- Separate facts from opinions.
- Check a fact for markers of quality: relevancy, currency, sources, and sufficiency.
- Spot common logical flaws in reasoninq.

Analyzing the Strength of the Evidence

When you study a hotly debated issue in a college course, you may be given a special kind of reading assignment that often arises from these important controversies. Your instructor may ask you to read the opinions of experts on both sides of an issue, list the arguments of each, and analyze the strength of the evidence for each side. Notice that you are not being asked whether you agree or disagree. Usually, the focus of the discussion is not on which side is "right." There would be no disagreement if all the evidence were on one side. When you analyze evidence for an opinion, you are checking to see whether the author

167

backed up his or her opinion with facts, and you are looking for certain qualities that make those facts more powerful and persuasive.

Facts versus Opinions. The first set of skills you need to analyze the strength of evidence used to support an author's points is the ability to separate facts from opinions. A problem is that students tend to label statements with which they agree as "facts" and those that they reject as "opinions." Special definitions of fact and opinion are used by the academic community. In this chapter, you will learn how statements are classified as fact or opinion for the purposes of scholarly debate.

Checking the Quality of a Fact. In general, we want to see that points are backed with facts. However, not all facts are equally strong. In this chapter, you will learn how to check a fact used to support an author's point for four markers of strength: relevancy, currency, sources, and sufficiency.

Spotting Common Logical Flaws. When authors have not found strong facts to back their points (either because of laziness or because there aren't any facts to be found), they often use certain junky kinds of reasoning as filler. These weak types of filler are so common that they have been given names like "circular reasoning" or "false alternatives." Learning to identify certain kinds of logical flaws is useful because you won't mistake them for strong support in other people's arguments, and you will know not to use them to support your own opinions.

The Importance of Research Studies

Many times the facts you see backing opinions will be research studies. This is particularly true in fields involving the behavior of human beings, such as counseling, law enforcement, social work, education, marketing and sales, financial advising, and health care. Research studies are considered the strongest type of factual support for opinions.

I have noticed that students are often troubled when they read a research study finding that conflicts with their own experience. For example, suppose that you read a research study result that said children of single parents tend to have lower grades than children in two-parent households. Suppose that you *are* a single parent, and both your children do very well in school. Clearly, your experience does not agree with the study finding. In these situations, many readers tend to dismiss the study results as "untrue," which is a mistake. Research studies tell us what is *usually* true. There are always exceptions. Your personal experience is true, but it may or may not be common. If you read a research study finding that does not agree with your own experience, it does not mean that either you or the study is wrong. More likely, it means that your experience is less common.

Research studies are particularly important when debating issues related to human behavior because of the limitations of personal experience. We all see the world through our own experiences. It is easy to assume that what has been true in our experience is commonly true. However, when you read arguments, pay special attention to the findings of research studies. They are a more reliable guide to what is *generally* true than one's personal experience.

Avoiding the Temptation to Choose Sides Too Quickly

When you read about a controversial issue, you will be tempted to choose a side immediately. Try to avoid doing this. There is no need to declare yourself for one opinion or the other right away. Instead, develop an understanding for the evidence on each side. When you read, try for the attitude of a good jury member, open to hearing all sides before coming to a conclusion.

Separating Facts from Opinions

After you have outlined the major points supporting an opinion, next look to see if each point has been backed with facts. Here, we should clarify what is meant by a "fact." In everyday speech, people often use the word "fact" to mean "something I believe is true." By contrast, "opinion" is used to mean "something I disagree with." For example, you may hear these kinds of conversations:

Person 1: It sure is hot today.

Person 2: That's a fact.

Person 1: I do all the work around here. You don't do your share.

Person 2: That's your opinion.

There is nothing wrong with using the words "fact" and "opinion" this way in ordinary conversation, but you need to use a second set of definitions when analyzing the evidence for opinions for academic purposes.

■ HOW TO DECIDE IF A STATEMENT IS A FACT

In the academic community, "fact" and "opinion" have another set of meanings. *Facts* are statements that can be checked. A fact may be proven to be true or false by checking records or interviewing witnesses. These are some examples of facts:

- College students take on an average of $17,000 in school loan debt.
- Today is Friday.
- In 1969, Neil Armstrong walked on the moon.
- A study conducted by researchers at the University of Minnesota found that the IQ scores of identical twins are more similar than those of non-twin siblings.

To say something is a fact does not necessarily mean it is true. A fact may be wrong, but that does not mean it becomes an opinion; it is simply an incorrect fact.

■ CATEGORIZING A STATEMENT AS AN OPINION

An *opinion* is a statement that cannot be proven true or false so as to end all argument. To say that a statement is an opinion does not mean it is wrong. It only means that the nature of the statement is such that there is no way to check it so as to end all debate. For instance, let's take the statement "Love exists." Can this statement be proven true by checking records or interviewing witnesses *in such a way as to end all debate?* No. No matter what evidence is brought forward, some people will still argue that it does not settle the question. Therefore, we would categorize it as an opinion. We talk about opinions as being "justified" or "unjustified," not "false" or "true." An opinion is said to be *justified* if factual evidence is brought forward to support it. An opinion is *unjustified* if the author does not bring forward any facts to support it. Notice that most of the great questions of humankind—love, right and wrong, the existence of God, the nature of justice—involve opinions, not facts. The questions are too large to be settled by a single record or a few witnesses. These are examples of opinions:

- Parents love their children.
- In the future, people will live longer than they do now.
- The gap between the salaries of the richest and poorest in the United States has become too large.

Notice that statements about the future tend to be opinions because they have not happened yet; therefore there are no records or witnesses to verify them.

When you are deciding whether a statement is a fact or an opinion, do not consider whether you believe the statement to be true. Decide based on whether the statement is checkable or not checkable. Can it be proven *beyond all debate* by looking at records or interviewing witnesses? If not, categorize it as an opinion.

SKILLS PRACTICE 1

Decide whether each of the following statements is a fact or an opinion, using the academic definitions of the words. Write "F" for fact or "O" for opinion in the blank.

_____ 1. Approximately 40 percent of couples in the United States cohabit or "live together" before getting married.

_____ 2. Cohabitation before marriage does not build a stronger marriage.

_____ 3. According to a study done by Rogers and Amato in 1997, couples who lived together before marriage rated their satisfaction with their marriages lower than couples that did not live together before marrying.

_____**4.** Couples that lived together before marriage divorce at higher rates than those that did not cohabit before marriage.

_____**5.** People that live together instead of marrying often have unhelpful attitudes toward commitment and a greater tendency to withdraw from a relationship at times of conflict.

_____**6.** Cohabitation before marriage will become the dominant pattern for couples in the future.

■ JUSTIFIED AND UNJUSTIFIED OPINIONS

When authors want to persuade you to a point of view, that position is typically an opinion. Here are some examples:

Psychology   Multiple personality disorder does not exist.

Education   The best way to teach children to read is through the heavy use of phonics.

Computer Science Advances in artificial intelligence will soon result in computers that can diagnose medical problems as well as people can.

In your college program, an instructor may give you a persuasive essay and ask you to evaluate the strength of the evidence for the author's point of view. The first thing you do is outline the points the author made in support of his or her position. Next, look to see if the points supporting an opinion are backed with facts (justified) or are not supported with any factual evidence (unjustified).

If we say that a statement is "unjustified," it doesn't mean that it is wrong or that there are no facts in existence that could back up that opinion. It simply means that the writer did not include any supporting facts. Unjustified opinions are seen as weak, not because they are necessarily wrong, but because they are not backed with facts.

■ WHERE TO LOOK FOR THE SUPPORTING FACTS

When you are reading an opinion, it is important to know *where* these supporting facts are supposed to be found. Take a look at the outline of this opinion and its supporting points.

Opinion: College students work too hard.

   Supporting Point 1: College courses are difficult and time-consuming.

   Supporting Point 2: Students work too many hours.

   Supporting Point 3: Many students have heavy family responsibilities.

Notice that all of the supporting points in the outline are opinions also. That's not a problem, as long as each reason is backed with facts. Here is the outline of the opinion and three supporting points with backup facts included for each supporting point:

> **Opinion:** College students work too hard.

> > **Supporting Point 1:** *College courses are difficult and time-consuming.* The average reading load assigned by college instructors is approximately forty pages per week.

> > **Supporting Point 2:** *Students work too many hours.* More than half of college students work over twenty-five hours per week; studies show that full-time students should work no more than fifteen hours per week.

> > **Supporting Point 3:** *Many students have heavy family responsibilities.* The number of undergraduate college students who have parenting responsibilities has more than doubled in the past twenty years.

Now each of the supporting points has been justified with facts. Notice that when we say an argument is backed with facts, we are talking about the support for the *points* that the author brought forward. Of course, an author might justify some supporting points with facts but not others.

SKILLS PRACTICE 2

The writer's opinion is that the increased used of computers is resulting in job loss. Check each of the underlined supporting points to see if it is backed with facts. Some are justified with facts and some are not.

Computers and Job Loss

Job loss due to migration of positions to countries offering cheap labor overseas has captured public attention and sparked public debate. However, people are less aware that the increased use of computers to streamline tasks has also resulted in the loss of thousands of jobs.

The losses are particularly severe in manufacturing. For example, one auto manufacturing plant in Japan runs around the clock without the use of human workers. Automobiles are assembled entirely by computer-controlled machinery. In addition to avoiding wage and health benefit expenses, the company saves money by lowering the temperature inside the factory to a cooler temperature than people could tolerate. Because computers don't require light to perform their functions, the automobiles are constructed in the dark.

It is true that all of society can benefit greatly through automating certain tasks. For instance, computers can reduce medication errors in hospitals. The Adverse Drug Event Prevention Study found that mistakes in patients' medication orders occurred in 6.5 out of every 100 adult hospital admissions. In one study, using computers in medication decision-making reduced errors by 83 percent.

Business managers cannot be expected to minimize use of computers to preserve jobs. Since they are evaluated on how well they improve efficiency and keep costs down, they have little incentive to combat these disturbing trends. Computer automation brings the interests of managers and workers into conflict because increasing productivity and reducing costs through automation inevitably results in job loss.

Defenders of computer automation systems argue that computers create new jobs while shrinking the demand for others; however, more jobs are lost than gained. According to the Bureau of Labor Statistics, only one job is created for every three that are lost to computer automation.

If this problem does not receive more attention, unemployment in the United States is likely to worsen. Young people will have great difficulty finding jobs that pay a living wage. We need an increased amount of attention on how to take advantage of the abilities of computers without throwing huge numbers of people out of work.

Notice that some of the supports for this opinion are justified with facts and others are not. Think of the unjustified points as weak spots in the writer's argument. To be made strong, they should be supported with facts.

We would say that this writer's position is partially justified. When you write your own persuasive essays, look for soft, mushy spots in your supporting points and strengthen them with facts.

Now take a look at this longer passage that is discussing the controversial practice of separating boys and girls for the purposes of education. To practice your skill at identifying facts and opinions, highlight only the facts you see. Don't mark any statements of opinion. When you have finished, see if you can identify the points mentioned that were nicely justified with facts and those were more poorly supported.

PRACTICE PASSAGE 6.1: EDUCATION

Does Single-Sex Education Enhance Learning?

SOME RESEARCHERS CLAIM SEPARATING BOYS AND GIRLS IMPROVES LEARNING

Australian researcher Kenneth Rowe examined the academic records of some 270,000 high school seniors in an effort to identify what factors really make a difference in students' learning. One of his key findings, according to a press release, was that both girls and boys attending single-sex schools scored 15–22 percentile points higher than their counterparts in coeducational schools.

Advocates of single-sex education in the United States point to the big differential as the strongest proof yet that separating boys and girls improves learning

FIGURE 6.1 ■ *Boys' reading circle.*
Source: Photograph by Cindy Charles. Courtesy of PhotoEdit Inc.

for both genders (Figure 6.1). "That's enormous," says Sax, a strong advocate of single-sex education.

OTHER RESEARCHERS SAY OTHER FACTORS ARE FAR MORE IMPORTANT

But Rowe, principal research fellow with the Australian Council on Education Research, himself insists that Sax and others are distorting his findings. In his formal paper, Rowe explained that the differences between single-sex and coeducational schools "pale into insignificance" compared to differences attributable to teacher training and ability. Today, Rowe says bluntly that the single-sex school debate amounts to "little more than epistemological claptrap."

WHY SOME RESEARCHERS CLAIM IT BENEFITS BOYS AND GIRLS TO BE SEPARATED

The advocates of single-sex education claim its benefits derive in part from biological realities. Boys' and girls' brains develop differently, they say—differences especially significant for learning in early years. Then, as they get older, boys and girls distract each other from academics because of normal social and sexual development. "If you put a 15-year-old boy next to a 15-year-old girl, his mind is not going to be on geometry, or Spanish or English," Sax says. "It's going to be on that girl sexually. He's got the hormones of a grown man, but the brain of a 10-year-old."

In earlier years, Sax and others say, girls typically begin to read at a younger age and are also less distractable in the classroom. Advocates of single-sex education say these differences set up a dynamic unhelpful for boys' learning. "To the extent that boys experience school in a competitive way and some boys aren't learning to read as readily, their response is to say that reading is girls' stuff, not boys' stuff," says Christopher Wadsworth, executive director of the International Boys' School Coalition. "That can lead to an attitude that is not conducive to development."

In addition, girls'-school advocates say, single-sex education helps girls overcome the male sexism that still exists in public schools. "Girls are at center stage with only girls in the audience," says Meg Milne Moulton, co-executive director of the National Coalition of Girls' Schools. "They get 100 percent of the attention." "No girl in a single-sex school is able to say, 'I can't do it because no girl can do it'—because there is some girl who is doing it," adds Cornelius Riordan, a professor of sociology at Providence College.

THE NEED FOR MORE RESEARCH

Critics of single-sex education say these claims are largely unsubstantiated. "People think it helps girls' self-esteem or makes boys calmer," the AAUW's Zirkin says. "This is anecdotal. This is pulling things out of the air. There is not the scientifically based research for anybody to make an informed decision."

Academics on both sides of the issue want more and better studies. "There is not definitive research," says Sadker, of American University.

THE BENEFITS OF SINGLE-SEX EDUCATION ARE STRONGER FOR DISADVANTAGED STUDENTS

Riordan, however, insists that although the subject is "overpoliticized and underresearched," the research favors single-sex schooling. "All of the studies consistently show small positive effects for boys and girls," he says. "The effects are stronger for girls than for boys, and the positive effects are always larger for disadvantaged students." Riordan cites a study he published more than a decade ago comparing boys and girls from the 1972 and 1982 graduating classes at American single-sex or coeducational Catholic high schools. After adjusting for ability and background, Riordan found that minority girls and minority boys in single-sex schools did better—about the equivalent of one grade year—than minority girls or boys respectively in coeducational schools. Girls from more representative cross-sections also did better in single-sex schools, but boys' scores were slightly higher in coeducational schools.

Today, Riordan has refined his argument. In a paper presented in various forums over the past several years, he says, "only females of low socioeconomic status are likely to show significant gains (along with boys) in single-sex schools."

Riordan posits a dozen "theoretical rationales" for why single-sex schools have positive effects—including such hypothetical advantages as reduced sex bias in teacher-student interactions, reduced sex differences in curricula, and more successful role models for girls. But, he points out, the fact that attendance at a single-gender school today requires an affirmative decision by students and parents—which he calls "a pro-academic" choice—is perhaps the single most important factor contributing to the positive effects. "That student realizes, 'I'm going to go to a school where it's not business as usual,' " Riordan explains. " 'I'm going to have to work.' "

CRITICS SAY THAT OTHER FACTORS PROBABLY ACCOUNT FOR THE SUCCESS OF SINGLE-SEX SCHOOLS

Critics of single-sex education say all the more explicitly that any benefits are most likely attributable to other factors. "A lot of the effects are [due to the fact that] they're good schools, not because they're single-sex," Sadker says. "The elements that make for good schools would work whether it's single-sex or coed," Zirkin says. "The elements are attention to core academics, qualified teachers, smaller classrooms, discipline and a sense of community, and parental involvement. These are the elements that will enable any child in any situation to learn. To say that it's a single-sex school that's achieved such good results really begs the question." Rowe says his research does indicate advantages from single-sex education, but "gender-class grouping" is not the critical factor, he insists. "Whether schools are single-sex or coed or have single-sex classes within coed settings matters far less than the quality of the teaching and learning provided," he says.

Source: Adapted from "Single-Sex Education," *CQ Researcher* 12, No. 25 (July 12, 2002). Used with permission.

Evaluating the Quality of Supporting Facts

You know that opinion statements gain persuasive power when backed up with facts. However, all facts are not equal in quality and strength. There are four markers of quality in a fact: relevancy, currency, sources, and sufficiency. To carry the maximum amount of persuasive power, a fact should possess all four qualities.

Talking about the quality of facts is a lot like evaluating the quality of a movie. Suppose we say that for a movie to be of the best quality, it needs an interesting plot, realistic dialogue, skillful acting, and excellent photography. You can see that a movie might be strong in some things, but weak in others. Movie raters award four stars to movies that are excellent in everything and fewer stars if there are problems in one or more areas. When people discuss movies, they say things like, "The story was interesting, but the acting was awful," or "The photography and acting were great, but the plot was pretty predictable—nothing special."

When you check the quality of facts used to back opinions, look for the four markers of quality. You may find that a fact is relevant, but the information was gathered so long ago that it is outdated, or the fact is is reasonably current, but no sources are mentioned. If there are problems in any of the areas, the persuasive power of the fact is reduced.

■ WAYS IN WHICH A FACT COULD BE WEAK

Not Relevant Here are some examples of facts that are not relevant to the point they are supposed to support:

> Cohabitation is responsible for the rising divorce rate. Over the past thirty years, the divorce rate has tripled.

> Small businesses are failing because corporate tax rates are too high. Over half of new businesses fail in their first few years of operation.

The supporting fact is supposed to relate directly to the point it is backing. Notice that in the first example, the link between cohabitation and divorce is not established. In the second, the relationship between taxes and business failure is not made plain. Because the connection between the point and the supporting fact is not clear, we would say the fact is "not relevant." A fact that is not relevant to the point it is supposed to support is nearly worthless.

Not Current These are examples of supporting facts that lack currency:

> Divorce is on the rise. According to a 1980 report from the Institute of Marriage and Family Studies, the divorce rate has doubled over the past fifteen years.

> Pollution in our state's lakes is not a problem. According to a 1995 report by the Department of Natural Resources, pollution levels are well under state guidelines.

If information is old and you have reason to believe that things could have changed since then, it is no longer reliable. Notice that the report from which the fact on divorce is drawn is more than 20 years old. If you looked at more recent data, you would see that the divorce rate peaked around 1980 and has gone down a bit since then. It is no longer on the rise. Similarly, over a period of more than ten years, pollution levels in lakes may have changed greatly. Although it is unlikely that you will always find facts that are up-to-the-minute, if there is reason to think that the situation may have changed since the information was gathered, then the fact is less reliable.

Be careful not to make a snap decision that a fact lacks currency just because you see an older date. For example, consider the statement, "Smoking causes lung cancer. According to studies done in 1979, the risk of lung cancer is many times higher in smokers than nonsmokers." There is no reason to think that lungs today are different from lungs in 1979, so this supporting fact would not necessarily be considered unreliable just because it isn't recent.

A similar situation holds for facts about historical periods. Look at this example: "Seabiscuit the racehorse was incredibly popular during the 1930s. In 1938, more articles appeared in the newspaper about Seabiscuit than about the president." You can see that given the nature of the point, it makes sense that the supporting fact should be drawn from the same time period.

Here is a final thought on the currency of a fact. Ideally, we would like to see that the information the author presents is no more than a year or two old. Unfortunately, studies are not done on all subjects every year. Sometimes, even though information is not perfectly current, it is the best we have available. When you start looking for research studies and other facts to support your own opinions, you may be surprised to find that it is hard to find data that is as current as you would like.

No Sources Given/Sources Are Biased   Here are some examples of supporting facts that lack sources:

> Some new fertility drugs are tremendously effective in helping infertile couples conceive a child. In a recent study, 80 percent of infertile couples became parents after using fertility drugs.

> According to a study published last year, cigarette smoking does not promote lung cancer in people who exercise regularly.

To know the source of a fact is important for at least two reasons. First, a fact is more reliable if readers can see that the source does not stand to profit by twisting the truth. For example, it may be that the first study was sponsored by a drug company that will make money if people use the new fertility drugs. The second study may have been sponsored by the tobacco industry. If the group that conducted a study has a strong interest in the outcome, people are often skeptical about the result.

Second, even if the study was not sponsored by a company, there should be enough information that you could check the accuracy of the fact by looking at the original report. Suppose you thought that the statement that cigarette smoking doesn't cause cancer if people exercise a lot sounded strange. You want to see the study they are talking about to see how it was set up. How would you begin to find the study? If you do a database search and type in the terms "smoking and exercise" you would see so much on that topic that the chances of finding the study would be very small. On the other hand, suppose that the writer said, "In a study conducted by researchers Smith and Jones at the University of Iowa in 2002, it was found that cigarette smoking did not promote lung cancer if people exercised regularly." Now you would have enough information to track down the original study report.

Not Sufficient   To be persuasive, a fact should be based on the experiences of more than one person or a small group. A fact can be true, but not reliable because it only speaks of what happened in a single case. We say that such a fact lacks sufficiency. Here are some examples of supporting facts that would not be considered sufficient:

> Marriage counseling has little power to save a troubled relationship. Martha Gutman and her husband, Frank, spent two years in weekly counseling sessions before finally filing for divorce.

> Copper bracelets reduce arthritis pain. Elizabeth Louanier of Paynesville, Ohio, reported that her arthritis pain was greatly diminished after she began wearing copper bracelets.

Although these facts may be true, one person's experience is not strong enough evidence to support such a general statement. Facts are stronger if they are based on the experience of large numbers of people, not a few isolated examples.

SKILLS PRACTICE 3

Each underlined opinion statement is followed by a supporting fact. Check each fact for relevancy, currency, sources, and sufficiency. If the fact is of decent quality, put a star in the space for that item. If there is a problem, leave the space blank.

	Relevant	Current	Sources	Sufficient
Family customs are quite different around the world. For instance, Murdock did a study of the Banaro people of New Guinea in 1949. A Banaro woman must give birth before she can marry, and she may not marry the father of the child.				
Some countries view same-sex marriage as legitimate. Denmark legalized same-sex marriage in 1989, Norway in 1993, and Holland in 1998.				
Wives typically carry more of the burden of house-work than husbands do, even when both work full time. According to a study done by Bianchi and Spain in 1996, wives with full-time jobs average eleven hours more child care and housework than their husbands.				
One way men avoid housework is through "needs reduction." Sociologist Hochschild (1989) cited one man who said he didn't need to shop because he didn't mind eating cereal and didn't need to iron because he didn't mind wrinkled clothes. This forced his wife to shop and iron since she had the "greater need" for nice dinners and pressed clothing.				
Children in homes filled with conflict do better if their parents divorce than if they stay together. According to the 2006 Statistical Abstract of the United States, over one million children in the United States learn their parents are divorcing each year.				
Most married people are content. In a survey of several thousand people, two out of every three married people say they are "very happy" with their marriages (Cherlin and Furstenberg 1988; Whyte 1992).				

Now try your skills at checking the strength of facts used to back up the supporting points in the essay "Adult Men Are Largely to Blame for Teen Pregnancy." Look at the points the author is making in support of her opinion. Are there studies backing up those points? Check each study for its relevance, currency, sources, and sufficiency. Then identify the points that were especially well defended with high-quality facts.

PRACTICE PASSAGE 6.2: SOCIAL WORK

Adult Men Are Largely to Blame for Teen Pregnancy

Most of the measures society takes to reduce teenage pregnancy are aimed at convincing teens to abstain from sex or promoting the reliable use of birth control. The underlying assumption of such measures is that if teenagers would just act more responsibly, most cases of adolescent pregnancy could be prevented. However, focusing on teen behavior does nothing to eliminate the primary cause of teenage pregnancy: the exploitation of adolescent girls by adult men. Take the case of twenty-nine-year-old Tyrone Gaskins, who was "dating" a twelve-year-old teen for several months before she became pregnant. Should society really fault the young girl—and not the grown man who took advantage of her—for this unwanted pregnancy? Yet in all too many cases, it is the girls who take the blame and bear the consequences when they are impregnated by adult men (Figure 6.2).

A WIDESPREAD PROBLEM

While the case of Gaskins obviously represents the extreme, the problem of adult men impregnating teenage girls is hardly uncommon. In fact, the results of two recent studies show that the vast majority of teen pregnancies are fathered by adults—not by "adult" eighteen-year-old high school students, but by men who are out of school and usually over the age of twenty. According to a 1995 study published in *Family Planning Perspectives*, almost two-thirds of adolescent mothers have partners older than twenty years of age. Furthermore, a 1998 report conducted by sociologist Mike Males concludes that "three fourths of the fathers in births among students aged sixteen to eighteen are postschool men" (Males, 1998).

The trends among younger teens are especially disturbing. Research suggests that the younger the adolescent mother, the greater the age gap between her and her partner, with one study revealing that "fathers are on average 9.8 years older than mothers 11 to 12 years of age and 4.6 years older than mothers 13 to 14 years of age" (Elders, 1998).

FIGURE 6.2 ■ *The stress of pregnancy may cause teenage girls to drop out of school.*
Source: Photograph by David Young-Wolff.
Courtesy of PhotoEdit Inc.

RAPE, PURE AND SIMPLE

These statistics offer a glimpse of the sickening reality behind so-called teen pregnancy. When a twenty-one-year-old man has sex with a twelve-year-old girl—or even a seventeen-year-old-girl—it is rape, pure and simple. It doesn't matter whether the girl says she wanted to. Statutory rape laws forbid even consensual sex between adults and minors as a way to protect children and adolescents from sexual exploitation. And, as columnist Leonard Pitts Jr. writes, "Who ever needed protection more than a teenage girl who is, or thinks she is, in love? Who was ever more vulnerable to exploitation by an older man willing to whisper the proper promises and tell the necessary lies?" (Pitts, 1999).

Just as a sexual relationship between an adult and a child is always exploitative, so is a sexual relationship between an adult and a teenage girl. Teenage girls may be physically mature, but they are still children, and possess a child's need for love and acceptance. Their youth and inexperience make them particularly vulnerable to older men who are looking for sex. Patricia, who first had sex at age fourteen with a twenty-one-year-old man, explains why: "They know more than you," she says. "If I'm going out with a twenty-five-year-old guy, what can I offer him that he hasn't already had? I'm just learning the rules. I have to show him that I can give him more" (Yang, 1999).

SEXUAL ABUSE

Even more alarming than these supposedly consensual relationships between adult men and teenage girls are those that are outright abusive. The problem of sexual abuse among teens who become pregnant is widespread, but barely acknowledged. However, a shocking 66 percent of pregnant teens have histories of sexual abuse—most perpetrated by adult family members or older boyfriends.

Sexual abuse makes teens prone to pregnancy for a variety of reasons. First, pregnancy may be the direct result of an episode of abuse. In a study of 455 teen mothers, researcher H. P. Gershenson found that "over 60 percent had coercive sexual experiences and 23 percent became pregnant by the perpetrator" (Elders, 1998). Second, the trauma of sexual abuse makes teenage girls more likely to engage in the types of behavior that increase their chances of an unplanned pregnancy. As Elders writes,

> A history of sexual abuse has been linked to high-risk behaviors that may account for increased risk of early unplanned pregnancy, including young age at initiation of sexual intercourse, failure to use contraception, prostitution, physically assaultive relationships, and abuse of alcohol and other drugs. Moreover, girls with histories of sexual abuse have been found to have a greater desire to conceive and increased concerns about infertility than girls without abuse histories. (Elders, 1998)

PROSECUTING STATUTORY RAPISTS

Some states are finally beginning to address the abusive relationships behind so many cases of teenage pregnancy. In California, officials have instituted aggressive efforts to prosecute and imprison adult men who have sex with minors. Since its inception in 1995, California's Statutory Rape Vertical Prosecution Program has convicted more than 1,454 offenders and has 5,000 more under investigation.

Other states must follow California's lead and treat statutory rapists as what they are: criminals. If older men know that they will suffer severe consequences for breaking statutory rape laws, perhaps they will think twice about taking advantage of young girls.

Source: Adapted from Jennifer A. Hurley, *Opposing Viewpoints Digests: Teen Pregnancy* (Pacific Grove, CA: Thomson Learning, 2000). Reprinted with permission of Thomson Learning: http://www.thomsonrights.com; fax 800-730-2215.

Recognizing Logical Flaws

When a position is well argued, the writer has spent a long time studying the issue and collecting factual evidence that supports it. Writers who have not done this kind of work won't have solid facts to back up their positions. Instead, they fill up space with opinions on top of opinions or facts of very poor quality. Some types of weak, unsound support for opinions are seen so often that they have names. It is nice to know these common logical flaws for two reasons:

1. You won't mistake any of them for quality support.
2. You can refer to a problem by name when discussing the opinion with others.

Also, once you become familiar with common logical flaws, you will never be able to listen to politicians' speeches in quite the same way. These faulty ways of arguing are amazingly prevalent in political debate.

Notice that when we say that a point is supported by a logical flaw, we are not criticizing the point itself—only the quality of the evidence offered for it.

■ CIRCULAR REASONING

Circular reasoning is saying the same thing over and over in different words. Example:

Alcoholism should not be regarded as a moral issue; it is a disease. No one should think that alcoholics are lacking in ethics. Alcoholics have as much moral fiber as others. They should be regarded as victims of a disease, not as people who have a character defect.

■ FALSE ALTERNATIVES

False alternatives involves framing the issue so that either the course of action proposed by the author is followed or the disaster will result. Example:

The best way to cure alcoholism is by changing the biochemistry of the alcoholic's brain. The U.S. government must intensify research in this area. Either we double the spending on brain chemistry research or the problem of alcoholism will worsen.

■ CARELESS COMPARISON

A *careless comparison* results when the author says that two things are just the same although there are important differences between them. Here is an example:

> Tax money should not be used for treatment for alcoholics. If the federal government provides funds for those who become victims of booze, then it should also aid those who are addicted to television, shopping, or the Internet.

■ ATTACKING THE PERSON

When a writer attacks the character or credentials of a person on the opposing side rather than addressing his or her argument, this is called *attacking the person*. Here is an example:

> Fitness specialist Susan Powter has argued that alcoholism is a disease, not a failure of character. However, Ms. Powter has a vested interest in denying the moral issues in alcohol addiction. She is herself an alcoholic.

■ APPEAL TO EMOTIONS

When writers use words or imagery designed to sway people through feelings rather than facts, this is called an *appeal to emotion*. Here is an example:

> The main reason more young men are turning to alcohol is the breakup of families and the absence of fathers. A boy should have the pleasure of being rocked and sung to by a mother as an infant. Later, he should be able to spend weekends throwing a football and building car models with a father.

■ ANECDOTAL EVIDENCE

The problem with *anecdotal evidence* is that the writer makes a broad generalization on the experience of a small number of people. Here is an example:

> The support group network Alcoholics Anonymous doesn't really help anybody. My uncle attended meetings for a few months, but then he went right back to drinking.

It would have been fine for the writer to say, "Alcoholics Anonymous didn't help my uncle." However, basing the effectiveness of hundreds of Alcoholics Anonymous groups on the experience of just one person is not reasonable. Saying that the writer's evidence is anecdotal is the same as saying that the fact offered was not sufficient.

■ BANDWAGON APPROACH

In the *bandwagon approach,* the writer says that we should do something because other people do. The problem is that no evidence is presented showing that such a way of doing things has benefited the other people. Here is an example:

> If children were introduced to alcohol use as a normal part of life, they would be less likely to abuse it later. Many other countries allow children to drink wine or beer. The United States should follow their example.

SKILLS PRACTICE 4

Match the name of each kind of logical flaw with its definition.

_____1. Circular reasoning

_____2. Attacking the person

_____3. False alternatives

_____4. Careless comparison

_____5. Anecdotal evidence

_____6. Bandwagon approach

_____7. Appeal to emotions

a. Saying that if the writer's ideas aren't followed, disaster will follow

b. Making a broad generalization based on a small example

c. Saying we should do something just because others do

d. Saying the same idea over and over in different words.

e. Saying that one situation is just like another while ignoring important differences

f. Using language and imagery designed to stir up people's feelings

g. Criticizing the character or credentials of an opponent instead of focusing on facts

Now see if you can identify common logical flaws in others' arguments.

SKILLS PRACTICE 5

Under the Americans With Disabilities Act, employers must make accommodations for people with mental illnesses just as they do for workers with physical illnesses. This aspect of the law has provoked a good deal of debate. See if you can identify the type of logical flaw represented in each statement.

_____ 1. Workers with clinical depression are just as effective as other employees. Abraham Lincoln suffered from recurrent bouts of depression, and he is widely regarded as the finest president that ever governed.

   a. circular reasoning

   b. anecdotal evidence

   c. bandwagon approach

_____ 2. Many people are afraid of the mentally ill. Such ideas are foolish and ignorant. Intolerant people who are fearful of working next to those with schizophrenia or obsessive-compulsive disorders should examine their own characters. They are a bigger problem than those with mental illnesses.

   a. false alternatives

   b. careless comparison

   c. attacking the person

_____ 3. Mentally ill people should not be tolerated in the workplace. If businesses are burdened with accommodating people displaying inappropriate behavior and disrupting the flow of the work, the United States will lose its competitive edge and more jobs will go overseas.

   a. attacking the person

   b. false alternatives

   c. circular reasoning

_____ 4. American companies should not have to hire or accommodate mentally ill workers. None of the other industrialized countries place such unreasonable expectations on employers.

   a. bandwagon approach

   b. false alternatives

   c. attacking the person

_____ 5. Mentally ill people are capable of productive work with appropriate accommodation. As long as employers provide support for mentally ill employees, they can work efficiently. Provided that workers with mental illnesses receive proper consideration, they will be able to function well in the workplace.

   a. appeal to emotions

   b. careless comparison

   c. circular reasoning

_____ 6. Mental illnesses should be treated the same as physical disabilities by employers. Just as we accommodate workers in wheelchairs, we need to be supportive of workers who are severely depressed and may need to miss work frequently.

    a. false alternatives

    b. attacking the person

    c. careless comparison

_____7. Americans should be proud that our laws protect some of our most vulnerable citizens—those suffering from mental illnesses. America stands for justice, tolerance, and equal opportunity. Mental illness strikes our mothers, fathers, brothers, sisters, neighbors, sons, daughters, and friends. How lucky we are to have laws that protect our nearest and dearest.

    a. circular reasoning

    b. appeal to emotions

    c. bandwagon approach

SKILLS PRACTICE 6

Suppose you are browsing through articles looking for information on the deinstitutionalization of people with severe mental illness. You have been assigned to identify and present the best evidence of both sides—that deinstitutionalizing people with mental illnesses has been either a great improvement or a disaster. Select the statements you might want to include in your paper. For the ones you passed up, note why you wouldn't cite them.

Controversies in Mental Illness:
Institutionalization of the Severely Mentally Ill

Background. Until the 1950s, thousands of people with schizophrenia, severe depression, and brain damage were committed to state-run institutions. Although they received food, shelter, and care, people in these institutions were not free to leave. With the development of new drugs, notably Thorazine, people with mental illnesses regained some of their lost abilities, and many were able to live with their families and take greater part in community activities.

In the 1970s, President Jimmy Carter's Commission on Mental Health conducted a study of severe mental illness and issued the opinion that as a general principle, it should be treated in the "least restrictive setting." This principle was based on the goal of maintaining "the greatest degree of freedom, self-determination, autonomy, dignity, and integrity of body, mind, and spirit for the individual while he or she participates in treatment or receives services."

Mental institutions were seen as too restrictive and not in keeping with the idea of allowing people with mental illnesses as much freedom as possible. Tens of thousands of people with mental illnesses were moved from institutions to group homes, which they were free to leave if they so desired. In 1955, there were over 500,000 people in government-run institutions. By the mid-1990s fewer than 75,000 lived in institutions.

Position #1: Deinstitutionalizing Mentally Ill People Was a Huge Mistake. Here are examples of statements you see while reading articles. Choose to save only those paragraphs that are justified with facts. Don't save those supported by logical flaws.

1. Most of the mentally ill people living in mental illnesses had various forms of brain dysfunction. People with problems involving the brain cannot make good decisions. We would not expect children with their undeveloped minds to make their own way in the world. Children are under the control of their parents for their own protection. Similarly, mentally ill people should not have been expected to look after themselves.

    a. Save.

    b. Don't save. Why not? _____

2. The majority of people released from institutions had brain disorders that would affect their judgment. The disorders affecting people in mental institutions were as follows: schizophrenia (50–60%); manic-depressive illness and severe depression (10–15%). Another 10–15% had organic brain diseases such as epilepsy, stroke, Alzheimer's disease, and brain damage following trauma. A smaller number had conditions such as mental retardation with psychosis, autism and other psychiatric disorders of childhood, and alcoholism and drug addiction with concurrent brain damage.

    a. Save.

    b. Don't save. Why not? _____

3. People with mental illnesses were discharged without making sure that each person had an appropriate rehabilitation plan and source of medication, and this situation continues up to the present. Consequently, approximately 2.2 million severely mentally ill people do not receive any psychiatric treatment.

    a. Save.

    b. Don't save. Why not? _____

4. Deinstitutionalization was meant to increase the freedom of the mentally ill. For thousands of people, however, it has been a psychiatric *Titanic.* Their lives are devoid of "dignity" or "integrity of body, mind, and spirit." "Self-determination" means that the mentally ill person has a choice of soup kitchens. The "least restrictive setting" turns out to be a cardboard box.

    a. Save.

    b. Don't save. Why not? _____

5. Deinstitutionalization has contributed to homelessness and crime. Of the 2.2 million Americans with untreated severe mental illness, an estimated 150,000 are homeless, living on the streets or in public shelters. Another 159,000 are in prison, incarcerated for crimes that they would have been unlikely to commit had they been sheltered in state-run institutions and treated for their mental illnesses.

    a. Save.

    b. Don't save. Why not? _____

Position #2: Deinstitutionalizing Mentally Ill People was the Right Thing to Do. Again, here are examples of statements you see while reading articles. Choose to save only those that are justified with facts. Don't save those supported by logical flaws.

1. Warehousing mentally ill people in institutions is a form of segregation. Its destructive and intolerant nature parallels the discrimination suffered by African Americans in the era when they were not allowed to attend the same schools, live in the same neighborhoods, or drink from the same water fountains as whites.

    a. Save.

    b. Don't save. Why not? _____

2. Legal scholars have argued that it is a violation of the Constitution to imprison people who have not committed a crime, and that forcing mentally ill persons to remain in institutions against their will amounts to incarceration. U.S. District Court Judge Myron Thompson observed that institutionalized individuals "suffer not only a dramatic loss of physical freedom, but . . . severely detailed control and invasive treatment, they also cannot enjoy those mundane, daily pleasures—working, shopping, the companionship of family or friends—the loss of which we on the outside would find to be not only intolerable but a threat to our very sanity."

    a. Save.

    b. Don't save. Why not? _____

3. Persons with mental illnesses living in institutions are frequently abused. A 1975 study revealed that between 10% and 30% of residents in the institutions studied had been struck or subjected to unnecessary restraint by staff members. Approximately 3% had been sexually molested. A report published last year by a commission on mental health treatment in the United States stated that neglect and abuse of severely mentally ill persons living in institutions remains a serious problem.

    a. Save.

    b. Don't save. Why not? _____

4. People committed to institutions lose the basic freedom to control their lives. Residents in institutions must live according to schedules that are based on the institution's needs. They cannot choose and prepare their own meals, they cannot decide how to spend their day, and they may not leave the grounds of the institution unless they are supervised.

   a. Save.

   b. Don't save. Why not? _____

5. Residents of institutions for the mentally ill are not safe. They are often victims of poor care, unnecessary restraint, and even assault. In one recent case, a woman with schizophrenia was raped by one of the staff members.

   a. Save.

   b. Don't save. Why not? _____

6. Mentally ill people need to interact with well people in order to regain their mental health. If persons with severe mental illnesses never have an opportunity to speak with well persons, they are likely to remain sick. Communicating with no one but others with severe mental illnesses does not provide the conditions necessary for recovery.

   a. Save.

   b. Don't save. Why not? _____

7. Mentally ill people recover more quickly if they are integrated into the community than they do in institutions. In one study conducted by the University of Michigan in 1992, a group of over 100 people with schizophrenia living in integrated settings was compared with a matched group in an institution. Over a period of three years, 40% of the people in the integrated setting made significant improvements in mental health, and 20% were able to go back to work. Only 5% of the people in the institutionalized group made significant gains in mental health over the same period.

   a. Save.

   b. Don't save. Why not? _____

When you read through an author's opinion, you may see that some points are well supported with facts and other points are not. In the places where there is little factual support, look for logical flaws.

In the essay that follows, Nadine Block brings forward a number of points in favor of making the practice of spanking children illegal. Which points are well supported with facts and which are not? Do you see any logical flaws in the support for points?

PRACTICE PASSAGE 6.3: CHILD DEVELOPMENT

Disciplinary Spanking Should Be Banned

Nadine Block*

Corporal punishment is the intentional infliction of physical pain for a perceived misbehavior. It includes spanking, slapping, pinching, choking, and hitting with objects. The practice is not permitted against prison or jail inmates, military personnel, or mental patients; nor is it allowed against a spouse, a neighbor, or even a neighbor's dog. Instead, in the United States, corporal punishment is legally preserved only for children. Children have been the victims since early colonial times and today remain so with the support of the courts and a significant percentage of the citizenry. Each year at least a million children are beaten in the name of "discipline," billions of dollars are spent on child abuse prevention, and the system devised to protect children fails. Yet, the subject is a divisive one that often pits generation against generation and family member against family member.

RELIGIOUS GROUPS SUPPORT CORPORAL PUNISHMENT

One reason for this divisiveness is corporal punishment's roots in theology. The strongest and most enduring support for the practice comes from the Bible, particularly the Old Testament. Many fundamentalist, evangelical, and charismatic Protestants use scripture to justify their use of corporal punishment to develop obedience and character in children. Their position is that God wills and requires it in order to obtain his blessing and approval; to not physically punish children for misbehavior will incur God's wrath.

For example, in "The Correction and Salvation of Children" on the Way of Life Web site, the Reverend Ronald E. Williams of the Believers Baptist Church in Winona Lake, Indiana, contends that the biblical "rod of correction" is a physical object, in most cases a wooden paddle for use in spanking a child's buttocks; any unwillingness to use physical correction is "child abuse." While he recognizes that using an object to hit a child increases the chances of injury, and while he cautions that bruising is not the goal of "correction," Williams counsels parents not to be overly concerned if bruising happens:

> But these opponents of God's methods may object, "What you are suggesting will hurt the child and may even bruise him!" My response would be, "That is correct." A child may in fact be bruised by a session of difficult correction. In fact, the Lord has already anticipated this

*Nadine Block is director of the Center for Effective Discipline and co-chair of End Physical Punishment of Children (EPOCH).

objection and has discussed it briefly in the Scriptures. "The blueness of a wound cleanseth away evil: so do stripes the inward parts of the belly" (Proverbs 20:30). One may say, "That is talking about a child who has bruised himself in an accident at play." No, the latter part of the verse explains that God is giving this passage in the context of physical chastening for correction. God makes the point that if a child is bruised during one of these sessions of correction that a parent should not despair but realize that the blueness of the wound cleanses away the evil heart of rebellion and willful stubbornness that reside in that depraved little body.

Williams also believes that corporal punishment should begin early in life:

> My wife and I have a general goal of making sure that each of our children has his will broken by the time he reaches the age of one year. To do this, a child must receive correction when he is a small infant.

However, the Reverend Thomas E. Sagendorf, a Methodist pastor and member of the advisory board of the Center for Effective Discipline's program, End Physical Punishment of Children (EPOCH)—USA, points out that Old Testament scripture can also be used to justify slavery, suppression of women, polygamy, incest, and infanticide. So, like many believers in the Bible, Sagendorf prefers to look for guidance on disciplining children in the New Testament. There, he says, children are shown great love and compassion, and violence is not tolerated.

SOCIAL ACCEPTANCE OF CORPORAL PUNISHMENT DECLINING

Fortunately, a growing willingness to challenge ingrained attitudes has resulted in a waning society acceptance of corporal punishment. For example, almost universally accepted in the 1950s, the practice has decreased each generation since. In 1985, only five states had banned it in public schools; today twenty-seven states have done so. Even in those states that still allow corporal punishment, many of the larger cities have banned it. In 1991, the American Academy of Pediatrics (AAP) called on parents, educators, legislators and other adults to seek the legal prohibition by all states of corporal punishment in schools. Unable to hush pro-spanking sentiments within its own ranks, however, the AAP stopped short of calling for a complete ban in 1998. Instead, it recommended that its members encourage and assist parents in developing nonviolent responses to misbehavior.

CORPORAL PUNISHMENT CONTRIBUTES TO INTERPERSONAL VIOLENCE

The changing perception of corporal punishment is being helped along by research in the field of physical abuse. Much of it is correlationship and retrospective in nature, given the difficulty of designing such experiments and the abhorrence of assigning children spanking and paddling treatment. It is, however, compelling.

FIGURE 6.3 ■ *A little girl spanks her doll.*
Source: Photograph by David S. Strickler.
Courtesy of The Image Works.

In his 1994 book *Beating the Devil out of Them: Corporal Punishment in American Families*, University of New Hampshire Family Research Laboratory co-director Murray Straus reviews the dozens of studies he has authored or coauthored that show corporal punishment contributes to interpersonal violence. Among his results, Straus found that children who were spanked regularly and severely have higher rates of hitting siblings, hitting their spouses as adults, and assaulting someone outside their family. Children who are frequently spanked for lying, cheating, hitting siblings, and being disobedient are more likely to display these kinds of antisocial behaviors (Figure 6.3).

Studies by Straus and others have also found that corporal punishment can escalate to the level of abuse prohibited by law. Since parents are more likely to spank when they are tired, stressed, depressed, and fatigued, and a majority of parents express moderate to high anger when spanking children, it is little surprise that parents who believe in corporal punishment are more likely to injure children than parents who do not. And children who are regularly spanked are more likely to continue the practice on the next generation and to show less remorse for wrongdoing as adults.

Even infrequent and moderate spanking in childhood can have deleterious effects in adult life, including a greater likelihood of depression and other psychological problems. Conversely, Straus found that children who are rarely or never spanked score higher on cognitive tests than those who are frequently spanked. He theorizes that parents who don't spank spend more time reasoning with and explaining to children, thus maximizing verbal ability.

PUNISHMENT IN SCHOOLS

A U.S. Department of Education survey indicates that about 500,000 students are hit each year in the nation's public schools. Physical injuries, including hematomas and broken bones, have resulted from adults hitting children in school with boards— sometimes in anger and in unobserved and unsupervised settings. The National Coalition to Abolish Punishment in Schools, another program of the Center for Effective Discipline, estimates that 2 percent of children who are paddled need medical care. Twenty years of Department of Education surveys analyzed by the coalition and the center reveal that corporal punishment in schools is used more frequently on children with disabilities, poor children, boys, and minority children.

ENDING CORPORAL PUNISHMENT IN SCHOOLS

Despite the compelling research, the task of ending corporal punishment in the United States is a daunting one. All too often repeated by those who grew up with violence are comments like "My parents hit me because they loved me" and "I got hit because I deserved it." Progress is likely to be slow and incremental, but it is not impossible.

The last fifteen years have seen a great deal of progress on a state-by-state basis. For example, nineteen of the twenty-seven states that have banned corporal punishment in public schools did so between 1985 and 1994. The remaining twenty-three states without bans—primarily southern and southwestern states—allow local boards of education to determine whether corporal punishment may be used.

And there is a slow but steady increase in the number of those school boards adopting voluntary bans—frequently to avoid potential litigation resulting from paddling injuries. In Ohio, child advocates were unable to get a complete ban, but they got so many restrictions put into law that only forty-two out of 611 school districts report using punishment. Each year a few more districts enact a local ban, making a statewide ban likely in the near future. The use of corporal punishment in other child-care settings (day care centers, foster care, and institutions) varies from state to state. State regulatory agencies are moving toward complete bans, and a great deal of legislative and regulatory progress has been made since 1980 because of extensive public education campaigns.

Perhaps an easier route is to get a federal ban on corporal punishment. Schools could be prompted to comply by tying federal funding to requirements for adopting bans, as Democratic Representative Major Owens of New York attempted in the early 1990s.

FOLLOWING THE EXAMPLE OF EUROPE

In all this, the United States is taking a lesson from Europe, where corporal punishment in schools was banned long ago. Nine European countries—Austria, Croatia, Cyprus, Denmark, Finland, Italy (by court decision), Latvia, Norway, and Sweden—have banned corporal punishment in all settings, including homes.

Sweden was the first country to act. It took away parents' specific authority to use punishment, then passed a comprehensive ban three years later in 1979, accompanied by a large-scale education effort. The law is generally used to require educational training of parents who hit children, but offenders can be subjected to criminal prosecution. The overall process has resulted in an overwhelming acceptance of the ban in Sweden and, more importantly, a decline in child abuse. U.S. child advocates are watching carefully as a number of countries—including Germany, Ireland, New Zealand, Switzerland, and the United Kingdom—are studying this model for possible adoption.

In Canada, an effort is underway to abolish Section 43 of the Criminal Code, which gives parents authority to use "reasonable chastisement" on children. Abolition of this section is likely to be followed by a complete ban that follows the Swedish model. Meanwhile, Susan Bitensky, a law professor and EPOCH advisory board member, has suggested criminalizing corporal punishment of children and making violators subject to the same criminal penalties imposed on adult assaults and batteries. In the winter 1998 *University of Michigan Journal of Law Reform*, Bitensky says that such a law could be effective if accompanied by prosecutorial restraint and a strong public education program, such as that used in the Swedish model.

Source: Adapted from Louise Gerdes, *Opposing Viewpoints Digests: Child Abuse* (Pacific Grove, CA: Thomson Learning, 2003). Reprinted with permission of Gale, a division of Thomson Learning: http://www.thomsonrights.com; fax 800-730-2215.

Putting It All Together

When you are given an opinion to read, make a simple chart outlining the author's major points and the evidence presented for each point. Don't recopy all the evidence you see for your outline, just note what it was (a study, a quote, a story) and whether the point made was justified by facts. Look at the following example:

"State Lotteries: More Curse Than Blessing" by John Smith

Thesis: State lotteries do more harm than good and should be banned.

Author's Major Points	Evidence for Major Points
State lotteries encourage gambling addiction.	Two studies—one showed that since state lotteries were legalized, gambling addiction has risen sharply. Other study gave percentages on how many buyers of lottery tickets have gambling addiction. (justified by facts)
Lotteries discourage people from getting ahead through hard work.	No evidence given—author just repeated this point several times using different words. (weak support: circular reasoning)
Many people that buy lottery tickets can't afford it.	Two studies—one showed that low-income people are more likely to buy lottery tickets than middle-class or wealthy people. Other study showed that when Power-ball jackpot is high and people buy more tickets, sales at grocery stores drop. (justified by facts)
Lotteries violate the moral values of many people.	One person was quoted. (weak support: anecdotal evidence)

Creating such a chart makes it very easy for you to participate in class discussions. Many times, instructors will assign you to read an opinion in preparation for a class discussion. Suppose your instructor were to call on you. Just by looking at the chart, see if you can answer these questions:

- What are the major points the author brings up in connection with his argument that the state lotteries should be banned?
- Which of the points were well supported with factual evidence and which were not?
- One of the points the author raised was that many people that buy lottery tickets can't afford them. What evidence did he present in support of this point?
- Another point the author made was that lotteries violate the moral values of many people. What evidence did he give in support of this point?

Notice that producing the chart enables you to give a good answer to any of these questions. You could also do well on an essay question asking you to outline the major points raised by people in favor of banning the lottery.

Read through the essay entitled "Helping Teens Quit Smoking." Create a chart of the author's six major supporting points and the evidence presented for each point.

FIGURE 6.4 ■ *Most smokers start in their teens.*
Source: Photograph by Michael Newman. Courtesy of PhotoEdit Inc.

PRACTICE PASSAGE 6.4: HEALTH CARE

Helping Teens Quit Smoking

Dr. Richard Hurt didn't hold out much hope the day he launched a drive to re-cruit volunteers for a Mayo Clinic study on smoking. Hurt was looking for teenagers. Teenagers who wanted to quit smoking. Teens who would have to have parental consent, visit a clinic weekly, and wear a nicotine patch for six weeks. So Hurt was pleasantly surprised when more than 100 volunteers—13- to 17-year-olds who smoked at least 10 cigarettes a day—signed up. There were so many vol-unteers that he had to turn away dozens. "There is a mythology out there that teen smokers don't want to stop," says Hurt, of the Mayo Clinic's Nicotine Depen-dence Center in Rochester, Minnesota. "That is not true. We just don't know how to help them very well." But a burgeoning movement focused on efforts to stop teenagers from smoking is gaining momentum in this country, targeting a group of smokers who have been largely ignored for years (Figure 6.4).

TEENS DO TRY TO QUIT—OFTEN

A landmark 1992 study from the University of Massachusetts Medical Center in Worcester found that 52% of 10th-grade smokers had already tried to quit two or more times. The study also found that one-quarter of the teens thought they were addicted. And nearly half were concerned about their health.

PROGRAMS TO HELP TEENS QUIT SMOKING HAVE A HIGH FAILURE RATE

While many teenagers apparently want to quit, they have an especially difficult time doing so. The few teen smoking cessation programs that have been scientifically evaluated show poor results. Hurt's work is a case in point. In his recent study, published in January, 2000 in the *Archives of Pediatric & Adolescent Medicine*, only 11 of 101 smokers had stopped at the end of six-week patch therapy. Six months later, only five remained abstinent. He attributes the poor results to the fact that the patch study did not include much behavior intervention, which teaches things like what to do when a craving strikes.

But others note that such intervention programs have fared poorly among adolescents. Steve Sussman, a professor of preventive medicine and psychology at the University of Southern California, examined 17 teen cessation programs using behavioral approaches (not including nicotine aids, like the patch) and found an average quit rate of 6% to 7%. In programs where kids seemed highly motivated, the quit rate was closer to 10%. The typical adult rate after a cessation program is 50%. "I think one of the problems with the programs developed early on is they were based on an adult model of cessation," Sussman says.

TEENS HAVE MORE PROBLEMS WITH WITHDRAWAL SYMPTOMS

Support may be the most vital component of teen programs. Like adult smokers, adolescents experience withdrawal symptoms. But adolescents appear less able or willing to put up with the irritability, headaches, or fatigue, and need more moral support during this phase. "These kids need support," says Rita Moncrief, a teacher who oversees smoking cessation programs at El Camino Real High School in Woodland Hills, California. Moncrief keeps a supply of chewing gum and plastic straws in her classroom for ex-smokers to gnaw on if a craving strikes.

TEENS HAVE PROBLEMS QUITTING IF FAMILY MEMBERS SMOKE

Helping adolescents deal with the people around them who smoke—family and friends—is also a huge issue, Hurt says. Surveys show that 30% of adult smokers have another smoker at home. But among teen smokers, 75% have another smoker in the home. The presence of another smoker often deters those trying to quit. "We asked the kids in our study if there was someone at home to help you, what would you want them to do?" Hurt says. "They said things like: Tell them not to smoke around me. Not to offer me cigarettes. Not to buy me cigarettes. As many teens wanted to bring a person in their household who is smoking into the study as wanted to stop smoking themselves."

THE SOCIAL ASPECT OF SMOKING ALSO COMPLICATES QUITTING

Perhaps especially for teenagers, the social aspect of smoking complicates quitting. One ex-smoker, who met many of her college friends in areas where smokers congregate, found she had to drop those friends in order to quit. "The reason I failed initially was because all my friends smoked," she said. "Finally my best friend decided to quit too, and he was really good at it. He really encouraged me. I'm not really friends with the smokers anymore."

James Chanthapak, a senior at Marshall High School in Los Angeles, tried to quit smoking in November 1999 on the American Cancer Society's Great American Smoke-out Day. During the last few years, the cancer group has stepped up its campaign to target teens during the Smokeout with a "Teens Kick Ash" motto. Chanthapak was enthusiastic enough to quit for two or three weeks. But he couldn't sustain the effort. "It's such a social thing," he says. "I would have had to change friends. Smoking is just what we do." In the meantime, his habit has grown from one pack a week to three packs. "I used to tell people that if you wanted to quit smoking, you could quit," he says, softly. "Now I think you need help. I didn't know it was as hard as it is."

MORE RESEARCH IS NEEDED TO IDENTIFY THE APPROACHES THAT WORK BEST

Should Chanthapak decide to try to quit again, there are a range of options. And within the next year, cessation experts will have a better idea of what works with kids, Sussman says. The enthusiasm to help teens is so great that some experts worry that programs may be implemented before they've been shown to work. "People are trying the Internet, CD-ROMs, school programs, patches, all kinds of ways to approach the topic," Sussman says. "But there is a push toward getting programs out there quickly, before they are evaluated."

Studies will also continue on nicotine aids, like the patch, gum, or the antidepressant medication Zyban. These aids shouldn't be ruled out for teens despite early poor results, Hurt says. Although few kids in his study quit smoking, the teens cooperated with wearing the patch and many dramatically cut back on the number of cigarettes they smoked. And then there was that most hopeful sign: They wanted to quit. "When we got the final results, we said, 'Oh, no,' " says Hurt. "But when we started peeling away the layers, there are some positive things happening."

Source: Adapted from Shari Roan, "Struggle to Quit," *Los Angeles Times*, February 14, 2000. Reprinted by permission.

PRACTICE TEST
Evaluating the Evidence for Opinions

PART I: PASSAGE TO PREPARE

Directions: Read the article entitled "The Debate over the Living Wage." Make two charts—one outlining the supporting points and evidence *against* the living wage, and the other outlining the supporting points and evidence *in favor* of it. You do not need to do anything with the first two paragraphs; they simply introduce the issue.

THE DEBATE OVER THE LIVING WAGE

OVERVIEW

1   According to a survey conducted in 2000, 94 percent of Americans agree that "people who work full time should be able to earn enough to keep their families out of poverty." Laws requiring employers to pay a minimum wage were established in 1938 with this goal in mind. In 1938, the minimum wage was 25 cents per hour. Today, it is $6.15 per hour. Many people believe that the current minimum wage is too low to keep families out of poverty, and that employers should be required to pay a wage that more closely reflects the cost of living. Others, however, argue that such a policy would do more harm than good.

2   Estimates of what an hourly "living wage" should be vary. Simply to reach poverty level, the hourly wage of those supporting families would need to be at least $8 per hour. Additionally, the cost of living in some cities, notably New York and Los Angeles, is much higher than in others. The Economic Policy Institute reviewed dozens of studies on what constitutes a "living wage" and came up with an average figure of $30,000 for one adult and two children, or $14 per hour. Sixty percent of Americans earn less than that amount. Proposals for a living wage range from $8 to $20 per hour depending on the city, with $12 per hour being the commonly cited amount.

ARGUMENTS AGAINST THE LIVING WAGE

3   Opponents argue that requiring employers to pay higher wages will result in job losses for the most vulnerable workers. They contend that employers will cut workers' hours or move their businesses to countries with cheaper labor costs. Foes of living wage proposals contend that such laws would create a hostile business climate, chasing away established companies and discouraging new companies from locating in an area. They maintain that either the current minimum wage must remain as it is or huge numbers of low-paid Americans will see their jobs disappear.

4   Critics of living wage proposals also claim that increases in the minimum wage will chiefly benefit teenagers, not adults who must support themselves and their

families. According to living wage opponents, most adolescents spend their earnings on luxury goods and entertainment. Few contribute toward household expenses. Therefore, raising the minimum wage would do little to reduce poverty.

5   Those who oppose living wage proposals also state that it is unreasonable to expect employers to pay high wages for unskilled labor. If workers want better pay, they contend, they must invest in their educations. It is unfair to burden employers with high payroll costs for workers that are not skilled.

ARGUMENTS IN FAVOR OF THE LIVING WAGE

6   Advocates of the living wage proposals argue that, contrary to the claims of their opponents, most low-wage workers are not teenagers. According to *The State of Working America* (Mishel et al., 2002), only 7 percent of the low-wage workforce is composed of adolescents. America's low-wage workforce is mostly white, female, high school educated, with family responsibilities. However, adult workers from minority groups are disproportionately represented.

7   Proponents of living wage proposals say that research evidence does not support the contention that higher wages cause low-paid workers to lose their jobs to cheaper labor overseas. Most low-wage jobs are in positions that must be done locally: caring for children, cleaning hotel rooms, waiting on tables, servicing office equipment, or checking out groceries (Freeman, 1997). In addition, when employers receiving government contracts in Baltimore were required to pay their workers a living wage, an evaluation study found that mandating higher pay did not result in job loss.

8   Supporters of living wage proposals also argue that low-wage jobs are not "unskilled." Meat processing, machine sewing, and care of children and the elderly all require specialized knowledge. Many low-wage jobs require sophisticated human relations skills. Unfortunately, skills related to caring for other human beings are not valued as much as technical knowledge.

9   Those in favor of the living wage argue that it would benefit employers as well as workers. Raising wages cuts employers' costs by reducing turnover, increases productivity, and improves employee morale. Responsible Wealth, an organization of

450 business owners that support living wage proposals, gathered a number of testimonials from employers that claim raising workers' pay has strengthened their businesses. Hal Taussig, the owner of a Philadelphia travel business, commented, "The benefits we get from paying living wages include low turnover, great staff spirit, and dedicated employees helping us find ways to keep other costs low and quality high." A study of home health care workers supported these employers' statements. Dawson (2000) found that as home health care workers' pay and benefits improved, turnover dropped dramatically.

10   Advocates also claim that paying a living wage will help people reduce their dependence on public assistance, thus cutting down on welfare costs. If people are paid enough to support their families, they don't need public assistance. Those who are getting food stamps, medical assistance, and housing subsidies could cover their own expenses.

PART II: TEST QUESTIONS

Directions: Using your charts of each side's points and any annotations you may have made on the article, answer the following questions on "The Debate over the Living Wage."

SEPARATING FACT FROM OPINION

Decide whether each statement is a fact or an opinion.

_____1. **Paragraph 1:** In 1938, the minimum wage was 25 cents per hour.

   a. a fact   **b.** an opinion

_____2. **Paragraph 2:** Sixty percent of Americans earn less than $14 per hour.

   a. fact   **b.** opinion

_____3. **Paragraph 5:** It is unreasonable to expect employers to pay high wages for unskilled labor.

   a. fact   **b.** opinion

_____4. **Paragraph 6:** Only 7 percent of the low-wage workforce is composed of adolescents.

   a. fact   **b.** opinion

_____5. **Paragraph 8:** Skills related to caring for other human beings are not valued as much as technical knowledge.

     a. fact   **b.** opinion

OUTLINING THE POINTS RAISED BY EACH SIDE

Questions 6–8: List the three reasons that those *against* living wage proposals offer in defense of their position. Keep your answers short and simple. (3 points)

6. _____

7. _____

8. _____

Questions 9–13: List the five reasons that those *in favor* of living wage proposals offer to explain their position. Again, keep your answers short. (5 points)

9. _____

10. _____

11. _____

12. _____

13. _____

CHECKING TO SEE IF POINTS WERE JUSTIFIED BY FACTS

For each statement, note whether the point made was justified by studies or other factual evidence or not.

_____14. **Paragraph 3:** Opponents argue that requiring employers to pay higher wages will result in job losses for the most vulnerable workers.

     a. justified by studies or other factual evidence

     b. not justified by studies or other factual evidence

_____15. **Paragraph 6:** Advocates of the living wage proposals argue that most low-wage workers are not teenagers.

     a. justified by studies or other factual evidence

     b. not justified by studies or other factual evidence

_____16. **Paragraph 8:** Supporters of living wage proposals also argue that low wage jobs are not "unskilled."

   a. justified by studies or other factual evidence

   b. not justified by studies or other factual evidence

_____17. **Paragraph 9:** Those in favor of the living wage argue that it would benefit employers as well as workers. Raising wages cuts employers' costs by reducing turnover, increases productivity, and improves employee morale.

   a. justified by studies or other factual evidence

   b. not justified by studies or other factual evidence

_____18. **Paragraph 10:** Advocates also claim that paying a living wage will help people reduce their dependence on public assistance, thus cutting down on welfare costs.

   a. justified by studies or other factual evidence

   b. not justified by studies or other factual evidence

RECOGNIZING LOGICAL FLAWS

Identify the type of logical flaw represented by the example given.

_____19. **Paragraph 3:** Opponents of the living wage maintain that either the current minimum wage must remain as it is or huge numbers of low-paid Americans will see their jobs disappear.

   a. attacking the person   **c.** careless comparison

   b. anecdotal evidence   **d.** false alternatives

_____20. **Paragraph 10:** Advocates also claim that paying a living wage will help people reduce their dependence on public assistance, thus cutting down on welfare costs. If people are paid enough to support their families, they don't need public assistance. Those who are getting food stamps, medical assistance, and housing subsidies could cover their own expenses.

   a. anecdotal evidence   **c.** circular reasoning

   b. false alternatives   **d.** bandwagon approach

Reading to Write Research Papers

OVERVIEW

LEARNING GOALS

After completing this chapter, you should be able to:

- Narrow the topic.
- Collect articles and research reports from scholarly sources.
- Develop a research question after doing a first read of the articles.
- Mark only those ideas in the readings that answer your research question.
- Make an outline of the answers you found to your research question.
- Organize the citable material from your readings onto note cards.

One of the most common writing assignments in college courses is the research paper. Students are asked to gather at least ten sources (books, news magazines, and journal articles) around a topic and produce a research paper of a specified length. An example of a short research paper (three to five pages) follows this overview. A common length for an undergraduate research paper is eight to ten pages. Students work on their research papers independently; instructors expect them to have developed the necessary reading and writing skills before beginning their programs.

Research papers are often weighted heavily; for example, they may be worth one-fourth of the final grade. College composition classes train students in how to manage various aspects of the research paper: writing grammatically correct paragraphs, developing a clear formal style, quoting correctly, citing sources, and avoiding plagiarism. However, the heaviest work of writing a research paper is handling the preparatory reading skillfully. Writing courses don't go into much detail on how to manage the reading side of a research paper. However, if the reading tasks are managed properly, the paper will almost write itself. ■

Common Problems in Managing Preparatory Reading

Unfortunately, many students don't know how to handle the reading portion well, and the result can be very painful. Here is what often happens:

Deciding on a Topic. Three weeks before the paper is due, the student, whom we will call Jane, takes out the syllabus and looks at the list of suggested topics. Let us suppose it is a psychology class. Jane runs an eye down the list of acceptable topics. "Clinical depression" is on the list. Jane decides that she will write her research paper on depression.

Collecting Material. The assignment specifies that the paper must have ten sources. Jane heads for the library and leaves two hours later with a stack of books with titles like *Depression in Children*, *Aspects of Depression*, and *Treating Depression in the Elderly*.

Reading through the Source Material. Over the next week, Jane dips into these books, looking for facts to include in her paper. Jane feels as if she is drowning in the reading, but spends more than thirty hours trying to cover as much as she can. There are dozens of little bits of paper sticking out of the books marking spots that might be quotable.

Citing from the Readings. With four days to go, Jane panics. She has not finished reading all the books, but writing can no longer be put off. She sits down at the computer to write. The bits of paper marking pages are of little help. Jane spends a lot of time re-reading sections of the books, trying to find the facts she vaguely recalls seeing. She keeps getting stuck, not sure what to write next. The paper starts out with a few statistics on how many people suffer from depression. From there, Jane writes a page or so on some different types of depression, another page on the causes of depression, a half page on the process of how it develops, a two-page section contrasting depression in children and adults, and finally, some ways in which it is treated (touching quickly on commonly prescribed drugs and various kinds of therapy).

When she finishes, Jane reads it over and feels uneasy. The paper seems to ramble and one section doesn't connect well with the next. However, it is too late to tinker with it now. She hands the paper in, hoping for the best. A week later, she gets her paper back with a grade of C minus and a note that says "Your paper has no thesis—see me if you want to rewrite."

The fix for a paper with no central point is painful. The writer must typically start all over again, this time with a more focused topic. Much of what was done before won't be relevant, and ends up getting tossed away. Unfortunately, such outcomes are common. Interestingly, the problem is nearly always in how the *readings* were prepared, not in the student's skill as a writer.

Building in Quality at Each Stage of the Reading Process

Making a few simple changes in how the readings are prepared makes all the difference in having a successful experience writing a research paper.

Overview of What to Do	Problem This Prevents
Narrow the research topic before collecting material. Collect news magazine and journal articles rather than books.	Drowning in the reading
Move from a topic to a research question early in the project. Mark only those ideas that directly relate to the research question.	Producing a paper that is a rambling mishmash of ideas with no clear thesis
Organize the source material so that putting paragraphs together is extremely simple.	Stress and wasted time trying to figure out where the source material to cite was located

If the readings are handled right, the tasks in writing a research paper can go smoothly, the job will be fairly stress-free, and the final result will be something of which you will be proud. Following is an example of a short research paper.

Sample Research Paper

Tyler 1

Jonathan Tyler

Instructor: Dr. James Foley

Chemical Dependency Counseling 1132

Spring Semester, 2007

Trends in Illegal Steroid Use among Teens

Public health specialists have become increasingly concerned about the rise in illegal steroid use among adolescents. According to a study conducted by the Centers for Disease Control, the number of boys who have used steroids increased from 4.1 percent to 6.8 percent between 1991 and 2003. The growth of steroid use among girls has been even more dramatic—from 1.2 percent to 5.3 percent. To design effective intervention policies, it is important to understand some recent trends in the use of illegal steroids among adolescents.

Teens are perceiving the use of steroids as less risky than they did previously. According to the National Center on Drug Abuse, the use of anabolic steroids by adolescents can permanently affect physical maturation, halting bone growth and damaging the heart, kidneys, and liver. In boys, steroid use may lead to impotence, shrunken testicles, and breast enlargement. Girls may experience irregular menstrual periods, growth of body hair, loss of scalp hair, a deepened voice, and reduced breast size (Bowman and Gehring 83). Despite these serious health hazards, a study conducted by the National College Athletic Association found that the percentage of teens who said steroid use is a "great risk" dropped from 70.7 percent in 1992 to 55 percent in 2003 (Lukas 22).

The age of first use is moving down for both boys and girls. The same NCAA study found that the percentage of college steroid users who began taking the drugs in junior high or earlier rose from 4.2 percent in 1989 to 15.4 percent in 2001 (Lukas 22). An annual study of 50,000 teens conducted by researcher Lloyd D. Johnston showed that among eighth-grade boys, steroid use jumped from 1.2 percent in 1998 to 1.7 percent in 1999 and 2000 (Bowman and Gehring 84). Approximately 5 percent of junior high and high school girls acknowledge using steroids at least once, and the percentage has risen steadily since 1991 (Johnson A8).

An increasing number of adolescent boys are taking steroids solely to improve their appearance. Dr. Kenneth Ginsburg, assistant professor of adolescent medicine at the University of Pennsylvania, noted, "It's pretty common knowledge that physical appearances have affected women for decades. While guys have always been concerned with their image, only recently have they become obsessed with achieving ultimate perfection" (Reyes 3). Between 1972 and 1997, the percentage of men dissatisfied with their appearance increased from 15 to 43 percent. Thirty-eight percent of the men surveyed want bigger chest muscles (Cloud 64).

Dr. Harrison Pope, a research specialist in body-image disorders in men, found that teenage boys have a mental image of an ideal masculine body that is unnaturally muscular and can

Tyler 3

typically only be obtained by using illegal steroids. Interestingly, young women have much more realistic views of ideal male bodies. When Pope asked them to rate the most desirable male bodies, the young women chose ones that had fifteen to thirty fewer pounds of muscle than those the young men rated as most ideal (Cromie 2).

One high school student named Tim began taking steroids in order to broaden his shoulders and chest when he was seventeen. "I was always the runt of the pack. I stood about 5'6" and weighed about 112," he said. "I always whined about my size until a friend offered me a way to bulk up. By the end of senior year I was huge. I had put on about 35 pounds of solid muscle, but then I started to get those tell-tale signs. I remember for my senior prom, I had an incredibly bad breakout of acne. But it wasn't only my face—my chest, back, arms, everywhere. Soon after I was benching about 250, 270, somewhere around there, when I felt something snap in my chest. I fell to the ground in the most excruciating pain I ever felt in my life, and had to be rushed to the hospital. I had torn two ligaments in my shoulder and a muscle in my chest. That's when I realized looking good wasn't worth killing myself" (Reyes 4).

Ironically, reading health and fitness magazines appears to increase the chances that adolescent boys will damage their health through taking steroids. Boys who compare their own physiques with those of the men in fitness magazines become dissatisfied with their bodies in the same way that girls may

Tyler 4

develop a distorted body image by looking at fashion magazines in which the models are unnaturally thin. According to a study conducted by Renee Blotta (49), the more time boys spent reading health and fitness magazines, the more likely they were to take steroids and other pills and supplements in order to gain muscle and the more committed they were to having a V-shaped, muscular body.

The number of girls taking steroids because of appearance concerns is also rising. A study conducted by the sports medicine division of the Oregon Health and Science University found that two-thirds of the Oregon high school girls who admitted to using steroids were not athletes and were also likely to engage in other unhealthful methods of losing weight. "They were more likely to have eating disorders and to abuse diuretics, amphetamines and laxatives," said Dr. Linn Goldberg, head of the division (Johnson A8).

Some of the increased use of steroids among young women does appear to be driven by greater opportunities in athletics. Participation rates of girls in high school athletics have risen sharply in the past decade, including a 160 percent increase in female wrestlers (Brady & Sylwester C1). Dr. Jim Peterson, a sports medicine consultant who was a professor of physical education at the U.S. Military Academy for nineteen years, stated, "The most disturbing part now is that females are involved too. They were supposed to be the smarter ones. But with the increased level of competition and so many female athletes after those few scholarships to their choice schools, they've gotten on board" (Davis A4).

Tyler 5

Adolescents' less cautious attitudes about steroids, the spread of steroid use to younger teens, the increased use of steroids to deal with appearance anxiety, and the rise of steroid use among female athletes has prompted calls for early intervention programs for all teens, not just student athletes. Dr. Eric Small, chairman of the American Academy of Pediatrics' committee on sports medicine, said adults should gently ask youngsters about possible steroid use. "Talking about supplements and steroids needs to start in the third grade," Small said. "If you wait until ninth grade, it's too late" (Johnson A8).

Works Cited

Blotta, R. "For Your Health? The Relationship between Magazine Reading and Adolescents' Body Image and Eating Disturbances." Sex Roles: A Journal of Research 26 (2003): 46–51.

Bowman, D. H., and J. Gehring. "Policymakers Tackling Teenage Steroid Abuse." Education Week 45 21 April 2004: 83–85.

Brady, E., and M. Sylwester. "More and More Girls Got Game." USA Today 1 July 2003: C1.

Cloud, J. "Never Too Buff." Time 24 April 2000: 64.

Cromie, W. "Drugs Muscle Their Way into Men's Fitness." Harvard University Gazette 15 June 2000: 1–2.

Davis, E. "Girls' Steroid Use Going up Fast." Houston Chronicle 14 July 2005: A4.

Johnson, L. "Dangerous Steroid Use Rises Among Girls." St. Louis Post-Dispatch 26 April 2005: A8.

Lukas, K. "Sports and Drugs." CQ Researcher 14.26 (2004): 21–23.

Reyes, D. "Boys Use Starvation, Steroids in Quest for Perfect Bod." Rutgers University Network for Family Life Education 19.3 (2004): 3–5.

Narrowing Your Research Topic

To write a good research paper, you must read deeply. A common mistake college students make is that they read broadly on their research topics, but not deeply. To illustrate this point, let me tell you about the research report my niece wrote when she was ten. Each child in her fifth-grade class was assigned a country. Stella got Scotland. The report was to cover the geography, principal industries, food preferences, history, and political organization of the country. Stella wrote one page on the major cities of Scotland, one page on favorite dishes, another page on sheep farming, and so on. Notice that this report was very broad (it covered many areas) but not deep (each area got a paragraph).

The higher up you go in the American educational system, the more depth is emphasized over breadth. For instance, Stella's report, written in fifth grade, was exactly what the instructor wanted, and it got an A. In high school, she might have been asked to write a ten-page paper on the history of Scotland. Notice that this is more narrow than writing on all of Scotland, but still quite broad.

In college, topics for research papers are narrowed further. A research paper on "the history of Scotland" would be viewed as too broad. Something like "the history of the sheep farming industry in Scotland" would be more appropriate. At the graduate level of college, people write papers on topics like "the sheep farming industry in Scotland between 1850 and 1920."

When people begin college, they often frame their research topics too broadly, at a level that would have been appropriate for high school, but isn't narrow enough for a higher level of education. This is a natural mistake, but it leads to two serious problems:

The broader the topic, the more likely the paper will have no thesis. Papers that try to cover too many areas sound rambling and disjointed.

The preparatory reading for a broad topic is incredibly heavy. For instance, if you write a paper on "depression" for a psychology course, you must read about the different types of depression, how it varies in children and adults, whether it affects racial and ethnic groups disproportionately, theories on its causes, how the various kinds of depression are treated (pros and cons of different approaches), and the controversies over certain medications. Imagine yourself at sea surrounded by an ocean of information on depression. That is what you let yourself in for when your topic is too broad.

Narrowing your topic solves two problems at once: It makes it much easier to develop a research question that can lead to a fine thesis, and it reduces the preparatory reading to more manageable levels. For instance, if you define your topic as "the treatment of manic-depressive disorder in children," your reading load will shrink considerably.

Therefore, before you begin gathering readings for a research paper, your first task is to ensure that your topic is sufficiently narrow. One good way to narrow a topic is by asking yourself if the larger topic is one that has smaller subfields. If so, you can focus on just one of the areas. For instance, one type of depression is manic-depressive disorder (also called bipolar disorder). The larger topic of depression can be narrowed by choosing to write on one of the subtypes.

SKILLS PRACTICE 1

Following is a list of topics that were suggested by the instructor for a ten-page research paper for a public health class. For each subject, narrow the topic by looking at a smaller piece of the issue. Write down one idea in the space provided. The first two have been done for you.

Suggested Topics for a Research Paper on a Public Health	Your Ideas for Narrowing the Topic
depression	*bipolar disorder*
smoking/tobacco use	*smokeless/chewing tobacco*
diabetes	
eating disorders	
chemical dependency/addiction	
problems in American diet	
advertising	

Another way to narrow a topic, particularly for areas in which there are no clear subfields, is to focus on a particular group. For example, "bipolar disorder" is still a fairly broad topic. "Bipolar disorder in teens" makes it narrower. Although some groups are not studied separately—you won't find much on "bipolar disorder in people with red hair and freckles"—you can often find a subject broken down further by age, gender, and race or ethnicity. You can also do combinations such as "smoking in African American teens." You don't want to make your topic so specific to one group that you can't find any information on it, but narrowing by demographic group is often a very effective way to make a topic more manageable.

SKILLS PRACTICE 2

Narrow the following public health research topics by specifying a group. The first one has been done for you as an example.

Heart disease in ___*women*_____

AIDS/HIV in _____

Diabetes in _____

Illegal steroid use in _____

Anorexia and _____

SKILLS PRACTICE 3

Now try using both techniques together—taking a smaller piece of a suggested topic *and* limiting yourself to a specific group. The first one has been done for you.

Suggested Topics for a Research Paper on a Public Health Issue	Your Ideas for Narrowing the Topic
maternal and child health	*pregnancy and mothers over 40*
cancer	
mental illnesses	
accidents	

■ COLLECTING READING MATERIAL: ADVANTAGES OF ARTICLES OVER BOOKS

When you have narrowed your topic and are ready to collect source readings, you should look first for articles and technical reports rather than books. Books are a wonderful way to get a broad view of a topic, but less useful when you are writing a research paper. Here is why:

Books are typically written as overviews of a general topic, whereas articles and technical reports focus on specific issues and groups. For instance, if you are writing about the treatment of bipolar disorder in children, you might have trouble finding much on it in a book. A general book on depression would probably have a chapter on bipolar disorder, but it isn't to be expected that it would have more than a paragraph or two about bipolar disorder in children. You would be more likely to find an article in a research journal specifically about bipolar disorder in children.

Articles and technical reports usually contain more current information. The length of time it takes to prepare and publish an article is much shorter than for a book. You will typically find the most up-to-date statistics and studies in a recently published article or technical report, not a book.

Research articles and technical reports commonly undergo a check for quality and accuracy to a greater extent than books do. For instance, research articles published in professional journals usually will have been reviewed by other specialists in the field before publication. If the reviewers feel that the information presented is not quite accurate, misleading in some way, or leaves out other relevant facts, then the author will be required to fix it or else the article won't be published. Books are not always subjected to such strict peer review.

There are some exceptions, of course—you may find a recently published book full of up-to-the-minute statistics and studies written by the world's greatest expert exactly focused on your particular research topic. In general, however, articles and technical reports are where you will find your best sources. An added benefit of using articles and technical reports as your main sources for a research paper is that it cuts down on your reading load. Would you rather read ten books on a subject or ten articles?

■ HOW TO FIND HIGH-QUALITY RESEARCH ARTICLES USING THE INTERNET

There is a right and a wrong way to use the Internet when finding source materials for your paper.

Don't Use Google. General search engines (like google.com) don't work very well in helping you find articles for your research paper. The problem with using a general search engine like google.com is that most of the scholarly articles are not stored on Web sites open to the public and so Google won't find them. What Google *will* find is a lot of Web sites containing information that is not considered appropriate for a research paper. For example, if you enter a topic like "treatment of bipolar disorder in children" on google.com you will find things like people's personal experience finding a doctor who correctly identified their child's problem, some Web pages that collect people's experience with various medications for bipolar disorder, and maybe a link to a newspaper article or two on the topic. These are not considered scholarly sources.

Use Library Databases. The research articles you need for your paper can be found by searching special databases that are not open to the public. Access to these databases is purchased by colleges so that their students and faculty can use them to research topics. No matter what college you attend, the system of accessing the databases through the Internet is pretty much the same. Here is what you do:

1. Go to your college's home page.

2. Once you are on the college's home page, click on the "library" link.

3. When you are on the library page, look for a link or button that says "databases." If there is any sort of choice that says "databases—complete list," click on that.

4. You will see dozens of databases to choose from. Notice that some are specifically for educational research, some for health research, some for business, and so on. Some are good for all areas, such as CQ Researcher or Academic Search Premier. You don't need to be familiar with all these databases—just try some until you find a few that are easy to use

and consistently pull up useful articles. You will soon find some databases that you like.

5. If you click on the link for one of these databases, you will see a box at the top of the screen where you can type in your search term. Type in the term (be careful about spelling) and click on the "go" or "search" button. A list of articles related to your search term will pop up.

6. Click on any article title that seems relevant. The article should appear, and if it looks useful, you can print it out. Usually there is a button toward the top of this screen that says "E-mail this article." If you don't have immediate use of a printer, then e-mail the article you want to save to yourself and print it out later.

You can search the college databases from your home computer as long as you have a user ID and a password. (When you get to the point where you click on the database links, the computer will usually ask for your user ID and password, because only students and staff are authorized users of the databases.) Ask the college librarian what you should enter in the user ID and password fields to use the databases from home. If you are using one of the on-campus computers, you won't usually be asked for your ID and password.

■ WHERE TO FIND RECENT STATISTICS AND TECHNICAL REPORTS ON YOUR TOPIC

Although most Web sites should not be used as sources for research papers, there is an exception. Government agencies and national research centers produce reports that may be downloaded from their Web sites. These reports often do not appear on the list that pops up when you do a library database search, so you need to go directly to the organization's Web site to search for them.

The reports produced by government agencies and national research centers are some of the most reliable and respected sources of information for research papers. When you decide on a field of study, ask the instructors in your program which government agencies and research centers put out the most useful reports and statistical updates. Write down their Web site addresses. You will use them over and over again. Here is a sample of some of the sites by field:

Health	Centers for Disease Control
	www.cdc.gov
	Information on major diseases, birth defects, disabilities, emergency preparedness, environmental health, injuries and violence, vaccination, workplace safety and health

	World Health Organization **www.who.int** Both U.S. and international data on health and safety issues
Housing	**Harvard University Joint Center for Housing Studies** **www.jchs.harvard.edu** Reports on the state of the nation's housing (demographics on who is buying houses, difficulties in finding affordable housing, and so on), plus information on home building and remodeling trends
Mental Health	**National Institute of Mental Health** **www.nimh.nih.gov** Statistics and reports on topics such as depression, schizophrenia, ADHD, and eating disorders
Criminal Justice	**Bureau of Justice Statistics** **www.ojp.usdoj.gov/bjs** Data and reports on various types of crimes, crime victims, the prison system, hate crimes, and terrorism
Juvenile Justice	**Office of Juvenile Justice and Delinquency Prevention** **www.ojjdp.ncjrs.org** Data on juveniles as both victims and offenders, and reports on the operation of the juvenile justice system
Education	**National Center for Education Statistics** **www.nces.ed.gov** Information on the educational achievements of students (reading and math scores), school safety, racial and ethnic backgrounds, languages spoken at home, higher education (common majors, debt taken on by students, rise in costs), and many other topics

■ LEARNING BASIC COLLEGE RESEARCH SKILLS

Many colleges offer a full-semester course in research skills in which students learn how to conduct database searches, evaluate the quality of sources, and assess the reliability of information. If your college offers such a course (often listed under something like "Information Literacy"), you should consider taking it during your first year of college. However, as a good start, do these two things:

1. Check out the databases available through your college library. Try different ones until you find two or three that you can use easily and that consistently locate useful research articles for you.

2. Write down the Web site addresses of one or two government agencies that maintain information on the issues relevant to your field.

If you do these two things, you will be prepared to gather information you need to write your research papers without trouble.

■ PRACTICING YOUR SKILLS

Go to the computer lab at your college. Try finding some articles using your college research databases and the relevant government agency Web site. For instance, suppose you are planning to be an elementary school teacher, and you are taking courses in child development. A good topic for a research paper would be "bullying." Try using your college research databases to find scholarly articles on bullying. You could also check for any government reports on that topic on the National Center for Education Statistics Web site at www.nces.ed.gov.

Developing a Research Question

After you have gathered the source readings on your narrowed topic and given them a first read-through, your next step is to develop a research question. Here is why you need to do this:

You use your research question as a guide when you mark ideas in your materials. It tells you which ideas to pay attention to and which to ignore. You can move more quickly through your readings if you know what kind of information you are looking for.

It keeps the focus of your paper tight. Information that is selected under the guidance of a clear research question all hangs together. Your paper will be coherent—it won't ramble or lack a thesis.

There is more than one good research question for a given topic. For example, let's say that you have gathered information on Type II diabetes in children. Here are some possible research questions:

- How has the rate of Type II diabetes in children changed over time?
- How is Type II diabetes different in children than adults?
- What are the causes of Type II diabetes in children?
- What are the effects of Type II diabetes on children's development?
- How can Type II diabetes in children be prevented?

If you were writing a research paper on Type II diabetes in children, you would focus on *only one* of these questions. You paper would not attempt to cover all of them. The questions might overlap somewhat (for example, it is hard to talk about how to prevent diabetes without mentioning its causes), but you choose just one.

■ BRAINSTORMING POSSIBLE RESEARCH QUESTIONS

Your first step in choosing a research question is to brainstorm a list of possibilities. Academic thought patterns are a great help at this stage. Notice how the research questions on Type II diabetes in children fit into certain of the academic thought patterns:

- How has the rate of Type II diabetes in children changed over time? (history)
- How is Type II diabetes different in children than adults? (comparison/contrast)
- What are the causes of Type II diabetes in children? (causes)
- What are the effects of Type II diabetes on children's development? (effects)
- How can Type II diabetes in children be prevented? (problem-solution)

There are other academic thought patterns, but the ones mentioned here are especially useful for shaping possible research questions.

CHANGES OVER TIME/RECENT TRENDS

(Frame your question in terms of trends or changes over time.)

How has the occurrence of heart disease in women changed over time?

What are some recent trends in teens' use of illegal steroids?

COMPARISON/CONTRAST

(Usually you are comparing groups—children versus adults, ethnic and racial groups, men versus women, old versus young, or people of one country versus another.)

How is television advertising in the U.S. different from TV advertising in Europe?

What are the similarities and differences in narcissistic personality disorder in men versus women?

CAUSES

(This one is easy.)

> *What are the causes of the growth in home size?*
>
> *What are the causes of anorexia in men?*

EFFECTS

(You usually need to specify what *kind* of effects: on quality of life, personal development, the economy, etc.)

> *How does schizophrenia affect children's social skills?*
>
> *How does air pollution affect the water quality of lakes?*

PREVENTION

> *How can strokes be prevented?*
>
> *How can obesity in children be prevented?*

TREATMENT

> *What is the best way to clean up old landfills that pollute groundwater?*
>
> *How is depression in children treated?*

You might think of other good research questions that are not based on academic thought patterns, but notice how useful these particular patterns are at helping you develop a list of possibilities quickly.

SKILLS PRACTICE 4

Suppose you are writing a paper on child development and your topic is bullying among children in elementary school. Use the following academic thought patterns to brainstorm a possible list of research questions.

Changes over Time/Recent Trends

Comparison

Causes

Effects

Prevention

Treatment

■ DECIDING ON A RESEARCH QUESTION

Your next step is to settle on a single question. There are several considerations in choosing a research question from a list of possibilities:

Based on what you know of the topic, is the answer to the question long enough for a research paper? For instance, "How many children are harassed by bullies each year?" is not a good research question because the answer will not fill up a research paper. The answer will be a number.

Is there plenty of information related to this question in the readings you found? Look through the readings you collected and make sure that many of the articles contain information that answers the question you are considering. If you don't see clear-cut answers to your possible research question on a fast skim of the readings you collected, then don't choose it.

Is the question one I can handle at this stage of my program? Some research questions lead you into a discussion that would be hard to follow if you are in the early stages of your program. For example, suppose you are in the first semester of a program in nursing. Choosing a research question like "What are the differences between Type II diabetes in children and adults?" may lead to a discussion of medical issues that would be over your head. This would be a research question you could manage at the end of your training, but not the beginning. It might be wiser to go with "Why has the occurrence of Type II diabetes in children been rising over the past thirty years?" The answers to that question (changes in diet, portion size, television watching, and exercise) would be easier for a beginning nursing student.

If there is plenty of information on your question and you already have enough training to follow the discussion for it, then just pick whichever question interests you most.

■ MARKING INFORMATION THAT ANSWERS YOUR RESEARCH QUESTION

Once you have gathered a number of articles on your research topic and developed a research question, your next task is to gather information that answers that question. The trick here is not to be distracted by facts that are interesting but not relevant to your question.

For instance, suppose that you have gathered ten articles on steroid use in adolescents. Your research question is, "What are some recent trends in steroid use among teens?" The first article is entitled "Steroid Use Among Student Athletes." You read through it, scanning for information on trends in steroid use among teens. Notice that the first paragraph is about the bad effects of steroid use on boys' health. No material here. You keep going. The next part is about how steroid use can affect girls' health. This is also interesting, but it does not have to do with trends (what has been changing recently) in teen steroid use. However, a little further on, the writer mentions that more nonathletes are using steroids, and this *is* a partial answer to your research question. You mark that idea.

STEROID USE AMONG STUDENT ATHLETES

Adolescent boys that take steroids are at risk for numerous health problems. Steroids can halt bone growth as well as damage the heart, kidneys, and liver. Males taking steroids may experience impotence, shrunken testicles, and breast enlargement.

The use of steroids by girls is of also of great concern to public health specialists. They may also suffer damage to vital organs. Additionally, girls using steroids may experience abnormalities in menstruation, loss of scalp hair, a deepened voice, and increased aggressive behavior.

Steroid use among adolescents can be hard to detect. Dr. Stephen G. Rice, a pediatrician at Jersey Shore University Medical Center in New Jersey that specializes in sports medicine, gives physicals to approximately 2,000 student athletes each year. "It's harder than you think to identify steroid use unless you're really, really, really looking hard," Dr. Rice said.

Randomly testing students for steroid use is prohibitively expensive, and few schools are willing to expend the funds. Schools that do regular steroid testing rarely find students that test positive. The school officials say they believe that testing acts as a deterrent.

More teens using steroids to improve looks, not to do better in sports One problem with testing for steroids, aside from the cost, is that it has been reserved for student athletes. However, in the past few years, there has been a sharp rise in the numbers of students that use steroids for reasons other than to enhance athletic performance. These adolescents are using steroids to improve their appearance.

When you find material that answers your research question, highlight the ideas in the text and put a note to the side that briefly mentions the point you found. Marking the point to the side is particularly important, because it will greatly speed up the task of organizing material later.

SKILLS PRACTICE 5

Read through the excerpt entitled "More Younger Teens Use Steroids" from the *CQ Researcher* article "Sports and Drugs." Mark only the ideas that answer the research question, "What are some recent trends in steroid use among adolescents?" Highlight the ideas you find and write a short phrase to the side about the author's point.

Special Focus: More Younger Teens Use Steroids

Forty percent of high school seniors say steroids are easy to obtain. The other 60 percent may never have seriously considered the question, but if they tried a quick Google search, they'd probably agree. Typing in a few simple keywords produces a wealth of information about steroids, including forums where users trade tips on the most reliable and discreet sources. Many sellers purchase "sponsored links" on Google, or advertisements that appear when a steroid-related search term is entered. One such site even offers prescriptions for sale.

Perhaps because of their easy availability, steroids increasingly are being used by high schoolers. The Centers for Disease Control and Prevention (CDC) says the number of boys who have used steroids at least once increased from 4.1 percent to 6.8 percent between 1991 and 2003. But girls' usage rocketed from 1.2 percent to 5.3 percent—more than a fourfold increase. That's a total of about 1 million high school steroid users.

But the real numbers are probably even higher, warns Charles Yesalis, a professor of health and human development at Pennsylvania State University and a leading expert on performance-enhancing drugs. At a recent Senate hearing on steroid use by teens and young adults, several witnesses said steroid use is widespread among adolescents and college students. A Division I college football player, testifying anonymously from beneath a hood, with his voice altered to protect his identity, told the panel: "My current friend and roommate lived with a player that supplied seven to eight other players on the team with these steroids." He said the NCAA's random testing program was weak because testing comes at roughly the same time each year.

Moreover, steroid users are getting younger. The percentage of college steroid users who began using in junior high or before jumped from 4.2 percent in 1989 to 15.4 percent in 2001, according to an NCAA survey of substance abuse among student athletes. In 1989, only 25 percent of NCAA steroid users had started taking the drugs before college; in 2001 the number had more than doubled to 57.2 percent. And steroid use among eighth graders is higher now than it was among seniors in the mid-1990s.

One reason for the increase may be that fewer teens view steroid use as dangerous. The percentage who said steroid use is a "great risk" decreased from 70.7 percent in 1992 to 55 percent in 2003. Some observers blame growing teen complacency about steroid risks on slugger Mark McGwire's use of the steroid precursor androstenedione. They also point to steroids' increasing popularity among professional athletes—or at least the perception among the young that more pros are using steroids.

Not surprisingly, Internet sellers and steroid-user forums play down the risks of usage, capitalizing on uncertainty in the medical community on the exact risks associated with steroid use and the multiplicity of steroids available, some of which are reputed to be safer than others. But the medical community unanimously opposes steroid use by adolescents. Steroids are definitively linked to permanent loss of height in adolescents due to the flood of artificial testosterone, which can cause bones to stop growing. Teenagers are also more likely to use extremely high doses or get steroids of questionable purity and production quality.

The motivations to use steroids by both girls and boys often reflect a striking reversal of gender stereotypes. Participation rates of girls in high school athletics have increased substantially in recent years, including a 160 percent increase in female wrestlers. The rising professionalism and profile of women's sports—like soccer and women's basketball—are probably also factors.

As girls begin taking sports more seriously, boys are becoming—like their female friends—increasingly dissatisfied with their bodies. The percentage of men dissatisfied with their overall appearance jumped from 15 percent to 43 percent between 1972 and 1997. Thirty-eight percent of men want bigger pectoral muscles, while only 34 percent of women want bigger breasts. According to a 2001 survey, 20 percent of young people who take muscle-building supplements or steroids do so to look better. The 2001 NCAA study supports that number. Harrison Pope, a Harvard psychiatrist who has studied body-image disorders among men, found that most teenage boys have an unnaturally muscular "ideal physique," attainable only by using steroids. "You feel a great sense of inadequacy, and steroids fill the gap," says "Joseph," an avid college weightlifter from New York who says he never used steroids but knew people who did. Ironically, Pope's research has found that when female college students selected the most desirable male bodies, they picked ones with 15 to 30 pounds less muscle than the bodies male college students rated as ideal.

For those trying to quit steroids, losing an artificially enhanced physique can be hard to bear. "There's a serious bout of depression, because it comes to a point where normally you're looking like Superman and you're lifting a phenomenal amount, but once you stop, it's a precipitous decline. So it almost compels you to continue and continue and creates an addictive cycle," Joseph says.

Source: Excerpt adapted from Kenneth Lukas, "Sports and Drugs," *CQ Research,* Vol. 14, no. 26 (July 23, 2004).

Developing a research question and marking only those ideas that answer your research question will keep your paper focused. In terms of time management, you might plan to read and mark up one or two articles per day. At the end of a week, you would have finished finding the points that answer your question. The next task is to organize the ideas you found in preparation for writing the paper.

Organizing Source Material Before You Write

Let's assume that you have narrowed your topic, developed a research question, and marked all the relevant spots on the articles you gathered. Are you now ready to begin writing? Not quite. You need to organize the ideas you marked before writing. In particular, you need to do two things:

1. Decide what the main parts of the answer to your question are.

2. List the citable material (research studies, expert quotes, and story-examples) that you have for each point you want to make.

Organizing your material before you sit down at the computer to type will cut hours off your writing time and help you produce a paper of which you will be proud.

■ MAPPING THE MAIN POINTS OF THE ANSWER TO YOUR RESEARCH QUESTION

A good way to see what the parts of your answer will be is to create a quick concept map. First, you take a piece of paper and write your research question in the middle. Then you go back through the side annotations on the articles you read. Write each piece of the answer on a spoke going out from your question. Here is an example.

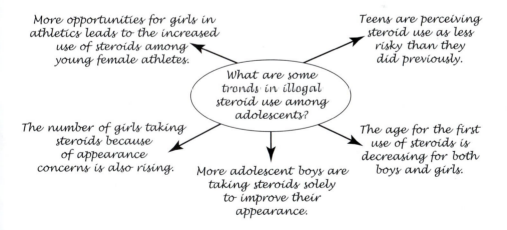

If you prefer, you can summarize what you found by writing your question across the top of a blank sheet of paper and then listing the points you found underneath. Then your summary would look like this:

What are some trends in illegal steroid use among adolescents?

1. *Teens are perceiving steroid use as less risky than they did previously.*
2. *The age of first use of steroids is moving down for both boys and girls.*
3. *More adolescent boys are taking steroids solely to improve their appearance.*
4. *The number of girls taking steroids because of appearance concerns is also rising.*
5. *More opportunity for girls in athletics is leading to use of steroids among young female athletes.*

Notice that now it is easy to see what the major parts of the paper are going to be. The writer will introduce the thesis—that it is important to understand recent trends in teens' use of illegal steroids. Then there will be about a page on each of the points mentioned.

■ LISTING THE CITABLE MATERIAL FOR EACH POINT

The next step is to list the citable material for each point. Studies, quotes by experts, and stories that illustrate a point are examples of citable material. To understand the importance of this step, let's look at a page from the sample research paper examining trends in illegal steroid use among teens. This page is elaborating on the point we saw in the concept map about how boys take steroids because they are unhappy with their looks.

> More adolescent boys are taking steroids solely to improve their appearance. Dr. Kenneth Ginsburg, assistant professor of adolescent medicine at the University of Pennsylvania, noted, "It's pretty common knowledge that physical appearances have affected women for decades. While guys have always been concerned with their image, only recently have they become obsessed with achieving ultimate perfection" (Reyes 2005). Between 1972 and 1997, the percentage of men dissatisfied with their appearance increased from 15 to 43 percent. Thirty-eight percent of the men surveyed want bigger chest muscles (Cloud 2000).
>
> Dr. Harrison Pope, a research specialist in body-image disorders in men, found that teenage boys have a mental image of an ideal masculine body that is unnaturally muscular and can typically only be obtained by using illegal steroids. Interestingly, young women have much more realistic views of ideal male bodies. When Pope asked them to rate the most desirable male bodies, the young women chose ones that had fifteen to thirty fewer pounds of muscle than those the young men rated as most ideal (Cromie 2000).

One high school student named Tim began taking steroids in order to broaden his shoulders and chest when he was seventeen. "I was always the runt of the pack. I stood about 5'6" and weighed about 112," he said. "I always whined about my size until a friend offered me a way to bulk up. By the end of senior year I was huge. I had put on about 35 pounds of solid muscle, but then I started to get those tell-tale signs. I remember for my senior prom, I had an incredibly bad breakout of acne. But it wasn't only my face—my chest, back, arms, everywhere. Soon after I was benching about 250, 270, somewhere around there, when I felt something snap in my chest. I fell to the ground in the most excruciating pain I ever felt in my life, and had to be rushed to the hospital. I had torn two ligaments in my shoulder and a muscle in my chest. That's when I realized looking good wasn't worth killing myself" (Reyes 2005).

Ironically, reading health and fitness magazines appears to increase the chances that adolescent boys will damage their health through taking steroids. According to a study by Renee Blotta (2003), the more time boys spent reading health and fitness magazines, the more likely they were to take steroids and other pills and supplements in order to gain muscle and the more committed they were to having a V-shaped, muscular body.

■ ANALYZING HOW A PAGE IS PUT TOGETHER

First, notice that the *entire page* is written around a single point from the concept map: More adolescent boys are taking steroids solely to improve their appearance. So how do you get a whole page out of a single point? You use three types of citable material. *To cite* means to mention something as part of your explanation or support for a point. These are the three kinds of material you use to flesh out your points:

1. a short description of a research study and its findings

2. a quote by an expert

3. a story example

To develop a point into a page or more, all you do is start with your point and add several of these types of support like beads on a string.

SKILLS PRACTICE 6

Analyze how the page from the research paper is put together. For each paragraph, circle the kind of citable material that is being used as supporting detail for the point "Adolescent boys often take steroids to improve their appearance."

a. research finding b. quote by expert c. story example	Dr. Kenneth Ginsburg, assistant professor of adolescent medicine at the University of Pennsylvania, noted, "It's pretty common knowledge that physical appearances have affected women for decades. While guys have always been concerned with their image, only recently have they become obsessed with achieving ultimate perfection" (Reyes 2005).
a. research finding b. quote by expert c. story example	Between 1972 and 1997, the percentage of men dissatisfied with their appearance increased from 15 to 43 percent. Thirty-eight percent of the men surveyed want bigger chest muscles (Cloud 2000).
a. research finding b. quote by expert c. story example	Dr. Harrison Pope, a research specialist in body-image disorders in men, found that teenage boys have a mental image of an ideal masculine body that is unnaturally muscular and can typically only be obtained by using illegal steroids. Interestingly, young women have much more realistic views of ideal male bodies. When Pope asked them to rate the most desirable male bodies, the young women chose ones that had fifteen to thirty fewer pounds of muscle than those the young men rated as most ideal (Cromie, 2000).
a. research finding b. quote by expert c. story example	One high school student named Tim began taking steroids in order to broaden his shoulders and chest when he was seventeen. "I was always the runt of the pack. I stood about 5'6" and weighed about 112," he said. "I always whined about my size until a friend offered me a way to bulk up. By the end of senior year I was huge. I had put on about 35 pounds of solid muscle, but then I started to get those tell-tale signs. I remember for my senior prom, I had an incredibly bad breakout of acne. But it wasn't only my face—my chest, back, arms, everywhere. I looked like a big zit. Soon after I was benching about 250, 270, somewhere around there, when I felt something snap in my chest. I fell to the ground in the most excruciating pain I felt in my life, and had to be rushed to the hospital. I had torn two ligaments in my shoulder and a muscle in my chest. That's when I realized looking good wasn't worth killing myself" (Reyes 2005).
a. research finding b. quote by expert c. story example	Ironically, reading health and fitness magazines appears to increase the chances that adolescent boys will damage their health through taking steroids. According to a study by Renee Blotta (2003), the more time boys spent reading health and fitness magazines, the more likely they were to take steroids and other pills and supplements in order to gain muscle and the more committed they were to having a V-shaped, muscular body.

Notice that the most common kind of support for points in a research paper is a description of the findings of a research study. If the area is relatively new, then there will be fewer research studies, and you will end up citing experts and using more story examples. However, research studies are the best kind of citable material to include.

■ SETTING UP FOR STRESS-FREE WRITING

Writing a research paper is easy as long as you have your citable material for each point listed. To write the sections of a research paper, you need to know where your research studies, expert quotes, and story examples are for each point you want to make. If you don't organize this *before starting to write*, you will find yourself pawing through a dozen research articles looking for the studies and quotes you marked every time you put a paragraph together, thus adding unnecessary time and frustration to the writing task.

■ MAKING A CARD FOR EACH POINT

The easiest way I know to organize citable material for writing is to make a card for each point. Large index cards (the 5 × 8 inch size) work well. Write the point itself across the top, and list the material from the articles you read in research study, expert quote, and story-example columns. The card should look like this:

More Adolescent Boys Are Taking Steroids Solely to Improve Their Appearance

Research Studies	Expert Quotes	Story-Examples
Cromie article (p. 8) Dr. Pope's research on young men's unrealistic image of ideal body type	Reyes article (p. 1) Boys are becoming obsessed with having perfect body.	Reyes article (p. 2) Story about Tim
Blotta article (p. 3) Connection between reading fitness magazines and taking steroids		
Lukas article (p. 2) 20% of young people who take steroids do so to look better		
Cloud article (p. 64) Percent of young men unhappy with appearance—37%		

■ HOW TO CREATE CARDS

1. Take out your concept map or outline containing your research question and the major points you found that answer the question. Make one card for each point. Write the point across the top of an index card.

2. Start with just one of the cards. Take out the stack of articles you read. Skim through the side annotations looking for spots that relate to the point you want to make.

3. When you find a place in one of the articles that relates to the card you're working on, check it for the three types of citable material: a research study result, a quote by an expert, or a story example. If you find any of these, list it on the card in the correct column. (Notice that you list an item by the last name of the author and the page number it was on.)

4. If the marked place doesn't contain any of those three things, then just keep going. Work your way through all the articles you read until you have listed all the material on that point.

5. When you finish one card, you do the others the same way. Depending on how many articles you read (usually around 10), it will take you about 20 minutes to do each card.

■ WRITING YOUR PAPER USING THE NOTE CARDS

A point card that has three or four studies, a quote or two, and a story example listed on it can be written up into about one full page. Since all the research studies, quotes, and story examples on a card are supporting the same point, you have a fair amount of freedom in how you want to arrange them. Open the section by stating your point. Then continue by describing the research studies, expert quotes, and story examples you found. Put the ideas in your own words, and be careful to cite the sources in your paper. Notice that it is easy to lengthen or shorten a section simply by adding or leaving out some of the studies, expert quotes, or story examples you have listed on the card.

Putting It All Together

Here are the steps to follow in managing the preparatory reading for a research paper:

1. Narrow the topic; then gather research articles from library databases.

2. Develop a research question. First, brainstorm a list of possibilities using academic thought patterns. Then choose the question that you think would work best, making sure that there is plenty of material to answer that question in the articles you found.

3. Read through all the articles, marking only those ideas that answer your research question. Make sure to annotate the point in the margin next to any spots you mark.

4. Make an outline or concept map of your research question and the major points of the answer you found.

5. For each point, create a note card listing the location of the relevant studies, expert quotes, and story examples you could cite from the articles you read.

Practice your skills on the set of research articles that follow. The first step has already been done for you. The topic of the articles is sleep deprivation in teens. Your job will be to develop a research question, mark the answers to that question you find in the articles, make a concept map of the major points you find, and create a note card for each point listing the citable material.

PRACTICE PASSAGE 7.1: YOUTH STUDY 1

Sleep Deprivation May Be Undermining Teen Health

Lack of sufficient sleep—a rampant problem among teens—appears to put adolescents at risk for cognitive and emotional difficulties, poor school performance, accidents, and psychopathology, research suggests.

Siri Carpenter
Monitor staff

On any given school day, teenagers across the nation stumble out of bed and prepare for the day. For most, the alarm clock buzzes by 6:30 a.m., a scant seven hours after they went to bed. Many students board the school bus before 7 a.m. and are in class by 7:30.

In adults, such meager sleep allowances are known to affect day-to-day functioning in myriad ways. In adolescents, who are biologically driven to sleep longer and later than adults do, the effects of insufficient sleep are likely to be even more dramatic—so much so that some sleep experts contend that the nation's early high school start times, increasingly common, are tantamount to abuse.

"Almost all teen-agers, as they reach puberty, become walking zombies because they are getting far too little sleep," comments Cornell University psychologist James B. Maas, Ph.D., one of the nation's leading sleep experts.

There can be little question that sleep deprivation has negative effects on adolescents. According to the National Highway Traffic Safety Administration, for example, drowsiness and fatigue cause more than 100,000 traffic accidents each year—and young drivers are at the wheel in more than half of these crashes.

FIGURE 7.1 ■ *An exhausted student asleep on his textbooks.*

Source: Photograph by Esbin/Anderson. Courtesy of Omni-Photo Communications, Inc.

Insufficient sleep has also been shown to cause difficulties in school, including disciplinary problems, sleepiness in class, and poor concentration (Figure 7.1). "What good does it do to try to educate teenagers so early in the morning?" asks Maas. "You can be giving the most stimulating, interesting lectures to sleep-deprived kids early in the morning or right after lunch, when they're at their sleepiest, and the overwhelming drive to sleep replaces any chance of alertness, cognition, memory, or understanding."

Recent research has also revealed an association between sleep deprivation and poorer grades. In a 1998 survey of more than 3,000 high-school students, for example, psychologists Amy R. Wolfson, Ph.D., of the College of the Holy Cross, and Mary A. Carskadon, Ph.D., of Brown University Medical School, found that students who reported that they were getting C's, D's and F's in school obtained about 25 minutes less sleep and went to bed about 40 minutes later than students who reported they were getting A's and B's.

In August, researchers at the University of Minnesota reported the results of a study of more than 7,000 high school students whose school district had switched in 1997 from a 7:15 a.m. start time to an 8:40 a.m. start time. Compared with students whose schools maintained earlier start times, students with later starts reported getting more sleep on school nights, being less sleepy during the day, getting slightly higher grades, and experiencing fewer depressive feelings and behaviors.

Also troubling are findings that adolescent sleep difficulties are often associated with psychopathologies such as depression and attention deficit hyperactivity disorder (ADHD). This research, combined with studies showing widespread sleep deprivation among teens, has propelled efforts to educate children and adults about the importance of a good night's sleep and to persuade schools to push back high school starting times.

"There is substantial evidence that the lack of sleep can cause accidents, imperil students' grades, and lead to or exacerbate emotional problems," says U.S. Rep. Zoe Lofgren (D-Calif.), who has introduced a bill that would provide federal grants to help school districts defray the cost of pushing back school starting times. Adjusting school schedules, Lofgren says, "could do more to improve education and reduce teen accidents and crime than many more expensive initiatives."

The research has also spurred further investigations into why teens need extra sleep, the effects of sleep deprivation on cognition, emotion regulation and psychopathology, and the long-term consequences of chronic sleep deprivation.

DOGMA REVERSED

For decades, experts believed that people require less sleep as they move from infancy through adulthood. It's easy to see why this belief persisted: Adolescents sleep less than they did as children, declining from an average of 10 hours a night during middle childhood to fewer than 7.5 hours by age 16. According to Wolfson and Carskadon's 1998 study, 26 percent of high school students routinely sleep less than 6.5 hours on school nights, and only 15 percent sleep 8.5 hours or more. The same study indicated that to make up for lost sleep, most teens snooze an extra couple of hours on weekend mornings—a habit that can lead to poorer-quality sleep.

But to researchers' surprise, in the past two decades studies have shown that teenagers require considerably more sleep to perform optimally than do younger children or adults. Starting around the beginning of puberty and continuing into their early 20s, Carskadon and colleagues have shown, adolescents need about 9.2 hours of sleep each night, compared with the 7.5 to 8 hours that adults need.

In addition to needing more sleep, adolescents experience a "phase shift" during puberty, falling asleep later at night than do younger children. Researchers long assumed that this shift was driven by psychosocial factors such as social activities, academic pressures, evening jobs, and television and Internet use. In the past several years, however, sleep experts have learned that biology also plays a starring role in adolescents' changing sleep patterns, says Carskadon.

Indeed, Carskadon's research is greatly responsible for that new understanding. In a pair of groundbreaking studies published in 1993 and 1997, she and colleagues found that more physically mature girls preferred activities later in the day than did less mature girls, and that in more physically mature teens, melatonin production tapered off later than it did in less mature teens. Those findings, Carskadon says, suggest that the brain's circadian timing system—controlled mainly by melatonin— switches on later at night as pubertal development progresses.

Changes in adolescents' circadian timing system, combined with external pressures such as the need to awaken early in the morning for school, produce a potentially destructive pattern of early-morning sleepiness in teen-agers, Carskadon argues. In a laboratory study of 40 high-school students published in the journal *Sleep* (Vol. 21, no. 8) in 1998, she, Wolfson, and colleagues examined the effect of changing school starting times from 8:25 a.m. to 7:20 a.m. Their results were disturbing: Almost half of the students who began school at 7:20 were "pathologically sleepy" at 8:30, falling directly into REM sleep in an average of only 3.4 minutes—a pattern similar to what is seen in patients with narcolepsy. Those findings, says Carskadon, persuaded her that "these early school start times are just abusive. These kids may be up and at school at 8:30, but I'm convinced their brains are back on the pillow at home."

ELUSIVE QUESTIONS

The evidence of adolescents' increased need for sleep and that many—if not most— teenagers are chronically sleep deprived has raised further questions. Particularly elusive, says Carskadon, has been the question of why adolescents' circadian clocks shift to a later phase around the beginning of puberty.

One possibility, she believes, is that the brain's sensitivity to light changes during adolescence. At the annual meeting of the Associated Professional Sleep Societies in June, she and colleagues presented research showing that in the evening, exposure to even very dim lighting delayed melatonin secretion for participants who were in middle or late puberty, but not for prepubertal participants.

Carskadon is also interested in how teenage alcohol use might affect the brain's sleep system. Following up on studies in adults that have established a link between drinking problems and changes in sleep patterns, for example, she and her colleagues plan to examine whether during early development, young people with a family history of problem drinking might have abnormalities in the brain mechanisms that govern sleep.

Just as important as the question of why sleep patterns change during adolescence is the issue of how sleep deprivation influences adolescents' emotion regulation and behavior. Many researchers have noted that sleep-deprived teenagers appear to be especially vulnerable to psychopathologies such as depression and ADHD, and to have difficulty controlling their emotions and impulses.

Although it's difficult to untangle cause and effect, it's likely that sleep deprivation and problems controlling impulses and emotions exacerbate one another, leading to a "negative spiral" of fatigue and sleepiness, labile emotions, poor decision making, and risky behavior, says Ronald E. Dahl, M.D., a professor of psychiatry and pediatrics at the University of Pittsburgh.

Despite the evidence that insufficient sleep affects young people's thinking, emotional balance, and behavior, the long-term effects of chronic sleep deprivation on learning, emotion, social relationships, and health remain uncertain.

"There's a real need for longitudinal studies to follow through later childhood and adulthood," says psychologist Avi Sadeh, Ph.D., a sleep researcher at Tel Aviv University. Although research has amply demonstrated that sleep problems affect young people's cognitive skills, behavior and temperament in the short term, he says, "It's not at all clear to what extent these effects are long-lasting."

RESEARCHERS PUSH FOR SCHOOL CHANGES, PUBLIC OUTREACH

With such a wealth of evidence about the prevalence of adolescent sleep deprivation and the risks it poses, many sleep researchers have become involved in efforts to persuade school districts to push back high school starting times so that teens can get their needed rest.

Some schools argue that adjusting school schedules is too expensive and complicated. But others have responded positively to sleep experts' pleas. The Connecticut legislature is considering a bill that would prohibit public schools from starting before 8:30 a.m., and Massachusetts lawmakers are also weighing the issue. And Lofgren's "Zzzzz's to A's" bill, first introduced in the U.S. House of Representatives in 1998, would provide federal grants of up to $25,000 to school districts to help cover the administrative costs of adjusting school start times.

These efforts are a move in the right direction, says Wolfson. But, she says, changing school start times isn't the entire answer. "I think we have to be educating children, parents, and teachers about the importance of sleep, just as we educate them about exercise, nutrition, and drug and alcohol use."

Toward that end, several public education efforts are now under way:

With a grant from the Simmons mattress company, Cornell's Maas recently produced a film on teenage sleep deprivation, its consequences, and the "golden rules" for healthy sleep. The film is scheduled for distribution through parent-teacher associations and school principals this fall. In August, Maas also published a children's book, *Remmy and the Brain Train,* which discusses why the brain requires a good night's sleep.

Next year, the National Center for Sleep Disorders Research at the National Institutes of Health plans to release a supplemental sleep curriculum for tenth-grade biology classes, addressing the biology of sleep, the consequences of insufficient sleep, and the major sleep disorders. In a related effort, the center is coordinating a sleep-education campaign aimed at 7- to 11-year-olds.

Wolfson and colleague Christine A. Marco, Ph.D., a psychologist at Worcester State College, are pilot-testing an eight-week sleep curriculum for middle-school students. As part of the curriculum, students keep sleep diaries, play creative games, and participate in role-playing about sleep, and set goals—for example, for the amount of sleep they want to get or for regulating their caffeine intake. Preliminary results indicate that the curriculum helps students improve their sleep habits.

"Changing school start times is one critical measure we can take to protect young people's sleep," says Wolfson. "And then, if we can only understand what's going on with sleep in these sixth-, seventh-, and eighth-graders, we can intervene to change their sleep behavior before it gets out of hand."

Source: Adapted from Siri Carpenter, "Sleep Deprivation May Be Undermining Teen Health," *Monitor on Psychology* 32, no. 9 (October 2001). Copyright © 2001 by the American Psychological Association. Reprinted with permission.

PRACTICE PASSAGE 7.2: YOUTH STUDY 2

Adolescent Sleep Needs and Patterns

INTRODUCTION

Sleep is a basic drive of nature. Sufficient sleep helps us think more clearly, complete complex tasks better and more consistently, and enjoy everyday life more fully. Although many questions regarding the role of sleep remain unanswered, scientific studies have shown that sleep contributes significantly to several important cognitive, emotional, and performance-related functions.

Sleep is, in essence, food for the brain, and insufficient sleep can be harmful, even life-threatening. When hungry for sleep, the brain becomes relentless in its quest to satisfy its need and will cause feelings of "sleepiness," decreased levels of alertness or concentration, and, in many cases, unanticipated sleep. Excessive sleepiness is also associated with reduced short-term memory and learning ability, negative mood, inconsistent performance, poor productivity, and loss of some forms of behavioral control (NIH, 1997).

Researchers have identified several changes in sleep patterns, sleep/wake systems, and circadian timing systems associated with puberty (Carskadon, 1999). These changes contribute to excessive sleepiness that has a negative impact on daytime functioning in adolescents, including increasing their risk of injury (Wolfson and Carskadon, 1998).

Scientists hypothesize that these sleep-related problems are due largely to conflicts between physiologically driven sleep needs and patterns, and behavioral and psychosocial factors that influence sleep habits.

Key changes in sleep patterns and needs that are associated with puberty include:

PHYSIOLOGICAL PATTERNS

- Adolescents require at least as much sleep as they did as preadolescents—in general, 8.5 to 9.25 hours each night (Carskadon et al., 1980).

- Daytime sleepiness increases—for some, to pathological levels—even when an adolescent's schedule provides for optimal amounts of sleep (Carskadon, Vieri, and Acebo, 1993).

- Adolescents' sleep patterns undergo a phase delay, that is, a tendency toward later times, for both sleeping and waking. Studies show that the typical high school student's natural time to fall asleep is 11:00 p.m. or later (Wolfson and Carskadon, 1998).

BEHAVIORAL AND PSYCHOSOCIAL PATTERNS

- Many U.S. adolescents do not get enough sleep, especially during the week. Survey data show that average total sleep time during the school week decreases from 7 hours, 42 minutes in 13-year-olds to 7 hours, 4 minutes in 19-year-olds (Wolfson and Carskadon, 1998). Only 15 percent of adolescents reported 8.5 or more hours on school nights, and 26 percent of students reported typically sleeping 6.5 hours or less each school night.

- Adolescents have irregular sleep patterns; in particular, their weekend sleep schedules are much different than their weekday schedules, to some extent as a direct consequence of weekday sleep loss. These differences include both the quantity and the timing of sleep. One study of more than 3,000 adolescents showed that the average increase of weekend over weekday sleep across ages 13–19 was one hour and 50 minutes (Wolfson and Carskadon, 1998). In 18-year-olds, the average discrepancy was more than two hours. In addition, 91 percent of the surveyed high school students reported going to sleep after 11:00 p.m. on weekends, and 40 percent went to bed after 11:00 p.m. on school nights.

- Irregular sleep schedules—including significant discrepancies between weekdays and weekends—can contribute to a shift in sleep phase (i.e., tendency toward morningness or eveningness), trouble falling asleep or awakening, and fragmented (poor quality) sleep (Dahl and Carskadon, 1995).

CONSEQUENCES OF POOR SLEEP IN ADOLESCENTS

Data on children, teens, and adults confirm that sleep loss and sleep difficulties can have serious detrimental effects. Research specifically on adolescents and young adults is relatively new and limited, but scientists believe that many effects demonstrated in studies and clinical observations of adults are similar in adolescents. Sleep researchers, therefore, believe that insufficient sleep in teens and young adults is linked to:

Increased risk of unintentional injuries and death. As noted, drowsiness or fatigue has been identified as a principal cause in at least 100,000 traffic crashes each year. In addition, about 1 million, or one-sixth, of traffic crashes in the United States are believed to be attributable to lapses in the driver's attention; sleep loss and fatigue significantly increase the chances of such lapses occurring. A North Carolina state study found that drivers age 25 or younger cause more than one-half (55 percent) of fall-asleep crashes.

The same symptoms of sleepiness that contribute to traffic crashes can also play a role in nontraffic injuries, such as those associated with handling hazardous equipment in the workplace or in the home. Furthermore, adolescents who have not received sufficient sleep and who consume even small amounts of alcohol are at greater risk of injury than those who are not lacking sleep because sleep loss has been shown to heighten the effects of alcohol (Roehrs et al., 1994).

Low grades and poor school performance. High school students who describe themselves as having academic problems and who are earning C's or below in school report getting less sleep, having later bedtimes, and having more irregular sleep schedules than students reporting higher grades. (Note: A causal relationship has not yet been established.) (Wolfson and Carskadon, 1998).

Negative moods (e.g. anger, sadness, and fear), difficulty controlling emotions, and behavioral problems. In one study, female high school students who went to sleep on the weekend two or more hours later than their typical weeknight bedtime reported feeling more depressed than those who did not stay up late on the weekends (Wolfson and Carskadon, 1998).

Studies also suggest that sleep loss may be associated with a decreased ability to control, inhibit, or change emotional responses (Dahl, 1999). Some signs of sleepiness, such as inability to stay focused on a task, impulsivity, difficulty "sitting still," and problems completing tasks, resemble behaviors common also in attention deficit hyperactivity disorder (ADHD) (Dahl, 1999). In addition, a 1995 study of students in transition from junior high to senior high school found that conduct/aggressive behaviors were highly associated with shorter sleep times and later sleep start time (Wolfson et al., 1995).

Increased likelihood of stimulant use (including caffeine and nicotine), alcohol and similar substances (Carskadon, 1990). Teens who are heavily involved in school and community activities, their jobs, and other responsibilities appear to be at greater risk for the above effects of sleepiness than those who are less involved in activities and do not hold jobs or who work fewer hours (Carskadon, 1990).

WHAT CAN BE DONE

The consequences of insufficient sleep among adolescents are particularly important to understand because they appear to be closely tied to key elements in human development. Achieving developmental goals during adolescence is essential for lifelong success and for what psychologists call social competency. In addition, the transition from childhood to adulthood is a critical time for "seeding" the values and habits that will shape their lives. Therefore, intervention to improve the sleep patterns of adolescents is important.

INFLUENCING PHYSIOLOGICAL SLEEP PATTERNS

Sleep researchers have established that basic sleep needs within individuals generally remain the same throughout their lifetime. Furthermore, insufficient sleep accumulates into a sleep debt that can ultimately be relieved only through additional sleep.

Circadian timing systems are also very resistant to change. Behavioral methods, such as controlled light exposure and chronotherapy, can sometimes help shift circadian timing to more socially appropriate sleep and wake times. Because the circadian rhythms in teenagers are typically highly sensitive to erratic schedules, to effectively adjust them requires making gradual, persistent and consistent changes. Adapting to an early school schedules following summer or other vacation periods during which very late schedules are typically kept, for example, can take several days to several weeks.

It is important to recognize that excessive sleepiness during the day and other sleep problems can be an indication of an underlying biological sleep disorder. Accurate diagnosis of disorders such as narcolepsy, sleep apnea, and periodic limb movement disorder usually requires examination by a qualified sleep specialist and an overnight stay in a sleep laboratory. In most cases, symptoms of early sleep disorders can be eliminated or minimized through the use of appropriate behavior modifications, medication, or other therapies.

CREATING SLEEP-FRIENDLY SCHOOLS

School systems can help positively influence adolescent sleep patterns in several ways. Suggestions include:

- Educate teachers, school health providers, and other school personnel about adolescent sleep needs and patterns, and about the signs of sleep loss and other sleep and alertness difficulties. Teachers and school staff should also be informed about accommodations that might be needed by some students with chronic sleep disorders.

- Integrate sleep-related education in curricula so that students can learn about the physiology and benefits of sleep and the consequences of sleep deprivation. Relevant academic subjects include, for example, biology, health, and psychology. In addition, driver's education courses should cover the prevalence and prevention of crashes related to drowsy driving.

- Structure the school schedule and related activities to accommodate adolescents' sleep needs and behaviors and circadian rhythm at this developmental stage. One approach is to start daily high school schedules when students are most likely to be alert and able to learn. Several school districts in the nation have adopted later school start times; countless more are considering doing so.

Preliminary findings and focus group studies conducted by the Center for Applied Research and Educational Improvement (CAREI) at the University of Minnesota reveal that after schools shifted from early to later start times, students from both urban and suburban high schools reported that they felt more rested and alert during the first hour of class and, in general, throughout the day (Wahlstrom and Freeman, 1997).

In addition, students in a suburban Edina high school whose schools delayed their start times reported increased hours of sleep, less erratic sleep behaviors and less depressive feelings and behaviors, better grades, and little restriction in time spent on extracurricular activities (Wahlstrom and Freeman, 1997). Findings in urban (Minneapolis) schools with later start times varied from the suburban schools somewhat; in particular, student mood appeared unchanged and schedule conflicts with extracurricular activities and employment were more pronounced (Wahlstrom and Freeman, 1997).

ESTABLISHING PUBLIC POLICIES

Governmental and organizational policies significantly influence social change. In addition to federal agencies, national medical and health care specialty organizations, education and parent associations, and youth groups can play a key role in developing and implementing recommendations, policies, and cooperative initiatives.

Furthermore, state, district, and local efforts may be spearheaded through voluntary, professional, and governmental organizations such as school boards and parent-teacher associations, state or district medical societies, motor vehicle administration departments, public health departments, and social service agencies.

Below are some examples of policy-related approaches that have been or could be used to better match adolescent sleep patterns and needs with cultural expectations and external demands, thereby increasing teens' overall safety and well-being.

- Legislation to encourage starting high schools no earlier than 9:00 a.m., and appropriations to help defray the school or school district's costs of changing school schedules.

- Legislation or policies to include age-appropriate sleep information in school curricula, grades K through 12.

- Initiatives to include information about the effects of drowsiness on driving ability in drivers' education courses and licensing tests.

- Graduated licensing regulations to reduce the number of adolescents driving unsupervised at night.

- Child labor laws to restrict the number of hours and the time of day that adolescents are permitted to work.

- Funding to support public education and scientific research on topics such as the interrelationships among sleep loss and injury, learning, and performance, as well as epidemiological data. Relevant federal oversight of funded agencies include the National Center for Sleep Disorders Research and other agencies of the National Institutes of Health, the Food and Drug Administration, the Department of Transportation, the Department of Education, the Centers for Disease Control and Prevention, and military branches.

- Initiatives to educate key adults who have frequent and regular contact with adolescents (e.g., caregivers and authoritarians) about sleep, the signs and hazards of sleepiness, and appropriate interventions for children and adolescents showing signs of sleep difficulties or disorders. Constituents include parents, teachers, school administrators, school nurses and counselors, coaches, employers, health providers (family practitioners, adolescent medicine specialists, and those who specialize in mental health or learning disabilities), and voluntary group leaders of youth-oriented organizations. In addition, police and emergency care personnel should be trained to recognize problem sleepiness and distinguish its signs from those associated with drug or alcohol use.

MAKING NEW DISCOVERIES

Sleep research has established clear relationships between sleepiness, health, safety and productivity. However, the sleep research field in general is relatively young, and scientists still have much to learn about the role of sleep and the effects of sleep loss in humans. Additional studies on the neurobiology, genetics, epidemiology, and neurobehavioral and functional consequences of sleepiness are needed (NIH, 1997). More studies specifically on the adolescent population are also needed, including interdisciplinary research to further examine sleep's role in adolescent development, health, and behavior.

Source: Used with permission of the National Sleep Foundation. For more information, visit http://www.sleepfoundation.org.

PRACTICE TEST
Reading to Write Research Papers

PART I: READING TO PREPARE

Suppose that you must write a very short (two- to three-page) research paper for a personal finance course you are taking. You decide to write your paper on identity theft. After collecting several articles, you settle on the following research question:

What actions can businesses and individuals take to reduce identity theft?

Two articles on identity theft have been provided for you. (Normally, you would collect about five articles, but two will be enough for you to demonstrate your skills.) Using the two articles, follow through on the next steps involved in handling the reading in preparation to write the paper.

1. Mark the places in the articles that answer your research question: What actions can businesses and individuals take to reduce identity theft?

2. Next, create a concept map of the research question and the major points you found that answer it. Find at least five points. Make sure that they all directly answer the research question.

LIABILITY FOR EMPLOYEE IDENTITY THEFT IS GROWING

A group of Michigan employees recently broke new legal ground when a jury awarded them $275,000 for the disasters that befell their lives when their union neglected to safeguard their Social Security and driver's license numbers. The verdict against Michigan Council 25 of the American Federation of State, County, and Municipal Employees (AFSCME) is the first in the nation to find that a custodian of employee information has a duty to guard the data with scrupulous care.

As reports of high-profile security breaches across the country continue to escalate, and the number of victims burgeons, many experts think that, with the Michigan case as a benchmark, courts across the nation are posed to find employers liable for the consequences of their failures to keep personal data private. And in the state capitols, lawmakers are starting to create new duties for employers, making them responsible for safeguarding sensitive information. Here's a look at what's going on in the courts and state legislatures.

"The Michigan case is the first I've seen that affirms the imposition of liability on the person who negligently handled sensitive information," says attorney Philip Gordon of law firm Littler Mendelson. "It's a national precedent that opens the door to employer liability for workplace identity theft in other jurisdictions that likely will follow Michigan's example."

"We know that identity theft is escalating," says Judith Collins, director of the Michigan State University–Business Identity Theft Partnerships in Prevention, suggesting that more decisions like Michigan's are waiting to happen. "Our phones are ringing off the hook. And we know that the majority of identity thefts happen in the workplace," said Collins.

According to David Parker of law firm Charfoos and Christensen, who represented Michigan employees, the situation occurred because officials of Michigan Council 25 of AFSCME allowed their union secretary, Yvonne Berry, to take work home, including lists of the Social Security numbers, dates of birth, and driver's license information of emergency service operators working for the City of Detroit. Berry's daughter, Dentry Berry, gained access to the employee data at the home, went on a spending spree, and brought havoc to the lives of 13 public employees.

"When the charges started rolling in, for almost two years, these people had to spend hours of their days, every day, dealing with angry creditors," Parker said. "One person had to postpone her retirement because her credit had been trashed. Another couldn't get credit at a time when she needed it badly. Another had to deal with an angry wife who looked at the charges and was convinced that he'd set up housekeeping with a honey." The jury award compensated them for the mental anguish of trying to straighten out their credit histories.

Why should HR be on the hook? As a central repository of employee data, Human Resources is particularly vulnerable to potential security breaches. "All aspects of the traditional Human Resources function, from recruitment, to selection, to socializing employees to the company culture, to rewarding employees for safeguarding security, are outdated because they don't incorporate security into every aspect," Collins says.

What to do:

- Develop uniform, industrywide standards for managing the threat of identity theft to customers, employees, and the business itself.

- Eliminate the use of Social Security numbers and set up an employee identification number system.

- Consider implementing policies that inform employees of their rights and the company's policies. In doing so, Gordon says, employers should go beyond the bare requirements of the law. For example, "employers should detail how documents should properly be destroyed."

Source: Adapted from Diane Cadrain, "Liability for Employee Identity Theft Is Growing," *HR Magazine,* June 1, 2005, 35. Reprinted with the permission of *HR Magazine,* published by the Society for Human Resource Management, Alexandra, VA.

CONSUMER PRACTICES TO REDUCE IDENTITY THEFT RISK: AN EXPLORATORY STUDY

Empirical results from an exploratory study of identity theft risk reduction behaviors using an online risk assessment quiz revealed that a majority of respondents did not follow the widely recommended practice of obtaining a credit report annually to check for errors and evidence of identity theft, even in states where reports are free of charge. Two other practices frequently reported were not securing incoming mail and carrying identification that includes one's Social Security number. These findings support the results of previous research on identity theft risks suggesting a need to educate consumers about certain identity theft risk factors and the strategies to reduce the risk of becoming a victim of fraud.

One way to create secure communities is to reduce the risk of crime. Identity theft continues to be one of the fastest growing white-collar crimes in the United States (Federal Trade Commission, 2003). Identity theft involves stealing a victim's personal information to commit a crime such as making fraudulent charges on a credit card or taking out loans in a victim's name (Zucker, 1999). An estimated 27.3 million Americans have been victims of identity theft in the past five years (Federal Trade Commission, 2003). Although primarily a crime that affects personal security and financial stability, identity theft also affects the broader community. All consumers pay higher prices for good and services to offset losses due to identity theft and fraud. Family and consumer sciences professionals can play an important role in educating consumers about how to reduce their risk of becoming an identity theft victim. This empirical study of the frequency of engaging in identity theft risk reduction practices using data from an online self-assessment tool can be useful in such educational efforts.

Identity thieves use a variety of methods to gain access to a victim's personal information, including rummaging through trash, stealing items such as wallets containing identification, mail, and personal information from a victim's home or from businesses or employer records (Federal Reserve Bank of Boston, 2003), and by posing as a business person or government official to scam information. A more high-tech method is "phishing," where fake e-mail messages that seem to come from legitimate sources are used to solicit personal data. Identity theft is typically not a standalone crime but, rather, part of a larger criminal act, such as credit card fraud.

Identity theft often goes undetected for months, allowing fraudsters the luxury of time to commit their crimes. According to the Federal Trade Commission (2003), nearly one-quarter of the victims of new account fraud and other frauds (as compared to victims whose existing accounts were misused) take six months or more to discover the crime. One reason is that fraudsters often use change-of-address forms or fraudulent addresses to divert mail such as credit card bills to another location (Federal Trade Commission, 2003).

Although identity theft cannot be prevented entirely, the risk of becoming a victim can be reduced. Information has been provided to consumers in recent years about identity theft and various risk reduction strategies (Consumer Action, 2000; Federal Reserve Bank of Boston, 2003; Federal Trade Commission, 2000; Privacy Rights Clearinghouse, 2003). Relatively few data exist, however, regarding consumers' individual risk exposures and actions they are taking, or not taking, to reduce their chance of becoming a victims of identity theft fraud.

Milne (2003) studied two small samples, one a cross-section of consumers and a second, of college students. Identity theft prevention-related actions performed least frequently by students were picking up new checks at a bank rather than having them mailed, ordering credit reports within the past year, and finding out how personal information will be used before revealing it to marketers. Actions performed least frequently by the consumer sample were avoiding carrying a Social Security card in their wallet, picking up new checks at a bank, and ordering an annual credit report. The low frequency of credit report requests by consumers also is confirmed by industry data (Welborn, 2003). More than 1 billion credit reports are generated each year, mostly for creditors, employers, and insurers, but only 16 million (less than 2%) are distributed to consumers.

METHODOLOGY

In 2003, the Rutgers Cooperative Extension introduced an online theft risk assessment quiz (O'Neill, 2003). The quiz, which is widely publicized during Extension's identity theft programs, includes 20 questions, each weighted on a scale of 1 to 5 points so that total scores can range from 20 to 100. The higher the total score, the more frequently a respondent reports practicing recommended identity theft risk reduction strategies. The quiz questions were based on risk reduction strategies suggested in Federal Trade Commission (2000, 2003) publications and an online identity theft IQ test developed by the Privacy Rights Clearinghouse (2003). Responses on the Likert-type scale included: 1—I never do this; 2—I rarely (every once in a while) do this; 3—I do this about 50 percent of the time; 4—I usually (almost always) do this; and 5—I always do this.

This analysis was conducted to determine the frequency with which consumers engage in 20 commonly recommended practices to reduce the risk of becoming an identity theft victim. Average scores for each individual risk reduction practice, by gender, age, education, household income, marital status, race, and state of residence, and differences in total scores are reported. The quiz includes seven demographic questions used in data analysis.

Data were collected from a convenience sample of respondents to the online self-assessment tool. There were 287 respondents from 41 states and Washington, D.C., and 4 non-U.S. residents, between January 29, 2003 and January 5, 2004. Data from the 4 non-U.S. residents were not included in the data analyses.

FINDINGS

The higher the score, the more frequently a specific identity theft risk reduction practice is performed. Using average scores, items are ranked from highest (1, most frequently performed risk reduction practice) to lowest (14, least frequently performed risk reduction practice).

Mean scores for individual quiz items ranged from 2.1 to 4.4. Medians and modes for most items were 4 or 3, except for three questions, which indicates that many consumers reported practicing a majority of recommended behaviors to reduce the risk of identity theft. The three areas of weakness were checking one's credit report annually (median of 2, mode of 1), using a post office box or locked mailbox for incoming mail (median and mode of 1), and carrying a Social Security card or anything with a Social Security number on it (median of 3, mode of 1). Most respondent scores ranged between 61 and 90. The mean, median, and modal total quiz scores were 71%, 73%, and 74% respectively. The risk reduction strategies that were performed most frequently included not divulging one's Social Security number, having mail held when away, not printing sensitive data on checks, and practicing "general security consciousness."

Analyses of variance were used to explore differences in frequency of identity theft risk reduction practices by demographic variables. Owing to small cell sizes, several variables were recoded to ensure that each cell had adequate observations.

Significant age differences were found for 11 items and the total score. Consumers less than 25 years of age were more likely to have a lower total score than older adults. Income differences were found for eight items and the total score. Lower income consumers had lower total scores than higher income consumers.

Education differences were found for four quiz items and the total score. Consumers at an education level of some college or less were more likely than consumers with more education to have a lower score. Racial differences were found in four quiz items and the total score. Non-White respondents had a higher average score than White respondents.

Differences in four quiz items and the total score were found in terms of marital status. Married consumers were more likely than single consumers to have a higher score. Gender differences were found in three quiz items, but there was no gender difference in terms of total score.

The most significant differences related to checking credit report annually and reviewing bank and brokerage statements and reconciling the balance. Age, income, education, and marital status related to reviewing bank and brokerage statements and reconciling the balance; age, income, race, and marital status had an effect on whether one checked credit reports annually.

Checking a credit report for evidence of identity theft was the least reported practice by this sample of consumers. Six states with respondents to this survey have laws requiring free credit reports to residents upon request. Consumers from these six states were grouped together and compared with consumers from other states. No statistically significant differences in frequency of requesting credit reports were found between these two groups of consumers.

DISCUSSION AND IMPLICATIONS

This exploratory study is limited in generalizability because the sample was small, convenient, and nonrandom. Selection bias is also present because some respondents were specifically directed to the quiz Web site. Also, online users tend to be better educated and have higher incomes than the general U.S. population. Nevertheless, the results indicate specific identity theft risk reduction strategies that are frequently practiced and those that need more attention by consumers. These findings also support the results of previous studies of identity theft risk factors.

EDUCATION

One of the major methods of uncovering identity theft, checking a credit report (Federal Trade Commission, 2003), was the least frequently performed identity theft risk reduction strategy in this study. Therefore, it is not surprising that many victims do not realize their identity has been stolen until months, or even years, later. Many people are not taking advantage of a valuable resource for limiting the amount of damage that an identity thief can cause, and this may be clue to cost, time, and the knowledge that it takes to make a credit file request. In this study, the cost of a credit report did not seem to be a significant factor.

These results suggest a need for educational programs and support services that help consumers regularly review their credit file. This is especially urgent in light of the 2003 Fair and Accurate Credit Transactions Act, which provides an opportunity for consumers nationwide to request a free copy of their credit report by the end of 2005 (Institute for Consumer Financial Education, 2004).

Another area of weakness indicated by quiz respondents was carrying a Social Security card or an identification card with their Social Security number on it, such as an employee ID or health insurance card. Many people apparently feel that carrying these cards is essential and do not heed warnings to "travel light" without ID that contains sensitive data. There are viable alternatives such as carrying an original card only when absolutely necessary (e.g., when visiting a lab or health care provider) and otherwise carrying a photocopy of the card with the Social Security number deleted.

Financial education professionals have a role to play in explaining various identity theft risk reduction strategies to consumers and providing them with tools such as a credit file request form to take action. Financial planning advisors also could include a credit report check as part of their clients' annual "financial physical."

PUBLIC POLICY

There were no significant differences in scores by state for the quiz item regarding checking credit reports annually. Residents of the six states that mandate free credit reports at the time of data collection did not perform this risk reduction task any more frequently than residents of other states. Perhaps cost is simply not a barrier to receiving a current credit report, or perhaps consumers in states that currently mandate free credit reports simply are not aware of this right or do not know how to obtain one.

One possible way to get credit file information in the hands of consumers would be to automatically send it to them. If the law required that credit reports were to be mailed annually to consumers, as Social Security benefits currently are, some of the identified barriers could be eliminated. However, this information would need to be transmitted securely, by means such as truncating Social Security and credit account numbers, in case mailed statements are stolen. In addition, a method to finance the costs to credit reporting agencies for preparing credit reports for all persons would need to be determined.

Source: Adapted from the article by Barbara O'Neill and Jing Jian Xiao, Journal of Family and Consumer Sciences (January 1, 2005), Volume 97, Number 1, page 33.

PART II: TEST QUESTIONS

The following twenty questions test how well you organized ideas from the readings on identity theft in preparation for writing a paper. To answer the questions, you may use

- the articles on identity theft that you annotated
- the concept map with the points you found that answer the research question

SELECTING INFORMATION THAT ANSWERS YOUR RESEARCH QUESTION

For each of the following statements, decide whether it is relevant to your research question (What actions could businesses and individuals take to reduce identity theft?).

_____1. Identity theft continues to be one of the fastest growing white-collar crimes in the United States (Federal Trade Commission, 2003).

   a. relevant/answers research question

   b. not relevant/does not answer research question

_____2. One of the major methods of uncovering identity theft, checking a credit report (Federal Trade Commission, 2003), was the least frequently performed identity theft risk reduction strategy by individuals in this study. Therefore, it is not surprising that many victims do not realize their identity has been stolen until months, or even years, later. Many people are not taking advantage of a valuable resource for limiting the amount of damage that an identity thief can cause,

   a. relevant/answers research question

   b. not relevant/does not answer research question

_____3. An estimated 27.3 million Americans have been victims of identity theft in the past five years (Federal Trade Commission, 2003).

   a. relevant/answers research question

   b. not relevant/does not answer research question

_____4. Businesses should eliminate the use of Social Security numbers and set up an employee identification number system.

   a. relevant/answers research question

   b. not relevant/does not answer research question

_____5. Although primarily a crime that affects personal security and financial stability, identity theft also affects the broader community. All consumers pay higher prices for good and services to offset losses due to identity theft and fraud.

   a. relevant/answers research question

   b. not relevant/does not answer research question

_____6. Businesses should consider implementing policies that inform employees of their rights and the company's policies. In doing so, Gordon says, employers should go beyond the bare requirements of the law. For example, "employers should detail how documents should properly be destroyed."

a. relevant/answers research question

b. not relevant/does not answer research question

_____7. Another area of weakness indicated by individual respondents was carrying a Social Security card or an identification card with their Social Security number on it. Many people apparently feel that carrying these cards is essential and do not heed warnings to "travel light" without ID that contains sensitive data.

a. relevant/answers research question

b. not relevant/does not answer research question

_____8. Businesses should develop uniform, industrywide standards for managing the threat of identity theft to customers, employees, and the business itself.

a. relevant/answers research question

b. not relevant/does not answer research question

_____9. Identity theft involves stealing a victim's personal information to commit a crime such as making fraudulent charges on a credit card or taking out loans in a victim's name (Zucker, 1999).

a. relevant/answers research question

b. not relevant/does not answer research question

_____10. Identity theft often goes undetected for months, allowing fraudsters the luxury of time to commit their crimes. According to the Federal Trade Commission (2003), nearly one-quarter of the victims of new account fraud and other frauds (as compared to victims whose existing accounts were misused) take six months or more to discover the crime.

a. relevant/answers research question

b. not relevant/does not answer research question

MAPPING THE ANSWERS TO YOUR RESEARCH QUESTION

Questions 11–15:   Refer to the concept map you created, and list five of the answers to the research question that you found.

What actions could businesses and individuals take to reduce identity theft?

11.   _____

12.   _____

13. _____

14. _____

15. _____

ORGANIZING CITABLE MATERIAL FOR POINTS (5 POINTS)

Questions 16–20: One of the points mentioned in the articles is that since employee information is vulnerable to theft, businesses should avoid using Social Security numbers to identify employees. They should use a special employee number instead. This point is written across the top of the following blank card.

Directions: Fill in the card with any research studies, quotes, or story-examples you saw that illustrate the point. Following the format you learned, note the author's name and the page number also.

Businesses Should Identify Employees by a Special Employee Number Instead of by Social Security Number		
Research Studies	Expert Quotes	Story-Examples

CHAPTER 8

Memorizing Ideas from Textbooks

OVERVIEW

LEARNING GOALS

After completing this chapter, you should be able to:

- Make an accurate judgment as to which ideas should be memorized.
- Create basic split-page notes.
- Simplify vocabulary from a text before transferring key ideas to notes.
- Organize review material that appears across multiple paragraphs.
- See the points to memorize in graphic material.
- Incorporate information from charts and graphs into split-page notes.

The most common college reading task is to read and memorize ideas from textbooks. You can expect your instructors to assign one or two chapters per week. No doubt you had thick textbooks to lug around in high school, but textbooks are used differently in college. In high school, textbooks are often used mainly for homework assignments. High school instructors frequently present the key points from the chapter as part of the lecture, and students read the textbook only if they missed class. ■

How Textbooks Are Used in College Courses

In college, textbook reading is much more important than in high school. Professors have a hard time covering all the topics that need to be addressed in the few short hours they have for lecture and other in-class activities. Splitting the lecture and the reading allows them to cover more material. For instance, a nursing instructor may assign the class to read a chapter on the respiratory system before giving a lecture on the treatment of asthma. Students that skipped the reading will have a hard time following the lecture. Additionally, many exam questions are pulled from textbook reading assignments even though these readings may never have been discussed in class.

When the instructor assigns a textbook chapter, the students are typically expected to identify and memorize important points. Additionally, students need to remember what they read over very long periods of time. For instance, a student in a counseling program may need to remember ideas presented in textbooks not only during the semester, but also for a licensure exam several years down the road.

Here it is useful to spotlight a common misconception that some students have. Many confuse understanding material with memorizing it. Students often think that if they understand ideas, they will automatically remember them. Studies have shown that even if people understand what they read perfectly, on average, after two weeks, they can remember only about 2–15 percent of the ideas. Without review, new information is quickly forgotten. Since it is not workable to read and re-read hundreds of pages of text as the semester progresses, students need to create notes that will capture the key ideas in a reading and provide a quick way to review. Although people tend to think of notetaking as something you do *after* you understand a reading, a good notetaking technique actually becomes an important tool in deepening your understanding and improving concentration while you read.

What Any Good Notetaking System Should Do for You

There are many ways to review material you have read: highlighting ideas, making annotations in the side margins of a text, creating idea maps, making flashcards for new technical terms, writing outlines and summaries, and so on. Each of these systems has advantages and disadvantages. All may be useful for certain tasks. Since taking notes uses up precious time, you should make sure your system provides you with these benefits:

- It helps you stay focused when you read. Maintaining concentration is often difficult in college reading, especially when you are tired.
- It gives you a more manageable, shortened list of ideas to memorize.

- Creating the notes should deepen your understanding. It should not be a mindless recopying of language from the text.

- Using the notes you create should make memorizing easy.

A good notetaking system sharpens your understanding while reducing your stress levels. It should result in successful performance on tests and projects. It should help you remember key ideas over a period of years, not just days. If your system does not do this for you, then you should switch methods.

Problems in Using Highlighting as a Review System. Many students have never created review notes for themselves. The more common strategy is to mark up sections of the text with a yellow highlighting pen. However, highlighting has some real disadvantages as a memorization system.

Highlighting doesn't require that you actually understand what you mark. It's easy to drift off mentally as you read and still mark up the text.

Highlighting does not force you to be selective about what you plan to memorize. It's easy to become too free with the yellow pen. Students often mark over half the text. Marking everything for review is the same as marking nothing.

The review process is miserable. You must re-read page after page of yellow sections, many of which you did not understand the first time around. Picture yourself up late at night before the final exam (which covers all chapters), staring at 400 pages' worth of yellow highlighting.

Split-Page Method. One of the most useful methods for taking notes is the split-page method. This is also called the Cornell method after the university at which it was widely promoted. In the split-page method, you first read through a section of text and pick out the ideas to be memorized. Then you set up notes in a question-and-answer format. Although there are many other good notetaking techniques, the split-page method is exceptionally useful and effective.

Time Management Issues

When you are assigned to read a long chapter, the first step is to break the reading into smaller bites. For example, suppose you have a week to read and memorize a forty-page chapter. Break it into eight five-page sections. Take out your schedule for the week and write in the eight times when you are going to sit down, read, and make notes. Avoid scheduling hours of reading at a time. You will become too tired and will lose efficiency. Don't plan to read anywhere that you will be interrupted. You will find that reading and creating notes is energy-intensive work. Take a ten-minute break every hour, and try not to schedule reading time late at night when you are exhausted.

Reading and Notetaking Sessions

1. Organize all your notes in a three-ring binder so that they don't get scattered and can be labeled and put on your bookshelf at the end of a semester for reference later.

2. Start each reading and notetaking session by reviewing the notes you took previously. Test yourself by covering up the answers to the questions you created. Spend about five minutes on review of past material. This will orient you to the ideas to come, and you will find you have very little to memorize right before a test.

3. Next, read a one- to two-page section at a time, and then go back and create notes for the ideas you think you should memorize. Check the text aids (learning goals and review questions) for guidance in selecting ideas to include in your notes.

4. After about forty-five minutes, you will be in need of a break. Before you stop, take a few more minutes to test yourself on the questions you just created for your notes.

The frequent, short memorization sessions are an important habit to build into your notetaking routines. If you train yourself to review old material at the beginning and end of every daily reading session, you will have almost no studying to do right before a test, your understanding of the class discussions will be much deeper, and you will feel less stressed.

Deciding What to Memorize

When you read a textbook chapter, you must decide what to memorize. Although there will be some variation depending on the subject and the instructor, information based on academic thought patterns is particularly likely to show up on a test. Here is a quick list of some common academic thought patterns for you to review:

- Definitions
- History/recent trends
- Types
- Comparison and contrast
- Causes
- Effects
- Process
- Parts (often accompanied by a diagram)
- Listing
- Problem-solution

Using the preceding guidelines, highlight the information in the following reading that should be memorized. Pay special attention to marking information based on academic thought patterns.

Births Outside Marriage

The birthrate among single women has been rising for most of this century, but it soared upward in recent decades. In 1990, single mothers had about a quarter of the babies born in the United States. By 2001, it was over a third. Among the more immediate causes, a rise in sexual activity among teenagers combined with failure to use appropriate contraceptive techniques stands out as the major contributor. Although American teenagers have about the same level of sexual activity as teenagers in Western Europe, Americans are less likely to use birth control and, consequently, their birthrate is far higher. Another important factor is the growing unwillingness of young couples to marry because the woman becomes pregnant. Studies of births in past centuries, when birthrates among single women were low, show that about 20 to 25 percent of all weddings occurred after the conception of a child. Today, the "shotgun wedding" (in which a pregnant woman's father threatens the man if he does not marry the virgin he has "spoiled") has gone out of style.

Source: Adapted from James William Coleman and Harold Kerbo, *Social Problems,* 9th edition (Upper Saddle River, NJ: Prentice Hall, 2005), 39–40. Used with permission of Prentice Hall, Inc.

Here are some other types of information you should typically memorize in addition to ideas based on academic thought patterns:

Information with practical value. Let's say you are reading a social work textbook chapter on child abuse and neglect. Here are two things that are discussed in the chapter:

1. a list of the signs that a child is being sexually abused
2. a discussion of one of the first cases of child abuse to be prosecuted in the courts, which occurred over 100 years ago (because there were no child abuse laws on the books at that time, the parents were prosecuted under the law forbidding cruelty to animals)

The first item is far more likely to appear on a test than the second because it has practical value. People studying to be social workers need that information to do their jobs competently. The second is interesting, but you don't need details of a 100-year-old child abuse case to be a competent social worker today.

Statistics. You will often run across a statistic on how common something is. Often, the statistic is describing the size of a problem. Here are some examples:

- An estimated 11 percent of American children suffer abuse or neglect.
- Approximately 25 percent of high school students drop out before graduation; however, most later earn their GEDs.

You should mark statistics such as these for memorization.

Study results. Often you will see studies mentioned in textbook chapters. For example, if you were reading a psychology textbook chapter on intelligence, you would probably read a discussion of a study done on twins. Identical twins were found to have more similar intelligence test scores than fraternal (nonidentical twins) or brothers and sisters that were not twins. The twin studies showed that intelligence is influenced by genetics, not just environment. The findings of studies should be marked for memorization.

Ideas mentioned in text aids. Many textbook chapters include text aids. Text aids are things like lists of learning objectives, summaries, and the review questions found at the beginning and end of the chapter. Take a look at the full-length sample chapter found at the end of your book for examples of text aids.

What you *don't* have to memorize. You don't typically have to memorize story examples. Textbook chapters often start with a story example to introduce a topic. You will also see story examples used to illustrate a point. However, you will not usually be expected to memorize these stories.

■ LOOKING ACROSS MORE THAN ONE PARAGRAPH

When you are looking for ideas to memorize, be careful to look across paragraphs. For instance, suppose you are reading a passage on teenage pregnancy. The section starts by saying that there are five factors that put young women at higher risk for early pregnancy. Although the discussion of the five factors may be spread across more than one paragraph, you want to consider them as a group in your mind. When you underline information to memorize, you can put a bracket or similar markings around information that goes together.

SKILLS PRACTICE 2

Highlight ideas that you think you should memorize, using the guidelines listed above.

Cohabitation

When they moved in together, Susannah, 24, and James, 29, had been dating for more than a year. Then their daughter, Elizabeth, was born. But the Albuquerque, New Mexico, couple is not quite ready to take the big step into matrimony. "We want to make sure we're doing the right thing," says Susannah, who also has a 4-year-old daughter from a previous marriage (Kantrowitz and Winger, 2001).

Susannah and James illustrate *cohabitation,* a living arrangement in which two unrelated people are not married but live together and have a sexual relationship.

The U.S. Census Bureau sometimes calls cohabitants *POSSLQs* (pronounced "possel-kews"), "persons of the opposite sex sharing living quarters." Unmarried couples also include same-sex relationships.

Cohabitation Trends and Characteristics

The number of unmarried couple households in the United States has increased tremendously, from an estimated 50,000 households in 1950 to almost 6 million in 2000 (Saluter, 1994; Simmons and O'Connell, 2003). Keep in mind, however, that only 9 percent of the population is cohabiting at any time. In contrast, married couples maintain 52 percent of all households.

Regional and State Variations. Cohabitation is more common in the Northeast and the West than the South or Midwest. The highest cohabitation rates are in the District of Columbia (21 percent), Alaska and Nevada (13 percent each), and Maine (12 percent). The lowest are in Utah (5 percent), Alabama (6 percent), and Arkansas and Kansas (about 7 percent each) (Simmons and O'Connell, 2003).

Duration. Most cohabiting relationships are short-lived, with a median duration of 15 to 18 months. When these relationships end, about 50 percent result in marriage (Smock and Gupta, 2002). Whether a cohabiting relationship ends in marriage or a breakup depends, among other things, on *why* people are living together.

Types of Cohabitation

Sociologists have identified several types of cohabitation. The most common types are coresidential dating cohabitation, premarital cohabitation, and cohabitation that is a trial marriage or a substitute for a legal marriage.

Coresidential Dating Cohabitation. Some people drift gradually into coresidential dating cohabitation when a couple that spends a great deal of time together eventually decides to move in together. The decision may be based on a combination of reasons, such as convenience, finances, companionship, and sexual accessibility. The couples are unsure about the quality of their relationship, and there is no long-term commitment.

Premarital Cohabitation. For many people, premarital cohabitation is a step between dating and marriage (Gwartney-Gibbs, 1986). In premarital cohabitation, the couple is testing the relationship before making a final commitment. They may or may not be engaged, but they have definite plans to marry their partners. Just 19 percent of Americans in 1988 said they lived with their spouse before marriage, compared with 37 percent in 2002 (Jones, 2002). Thus, increasing numbers of Americans are cohabiting before marriage.

Trial Marriage. In a trial marriage, the partners want to see what marriage might be like—to one another or someone else. This type of living together is similar to premarital cohabitation, but the people are much less certain about their relationship. Such "almost married" cohabitation may be especially attractive to partners who doubt that they can deal successfully with problems that arise from differences in personalities, interests, age, ethnicity, religion, or other issues.

Substitute Marriage. A substitute marriage is a long-term commitment between two people without a legal marriage. Motives for substitute marriage vary widely. For example, one or both partners may be separated but still legally married to someone else or may be divorced and reluctant to marry. In some cases, one partner may be highly dependent or insecure and thus prefer any kind of relationship to being alone. In other cases, partners may feel that a legal ceremony is irrelevant to their commitment to each other.

Source: Adapted from Nijole V. Benokraitis, *Marriage and Families: Changes, Choices, and Constraints,* 5th edition (Upper Saddle River, NJ: Prentice Hall, 2004), 245–47. Used with permission of Prentice Hall, Inc.

PRACTICE PASSAGE 8.1: FAMILY COUNSELING

In the next practice passage, focus on these two things: (1) using the title of the section as a cue for what you should memorize, and (2) looking for points that are spread across more than one paragraph. Pay attention to the main idea of each paragraph.

Problems of Men

Women are not alone in suffering gender stereotypes. While women frequently complain about being only sex objects in the eyes of men, an increasing number of men complain that they are only "success objects" for women. Three-fourths of young women, but only one-fourth of young men, polled by *Time* magazine said that a well-paying job was an essential requirement for a spouse. Obviously, three-fourths of all men do not have well-paying jobs. In fact, the income of the average man has dropped significantly in recent years, and the income of young men has been declining faster than that of any other group in our society. Between 1979 and the mid-1990s, the median wage for women increased by about $0.35 an hour (after controlling for inflation), while the average wage for men declined about $2.00 an hour. Of course, men's incomes are still higher on the average, but these changes have placed enormous psychological pressure on many men, a pressure not felt by women. Success as a man has traditionally been defined by the ability to earn. The erosion of their incomes and their growing dependence on their wives' earnings to help make ends meet are, therefore, a serious blow to the self-esteem of many men.

Another common complaint among men is that although they are being encouraged to take a greater role in child rearing, the deck is still stacked against them when it comes to child custody after a divorce. When both parents seek custody, many courts assume that the mother will make the better parent. Yet, although the mother is usually given custody of the children, the father still has to pay to support them while being given only limited visitation rights. In addition, when the separation is a bitter one, many husbands complain that their wives have tried to turn their children against them.

Finally, the increasingly negative stereotypes of men have become a staple of the contemporary media. A study of 1,000 television commercials in which there was a negative portrayal of one side of a male-female interaction found that the male was cast as the "bad guy" in every case. Today's media repeatedly stereotype men as either violent, sexually aggressive, and emotionally distant, or as fumbling nerds who are good for a laugh but not much else.

Source: Adapted from James Coleman and Harold R. Kerbo, *Social Problems,* 9th edition (Upper Saddle River, NJ: Prentice Hall, 2005), 295–96. Used with permission of Prentice Hall, Inc.

Creating Useful Notes

■ MEMORIZATION METHOD #1: ANNOTATING THE TEXT

You may have noticed that simply underlining ideas in a text produces a set of markings from which it would be hard to study. Think of texts you have seen all marked up with yellow highlighter. Imagine how hard it would be to stare at all those yellow markings the night before a midterm, trying to memorize the ideas.

There is a way to highlight a text that produces a nicer set of notes. You write a question indicating what you think you should memorize to the side of the text. Then you highlight or underline only the information that answers the question in the text.

SKILLS PRACTICE   3

The following passage on foodborne illness is typical of what culinary arts students must read and memorize. Off to the side of each paragraph, write what you would expect to be asked on a test, such as "number of cases of food poisoning" or "causes of food poisoning." Then highlight or underline the information in the text that answers the question.

Foodborne Illness

It is estimated that as many as 76 million Americans fall victim to a foodborne illness each year, and food poisoning is responsible for approximately 5,000 deaths annually. As shocking as these numbers are, public health experts believe that numerous cases of food poisoning go unreported. Sufferers may mistakenly believe they have the "flu" and fail to seek medical help. Even if the illness is grave enough to require medical attention, the victim may not link his or her symptoms to tainted food. Additionally, cases may go underreported because physicians fail to report them to public health authorities.

Although many people believe that chemicals or food additives are the likely culprits in cases of food poisoning, the majority of foodborne illness can be traced to mishandling of food resulting in microbial contamination by bacteria or viruses. The following are the most common causes of food poisoning ranked in order of concern: microbial contamination, naturally occurring toxicants, environmental contaminants such as metals and pesticide residues, food processing, and food additives.

Experts in foodborne illnesses have classified them into two types: food intoxications and foodborne infections. Food intoxication occurs when a person eats a food containing a toxin that affects the gastrointestinal tract or the nervous system. For example, a potato salad contaminated with *Staphylococcus aureus* bacteria would cause anyone that ate it to experience vomiting and abdominal cramps as the toxins produced by the bacteria acted on the gastrointestinal tract.

Botulism is an example of food intoxication in which the nervous system is affected. The toxin produced binds to nerve endings, making it difficult for the victim to swallow or breathe. Food intoxication may also occur in the case of a person ingesting a food contaminated with a metal, such as lead.

Foodborne infections occur when a microorganism such as bacteria, viruses, or parasites are introduced into the body through food. These microorganisms multiply within the body and cause sickness. For example, the microbial pathogen *Campylobacter jejuni* causes a disease called campylobacteriosis. The symptoms include diarrhea, abdominal pain, and fever. Another example of foodborne infection occurs when people eat oysters or clams contaminated with *Vibrio* bacteria. The bacteria spreads rapidly through the body, causing chills, fever, and prostration.

■ LIMITATIONS OF USING TEXT ANNOTATIONS AS A REVIEW SYSTEM

It is possible to study directly from an annotated text. Combining highlighting with side notes on the key concepts makes it a much more powerful system than just marking phrases with a yellow highlighting pen. However, studying from text annotations has some limitations.

You are stuck with the language of the original text during review. The ideas have not been translated into your own way of expressing the same thought. This is not a huge problem if the writer's style is clear, but some authors write in a style that takes a lot of energy to translate mentally.

It is often hard to mark up a text to show that certain ideas belong together. For instance, suppose you are reading a food science chapter on freezing foods. The writer is describing eight problems that can occur when foods are frozen, and each problem is explained in a separate paragraph. How will you mark up the text to show that these ideas go together? It is particularly hard to do when a discussion is spread over more than one page.

Sometimes there is very little space in the margin to pencil in anything at all. The annotations get messy and disorganized as you start running them around the edges of the page.

Annotation is a workable review system when you are comfortable with the language of the original text, there is enough space in the margin to pencil in ideas, and you already have some background knowledge on the topic so there is not a lot to memorize.

■ MEMORIZATION METHOD #2: CREATING SPLIT-PAGE NOTES

A great advantage of taking notes rather than marking up a text is that it enables you to combine ideas from across paragraphs, simplify the language of the text, and make review much easier. Here is how to set up your page:

1. Put the name of the chapter on which you are working across the top of the first page.

2. Next, draw a vertical line down the page so there is a question column to the left and a wider answer column to the right.

3. It is important to express answers to your questions in simple, short phrases, not long sentences copied word-for-word from the textbook.

4. After you record the answer to each question you find, draw a line under it so sets of questions and answers don't run together in your notes.

■ EXAMPLE OF SPLIT-PAGE NOTES

If you compare the annotated passage on foodborne illness to the split-page notes, you can see that it would be easier to memorize from the split-page notes. A useful feature of split-page notes it that it is easy to test yourself. Cover up the answers on the right side of the page with your hand, and ask yourself the questions in the left question column.

Many students are in the habit of waiting to memorize until the day before a test. Last-minute memorizing is stressful and far less effective than doing a little bit each day. If you start and end each reading and notetaking session with a few minutes of memorization, by the time the test comes around, you will already know everything.

FOODBORNE ILLNESS (pages 124-126)

Cases of foodborne illness in the U.S. each year	About 76 million
How many die	About 5,000 people
Why public health specialists think there are even more cases	• people think they have flu and don't go to the doctor • sick person doesn't connect illness to food • doctors may fail to report cases they see
Causes of food poisoning	1. microbial contamination 2. naturally occurring toxicants 3. environmental contaminants (metals/pesticides) 4. food processing 5. food additives
Two types of foodborne illness	food intoxication - Person eats food containing toxin that hurts the gastrointestinal tract or the nervous system - examples: botulism, Staphylococcus aureus, lead foodborne infection - person eats food containing bacteria, virus, or parasite - examples: campylobacteriosis, Vibrio bacteria

SKILLS PRACTICE 4

Read the excerpt from the government report on preventing *E. coli* infection from hamburgers. On a separate piece of notebook paper, create split-page notes for the ideas you think you should memorize. Remember to simplify the language for your notes.

Preventing *E. coli* Infection from Hamburgers

E. coli is a strain of bacteria that produces a toxin that can cause hemorrhagic colitis. This illness can develop into an extremely serious condition known as hemolytic uremic syndrome, which can cause kidney failure, brain damage, strokes, and seizures in young children and the elderly. This pathogen can survive both refrigerator and freezer storage. A number of *E. coli* outbreaks recorded since 1982 have been linked to undercooked ground beef as the primary source of infection. For example, in 1993, more than 500 people became sick, 150 were hospitalized, and four died after eating undercooked hamburgers contaminated with *E. coli* bacteria at a fast-food restaurant. Had the contaminated meat been cooked at a higher temperature, the bacteria would have been destroyed and no one would have become ill. Hamburgers, steaks, and other beef items should always be ordered well-done, not rare.

The Food Safety and Inspection Service has long advised consumers to use a food thermometer when cooking meat and poultry to ensure that a temperature sufficient to destroy bacteria has been reached. In June 1997, the FSIS expanded this recommendation to include ground beef patties. Pathogens (including *Salmonella* and *E. coli*) die when exposed to heat for a specific amount of time. A ground beef patty cooked to 160 degrees Fahrenheit is safe.

Many food handlers and consumers believe that visible signs, such as color changes in the food, are indicators that the food is safely cooked. However, recent research has shown that color and texture indicators are not reliable. First, some ground beef will lose all pink color before it is fully cooked. A 1995 study done by Kansas State University (Hunt et al., 1995) found that a number of ground beef patties were turning brown well before they reached 160 degrees Fahrenheit, making color an unreliable indicator of doneness. A consumer who believes a brown color always means a safe hamburger is taking a chance on foodborne illness. Second, some lean ground beef may remain pink at temperatures well above the 160 degree final cooking temperature recommended for consumers.

The only way to be sure a ground beef patty is cooked to a high enough temperature to destroy any harmful bacteria that may be present is to use an accurate instant-read thermometer. For ground beef patties, a digital instant-read food thermometer may be used toward the end of the cooking time and inserted at least 1/2 inch into the thickest part of the patty. If the ground beef patty is not thick enough to check from the top, the thermometer should be inserted sideways. Ground beef should be cooked to an internal temperature of 160 degrees Fahrenheit on an instant-read food thermometer.

Thermometer use to ensure proper cooking temperature is especially important for those who cook or serve ground beef patties to people most at risk for foodborne illness because *E. coli* bacteria can lead to serious illness or even death. Those most at risk include young children, the elderly, and those who are immunocompromised.

Source: Adapted from "Color of Cooked Ground Beef as It Relates to Doneness," United States Department of Agriculture Report, April 2003.

PRACTICE PASSAGE 8.2: CULINARY ARTS

Now make split-page notes on a longer passage. When you develop questions, try to write slightly broader questions that capture a related group of ideas. For instance, in the beginning of the passage, write the question, "What are some problems with American kids' eating habits?" The multi-part answer to this will include information on how much fat, fiber, calcium, and sugar they eat. This is better than writing a lot of small questions like "What percentage of kids eat too much fat?" "What percentage eat enough fiber?" and so on.

The Controversy over School Lunches

Good nutrition during the school years is vitally important for helping children grow strong, succeed in school, and establish health habits for a lifetime. Sadly, the current eating habits of some American children are falling far short of the mark.

■ More than 60 percent of children in the United States eat too much fat.

■ Only 39 percent of children eat enough fiber, found in fruits and vegetables, whole grains, and legumes such as lentils, chickpeas, and black beans.

■ Adolescents do not drink enough milk. Over 85 percent of adolescent girls lack sufficient calcium in their diets. During the past 25 years, consumption of milk, the largest source of calcium, decreased 36 percent among adolescent females. At the same time, soft drink consumption almost doubled among girls, and nearly tripled among boys.

■ Between 18 and 20 percent of calories consumed by children and adolescents come from added sugars. The Dietary Guidelines for Americans express concern that consuming excess calories from foods high in added sugars may "contribute to weight gain or lower consumption of more nutritious foods."

Poor eating habits, along with physical inactivity, contribute to obesity and other serious health problems. Overweight children have higher rates of Type 2 diabetes. Atherosclerosis, the most common cause of heart disease, begins during childhood and is related to blood cholesterol levels, which can be affected by what children eat. Young people who do not get enough calcium are at greater risk for later development of osteoporosis. Poor eating habits can also contribute to dental caries, which remains a major cause of school absences.

Although schools should encourage children to eat nutritious foods, much of what is sold on school campuses is of little nutritional value. The school lunches are prepared according to federal nutrition guidelines. However, many public schools are facing budget crises, and they can raise extra money by selling the nonnutritious foods children prefer through two channels. First, candy, salty snacks such as potato chips, and soda are sold through vending machines. No national data are available on the income that schools earn from selling food and beverage items in vending machines. However, a survey of school districts in Texas estimated that the total annual income from vending machines was over $54 million. Second, schools can raise money by selling individual items that are not part of school meals (called à la carte sales), such as cookies, pizza, and hamburgers. Several studies have documented that the majority of foods sold in à la carte settings are high in fat and/or added sugars. A survey conducted in 2000 in California found that à la carte items contributed up to 70% of all food sales in the school districts surveyed.

National nutrition groups have expressed concern about the sale of competitive foods and beverages in schools and their effects on student health. According to a joint position paper from the American Dietetic Association (ADA), Society for Nutrition Education (SNE), and the School Nutrition Association:

Schools' child nutrition programs should serve as a learning laboratory for developing healthful eating habits and should not be driven by profit-making ventures that may undermine nutrition goals.

In spite of criticism, schools are reluctant to give up the money earned through the sale of non-nutritious foods. In a 2001 national survey, 832 school principals reported using income from beverage sales in six key areas: sports and physical education equipment, after-school student activities, instructional materials, field trips, arts and theatre programs, and computers and technology equipment.

The good news is that many schools and districts across the United States are improving their nutrition environments while still earning profits from the sale of foods that compete with school lunches. Some schools are establishing nutrition standards for competitive foods, others are using marketing techniques to promote healthful food choices, and others have made more healthful foods and beverages available. Of 17 schools and districts that reported sales data after making these kinds of changes, 12 made more money and four made the same amount of money after making nutrition improvements.

Source: Adapted from "Making It Happen: School Nutrition Success Stories," a publication of the Centers for Disease Control.

READING FOR REAL LIFE

The Controversy over School Lunches

Do you think the food served at your college cafeteria is nutritious? How could it be improved?

Making Notes from Charts, Graphs, and Diagrams

When you create review notes to memorize information in textbooks, don't forget the charts, graphs, and diagrams. Test questions are taken from these sources as well. Notes from graphic sources can be combined with notes from the text.

When the text directs you to look at a certain chart or graph, add any potential test questions from those sources to your notes. For instance, suppose you are reading a health sciences textbook chapter on headaches. Here are the split-page notes you created so far:

HEADACHES (pages 83-98)

How are headaches classified?	*Fourteen types divided into three groups*
	 Primary headache disorders
	   (migraine, tension, and cluster headaches)
	 Secondary headache disorders
	   Caused by other medical problems like trauma or infection
	 Pain associated with nerve fibers
	   Cranial neuralgia, facial pain

Most common type	*Primary headache disorders—over 90%*
Causes of primary headache disorders	*Sometimes triggered by coughing, sneezing, or exercising too long, but most have no clear cause*

Now suppose that this is what the next part of the text says:

> The three types of primary headache most often seen in clinical practice are migraines, tension-type headaches, and cluster headaches. To make an accurate diagnosis, it is important to be aware of the differences between these major types of primary headache (see Table 8.1).

TABLE 8.1   **Differential Diagnosis of Common Headache Disorders**

	Migraine	Tension-Type	Cluster
Location	one side	both sides	one side or periorbital
Duration	several hours to 3 days	30 minutes to more than a week	30–120 minutes
Frequency and Timing	variable	variable	1–8 times per day; nocturnal attacks
Severity	moderate to severe	dull ache	excruciating
Pain Quality	throbbing, steady	viselike pressure	boring, piercing
Associated Features	nausea, vomiting, avoidance of sound or light, visual aura	usually none	lacrimation, runny nose, facial sweating

Source: Adapted from the *Headache Management: Office-Based Strategies for Nurse Practitioners.* National Headache Foundation, 2005. Reprinted by permission.

You can see that the question you should add to your notes is, "What are the differences between the types of primary headaches?" When you create split-page notes for charts and graphs, remember to simplify vocabulary the same as you would for notes from the text.

SKILLS PRACTICE 5

Annotate any unfamiliar words on Table 8.1 on the previous page and then create split-page notes for the question the table answers.

READING FOR REAL LIFE

Common Headache Disorders

You are a physician's assistant. A patient comes to your office complaining of extremely painful headaches. The patient is a twenty-year-old college student. He says the headaches start behind his right eye and often prevent him from sleeping at night. The patient describes the pain as similar to "being stabbed by a knife," and says that it makes his eyes water. Can you diagnose the type of headache disorder he has?

■ HANDLING GRAPHS OF NUMERICAL INFORMATION

Many of the graphs you will run across will display numerical data of some kind. It is important not to get overwhelmed by thinking that you are supposed to memorize all those numbers. Only rarely would an instructor expect that. Instead, look for the *points* that those numbers illustrate. Pay special attention to

- changes over time (trends)
- differences between groups
- the largest versus the smallest

SKILLS PRACTICE 6

Add to your split-page notes on headaches by creating a question and answer for the following graphs (Figures 8.1, 8.2, and 8.3).

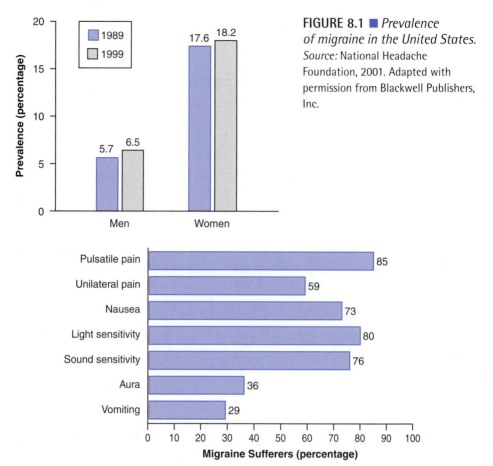

FIGURE 8.1 ■ *Prevalence of migraine in the United States.* *Source:* National Headache Foundation, 2001. Adapted with permission from Blackwell Publishers, Inc.

FIGURE 8.2 ■ *Prevalence of migraine complications in U.S. patients.*
Source: National Headache Foundation, 2001. Adapted with permission from Blackwell Publishers, Inc.

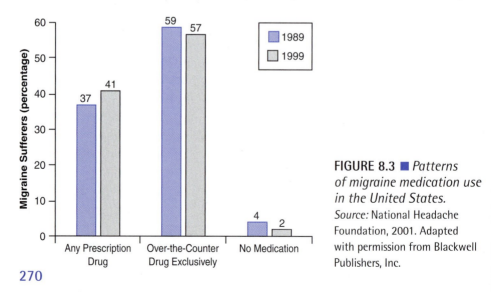

FIGURE 8.3 ■ *Patterns of migraine medication use in the United States.* *Source:* National Headache Foundation, 2001. Adapted with permission from Blackwell Publishers, Inc.

■ HANDLING DIAGRAMS

In many fields, students are tested on the parts of something. For example, in auto repair technology courses, the textbook will include a diagram of an engine. On the test, students may be shown a line drawing of an engine and asked to label the carburetor, the alternator, and so on. Memorizing diagrams is also important in health-related programs. Health care practitioners must learn the names and locations of parts of the respiratory system, circulatory system, muscles, and bones.

The importance of learning the locations of parts was illustrated wonderfully in a memoir written by William A. Nolen called *The Making of a Surgeon*. Nolen writes about his days as a new graduate of medical school learning surgery as the apprentice of an experienced surgeon. He was excited when his mentor, George, announced that he could remove an infected appendix under supervision. Taking out an infected appendix is a relatively easy job. All the surgeon has to do is find the appendix, cut it off, and tie a knot in the stump. After Nolen managed (with great difficulty) to cut through the layers of fat and muscle to get to the abdomen, George started guiding him through the next part of the operation:

> "Now," said George, "put your fingers in, feel the cecum (the portion of the bowel to which the appendix is attached) and bring it into the wound."
>
> I stuck my right hand into the abdomen. I felt around—but what was I feeling? I had no idea. It had always looked so simple when the senior resident did it. Open the abdomen, reach inside, pull up the appendix. Nothing to it. Everything felt the same to me. I grabbed something and pulled it into the wound. Small intestine. No good. Put it back. I grabbed again. This time it was the sigmoid colon. Put it back. On my third try I had the small intestine again.
>
> "The appendix must be in an abnormal position," I said to George. "I can't seem to find it."
>
> "Mind if I try?" he asked.
>
> "Not at all," I answered. "I wish you would."
>
> Two of his fingers disappeared into the wound. Five seconds later they emerged, cecum between them, with the appendix flopping from it.
>
> "Stuck down a little," he said kindly. "That's probably why you didn't feel it."

Memorizing the names and locations of parts from a diagram is not easy to do. Try staring at the diagram of the skin in Figure 8.4. How long before your mind starts to wander? Notice that it is very difficult to maintain concentration.

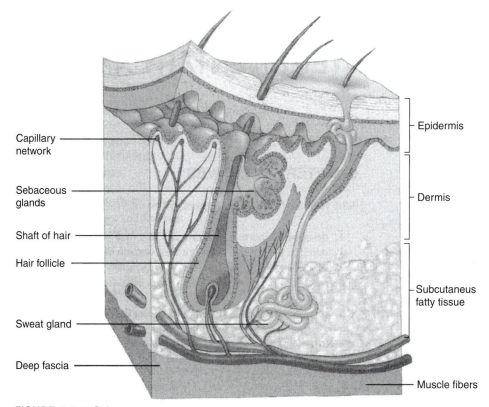

Capillary network

Sebaceous glands

Shaft of hair

Hair follicle

Sweat gland

Deep fascia

Epidermis

Dermis

Subcutaneus fatty tissue

Muscle fibers

FIGURE 8.4 ■ *Skin structure.*
Source: Adapted from Daniel Limmer, Michael O'Keefe, Harvey D. Grant, Robert H. Murray, and J. David Bergero, *Emergency Care,* 9th edition (Upper Saddle River, NJ: Pearson Education, 2001), 2. Used with permission of Prentice Hall, Inc.
Note: The superficial lymphatics are not shown in this schematic.

The best way to memorize a diagram is to draw and label the parts yourself. Make sure you have enough space. If the diagram is too detailed, just choose a few parts to learn first, and then add to the sketch later. Use a pencil, because you will find you need to fix a line or correct a shape. Figure 8.5 shows how you make split-page notes for diagrams:

Notice that the sketch doesn't have to be a professional-quality drawing. The benefit of making the sketch is that it keeps your mind focused on the diagram. Drawing forces you to notice shapes and the relationship of one part to another. You will learn the parts far more quickly than if you just stare at the diagram, hoping the information will stick.

Now suppose you are continuing along in the chapter about headaches, and you run across Figure 8.6, a diagram of the parts of the brain. If you are in a health sciences program, your instructor will certainly expect you to memorize it.

What are the parts of the skin?

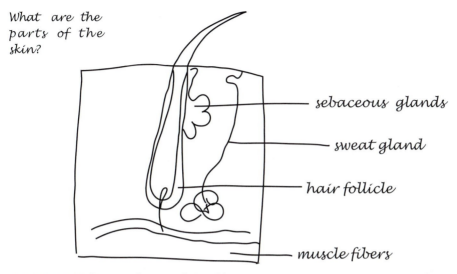

— sebaceous glands

— sweat gland

— hair follicle

— muscle fibers

FIGURE 8.5 ■ *Sketch of parts of the skin.*

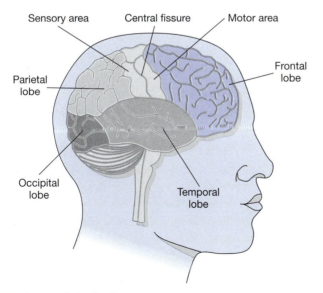

FIGURE 8.6 ■ *Areas of the brain.*
Source: Adapted from Jeffrey S. Nevid, Spencer A. Rathus, and Beverly Greene, *Abnormal Psychology in a Changing World,* 6th edition (Prentice Hall, 2006). Used with permission.

SKILLS PRACTICE 7

Add to your split-page notes on headaches, using the information in Figure 8.6. Write the question "Where are the different lobes of the brain?" in the left question column. In the answer space, draw and label the parts of the brain.

You know that to review using split-page notes, you cover up the answers on the right side. Then you test yourself on the questions in the column to the left to see you if you remember the correct answer. When you come to a question that is answered by a diagram, you don't want to just say the parts aloud. Instead, test yourself by taking out a piece of scratch paper to see if you can make a quick sketch of the answer. Then compare your sketch to the more elaborate diagram to see if it is right.

Many times, information on diagrams is tested through the use of matching questions.

SKILLS PRACTICE 8

Following is an example of a diagram-related question you could expect to see in a test. See if you can label all the parts of the brain correctly without looking back at your notes.

Label the following areas of the brain: temporal lobe, central fissure, parietal lobe, occipital lobe, motor area, sensory area, frontal lobe.

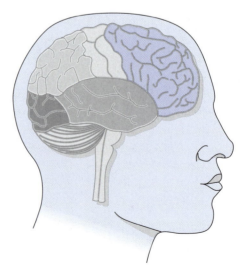

PRACTICE PASSAGE 8.3: PHARMACOLOGY

Next, try making a complete set of notes from this passage on colds and flu.

The Respiratory System

ANATOMY OF THE RESPIRATORY SYSTEM

The respiratory system is divided into two parts. The upper respiratory tract consists of the nasal cavity (nose), paranasal sinuses, and pharynx (throat) and ends at the larynx. The larynx acts in conjunction with the epiglottis to guard the entrance to the trachea and lower airways. It also functions as the voice box. The lower respiratory tract consists of the trachea (which enters the thoracic cavity), two lungs, two main bronchi (one to each lung), secondary and tertiary bronchi, bronchioles ending with the terminal respiratory bronchioles, alveolar ducts, and alveoli (see Figure 8.7).

The upper respiratory tract gets afflicted with diseases such as sinusitis, colds with either rhinitis or nasal congestion, and allergies, while the lower respiratory tract is affected by bronchial infections, bronchoconstriction, and chronic obstructive diseases such as asthma and emphysema.

FUNCTION OF THE RESPIRATORY SYSTEM

The primary function of the respiratory system is to supply oxygen to the blood, which carries it to all parts of the body. The blood carries oxygen via the "freeways" of the circulatory system, or the blood vessels known as the veins, arteries, and capillaries. The heart is the pump that propels the blood to and from the lungs. The purpose of the respiratory system is twofold in that it (1) transports air to and from the lungs and (2) exchanges gases within the blood vessels—oxygen for carbon dioxide. During its journey, air is humidified, warmed, and purified (suspended particles removed).

Respiration or breathing is the mechanism through which gas exchange is accomplished. When we breathe, we inhale air, which has oxygen in it, and when we exhale, we release carbon dioxide, a by-product of the usage of oxygen that plants utilize. This exchange of gases is the way in which the respiratory system gets oxygen to the blood. If oxygen does not get to a specific part of the body, that part would die. When blood stops moving, oxygen does not get to the tissue that it needs to "feed." This is called *ischemia*.

The supportive functions of the lymphatic system of the lungs are threefold: (1) maintains fluids, (2) provides respiratory immunity defenses, and (3) removes inhaled solid material and microorganisms. The sizable flow of lymph from the lung tissue interstitial spaces into the blood help to eliminate excess fluid, and the lymphoid tissue of the tonsils protect against infection at the entrance to the respiratory tract.

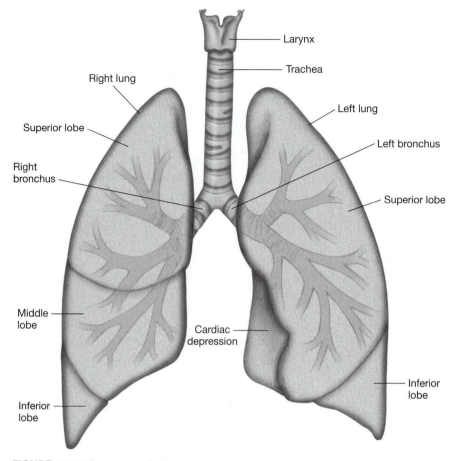

FIGURE 8.7 ■ *Lower respiratory tract.*
Source: Adapted from Mike Johnston, *Pharmacology* (Prentice Hall, 2006). Used with permission.

In essence, there are two ways to get oxygen to the body: (1) via the respiratory system, which brings oxygen into the body and blood, and (2) the circulatory system, which takes the oxygen in the blood to various parts of the body. The respiratory and circulatory systems work in tandem to accomplish their mutual goal of keeping the body alive.

A DIFFERENCE BETWEEN AIR AND OXYGEN

Air is a mixture of gases, not one pure element. The normal composition of air by volume is approximately 78 percent nitrogen, 21 percent oxygen, and 0.03 percent carbon dioxide. The balance is made up of other gases, like argon, helium, krypton, neon, and xenon, which occur in trace (small) amounts. In addition, air contains water vapor, traces of ammonia, and suspended matter such as bacteria, dust, spores, and plant debris. Oxygen is a gas that is one pure element. Oxygen is just one of the components of air.

ACTUAL RESPIRATION AND THE EXTERNAL EXCHANGE

Respiration is achieved through the mouth, nose, trachea, lungs, and diaphragm. Inspiration of air occurs when the pressure inside the lung, known as intrapulmonary pressure, becomes lower than the outside (atmospheric) pressure. This change in pressure allows the air to flow into the alveoli (tiny air sacs) of the lungs. During inspiration the intrapulmonary pressure would be less than the atmospheric pressure of 760 mm Hg. During inspiration, oxygen enters the upper respiratory system through the mouth and nose, where it is warmed and filtered by *cilia*, the tiny hair-like organelles found in the nose and bronchial passageways.

Cilia provide another important function by adhering to inhaled dust, smoke, and other pollutants and then moving in a specific manner to eliminate the irritants. The oxygen then passes through the larynx (the voice box) and the trachea (windpipe). The trachea is a tube that enters the chest cavity, where it splits into two smaller tubes called the bronchi. Each bronchus then splits off into the bronchial tubes. The bronchial tubes lead into the lungs, where they split off into many smaller tubes, which connect to tiny air sacs know as alveoli.

The average adult human lungs contain about 600 million spongy alveoli, which are surrounded by capillaries. These alveoli are often referred to as grape-like clusters of air sacs. Inhaled air with oxygen passes into the alveoli and then diffuses oxygen through the capillaries. The oxygen then travels into the arterial blood (oxygen-rich blood). During this same time, the blood that is full of waste, from the veins and capillaries, releases its carbon dioxide into the alveoli. The carbon dioxide leaves the lungs by the same capillaries during exhalation.

In review, alveoli bring new oxygen from the breathed-in air to the bloodstream. These alveoli, or "air sacs," exchange oxygen for waste products, like carbon dioxide, which the cells in the body have made and cannot use. In fact, if the waste does not leave the body, it will accumulate in the blood and cause suffocation to all body parts due to the lack of external exchange. There must be an external exchange of carbon dioxide for air, from which oxygen can be extracted. This external exchange that keeps the human body alive is directed by the brain, which does it automatically.

Source: Adapted from Mike Johnston, *Pharmacology* (Upper Saddle River, NJ: Prentice Hall, 2005), 359–60. Used with permission of Prentice Hall, Inc.

Putting It All Together

In this practice passage, pay special attention to seeing the big questions that have answers spread across several paragraphs. For each of the two sections, try to form one or two broad questions that have multi-part answers rather than writing a series of smaller questions.

PRACTICE PASSAGE 8.4: LAW ENFORCEMENT

Police Stress and Burnout

POLICE AND ALCOHOL

In his novel, *The Choirboys,* former Los Angeles policeman Joseph Wambaugh portrayed the police as consuming excessive amounts of alcohol to cope with the stresses of the job. After their shift ended in the early morning hours, the squad would go to what is euphemistically called "choir practice" at Los Angeles' MacArthur Park, where they would get drunk and tell each other stories about their night on patrol. Although the book can be very funny at times, there is an undercurrent of tension caused, in part, by the excessive consumption of alcohol that Wambaugh linked to the stress of policing (Figure 8.8).

This theme of policing and alcohol abuse is also present in the academic literature on the occupation. For example, one study looked at psychological stress, the demands of police work, and how police coped with these issues. The study

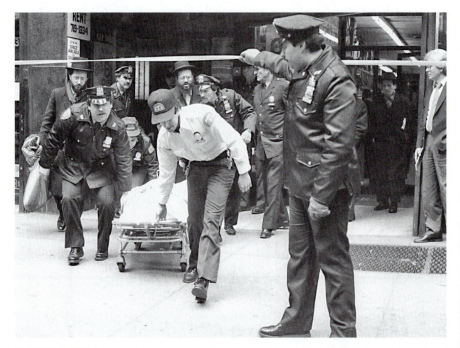

FIGURE 8.8 ■ *Law enforcement and emergency personnel removing the body of an employee killed during a robbery. Police officers see more tragedy than those in most other professions.*
Source: Photograph by Arnold J. Saxe. Courtesy of AP Wide World Photos.

found that the stress of police work was highly related to alcohol abuse. Other coping mechanisms such as emotional dissonance (officers learn to objectify their emotions when faced with dead or injured people, crime victims, abused children, etc.) and cynicism were found to be related either directly or indirectly to alcohol use. What is important to learn from this study is that alcohol was used as a method to relieve the inherent stress of police work 20 times more often than cynicism or emotional distancing. In fact, when those methods failed, alcohol use became more likely.

The stress of police work may not be the only factor, however, in influencing law enforcement officers to turn to alcohol. The police subculture may also exert a powerful influence on drinking patterns. Additionally, it may act as an obstacle to the reporting of a fellow officer with a drinking problem. Consider the following:

1. **The police subculture may socialize new officers into accepting a pattern of after-shift drinking.** New employees are anxious to fit into the group. In many occupations, the older workers want to know whether the new person can be trusted. In police work, in which the officer must depend on his or her partner, there is a pressure to judge each other's reliability quickly. Learning what "makes the other person tick" through after-hours socializing is an important part of this judgment process. New officers are judged by their peers to "fit in" to the extent that they can hold their liquor; articulate the occupational worldview of the police subculture; and accept and participate in the complaining about citizens, politicians, and superiors.

2. **Socialization in the police subculture establishes that drinking is not deviant.** Because "everyone drinks after work," the consumption of alcohol is soon viewed as normal behavior. Whereas in other circumstances, consistent and excessive drinking might be viewed as a problem, in police work it just means that an officer is "one of the guys." When embarrassing incidents happen or problems with family emerge because of drinking, these issues are turned into amusing stories that are told over and over in future drinking bouts as evidence that "civilians don't understand police work."

3. **This normalization of drinking may preclude treatment because "every one of my friends drinks."** One of the issues that can lead people to seek treatment for their drug or alcohol addiction is the embarrassment it can cause in the workplace. To the extent that alcohol use is the norm among one's contemporaries, its abuse is not a cause for concern and its treatment may actually be viewed as a weakness or even a betrayal of the work group. When a fellow officer is forced to admit that drinking is a problem, other officers may feel uncomfortable in examining their own drinking patterns. A reformed drinker can sometimes help his or her friends, but often the friends continue to maintain their lifestyle, and an unspoken barrier is erected.

The impact of alcohol on the police force has not been lost on police administrators. As with many other agencies and corporations, personnel policies are geared toward ensuring that the police maintain good health and do not put the force at risk of lawsuits because of unfitness for duty. In the past several years, many public safety organizations have instituted drug and alcohol testing to ensure that police officers are capable of performing their assignments. Assistance is offered to those who are determined to need help, and continued failures to meet departmental standards can be cause for dismissal.

FAMILY PROBLEMS AND THE POLICE

The individual police officer is not the only one affected by the stress of police work. Often, family members experience a variety of stressful concerns. The first of these is the change in the personality of the police officer and his or her relationship with the spouse and/or children. Jerome Skolnick coined the term "the policeman's working personality" to explain how the police must cope with danger, isolation, authority, and suspicion. Police families experience stress when the police officer brings the job home and starts to treat his or her spouse and children like potential suspects. The simple question, "Where are you going?" may be viewed as an interrogation rather than a normal concern. Children of police officers may be held to a higher standard of etiquette as the officer demands that they show proper respect and deference.

The issue of isolation can take on two forms. First, the officer may not express the stress that comes from the job to the family, and he or she may appear withdrawn and disinterested in the family's concerns. Second, the family members may be treated with hostility by neighbors who believe they are being watched by the police officer.

The dangers associated with police work can also be a source of stress for officers' family members. Knowing that one's spouse or parent is potentially just one radio call away from a deranged person with a gun can keep one in an uneasy state of mind. If each phone call could be the police commissioner calling to say there has been a shooting, it is only natural that some family members would suggest the police officer find less dangerous work. Having a spouse or parent as a police officer can be a source of pride, but it can also be a source of worry and concern. Family members' pressure on the police officer about the job can create a dilemma. Feeling a loyalty to the job and responsibility to the family can result in the officer internalizing stress and, as a result, doing a bad job at both family life and policing.

Finally, the nature of police work can cause hardships in the family because of rotating shifts. Depending on the department, the nature of shift work can exert an extreme hardship on both the police officer and the family. Scheduling day care, vacations, children's after-school activities, and a host of other domestic duties is difficult when the officer's shift is always in flux. Most people work best when they have a routine to which their bodies can adjust. In police work, the routine is lost with constant changes in shift. People become irritable when their sleeping patterns are altered and, by the time an officer adjusts to a shift, the shift changes again.

Source: Adapted from John Randolph Fuller, *Criminal Justice: Mainstream and Crosscurrents* (Upper Saddle River, NJ: Prentice Hall, 2005), 237–40. Used with permission of Prentice Hall, Inc.

PRACTICE TEST
Memorizing Ideas from Textbooks

PART I: READING TO PREPARE

Directions: Read through the article entitled "Understanding Your 401(k) Plan Choices." Then create split-page notes for the ideas you decide you should memorize. Study from these notes, testing yourself by asking yourself the questions you created in the left column while covering the answers to the right.

UNDERSTANDING YOUR 401(k) PLAN CHOICES

When you begin your first full-time job after college, it is likely that your employer will offer a 401(k) or similar retirement plan as a benefit of working at the organization. It is important to understand how these plans function and why it is so important to begin building your retirement accounts from the first day you start work.

RETIREMENT IN THE LAST CENTURY

In the early decades of the 1900s, retirement required little thought on the part of the individual. Until the mid-twentieth century, people expected to work full-time until health problems forced them to stop. There was no idea of a golden age of rest and relaxation in the last stage of life. Retirement was equated with illness followed shortly thereafter by an obituary notice. On average, people were retired for less than five years before they died. If necessary, elderly people moved in with one of their grown children if they were unable to support themselves financially or were in poor health. However, elderly people too sick to work and without family resources could quickly exhaust their savings and suffer terrible poverty.

PROBLEMS WITH RELYING ON SOCIAL SECURITY

The Social Security system was started in 1935. Everyone does not qualify for retirement benefits under the Social Security system—only those who have contributed to it during their working years are eligible for benefits. Even for those who do qualify, the benefits are not very large. The purpose of the system is to prevent widespread poverty among elderly and disabled people. It is not designed to cover the full cost of living for retired people. For instance, the average monthly payment to a retired individual in 2006 was $1,044. On average, men receive approximately $200 more per month than women do because they tend to earn more money and pay into the system for more years. In 2006, the average monthly Social Security check was only $904 for women and $1,177 for men. A problem with the Social Security system is that it is funded through the payroll taxes shared between current workers and their employers. The large number of retired workers is straining the capacity of the system. It is likely that in the future, Social Security benefits will be reduced, the age of eligibility will have to be increased, or the benefits will be restricted to only those retirees with no other financial resources.

A sizeable number of older workers were not employed in positions with Social Security benefits. These workers—who did not pay into the Social Security system while they were employed and are therefore ineligible for benefits—may apply for Supplemental Social Security. However, the amounts that retired persons can get from Supplemental Social Security are very low. The maximum monthly Supplemental Social Security benefit for an individual in 2006 was only $603. Additionally, to qualify for Supplemental Social Security benefits, applicants may not own assets worth over a certain amount.

POVERTY AMONG OLDER WOMEN

Older women are at greater risk for poverty than men. Approximately 40% of older single women live in poverty; for women over 85, the percentage rises to 58%. Women who stay at home to raise children and don't develop the kinds of skills that will earn them high wages are at especially high risk of poverty in old age. In their book, *Quality of Life for Older People: An International Perspective*, authors William and Marie Lassey cite the example of Joan, a woman who married at 19 shortly after completing high school. Joan did not work except occasionally for 25 years while she raised five children. Her husband had a manager's job with a major supermarket chain, and he provided generally good support for the family. However, he turned to alcoholism, became abusive, and eventually the marriage ended in divorce. After the divorce, Joan worked as a waitress until health problems forced her to retire at age 62. She had no health insurance, very little money saved, and a Social Security income of only $470 per month—scarcely enough to pay for food and rent on a small apartment.

THE DECLINE IN EMPLOYER PENSION PROGRAMS

In the past, retired employees could combine their Social Security checks with income from pensions. A pension is a fixed amount of money paid regularly to a retired worker by their former employer. For example, a retired teacher that taught at the same school for 30 years might continue to receive pension checks each month from the school system with whom she was employed.

Unfortunately, few employers are willing to offer pensions any more. There are two main reasons for the discontinuation of pension benefits at most organizations. The first cause is greater worker mobility. When workers spent their entire work lives with one company, employers were more willing to undertake the full responsibility for their support after retirement. However, many workers now change employers every few years. Second, increases in life expectancy have had an enormous impact on the expenses of offering pensions to retired workers. Employers are reluctant to promise to send monthly pension checks to workers that may live twenty-five years past their last day of work.

401(k) PLANS

Pension plans are being replaced by defined contribution plans such as the 401(k). The defined contribution plans allow the employee to build retirement savings through investments that can usually be rolled over from one employer's plan to that of another. Here is a simplified explanation of how 401(k) plans work:

1. The employer works with a financial services company to put together a list of investments—mostly stock and bond funds—which employees can choose from. Investments such as stock and bond funds are selected because they have the potential to build savings faster than simply depositing the money in a bank.

2. The employer takes a certain amount of money from the employee's paycheck each pay period and invests it in whichever stock or bond fund the employee chose. Often the employer will match the funds going into the 401(k) investment fund. For instance, if $100 was taken from the employee's paycheck for retirement, the employer will match the amount so that $200 is invested into the fund.

3. When the employee leaves the job, he or she is allowed to take *all* the money he or she invested into the 401(k) plan and roll it over into the 401(k) plan of the new employer. Employees can also take all or part of the employer's matched amounts, depending on how long they were employed at the organization.

Under the pension system that is fast dying out, the workers did not have to "manage" their retirement accounts during the time they were employed. The worry of saving enough money and investing it properly was the concern of the employer, not the employee. Under the defined contribution plans such as a 401(k), it is now the employees' responsibility to understand the advantages and disadvantages of different kinds of stock and bond funds and make the decision as to where to invest the retirement money. To make an informed decision, all workers need to understand the basics of investing in stock and bond funds.

AN INTRODUCTION TO STOCK AND BOND FUNDS

There are many kinds of investments, but the two most basic types—the chocolate and vanilla of investments—are stocks and bonds. The nature of these investments is quite different. In one case, you are lending money and in the other, you are part owner in a company.

BOND FUNDS

When you buy a bond, you are loaning money at interest. Let's say a fast-food company—Southern Chicken Express—has done well and wants to expand the business to a new state. To make this big jump, they need more money than they have. One way of raising the money would be to offer bonds to investors. A bond is a loan agreement. The investor who buys the Southern Chicken Express bond acts like a bank; he or she is lending them money and gets paid back with interest.

Companies are not the only kind of organizations that issue bonds to raise money. Cities, states, and the national government also issue bonds. Governments are often faced with too many needs and not enough tax money to fund all the programs people want. In this situation, they can issue bonds the same way that people run up debt on their credit cards to buy things they can't really afford. Investors can buy government bonds and get paid back later with interest. The problem for the government in issuing bonds is the same as for individuals—all these debts must be paid out of future income, making it harder to pay for things later. When people complain about the national debt, they are talking about the number of bonds the government has issued. All those investors that bought government bonds must eventually be paid back with future tax money, leaving less money for new programs.

You won't usually have the choice of investing in bonds for a single company as one of your 401(k) plan options. Instead, you invest in a group of bonds from many different companies or other organizations. Here are some types of bond funds that might be included in your 401(k) plan:

Corporate Bond Funds. These funds invest in the bonds issued by American companies.

Municipal Bond Funds. The government of a city or state issues a municipal bond.

U.S. Government Income Funds. These funds invest in bonds issued by the federal government such as U.S. Treasury bonds.

Global Bond Securities. These funds invest in bonds issued by both foreign and U.S. companies.

Balanced Funds. A balanced fund is made up of a mix of stocks and bonds.

STOCK FUNDS

The other kind of investment you will see listed as a choice on your 401(k) plan is stock funds. When you invest in stocks, you are not lending money. A person who owns stock has bought part ownership in a company. Here it is useful to think about the birth of a company and how it grows. Let's take a simple example. Suppose a woman—we will call her Sofie—was taught to make homemade soap by her mother and has developed a great formula for a mint-scented soap. Sofie gives mint soap away as presents, and before long, people are asking to buy some. Sofie makes up batches of mint soap to sell to friends and asks a local gift shop if they would like to carry it. Pretty soon, the demand for the soap is taking up all Sofie's time. She decides she needs to rent space, buy soap-making materials and equipment in bigger quantities, and hire an employee. She goes to the bank and asks for a business loan for $20,000.

Unfortunately, the bank turns her down. They say she has too little business experience for them to risk making a loan. Sofie decides to raise the money to expand by incorporating her business and offering stock (partial ownership) to friends and others who think the business has potential to grow and be profitable. To raise $20,000, Sofie decides to offer 2,000 shares in Sofie's Soaps at $10 per share. A lawyer will draw up the paperwork to incorporate the company and issue the shares. When Sofie decides to offer shares in her company, she is giving up complete ownership in exchange for help raising the money to grow a bigger company than she can nurture on her own funds. She buys 500 shares herself. Friends, family members, and others buy the rest. After all the shares are sold and the $20,000 is raised, a shareholders' meeting is held. The shareholders elect a board of directors. The board of directors decides that Sofie will be in charge of soap production and a person with business experience will be hired to manage the new company.

HOW STOCKHOLDERS MAKE MONEY

So how will the people who bought shares of stock in Sofie's Soap make money? There are two ways: through dividends and by selling off the stock after its price rises. Let's look at dividends first. Suppose that after a year, Sofie's Soaps has made a profit of $10,000. These profits belong to the stockholders and they could be shared out. Since there are 2,000 shares of stock in Sofie's Soap, the total profits for the year ($10,000) could be divided by the total number of shares (2,000). Each person who owned a share of Sofie's Soap would get a check for $5 in the mail. People who owned 10 shares would get a check for $50. The share of company profits that stockholders receive are called dividends.

However, suppose the board of directors for Sofie's Soap decides that since the company is doing so well, they should not share out the profits by sending dividend checks. Instead, they will use the profits to expand the company further. This is usually the choice that young, growing companies will make. As the company grows, each share of stock in it becomes more valuable and the price will rise. Stockholders can make money by selling their shares for more than they paid for them.

TYPES OF STOCK FUNDS

On the list of your 401(k) choices, you won't usually be given the option to invest your retirement money in the stock of a single company. Instead, you will have the choice of investing in various kinds of stock funds—collections of stock from different companies. For example, some stock funds are made up of shares of stock in large, established companies like Coca-Cola or Microsoft. Other stock funds are focused on small companies—a riskier kind of investment. Still others focus on companies in foreign countries. Common types of stock funds are listed below.

Aggressive growth. These are considered a high-risk investment. The fund manager might select the stocks of small companies with good growth potential or those developing new technologies such as wind power. While these companies are most likely to show spectacular growth and profits, they are also running the highest risk of failure.

Growth. The holdings in these funds might include both smaller and better-established companies with potential to grow.

Growth and income funds. The stocks in a growth and income fund represent a mix of companies that show promise of growth as well as older, established companies that pay dividends. They are considered a less risky investment than growth funds.

Value funds. Managers of value funds seek out underpriced stocks that are out of favor with investors but could become more sought after in the future. For example, the price of stocks in airline companies dropped after the September 11th attacks. If a value fund manager thinks that these companies are ready to make a comeback, he or she will buy the stocks of airline companies while the price is still low, figuring that they will rise in the future.

Small company funds. These funds are also referred to as *small cap* funds.

Large company funds. Stocks in these funds, also called *large cap funds,* are selected from well-established companies like General Mills or McDonald's.

Sector funds. The stocks in a sector fund are chosen from companies in one industry or portion of the economy. A sector fund may focus, for example, on health care or computer technologies. Investors should be aware that sector funds are riskier than some other types of funds because of the lack of diversity. Even though the fund may include stocks in many companies, an industry can suffer unforeseen setbacks. For example, sector funds focused on computer technologies took a hit when many Internet companies failed.

Global and international funds. Although both global and international funds invest in foreign companies, an international fund is made up of only foreign stocks, while a global fund also includes the stock of U.S. companies.

Emerging Market Funds. The stocks in an emerging market fund are chosen from companies based in newly industrialized countries and those moving away from a socialist economy. For instance, the manager of an emerging market fund might invest in companies in Russia.

Index funds. Investors in index funds are reasoning that since there are so many variables that can affect the performance of a company, the best strategy is to buy stocks in all companies. The stocks in these funds are chosen to match those in a standard group, such as the S&P 500 (larger companies) or the Wilshire 5000 (all companies). The risk of investing in stocks is lessened because of the diversity of stocks in the fund.

INDIVIDUAL RETIREMENT ACCOUNTS (IRAs)

All workers—both those who are employed with companies that offer 401(k) plans and those that are not—can invest in these same kinds of stock and bond funds for retirement through individual retirement accounts (IRAs). You simply contact a financial services company such as T. Rowe Price or Morgan Stanley and say that you want to open an IRA. An IRA is not a kind of investment; it's just a label on an investment that shows that its purpose is to build money for retirement. Labeling an investment as an IRA allows the profits you make to grow without being taxed until you withdraw them when you retire. The government will allow you to invest up to several hundred dollars a month for your retirement that will grow tax-free through an IRA.

The advantage of investing for retirement through an IRA rather than through your employer's 401(k) plan is that you have a much wider range of investment choices. A 401(k) plan may only offer a selection of a dozen different stock or bond funds. By contrast, when you open an IRA, you can choose any kind of investment—the selection is huge. The disadvantage of saving for retirement through an IRA instead of a 401(k) plan is that there are no matching funds from the employer.

THE IMPORTANCE OF STARTING EARLY

The earlier you start, the easier it is to build up a large sum of money for retirement. The reason you must start early is that if you do, you will have the tremendous power of compounding working in your favor. *Compounding* means that the profits you make on your investments are not spent, but instead are rolled over for making more investments.

Here is a simple example of what it means to let investment gains compound. Suppose that you set aside $1,000 for investing in loans. If you lent out $1,000 and required that the borrower pay you 10% in interest, at the end of a year, you would get your $1,000 back plus the extra $100 for interest. Now you have a choice—will you spend the $100 profit you made on your investment or will you roll it over to make new investments (let it compound)? If you let it compound, then the following year, you will have $1,100 to loan out at interest.

If people begin investing early, rolling over the profits each time, the total can become enormous. For example, let's say you were to invest $2,000 each year from the time you were 25 until you were 35 years old. You invest the money and it earns a return of 10%. (The *return* is a measure of how much the money you invested grew in a year. It is expressed as a percentage.) Since you invested $2,000 for a total of ten years, the total amount you invested would be $20,000. However, if you didn't invest another penny from the time you were 35, but simply rolled over the profits each year, allowing your investment gains to compound, by the time you were 65 years old, you would have $556,197. Allowing money to compound over a period of several decades is like rolling a snowball down a hill. The snowball is small at the top, but it gains enormously on each roll as it get close to the bottom of the hill.

Notice that in the example, the money compounded for thirty years. It takes several decades for the complete effect of compounding to kick in. People who don't start investing for retirement until middle age don't have the full power of compounding working for them, and they must save much larger amounts each month to make up for the late start.

READING FOR REAL LIFE

Understanding Your 401(k) Choices

Having to learn investing in order to provide for one's retirement is a new system in the United States, and it is something of a headache, especially since we don't require that people learn personal finance skills in our public schools. In most other countries, people do not have to develop a knowledge of investing to provide money for their old age. Most other countries use one of two systems:

1. Everyone is taxed very heavily, and the government uses the funds to send enough money to retired persons that they can live comfortably.

2. You make sure to have many children and hope that one of them will be wealthy enough to care for you in old age. You plan on moving in with this child later.

Do you think that people in the United States should follow one of these systems? Why or why not?

PART II: TEST QUESTIONS

Directions: Using the split-page notes you created for "Understanding Your 401(k) Plan Choices," answer the following questions. Do not refer back to the original article.

_____1. In the early 1900s, everyone looked forward to retirement as a time when they would relax, travel, and enjoy spending time with their grandchildren.

  a. true

  b. false

_____2. During what decade was the Social Security system started?

  a. 1930s

  b. 1950s

  c. 1960s

  d. 1970s

_____3. Social Security benefits cover the full cost of living for retired persons.

  a. true

  b. false

_____4. All retired adults are entitled to some kind of retirement benefits from the government—either through Social Security or Supplementary Social Security.

   a. true

   b. false

_____5. On average, men receive a higher monthly Social Security benefit than women.

   a. true

   b. false

_____6. In 2006, the *average* monthly Social Security benefit to a retired individual was

   a. $302.

   b. $568.

   c. $1,044.

   d. $2,532.

_____7. Supplemental Social Security benefits are higher than Social Security benefits.

   a. true

   b. false

_____8. Supplementary Social Security is designed to help retired workers that don't qualify for Social Security benefits. What was the maximum *Supplemental Social Security* benefit for an individual in 2006?

   a. $302

   b. $470

   c. $603

   d. $1,433

_____9. What percentage of older single women live in poverty?

   a. 10%

   b. 20%

   c. 30%

   d. 40%

_____10. What are the two main reasons employers are less likely to offer pension benefits now than in the past?

   a. Greater worker mobility and increased life expectancy.

   b. Increased inflation and instability in the stock market.

    c. Competition from overseas and improved family resources.

    d. Improvements in Social Security and declines in worker loyalty.

_____11. A problem with 401(k) plans is that they require the employee to take responsibility for understanding the advantages and disadvantages of different kinds of investments.

    a. true

    b. false

_____12. In which kind of investment does the investor lend money to an organization in exchange for interest?

    a. stocks

    b. bonds

_____13. Which kind of bond fund would be made up of bonds from cities or states?

    a. corporate bond funds

    b. municipal bond funds

    c. U.S. government bond funds

    d. balanced funds

_____14. Which kind of bond fund contains both bonds and stocks?

    a. corporate bond funds

    b. U.S. government income funds

    c. global bond securities

    d. balanced funds

_____15. A person who buys a share of stock in Coca-Cola is a partial owner of the company.

    a. true

    b. false

_____16. What are the two ways that stockholders can make money?

    a. Through inflation or by purchasing the stock after its price drops.

    b. Through diversifying and selling stock after its price drops.

    c. Through dividends and by selling the stock after its price rises.

    d. Through deflation and getting interest payments on their shares.

____17. Which would be considered the riskiest kind of stock fund?

    a. aggressive growth

    b. large company funds

    c. growth and income funds

    d. index funds

____18. Which kind of stock fund buys the stocks of companies from a single industry such as computer technologies or health care?

    a. emerging market funds

    b. sector funds

    c. value funds

    d. growth funds

____19. Rolling over the profits you earn on investments to make more investments (instead of spending the money) is called

    a. compounding.

    b. return.

    c. dividends.

    d. hedging.

____20. People should start saving for retirement in middle age when their earning power is higher; this is not an issue that young adults need to worry about.

    a. true

    b. false

Preparing to Take Standardized Reading Tests

LEARNING GOALS

After completing this chapter, you should be able to:

- Understand how to handle items testing vocabulary skills.

- Manage test items assessing your knowledge of the organization of ideas.

- Deal with test items on the author's purpose, bias, tone, and evidence for opinions

It is likely that before entering your college program, you will be required to take a high-stakes standardized reading test. By "high stakes," I mean that the test has great importance; the results often determine whether or not you will be allowed to enter a program or continue to the next level. "Standardized" means that the same test is given to everyone, and it is easy to compare the performance of one student with another. ■

Examples of Standardized Reading Tests

Here are some examples of standardized, high-stakes tests that include reading comprehension sections:

GED	Students that pass this test are awarded the equivalent of a high school diploma.
ACT and SAT	These are the two most common exams given to students that are applying to college.
TOEFL	This test is given to international students desiring to study in U.S. colleges and universities. They take the test to demonstrate their competence in English.
College placement tests	Students are often given assessment tests when they apply to a college. The college uses the assessment test results to decide whether the student will be required to take preparatory reading, writing, or math classes before starting college-level coursework.

Additionally, students finishing preparatory work in college reading must often pass an exit exam that documents their readiness for the reading demands of college courses. Sometimes these exams are mandated by the state; at other times, they are required by individual reading and study skills departments.

Doing poorly on these exams means postponing your hopes of entering a program or profession and spending additional months preparing for a second attempt at passing the exam. Therefore, even though you may only have to take a standardized, high-stakes reading test a few times in your life, it is worthwhile to spend some time making sure you do well.

How to Do Well

The first thing to understand about standardized, high-stakes reading tests is that the greater the number of people that must take the test, the more likely the test is to be composed of multiple-choice questions. Although asking a student to create an outline of the key ideas in a passage is an excellent way to see how well the student understood the reading, evaluating the quality of the outlines is more time-consuming than scoring a multiple-choice test. Multiple-choice tests are often relied on when large numbers of students are sitting for the exam at the same time and they need a fast answer as to whether or not they passed the exam.

Second, high-stakes reading tests tend to follow similar formats. Students are given a passage to read, and then they are asked a series of comprehension questions about the meanings of words, the organization of ideas within the passage, important facts presented in the reading, the quality of the evidence offered for opinions, and the conclusions that can be drawn from the passage. Some tests include questions on reading and interpreting charts and graphs.

Third, practice is vitally important. Even if you have developed good basic college reading skills, you need to be familiar with the test you must take to document those skills. There are almost always sample exams available so that students can practice taking the test and can identify areas for review. Studies have shown that practice can substantially raise students' scores on reading exams, often making the difference between passing or failing the exam.

Fourth, work for speed as well as accuracy. High-stakes, standardized reading tests typically have time limits. When you practice, make sure that you allow yourself the same amount of time you will be given on the exam. Set a timer. The reason that many people do poorly on high-stakes reading tests is that they simply run out of time halfway through.

Finally, make sure that your mind is alert and you can do your best job on the day of the test. Take steps to reduce your stress levels, make sure you get enough sleep, and be sure to eat balanced meals in the days leading up to the exam.

Skills Review: Vocabulary Questions

Most standardized reading tests contain vocabulary questions. Typically, you will be given a word in a passage and asked to select its meaning. Here is an example:

> Businesses accumulate a lot of data. Sometimes businesses have so much data that they find it difficult to separate the anomalies from the trends. How do businesses manage to make meaning of all this data? They use a process known as data mining.

The word "anomalies" as it is used in this passage refers to something that is:

a. common; typical

b. unusual; not fitting a pattern

c. having to do with mining

d. profitable

Questions like this one test two kinds of vocabulary knowledge:

■ how many words you know

■ how well you can use context to guess word meanings

Obviously, if you know the word "anomalies," you can select the correct answer. However, you can also figure it out from the context if you know the meaning of "trend." Look at the phrase "separate the anomalies from the trends." An anomaly has to be different from a trend. If you know that a trend is a pattern, something that is happening in most cases, then you can see that the correct meaning of "anomalies" is choice b.

■ DOING WELL ON VOCABULARY ITEMS

Vocabulary Building. It is worthwhile to make a conscious effort to expand your vocabulary. One of the best ways to build your vocabulary is to read the newspaper every day. About 4 percent of the words in newspaper articles are the same as those that appear in college textbooks and on vocabulary tests for adults. If you read articles that use these words, eventually they will become part of your vocabulary. However, vocabulary building is a long-term project; there is no quick way to learn all the words that might appear on a standardized reading test.

Sharpening Awareness of Context. Vocabulary items on standardized tests don't just measure how many words you know. Many also assess your ability to use surrounding words to guess what a word might mean. Sharpening your sensitivity to context is something that can be done in a short time, and you should review this skill before taking a high-stakes reading test.

When you are asked for the meaning of a word you don't know, try this. Cover up the word itself. Then read through the passage, asking yourself what idea belongs in that place.

SKILLS PRACTICE 1

Read the following paragraph and see if you can figure out the meanings of the underlined words. Don't look at the words themselves. Cover them up and let your mind fill in a word that would make sense.

Technology is being used to <u>thwart</u> graffiti artists. A company called Traptec has <u>pioneered</u> a graffiti detection system called Taggertrap. When the Taggertrap system detects the telltale sound of a spray can being used, the system alerts the police by cell phone and uses miniature cameras to record the crime in progress.

<u>thwart</u> probably means something like _____
<u>pioneered</u> probably means something like _____

■ WATCH OUT FOR COMMON WORDS WITH MORE THAN ONE MEANING

It's important to use this technique even on words that look familiar because common words often have more than one meaning. Suppose that you see this sentence:

It is often difficult for young people to appreciate what daily life was like before telephones, television, and computers were invented.

In this sentence, the word "appreciate" means

a. to be grateful.

b. to increase in value.

c. to understand.

The most common meaning of "appreciate" is "to be grateful." However, that is not what it means in this sentence. Try covering up the word "appreciate." Which of the three meanings makes the most sense? You can see that it is the last one—to understand.

PRACTICE PASSAGE 9.1: COMPUTER TECHNOLOGY

Read the following passage, and see if you can figure out the meanings of the underlined words. Don't look at the words themselves. Cover them up and let your mind fill in a word that would make sense.

 # Biomedical Chip Implants: Combining Humans with Machines?

1   The goals of modern-day biomedical chip research are to provide technological solutions to physical problems and to provide a <u>means</u> for <u>positively</u> identifying individuals.

    One potential application of biomedical chip implants is to provide sight to
5   the blind. Macular degeneration and retinitis pigmentosa are two diseases that account for the majority of blindness in developing nations. Both diseases result in damage to the photoreceptors contained in the retina of the eye. (Photoreceptors <u>convert</u> light energy into electrical energy that is transmitted to the brain, allowing us to see.) Researchers are experimenting with chips
10 that contain microscopic solar cells and are implanted in the damaged retina of patients. The idea is to have the chip take over for the damaged photoreceptors and transmit electrical images to the brain. Although these chips have been tested in patients, they have not yet restored anyone's sight. But uses of biomedical chips such as these are <u>illustrative</u> of the type of
15 medical devices you may see in the future.

    One form of biomedical chip already entering the market is a technology that can be used to <u>verify</u> a person's identity. Called the VeriChip, this "personal ID chip" is being marketed by a company called Applied Digital Solutions. VeriChips, about the size of a grain of rice, are <u>implanted</u> under the skin (Figure 9.1).
20 When exposed to radio waves from a scanning device, the chip <u>emits</u> a signal that transmits its unique serial number to the scanner. The scanner then connects to a database that contains the name, address, and serious medical conditions of the person in whom the chip has been implanted.

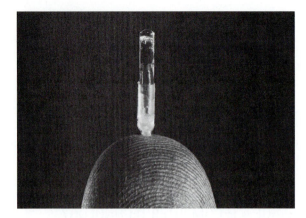

FIGURE 9.1 ■ *The VeriChip is a small device implanted directly under the skin. A special scanner is then able to read the information stored on it.* Source: Photograph by Sarah Leen. Courtesy of National Geographic Image Collection.

25 The company <u>envisions</u> the VeriChip speeding up airport security and being used together with other devices (such as electronic ID cards) to provide tamperproof security measures. If someone stole your credit card, that person couldn't use it if a salesclerk verifies your identity by scanning a chip before <u>authorizing</u> a transaction. Chips could eventually be developed so that they contain a <u>vast</u> wealth of information about the person in whom they are
30 implanted. However, it remains to be seen whether the general public will accept having personal data implanted into their bodies.

Source: Adapted from Alan Evans, Kendall Martin, and Mary Anne Poatsy, *Technology in Action,* 2nd edition (Upper Saddle River, NJ: Prentice Hall, 2005), 16–17. Reprinted by permission of Prentice Hall, Inc.

READING FOR REAL LIFE

Biomedical Chip Implants

Would you agree to have a chip implanted under your skin if it reduced your chances of being a victim of financial fraud? Improved the medical care you received? Sped you through airport security?

_____1. The word "means" (line 2) refers to

  a. money or other resources.

  b. a method.

  c. unpleasantnesses.

  d. a period of time.

_____2. In this passage, the word "positively" (line 3) refers to something that is

   a. certain, not in doubt.

   b. confident and cheerful.

   c. in agreement.

   d. final.

_____3. The word "convert" (line 8) means

   a. to adopt new opinions.

   b. to change.

   c. to reverse.

   d. to calculate.

_____4. The word "illustrative" (line 14) means

   a. having to do with drawing.

   b. expensive.

   c. experimental.

   d. an example.

_____5. "Verify" (line 17) refers to

   a. duplicate.

   b. check for truthfulness or accuracy.

   c. eradicate; wipe out.

   d. enhance; improve.

6. The word "implanted" (line 19) means

   a. placed.

   b. removed from.

   c. broken; destroyed.

   d. subjected to stress.

_____7. "Emits" (line 20) means

   a. stops.

   b. sends.

   c. copies.

   d. renders inaudible.

_____8. The word "envisions" (line 24) means

 a. imagining something to be possible.

 b. speeding up an action.

 c. slowing down a process.

 d. checking carefully.

_____9. The word "authorizing" (line 28) refers to

 a. refusing; declining an action.

 b. approving an action.

 c. having power.

 d. writing a text.

_____10. "Vast" (line 29) means

 a. small; limited.

 b. incorrect; unreliable.

 c. impressively large.

 d. having to do with money.

Skills Review: Organization of Ideas

Reading tests also typically assess your awareness of the organization of ideas in a text. For instance, you may be asked to select the main idea of a paragraph or identify the academic thought pattern that a portion of the text follows. You learned these skills in Chapters 2 and 3.

Many questions ask about details that were presented in the passage. These kinds of questions also test your awareness of the organization of ideas. For instance, suppose that you are reading a passage on types of blood vessels. The first paragraph is on capillaries, the second focuses on veins, and the third is centered on arteries. Let's say you are asked this question: "What is the name of the largest artery in the body?" If you were aware of the focus of each paragraph as you read, you could zip back quickly to the third paragraph without wasting time reading from the beginning. Remember that high-stakes, standardized tests are timed. You must be fast. Saving time by noticing the organization of ideas in texts can make the difference between passing or failing a standardized reading test.

If you are taking a paper-and-pencil version of the test and you can quickly mark the topics of paragraphs as you go, doing so will help you find information without having to re-read the entire passage. Even if you are taking the test on a computer and can't annotate the passage, make a special effort to notice the layout of ideas as you read.

PRACTICE PASSAGE 9.2: INTERIOR DESIGN

As you read through the following passage on the physiological effects of color, circle or write in the topic of each paragraph. Be very fast—select just a few words that express the focus of that paragraph. Then answer the questions that follow.

Physiological Effects of Color

1   Mystics have long held that we emanate a colored glow, or aura. Some feel that its presence has been verified by Kirlian photography, a special process for capturing the usually invisible energies that radiate from plants and animals. The color of the aura, as seen by clairvoyants, is thought to reflect
5   the state of a person's health and spirituality. According to the mystic Corinne Heline, gold is the auric color of spiritual illumination, clear blue or lavender indicates a high spiritual development, orange a predominantly intellectual nature, clear green a sympathetic nature, and pure carmine or rose-red an unselfish, affectionate quality. Duller colors are associated with
10   materialistic, fearful, or selfish qualities. A dark grey aura with brown and red in it accompanies depression.

According to physiological research with the effects of colored lights, red wavelengths stimulate the heart, the circulation, and the adrenal glands, increasing strength and stamina. Pink has a more gently stimulating quality
15   and helps muscles to relax. Orange wavelengths stimulate the solar plexus, the immune system, the lungs, and the pancreas, and benefit the digestive system. Yellow light is stimulating for the brain and nervous system, bringing mental alertness and activating the nerves in the muscles. Green lights affect the heart, balance the circulation, and promote relaxation and healing of
20   disorders such as colds, hay fever and liver problems. Blue wavelengths affect the throat and thyroid gland, bring cooling and soothing effects, and lower blood pressure. Deep blue lessens pain. Blue-green light helps to decrease infections, soothe jangled nerves, and correct weakness in the immune system. Indigo light helps to counteract skin problems and fevers.
25   Violet light affects the brain, has purifying, antiseptic, and cooling effects, balances the metabolism, and seems to suppress hunger.

Given these apparent physiological effects of colored lights, there is a science of healing with colors, or chromotherapy. People are bathed with colored lights, placed in colored environments, or asked to meditate on specific colors
30   thought to stimulate particular glands. This form of treatment dates back thousands of years to the "color halls" of the ancient Egyptians, Chinese, and Indians. Although color healing has remained largely an occult science, chromotherapy is being taught in some nursing schools and alternative medical centers, and the medical profession as a whole makes use of color in

35   certain treatments. For example, premature babies with jaundice are cured by exposure to blue light.

A more prominent use of color therapy occurs in interior design. Psychological literature is full of attempts to determine how specific colors affect human health and behavior and how best to put the results into effect.
40   Bright colors, particularly warm hues, seem conducive to activity and mental alertness and are therefore increasingly being used in schools. Cooler, duller hues, on the other hand, tend to sedate. Henner Ertel studied the effects of environmental color among schoolchildren in Munich. The interior design colors with the most positive intellectual effects in Ertel's study were yellow,
45   yellow-green, orange, and light blue. Surrounded by these colors, children's IQ scores rose up to 12 points. In white, brown, and black environments, IQ scores fell. In addition, Ertel found that an orange environment made the children more cheerful and sociable and less irritable and hostile.

In some institutional situations, a calming environment is beneficial. In a
50   study conducted by Harry Wohlfarth and Catharine Sam of the University of Alberta, the color environment of 14 severely handicapped and behaviorally disordered eight-year-olds was radically altered. It was changed from a white fluorescent-lit classroom with bright orange carpeting and orange, yellow, and white colored walls and shelves to one with full-spectrum fluorescent lighting
55   and brown and blue walls and shelves. The children's aggressive behavior diminished and their blood pressure dropped. As one nurse reported:

> I found the children and myself considerably more relaxed in the new room. The afternoons seemed less hectic and instead of running out of time for our activity, we ran out of activities. I also found at lunch I
60   > was more relaxed and was able to eat something without feeling sick . . . . The noise level really went down in the Phase II room, which seemed to keep everyone from getting upset as the day went on.

When the environment was then experimentally changed back to the way it had been before, aggressive behavior and blood pressure returned to their
65   previous levels.

Interestingly, the same effects were found in both blind and sighted children in Wohlfarth and Sam's study, suggesting that we are affected by color energies in ways that transcend seeing. One hypothesis is that neurotransmitters in the eye transmit information about light to the brain even
70   in the absence of sight, and that this information releases a hormone in the hypothalamus that has numerous effects on our moods, mental clarity, and energy level.

The legendary Notre Dame football coach Knute Rockne attempted to use awareness of the physiological effects of colors competitively. To stir up his
75   own players, he painted their locker room red. He had the visiting team's locker room painted in blue-greens, thus sedating them both before the game and when they returned to relax at half-time.

80 Similarly, the influence of environmental color was demonstrated in one factory where workers were complaining about feeling cold. Rather than raise the thermostat, management decided to paint the blue-green walls coral. The complaints stopped.

85 Lest we hasten to repaint everything in attempts at behavior modification, we should note that physiological color responses are complex. The precise variation of a hue has a major impact, but one that is rarely addressed by psychological research. One shade of pink may be calming while another can be stimulating. Although mystics find certain blue-violets conducive to a very high spiritual state, a group of college students said that a blue-violet they were shown made them feel sad and tired. These same students found that a color described as "cool green" made them feel angry and confused.

90 Furthermore, initial responses to a color environment may be reversed over time as our body adjusts to the new stimulus. It is known that some time after blood pressure is raised by red light it drops below normal level; after blood pressure is lowered by blue light, it eventually rises to a higher-than-normal level.

Source: Adapted from Paul Zelanski and Mary Pat Fisher, *Color,* 4th edition (Upper Saddle River, NJ: Prentice Hall, 2003), 36–39. Reprinted with permission of Prentice Hall, Inc.

_____1. The implied relationship (academic thought pattern) expressed in lines 27–29 is best described as

a. time order.

b. comparison.

c. definition.

d. spatial order.

_____2. Color has been used to improve the mental alertness of children in school. In the study conducted by Henner Ertel, how much did changing the color of the classroom to warm colors cause children's IQ scores to rise?

a. None—the study found no measurable difference.

b. 4 points

c. 12 points

d. 18 points

_____3. Blind children are not affected by the color of their environment.

a. true

b. false

_____4. The implied relationship (academic thought pattern) expressed in the sentences of paragraph 2 (lines 12–26) is

a. cause and effect.

b. time order.

c. spatial order.

d. definition.

_____5. According to the passage, color can be used to promote a feeling of calm and reduce aggressive behavior in children. In the study by Wolfarth and Sam, which colors were used to relax children with behavior problems?

a. blue and brown

b. orange and yellow

c. shades of green

d. gray and violet

_____6. The implied main idea of paragraph 10 (lines 78–81) is that

a. management did not want to spend money by raising the thermostat.

b. employees were imagining that they felt cold.

c. the color of an environment can make people feel warmer or cooler.

d. painting the walls blue makes workers less productive.

_____7. The main idea of the last paragraph (lines 90–94) is that

a. some physiological responses to color may be only temporary.

b. red raises blood pressure.

c. color can be used to change blood pressure.

d. blue lowers blood pressure.

_____8. According to the passage, the aura of a person who has an affection-ate, unselfish nature is

a. rose-red.

b. light green.

c. deep blue-violet.

d. pale yellow.

_____9. The main idea of paragraph 11 (lines 82–89) is that

a. there are many shades of pink.

b. variations of the same color may cause different effects.

c. young adults do not perceive color the way others do.

d. everyone is affected differently by color; it is completely individualistic.

_____10. In experiments with colored lights, which color was found to lessen pain?

a. deep blue

b. violet

c. blue-green

d. orange

Skills Review: Author's Purpose, Bias, and Support for Opinions

Reading comprehension questions also commonly include items related to the quality of support for opinions. To do well on these questions, make sure you remember what is meant by the terms *bias, fact, opinion, justified,* and *unjustified.*

We say that an author is biased if he or she does not have a neutral position on an issue. Bias is often revealed through tone. For example, if an author is opposed to state-sponsored gambling, then he or she may use words that sound negative when referring to the state lotteries.

You should also review the difference between a fact and an opinion. Remember that a fact is checkable; it can be verified by looking at records or interviewing witnesses. "Over half of all high school graduates enroll in college" is an example of a fact. Just because you think a statement is true does not make it a fact. A fact doesn't have to be correct; it just has to be checkable. A fact that is untrue is an incorrect fact, not an opinion.

Opinions cannot be directly verified by checking records in such a way as to end all debate. "Everyone should have some education beyond high school if at all possible" is an example of an opinion. Also, recall that opinions should be backed by factual evidence. If they are, we say that they are justified. If no factual support is given, we say the opinion is not justified.

PRACTICE PASSAGE 9.3: CRIMINAL JUSTICE

Read through the passage entitled "Drug Use and Drug Abuse." Then answer the comprehension questions related to the author's bias and the support for his opinion.

Drug Use and Drug Abuse

[1] It is important to keep in mind the clear distinction between drug use and drug abuse. Drug use is generally understood as any consumption of a drug, including recreational or occasional use. Drug abuse implies a problematic level of use, or overuse, of drugs. Lyman and Potter (1998) define drug abuse
[5] as "illicit drug use that results in social, economic, psychological or legal problems for the drug user." They also note that the Bureau of Justice Statistics defines drug abuse as "the use of prescription-type psychotherapeutic drugs for nonmedical purposes or the use of illegal drugs."

Drug use, even of illegal substances, is not the same as drug abuse. It is
[10] possible to use illegal drugs without abusing them, although this is a lesson that seems to be lost on the criminal justice agencies. We treat drug use as a crime rather than a recreational habit and do not recognize that most people who use drugs do not abuse them. Most drug-related arrests are for simple possession, not for manufacturing, distributing, or selling drugs (Beckett and
[15] Sasson, 2000).

Drug abuse varies by individual: "Abuse occurs when the use of the drug—whether aspirin, beer, caffeine, cigarettes, marijuana, diet pills, or heroin—becomes a psychological, social, or physical problem for the user" (Gaines and Kraska, 1997). Only a small portion of drug users, somewhere between
[20] 7% and 20%, depending on the type of drug in question, actually become drug abusers (Kraska, 1990). In fact, depending on one's definition of a drug, we all use drugs as part of our everyday lives: "Some form of drug use is an everyday part of living for most Americans" (Lyman and Potter, 1998).

Drugs are useful because they can alter our moods, create feelings of pleasure,
[25] stimulate brain activity, or aid in sedation or enhanced physical and psychological performance (Lyman and Potter, 1998). Some suggest that drug use is innate or natural, as much as the need for food or sex. Weil (1998) writes "The use of drugs to alter consciousness is nothing new. It has been a feature of human life in all places on the earth and in all ages of history."
[30] Hamid (1998) suggests that "the human use of psychoactive drugs is both primordial and nearly universal. In almost every human culture in every age of history, the use of one or more psychoactive drugs was featured prominently in the contexts of religion, ritual, health care, divination, celebration (including the arts, music and theater), recreation, and cuisine."
[35] People use drugs in certain rituals in groups, such as during "Happy Hour" or at parties with friends. People may use drugs to relieve boredom (Glassner and Loughlin, 1987), to alter their moods, to inspire creativity, and sometimes for medicinal and religious purposes.

For numerous reasons, then, people use drugs without experiencing
[40] significant problems associated with drug abuse. This does not mean that drug use should be promoted or supported by government, but it does raise

the question of why we spend so many physical and financial resources fighting something that is considered normal by most people at some point in their lives, is relatively harmless, and is not likely to be stopped through
45 criminal justice mechanisms. I would argue that drug abuse (which is only a small portion of all drug use) should be of concern to our government because of its possible outcomes, regardless of whether the drug being abused is legal.

Source: Adapted from Matthew B. Robinson, *Justice Blind?*, 2nd edition (Upper Saddle River, NJ: Prentice Hall, 2004), 318–19. Used with permission of Prentice Hall, Inc.

_____1. The author's primary purpose in this passage is to

   a. defend the current drug laws.

   b. persuade us that drug use is not the same as drug abuse.

   c. trace the history of the use of drugs in the United States.

   d. argue that many drug users go on to become drug abusers.

_____2. In this passage, the author expresses a biased attitude against

   a. government efforts to stop illegal drug use.

   b. people who use illegal drugs.

   c. the tendency of doctors to overprescribe drugs.

   d. use of drugs in religious rituals.

_____3. In this passage, the author expresses a biased attitude in favor of

   a. avoiding the use of all drugs, whether legal or illegal.

   b. increasing drug use prevention efforts in public schools.

   c. use of illegal drugs as long as they are used responsibly.

   d. making the sale of alcohol illegal, since it is often abused.

_____4. The author's tone in this passage can best be described as

   a. worried and pessimistic.

   b. sarcastic and insulting.

   c. playful and humorous.

   d. neutral and straightforward.

_____5. The assertion "Most drug-related arrests are for simple possession, not for manufacturing, distributing, or selling drugs" (lines 13–14) is a statement of

   a. fact.

   b. opinion.

_____**6.** The claim that "drug use is innate or natural, as much as the need for food or sex" (lines 26–27) is a statement of

a. fact.

b. opinion.

_____**7.** The statement that drug abuse is commonly understood to include "a problematic level of use, or overuse, of drugs" (lines 3–4) is

a. adequately supported by factual evidence and respected sources.

b. inadequately supported because of lack of factual evidence.

_____**8.** The statement that "Depending on one's definition of a drug, we all use drugs as part of our everyday lives" (lines 21–22) is

a. adequately supported by factual evidence and studies.

b. inadequately supported by facts.

_____**9.** It could be inferred that this author would support which of the following actions?

a. Increased funding for the government's War on Drugs program.

b. Teaching children that drug use is bad.

c. Legalizing the use of many drugs that are currently illegal.

d. Banning the use of alcohol.

_____**10.** A conclusion that can be drawn from this passage is that

a. drug abuse is always bad, whether the drug is legal or illegal.

b. the government should not try to prevent drug abuse.

c. some legal drugs, such as nicotine, should be made illegal.

d. all religious ceremonies should include the use of drugs.

Putting It All Together

The practice sets that follow have a mix of the three common kinds of questions: vocabulary items, questions that test awareness of the organization of ideas, and questions on bias and evidence for opinions.

- Circle a phrase that expresses the topic of each paragraph as you read through the passage. Alternately, you might jot down the topic of each paragraph to the side.

- If you are asked about the meaning of a particular word, try covering up the target word and letting your mind fill in the idea that is called for to complete the thought.

PRACTICE PASSAGE 9.4: ELECTRONIC PUBLISHING

Planning a Website

1 There are many things that all come together on a website. However, even
after you learn all the code, the different ways of preparing images, and
perhaps even some JavaScript, the most important considerations come before
you sit down at the computer. A website usually contains a series of inter-linked
5 pages, each of which covers part of the particular content you wish to present.
The first questions asked should not deal with HTML code, but with the nature
of the site itself.

As in any multimedia production, before you begin you should ask several
important questions: Who is your audience? What do you wish to convey?
10 What ideas do you have for the "look" of the page—the format of the basic
design? While the Web does have its own special properties, you are still
designing space that must not only make sense and be visually appealing, but
must also convey the content (what the site is about) clearly and coherently
with a minimum of distraction. A site for "John Smith—Party Clown" would
15 not have the same look and feel as one for "John Smith: Corporate Law."

All of the skills that a graphic designer brings to print publication—selection,
size and spacing of type; use of graphics and photographs; judicious use of
color; and so on—apply to designing for the Web. Many students interested in
Web design feel they should spend most of their time learning the latest in
20 HTML code, JavaScript, and other Web languages. However, even the best
HTML skills will be wasted if the underlying design is poor and navigational
elements are difficult to use. Strong design skills still go a long way and are
absolutely the best preparation for Web design.

That said, consider the site's content. Who is actually going to write the
25 information that will appear on the website? Clear, cogent writing that gets to
the point quickly and without obvious errors in the use of language says
something about the professionalism of the site you prepare. If you don't like
to write, find someone who does. Many websites are the result of a
collaboration between visual artists, writers, photographers, and technology
30 experts.

The website interface is the next issue to consider. Once your content is
clearly delineated, it makes sense to plan the various ways in which that
information can be presented within the website. As already mentioned, a
website is usually composed of inter-linked pages, each of which contains
35 some portion of the information you wish to present. Based on the content of
the page, how should the information be accessed? Usually there is a home or
opening page, often referred to by professionals as the index page, which
introduces the site and offers links to additional information/pages on the

40 site. Because this is an HTML page, items will be linked to other information on later pages. However, once again there are questions to be addressed before jumping into the coding of the page.

45 One of these considerations relates to page size. Different size monitors, while able to display various screen resolutions, have a default resolution for their relative size. A 14-inch monitor's screen resolution is 640 × 480 pixels, while a 17-inch monitor has a default screen resolution of 1,024 × 768 pixels. When designing a website, a decision has to be made to design for a particular screen size and its pixel dimensions. In the past, designers automatically designed for 14-inch monitors because they were used by the majority of viewers. Evolving technology has changed that. Many people are now using 50 a 15-inch, 17-inch or larger monitor. Again, you must consider the purpose of your site when making the decision to design for a particular screen size. A site designed for the 800 × 600 pixel size of a 15-inch monitor may look smaller on a 17-inch monitor, but it will display just fine. A site designed for the 1,280 × 1,024 pixel size of a 19-inch monitor will require someone with a 55 smaller monitor to scroll from side to side to see the entire page, resulting in viewer frustration and perhaps loss of interest in your content.

The next issue to consider is navigation. Once you have made a few of the decisions previously outlined, it often helps to draw out a schematic of the site you wish to create. This can be a simple series of boxes that indicates the 60 "flow" of information on the website and how you intend to get from one place to another. This flowchart, outlining how information is to be connected, can indicate when a website might be too "deep." In other words, users may have to click and click from one page to another to another and so on, making it difficult for someone to backtrack to an earlier page. However, 65 a site that is too shallow, with one page leading to a series of parallel pages, might not offer the depth of information necessary. Planning at this step is crucially important to creating a good site.

The schematic you prepare in planning your website will not only provide a clear sense of how information on one page will lead to another, but also a 70 clear outline of the kinds of navigational elements that should be included on the page. Getting from one page to another and back again, without confusion, is an important element of Web design. If your pages are longer than a single screen, it makes sense to include navigational controls both at the top and bottom of the page. If your page is complex enough to require 75 many pages of information, it is important to include navigational aids beyond the browser's back button. For example, in addition to clickable buttons that can move you backward and forward on the site, there should also be a button that will take you home to the main or index page of the site.

Source: Adapted from Richard Lewis and James Luciana, *Digital Media: An Introduction* (Upper Saddle River, NJ: Prentice Hall, 2005), 274–77. Reprinted by permission of Prentice Hall, Inc.

_____1. The author's primary purpose in this passage is to

    a. explain important first steps in designing a website.

    b. argue that technical expertise is more important than skills in design.

    c. describe the HTML codes used to create websites.

    d. trace changes in the size of monitors over the years.

_____2. The word "convey" (line 9) means

    a. communicate.

    b. carry or move.

    c. put into computer code.

    d. design.

_____3. In discussing the training of future website developers (paragraph 3, lines 16–23), the author expresses a bias

    a. against spending much time on graphic arts/design training.

    b. against learning HTML and JavaScript.

    c. in favor of learning as much about design as possible.

    d. in favor of emphasizing coding techniques over design.

_____4. The word "cogent" (line 25) means

    a. spelled correctly.

    b. persuasive; convincing.

    c. confusing; unclear.

    d. similar to.

_____5. The home page is also called the

    a. interface page.

    b. navigation page.

    c. screen page.

    d. index page.

_____6. Pixels and resolution are issues in

    a. interface design.

    b. navigation.

    c. screen size.

    d. using HTML or JavaScript for coding.

_____7. The word "delineated" (line 32) means

    a. set aside; put off until a later time.

    b. arranged in a line.

    c. described; outlined.

    d. reduced or eliminated.

_____**8.** In lines 63–64, we read that a website is hard to use if, in order to find the information they need, people "have to click and click from one page to another to another and so on, making it difficult for someone to backtrack to an earlier page." Another way of describing this problem is to say that

    a. the website is too shallow.

    b. the website is too deep.

    c. there is a problem with screen size.

    d. there is an error in the code.

_____**9.** The word "element" (line 72) means

    a. part.

    b. small amount.

    c. cause or factor.

    d. substance that can't be broken down.

_____**10.** A conclusion that could be drawn from the author's discussion of screen size (lines 42–56) is that

    a. it is better to design for a slightly smaller monitor than a larger one.

    b. it is better to design for a slightly larger monitor than a smaller one.

    c. designers should assume all users will have a 14-inch monitor.

    d. monitor size doesn't matter because the pages will automatically expand or shrink to fit the user's monitor.

PRACTICE PASSAGE 9.5: BUSINESS LAW

Joe Camel Exhales

1 From his introduction in 1988, Joe Camel was a cartoon icon. R.J. Reynolds Tobacco Company splashed the cool camel on billboards, in magazines, and in other media across the country. Joe Camel could be seen riding motorcycles, playing pool, jamming with a jazz band, and hanging out with
5 his female comrade, Josephine Camel. Joe and his buddies were used to promote R.J. Reynold's Camel cigarettes.

Why would a cigarette company choose a cartoon character to advertise its cigarettes? In December 1991, San Francisco attorney Janet Mangini thought she knew when she read results of three studies that were published by the
10 *Journal of the American Medical Association (JAMA).* These studies concluded that the popularity of Camel cigarettes had increased 66-fold with teen smokers in the three years following the introduction of Joe Camel. Joe Camel was right up there with Mickey Mouse in recognition by children. Mangini concluded that R.J. Reynolds had gone after children and teens to
15 promote cigarette smoking, so she decided to go after Joe Camel.

But how do you successfully sue a monolith like R.J. Reynolds? Mangini enlisted the lawyers at the five-attorney firm of Bushnell, Caplan & Fielding in San Francisco to help brainstorm the attack on R.J. Reynolds. They were aware that traditional personal injury lawsuits against cigarette companies had
20 not been successful, so they turned to California Business and Professional Code Section 17200 et seq., also known as the Unfair Business Practices Act. This act permits any individual to act as a private attorney general for the state of California and to file a suit against a company to halt a harmful or unfair business practice.

25 Mangini and the small law firm knew they were in over their heads in taking on R.J. Reynolds, so they sought the help of Milberg Weiss, a large law firm in San Diego known for filing shareholder class-action lawsuits. Patrick J. Coughlin, a partner at the firm whose father was a smoker who had died of lung cancer, became interested. Milberg Weiss joined the team and agreed to
30 shoulder 80 percent of the work. Mangini became the plaintiff. The law firms filed an unfair business practice lawsuit against R.J. Reynolds to try to eliminate Joe Camel and his cohorts.

R.J. Reynolds's first action was to try to get the case thrown out of court. The company argued that Joe Camel was protected by the freedom of speech
35 clause of the First Amendment of the U.S. Constitution and that the state law claims were preempted by the Federal Cigarette Labeling and Advertising Act, the act that requires warnings on cigarette packages. The trial court threw the case out of court, but the California Supreme Court reinstated the case, stating

40   *The targeting of minors is oppressive and unscrupulous, in that it exploits minors by luring them into an unhealthy and potentially life-threatening addiction before they have achieved the maturity necessary to make an informed decision whether to take up smoking despite its health risks.*

45 R.J. Reynolds appealed to the U.S. Supreme Court, which declined to hear the case. With the courtroom door finally open, the real work began. The plaintiff's attorneys reviewed more than 30 million pages of documents over a five-year period. The evidence showed that R.J. Reynolds's advertising was aimed at the "youth market." Company reports outlined the importance of

50 attracting "presmokers," aged 12 to 24, and stated that "young adult smokers are the only source of replacement smokers." R.J. Reynolds's market research reports: "Less than one third of smokers start after age 18. Only 5 percent of smokers start after age 24."

Twenty states, the U.S. Surgeon General, the American Lung Association, the 55 American Cancer Society, and the American Heart Association backed Mangini's claim against R.J. Reynolds. Eventually, the parties entered into settlement negotiations. The plaintiff and her lawyers agreed that there was no amount of money they would accept to settle the case; Joe Camel must go! With mounting pressure and facing trial, in July 1997, R.J. Reynolds formally 60 agreed to terminate the Joe Camel campaign across the nation.

Source: Adapted from Henry R. Cheeseman, *The Legal Environment of Business and Online Commerce,* 4th edition (Upper Saddle River, NJ: Prentice Hall, 2004). Reprinted by permission of Prentice Hall, Inc.

_____1. The author's purpose in this passage is to

    a. criticize tobacco companies for marketing to minors.

    b. describe the events that led up to the end of the Joe Camel advertising campaign.

    c. praise the U.S. Supreme Court for protecting the health of children.

    d. list all the groups that are opposed to the actions of tobacco companies.

_____2. Overall, which academic thought pattern does the relationship of the ideas in this passage follow?

    a. history; time order

    b. spatial order

    c. comparison

    d. simple listing

_____3. The word "icon" (line 1) means

    a. object used in worship.

    b. something widely recognized.

    c. small image on a computer screen.

    d. an animal.

_____4. The implied main idea of paragraph 2 (lines 7–15) is that

    a. it is questionable whether R.J. Reynolds' ads targeted children.

    b. the AMA was interested in the attitudes of children toward smoking.

     c. attorney Janet Mangini decided to go after R.J. Reynolds after reading research that convinced her they were deliberately targeting children.

     d. attorney Janet Mangini specializes in smoking-related litigation.

_____**5.** The word "monolith" (line 16) means

     a. a tall structure made of stone, like a monument.

     b. a huge and long-established organization.

     c. an isolated and vulnerable group.

     d. a group organized for the public good.

_____**6.** The statement "R.J. Reynolds's market research reports: 'Less than one third of smokers start after age 18. Only 5 percent of smokers start after age 24'" (lines 51–53) is

     a. a fact.

     b. an opinion.

_____**7.** The assertion that R.J. Reynolds was deliberately targeting the youth market was

     a. justified by facts and studies.

     b. not justified by factual evidence.

_____**8.** The opinion of the California Supreme Court (lines 40–44) was biased

     a. in favor of the free speech rights of tobacco companies.

     b. against the practice of directing cigarette ads at children and teens.

     c. in favor of of allowing young people to make up their own minds.

     d. in favor of banning all tobacco sales.

_____**9.** Mangini sued R.J. Reynolds under the

     a. freedom of speech clause of the First Amendment.

     b. Federal Cigarette Labeling and Advertising Act.

     c. Unfair Business Practices Act.

     d. U.S. Surgeon General's Report.

_____**10.** The word "terminate" (line 60) means

     a. stop.

     b. continue.

     c. lessen or reduce.

     d. increase.

PRACTICE PASSAGE 9.6: CHILD DEVELOPMENT

Superhero Play

1   Rough-and-tumble play and superhero play are closely related. Indeed, teachers often fail to notice any difference between the two because super-hero play is often a part of rough-and-tumble play. Rough-and-tumble play has been characterized as "friendly chasing and playfighting" (Berk, 1996). It may also

5   entail hitting and wrestling, but it is significantly different from real fighting. Jones (1976) described seven movement patterns that tended to occur in this type of play: "These are running, chasing, and fleeing; wrestling; jumping up and down with both feet together . . . ; beating at each other with an object but not hitting; laughing." A major difference between real fighting and rough-and-tumble

10   play is the fact that children are laughing and smiling as they play. An important distinction between rough-and-tumble play and superhero play is that superhero play will include rough-and-tumble play while rough-and-tumble play can occur without superhero play.

Superhero play is the result of television programming for young children. As

15   children reflect their favorite programs in their dramatic play, superhero play results. Boyd (1997) defines superhero play as follows: "Superhero play refers to the active, physical play of children pretending to be media characters imbued with extraordinary abilities, including superhuman strength or the ability to transform themselves into superhuman entities."

20   Superhero play appeals particularly to boys for several reasons. First, it permits young boys to engage in running, wrestling, jumping, and shouting that are characteristic of rough-and-tumble play. Second, superheroes possess powers children wish they had; they can feel that they are strong and powerful when they engage in superhero roles. Third, preschool boys are attracted to

25   superhero play because they can pit good against evil and play roles that are always "good" (Bauer & Dettore, 1997).

As is the case with rough-and-tumble play, teachers commonly ban superhero play in their classrooms and on the playground. They might be concerned about the violent content, viewing it as aggressive and frightening as well as

30   bizarre (Carlsson-Paige & Levin, 1995). As is the case of rough-and-tumble play, they are concerned that children can get hurt when the play gets out of control and because it can escalate into noisy and chaotic play (Bauer & Dettore, 1997).

Part of the concern about superhero play is the perception that it is escalating.

35   There is little concrete evidence, however, that this is so. Boyd (1997) asserts that much of the data used to support the increase is based on anecdotal reports and may include a lack of objectivity on the part of teachers.

40 Furthermore, teachers describe superhero play as characterized by fighting, martial arts moves, and kicking. These play behaviors are reportedly the main source of teachers' concerns (Bergen, 1994; Carlsson-Paige & Levin, 1995). Teachers also make a connection between preschool play and later membership in adolescent gangs (Boyd, 1997).

45 Superhero play actually offers benefits, again similar to benefits of rough-and-tumble play. First, superhero play is engaged in by friends, thus promoting friendships between children. Second, children can use superhero play to elevate their status within the group. They select players similar in strength or choose a slightly stronger partner (Smith & Boulton, 1990).

50 Banning superhero play can have negative results. Undesirable behaviors that can result when teachers ban superhero play include children feeling guilty about engaging in superhero play or learning to be deceptive when engaging in superhero play. They can fear talking to adults about their interests in superhero play (Carlsson-Paige & Levin, 1990). Teachers send the message that such play is wrong for them, as is being interested in some of the values such as good and evil that are part of superhero themes (Boyd, 1997).

55 Teachers also lose opportunities to incorporate superhero characters as a positive influence in children's development and learning (Bauer & Dettore, 1997). Carlsson-Paige & Levin (1995) suggest to teachers that superheroes can be used to instill positive behaviors in children if they are used as a motivational tool.

Source: Adapted from Joe L. Frost, Sue C. Wortham, and Stuart Reifel, *Play and Child Development,* 2nd edition (Upper Saddle River, NJ: Prentice Hall, 2004), 145–47. Reprinted by permission of Prentice Hall, Inc.

_____1. The author's primary purpose in this passage is to

   a. put to rest teachers' concerns about superhero play and explain its benefits.

   b. explain why superhero play is inferior to rough-and-tumble play.

   c. encourage teachers to ban superhero play on the play-ground.

   d. trace the history of superhero play in the United States.

_____2. In the passage, we read "Rough-and-tumble play has been characterized as 'friendly chasing and playfighting'" (lines 3–4) The relationship (academic thought pattern) that this sentence follows is

   a. spatial order.

   b. comparison and contrast.

   c. problem-solution.

   d. definition.

_____3. The phrase "imbued with" (line 18) means

    a. possessing; having.

    b. lacking; without.

    c. losing control of.

    d. transferring.

_____4. In the passage, we read: "Jones (1976) described seven movement patterns that tended to occur in this type of play: 'These are running, chasing, and fleeing; wrestling; jumping up and down with both feet together . . . ; beating at each other with an object but not hitting; laughing.'" (lines 6–9). What relationship (academic thought pattern) do these ideas follow:

    a. problem-solution

    b. time order

    c. comparison

    d. simple listing

_____5. According to the passage, teachers tend to exhibit a bias

    a. in favor of superhero play.

    b. against superhero play.

_____6. The word "incorporate" (line 55) means

    a. include.

    b. exclude.

    c. start.

    d. prevent.

_____7. The main idea of paragraph 4 (lines 27–33) is that

    a. superhero play can cause injuries.

    b. superhero play is often discouraged by teachers.

    c. superhero play encourages children to be violent.

    d. superhero play results in unacceptable levels of noise.

_____8. According to the passage, why does superhero play appeal to boys in particular?

    a. It allows them to run, wrestle, jump, and shout.

    b. It allows them to feel superior to adults.

    c. It is a way to express aggression in socially acceptable ways.

    d. It is a precursor of membership in adolescent gangs.

_____**9.** The word "escalate" (line 32) means

    a. stop.

    b. grow.

    c. loud.

    d. break into steps.

_____**10.** A conclusion that readers of this passage could reasonably make is that

    a. superhero play is harmless, and even offers some benefits.

    b. girls do not enjoy superhero play.

    c. parents and teachers should discourage superhero play.

    d. superhero play is associated with a rise in youth violence.

PRACTICE TEST

PART I: READING TO PREPARE

Directions: Read through the passage, making quick annotations on the likely meanings of unknown words and the focus of each paragraph. Don't use a dictionary, because dictionaries are not usually permitted for this type of test.

MICROLOANS: BANKING ON THE POOR

1   In 1974, a man named Muhammad Yunus was a professor of economics at Chittagong University in Bangladesh, one of the poorest countries in the world. One day while out for a walk in a village near the university, he spoke to a woman who made bamboo stools. Yunus asked her how much the materials for the stools cost

5   and how much profit she could make. The woman replied that after repaying a middleman who charged her extremely high prices for small quantities of raw bamboo, she was left with only a penny profit, hardly enough to buy a handful of rice for her family. The woman could not circumvent the middleman by purchasing the bamboo directly from the wholesaler because it had to be bought in larger

10   quantities and she had no savings.

Yunus interviewed other small businesspeople in the neighborhood and discovered 42 others with similar problems. He discovered that each needed less than a dollar

in order to free themselves from the power of the usurious middlemen. All 42
people could be helped for $27. Professor Yunus stated, "I realized that it was in
my capability to solve the problem, so I gave the money, the $27, and got them
liberated from the clutches of the money lenders. This created such excitement
among the people in the village that I wanted to continue. I said to myself, if
you can make so many people happy with such a small amount of money, why
shouldn't you do more of it."

Professor Yunus tried to persuade a local bank to make small loans to the poor, but
the bank officials refused, stating that they believed that the poor borrowers would
fail to pay back their loans and that the amounts were so minute that it was
unprofitable for bank staff to process the paperwork. Yunus responded by taking
out bank loans himself and then lending the money to small business people for their
entrepreneurial activities. Yunus found that, contrary to the bank officials'
predictions, poor borrowers did not default on their loans—their repayment rate was
100%.

Yunus was so enthusiastic about the potential of the microloans to help villagers
extricate themselves from poverty that he went on to found the Grameen Bank in
1983. Today the bank has 3.5 million borrowers, 95 percent of whom are extremely
poor women. The Grameen Bank has lent over $4 billion in loans. The repayment
rate is 99%. The women that start or expand small businesses using loans from the
Grameen Bank have used their increased earnings to buy more nutritious food for
their children and send them to school, thereby reducing the rates of child mortality
and illiteracy in Bangladesh.

PART II: TEST QUESTIONS

Directions: Using the annotations you made, answer the questions below.

_____1. The term "circumvent" (line 8) means

    a. satisfy.

    b. get around; avoid.

    c. pay back.

    d. go back to; give repeat business to.

_____2. The main idea of the story-example about the woman who made bamboo stools (lines 2–9) is that

 a. women earn less money than men.

 b. people cannot make a profit constructing stools.

 c. greedy middlemen made it impossible to make a profit.

 d. small businesses are not usually successful.

_____3. The word "usurious" (line 13) refers to

 a. fair; just.

 b. greedy and exploitive.

 c. necessary; essential.

 d. weak; vulnerable.

_____4. In lines 11–14 we read: "Yunus interviewed other small businesspeople in the neighborhood and discovered 42 others with similar problems. He discovered that each needed less than a dollar in order to free themselves from the power of the usurious middlemen. All 42 people could be helped for $27." The relationship (academic thought pattern) that the ideas in lines 11–14 follow is:

 a. types; classification

 b. process

 c. problem-solution

 d. definition

_____5. According to the passage, what year was the Grameen Bank founded?

 a. 1974

 b. 1983

 c. 1992

 d. 1999

_____6. The word "minute," as used in line 22, refers to

 a. a short period of time.

 b. problematic.

 c. small; tiny.

 d. having to do with money.

_____7. Professor Yunus' assertion that poor borrowers will repay their loans was

 a. justified by supporting facts.

 b. not justified by supporting facts.

_____8. What percentage of Grameen Bank borrowers are women?

   a. about 95%

   b. about 97%

   c. about 99%

   d. 100%

_____9. This author exhibits a biased attitude against

   a. Professor Yunus.

   b. poor borrowers in villages.

   c. the middlemen that lent money at high rates of interest.

   d. small businesses.

_____10. A conclusion that can be drawn from this passage is that

   a. bank officials are not competent at their jobs.

   b. little can be done to help the world's poorest people.

   c. microlending can help poor people raise their incomes.

   d. people should avoid debt of any kind.

SAMPLE CHAPTER

The Changing Family

T he most common homework assignment in college is to read a textbook chapter. To complete this task, students are expected to use the skills taught in this book: troubleshooting unfamiliar words, marking main ideas, interpreting charts and graphs, noticing whether statements of opinion have been backed with facts, and creating notes or other study aids to remember important information. The sample textbook chapter entitled "The Changing Family" has been included so that you may practice the skills you learned on a text that is typical in length and difficulty of the material you will be given to read in college.

OUTLINE

What Is Marriage?
What Is a Family?
Family Structure and Social Change
Functions of the Family
Diversity in Marriages, Families, and Kinship Systems
Myths About Marriage and the Family
Family Values: Three Perspectives on the Changing Family
Trends in Changing Families
Why Are Families Changing?
A Cross-Cultural and Global Perspective
Conclusion

Source: Adapted from Nijole V. Benokraitis, *Marriage and Families: Changes, Choices, and Constraints,* 5th edition (Upper Saddle River, NJ: Prentice Hall, 2004). Reprinted by permission of Prentice Hall.

DATADIGEST

- The "traditional" family (where the husband is the breadwinner and the wife is a full-time mother) declined from 60 percent in 1972 to 30 percent in 2001.
- Almost 19 million people aged 25 to 34 years have **never been married**, representing 41 percent of all people in that age group.
- Today the **median age at first marriage** is higher than at any time in the twentieth century: 26.8 years for men, 25.1 years for women.
- On average, **first marriages that end in divorce** last 7 to 8 years.
- The percentage of children under age 18 **living with one parent** rose from 11 percent in 1970 to 27 percent in 2000.

Sources: Fields, 2001; Fields and Casper, 2001; Smith, 2001; Kreider and Fields, 2002; U.S. Census Bureau, 2002.

Two generations ago, the typical American family consisted of a father, a mother, and three or four children. In a recent survey on what constitutes a family, in contrast, a woman in her 60s wrote the following:

> My boyfriend and I have lived together with my youngest son for several years. However, our family (with whom we spend holidays and special events) also includes my ex-husband and his wife and child; my boyfriend's ex-mother-in-law and her sister; his ex-wife and her boyfriend; my oldest son who lives on his own; my mom and stepfather; and my stepbrother and his wife, their biological child, adopted child, and "Big Sister" child. Needless to say, introductions to outsiders are confusing. (Cole, 1996: 12, 14)

Clearly, contemporary family arrangements are more fluid than in the past. Does this shift reflect changes in individual preferences, as people often assume? Or are other forces at work? As this chapter shows, although individual choices have altered some family structures, many of these changes reflect adaptations to larger societal transformations.

You will also see that, despite both historical and recent evidence to the contrary, we continue to cling to a number of myths about the family. Before we examine these and other issues, we need to define what we mean by *marriage* and *family*. . . .

What Is Marriage?

Defined broadly, **marriage** is a socially approved mating relationship that is expected to be stable and enduring. Marriage forms vary across many different groups because the members of a society construct its **norms,** or culturally defined rules for behavior. Norms that define marriage include formal laws and religious doctrines. To be legally married, for example, we must meet specified requirements in every state, such as a minimal age. Although the laws are rarely enforced, 31 states prohibit marriage between first cousins. And because the Catholic Church forbids the dissolution of what it considers the holy sacrament of marriage, devout Catholics may seek annulments but not divorces.

Despite numerous societal and cultural variations, marriages in most Western industrialized countries have some common characteristics. In general, married couples are expected to share economic responsibilities, to engage in sexual activity only with their spouses, and to bear and raise children.

In the United States, laws governing marriage have changed more rapidly than social customs or regional practices. In 1967, for example, the U.S. Supreme Court declared miscegenation laws, which prohibit interracial marriages, unconstitutional. However, local customs and attitudes among many groups still discourage interracial marriages. And as recent violent outbursts in white neighborhoods in Massachusetts, New York, and New Jersey have shown, intolerance of interracial dating is not limited to the South or to rural areas.

Marriages in the United States are legally defined as either ceremonial or nonceremonial. A *ceremonial* marriage is one in which the couple must follow procedures specified by the state or other jurisdiction, such as buying a license, getting blood tests, and being married by an authorized official. Some states also recognize **common-law marriage,** a *nonceremonial* form of marriage that people establish by cohabitation (living together) or evidence of *consummation* (sexual intercourse). Common-law marriages are recognized as legal in 14 states and the District of Columbia. In both kinds of marriage, the parties must meet minimal age requirements, and they cannot engage in **bigamy,** that is, marrying a second person while a first marriage is still legal.

When common-law relationships break up, the legal problems can be complex, including the child's inheritance rights and the father's responsibility to pay child support. Even when common-law marriage is considered legal, ceremonial marriage provides more advantages (such as health benefits and social approval).

What Is a Family?

Although it may seem unnecessary to define familiar terms such as *family*, meanings vary between groups of people and change over time. The definitions also have important consequences for policy decisions, often determining family members' rights and obligations by legal and other social institutions. Under Social Security laws, for example, only a worker's spouse, dependent parents, and children can claim benefits based on the worker's record. And in most adoptions, a child is not legally a member of an adopting family until social service agencies and the courts have approved the adoption. Thus, definitions of family affect people's lives by limiting their options.

Traditionally, *family* has been defined as a unit made up of two or more people who are related by blood, marriage, or adoption and who live together, form an economic unit, and bear and raise children. The U.S. Census Bureau defines the family simply as two or more people living together who are related by birth, marriage, or adoption.

Many social scientists have challenged such traditional definitions because they exclude a number of diverse groups who also consider themselves families. Social scientists have asked, Are childless couples families? What about cohabiting couples? Foster parents and their charges? Elderly sisters living together? Gay and lesbian couples, with or without children? Grandparents raising grandchildren?

There is no universal definition of the family because contemporary household arrangements are very complex. For our purposes, a **family** is as an intimate environment in which two or more people: (1) live together in a committed relationship, (2) see their identity as importantly attached to the group, and (3) share close emotional ties and functions. However, not all social scientists will agree with this definition because it does not explicitly include legalized marriage, procreation, or child rearing.

Definitions may become even more complicated—and more controversial—in the future. As reproductive technology advances, a baby might have several "parents": an egg donor, a sperm donor, a woman who carries the baby during a pregnancy, and the couple who intends to raise the child. If that's not confusing enough, the biological father may be dead for years by the time the child is actually conceived because his sperm can be frozen and stored.

Some believe that definitions of the family should emphasize affection and mutual cooperation among people who are living together. Particularly in African American and Latino communities, ties with **fictive kin,** or nonrelatives who are accepted as part of the family, may be stronger and more lasting than the ties established by blood or marriage (Dilworth-Anderson et al., 1993). James, one of my black students now in his forties, still fondly recalls Mike, a fictive kin, who was a boarder in their home:

> *Mike was an older gentleman who lived with us from my childhood to my teenage years. We considered him part of the family. He was like a grandfather to me. He taught me how to ride a bike, took me fishing, and always told me stories. He was very close to me and my family until he died. When the family gets together, we still talk about old Mike because he was just like family and we still miss him dearly. (Author's files)*

A recent variation of fictive kin among Unitarian congregations is "intentional families," made up primarily of white, professional people. They are separated by distance or estrangement from their own relatives but yearn for familial closeness. Intentional families live apart but meet regularly for meals, holidays, and milestones. They also plan outings together, help each other during crises, and sometimes find stand-in grandparents (E. Graham, 1996).

🖳 Family Structure and Social Change

For nearly a century, the nation's family structure remained remarkably stable. Between 1880 and 1970, about 85 percent of all children lived in two-parent households. Then, in the next two decades, the number of divorces and single-parent families skyrocketed. By 1996, almost one in four children was living in mother-only homes. . . . Some people have been concerned that the **nuclear family**—made up of a husband, a wife, and their biological or adopted children—has dwindled. Some groups were very optimistic when the nuclear family "rebounded" from 51 percent in 1991 to 56 percent in 1996 (Fields, 2001).

Despite the recent increase in the number of nuclear families, many social scientists contend that using the nuclear family as the only "normal" or "natural" type of family ignores many other prevalent household forms. One researcher, for example, has identified 23 types of family structures, and some include only friends or group-home members (Wu, 1996). Various family structures exist not only across cultures and eras but also within any particular culture or historical period.

As reflected in many television shows, diverse family households are more acceptable today than ever before. At the same time, the lineup of shows is rarely representative of "real" families. For example, at least 11 shows have focused on single-father households, but only 4 have portrayed single-mother households. In real life, only 3 percent of all children live in father-only families. The star of the only show that featured an unwed mother—*Murphy Brown*—was white, upper middle class, and a successful professional. In real life, most unwed mothers are poor and have little education (Fields and Casper, 2001). And although the number of traditional families has decreased since the 1970s (see "Data Digest"), such programs increased during prime time in the early 2000s (for example, *The Hughleys, 7th Heaven, Everybody Loves Raymond, American Dreams*, and *Yes, Dear*).

🖳 Functions of the Family

Although family structures differ, most contemporary families fulfill five important functions. They legitimize sexual activity, bear and raise children, provide economic security, offer emotional support, and establish family members' places in society. As you read this section, think about your own family. How does its structure—whether nuclear, divorced, stepfamily, or another form—fulfill these functions?

■ Regulation of Sexual Activity

Every society has norms regarding who may engage in sexual relations, with whom, and under what circumstances. One of the oldest rules is the **incest**

taboo, cultural norms and laws that forbid sexual intercourse between close blood relatives, such as brother and sister, father and daughter, uncle and niece, or grandparent and grandchild.

Incest Taboos

Sexual relations between close relatives can increase the incidence of inherited genetic diseases and abnormalities by about 3 percent (Bennett et al., 2002). Incest taboos have primarily social bases, however, and probably arose to maintain the family for several reasons:

■ Incest taboos minimize jealousies and destructive sexual competition that might interfere with the functioning of the family circle.

■ Incest taboos ensure a group's survival. If family members who are sexual partners lose interest in each other, for example, they may avoid mating.

■ Because incest taboos ensure that mating will take place outside the family, a wider circle of people can band together in cooperative efforts (such as hunting), in the face of danger, or in war (Ellis, 1963).

■ By controlling the mother's sexuality, incest taboos prevent doubt about the legitimacy of her offspring and their property rights, titles, or inheritance.

   Most social scientists believe that incest taboos are universal. There have been exceptions, however. The rulers of the Incan empire, the native Hawaiian royalty, the ancient Persian rulers, and the Ptolemaic dynasty in Egypt practiced incest while it was forbidden to commoners. Cleopatra, for example, was purportedly the issue of at least 11 generations of incest and married her younger brother. Some anthropologists speculate that wealthy Egyptian families practiced sibling marriage to prevent losing or fragmenting their land. If a sister married a brother, the property would remain in the family in cases of divorce or death (Parker, 1996).

Endogamy and Exogamy

Two other cultural rules define the "right" marriage partner. The principle of **endogamy** requires that people marry or have sexual relations within a certain group, such as Jews marrying Jews or African Americans marrying African Americans. **Exogamy** requires marriage outside the group, such as not marrying one's relatives. Even in the United States and other countries where marriages are not arranged, societal, religious, subcultural, and familial rules, however implicit, usually govern our choice of sexual and life partners. (We will discuss two related terms—*homogamy* and *heterogamy*—in several later chapters.)

■ Procreation and Socialization of Children

Procreation is an essential family function. Although some married couples choose to remain childless, most plan to raise families. Some go to great lengths to conceive the children they want through reproductive technologies. Once a couple becomes parents, the family embarks on socialization, another critical function.

Through **socialization,** children acquire language, absorb the accumulated knowledge, attitudes, beliefs, and values of their culture, and learn the social and interpersonal skills needed to function effectively in society. Some of our socialization is unconscious and may be unintentional, such as teaching culturally accepted stereotypical gender traits. Much of the socialization is both conscious and deliberate, however, such as carefully selecting preschoolers' playmates or raising children in a specific religion.

We are socialized through **roles,** the obligations and expectations attached to a particular situation or position. Families are important role-teaching agents because they delineate relationships between mothers and fathers, siblings, parents and children, and other relatives and non-family members.

Some of the rights and responsibilities associated with our roles are not always clear because family structures shift and change. For example, if you or your parents have experienced divorce or remarriage, have some of the new role expectations been fuzzy or even contradictory? Children often are torn between their allegiance to a biological parent and that to a stepparent because stepparent–stepchild roles are often ambiguous.

Some claim that the family is less powerful today in socializing its young than it was in the past. With more mothers of young children in the work force, for example, child-care centers and preschool programs are playing an increasingly important role in socialization. Especially on such politically charged issues as sex education, some parents feel that schools have become too intrusive in socializing their children and have undermined parental authority.

■ Economic Security

The family is an important economic unit that provides financial security and stability. Families supply food, shelter, clothing, and other material resources for their members. If such economic cooperation did not exist, a family's survival would be jeopardized. There is a large number of homeless families. They often wind up on the streets or in shelters not because the parents are mentally ill or drug users but simply because they can't produce the income to purchase some of life's basic necessities such as housing and food.

In traditional families, the male is the breadwinner and the female does the housework and cares for the children. Increasingly, however, many mothers are entering the labor force. Among married couples with children under 18, the proportion of traditional homes has declined significantly (see "Data Digest"). The traditional family, where Mom stays home to raise the kids, is a luxury that most families today can't afford. Because of high unemployment rates, depressed wages and salaries, and a lack of job security, many mothers must work outside the home whether they want to or not.

■ Emotional Support

American sociologist Charles Horton Cooley (1864–1929) explored the concept of **primary groups,** those characterized by close, long-lasting, intimate, and face-to-face interaction. Later writers introduced the notion of **secondary groups,** those characterized by impersonal and short-term relationships where people work together on common tasks or activities. The family is a critical primary group because it provides the nurturance, love, and emotional sustenance that people need to be happy, healthy, and secure.

In contrast, secondary groups have few emotional ties, and its members typically leave the group after attaining a specific goal. While you're taking this course, for example, you, most of your classmates (except for a few close friends, perhaps), and your instructor make up a secondary group. You've all come together for a quarter or a semester to study marriage and the family. Once the course is over, most of you may never see each other again.

You might discuss your course with other secondary groups, such as co-workers. They might listen politely, especially if you're the boss, but they probably won't care how you feel about a class. Such primary groups as your family and close friends, in contrast, usually will listen sympathetically, drive you to class or your job when your car breaks down, offer to do your laundry during exams, and console you if you don't get that much-deserved "A" in a course or a promotion at work.

A simple test distinguishes my primary and secondary groups. I don't hesitate to call the former at 3:00 A.M. to pick me up at the airport, for example, because I know they'll be happy (or at least willing) to do so.

■ Social Class Placement

A **social class** is a category of people who have a similar standing or rank based on wealth, education, power, prestige, and other valued resources. People in the same social class tend to have similar attitudes, values, and leisure interests.

Social class affects many aspects of family life. There are class variations in terms of when we marry, how many children we have, how parents socialize their children, and even how partners and spouses relate to each other. Middle-class couples are more likely than their working-class counterparts to share more equally in housework and child rearing, for example, [and] families on the lower rungs of the socioeconomic ladder face a greater risk than their middle-class counterparts of adolescent nonmarital childbearing, dropping out of high school, committing street crimes, neglecting their children, and domestic violence.

Diversity in Marriages, Families, and Kinship Systems

Although the basic family functions you have just read about are common to most cultures, each society has its own norms that specify acceptable marriage and family forms. Thus, there is much diversity among families both across and within cultures.

Most people are born into a biological family, or *family of origin*. If the person is raised in this family or is adopted, it is her or his **family of orientation.** By leaving this family to marry or cohabit, the individual becomes part of the **family of procreation,** the family a person forms by marrying and having or adopting children. This term is somewhat dated, however, because in several types of households—such as childless or gay and lesbian families—procreation may not be part of the relationship.

Each type of family is part of a larger **kinship system,** or network of people who are related by blood, marriage, or adoption. In much of the preindustrial world, which contains most of the world's population, the most common family form is the **extended family,** in which two or more generations (such as the family of orientation and the family of procreation) live together or in adjacent dwellings.

Some researchers predict that in industrialized societies where the numbers of single-parent families are increasing, extended families living together or nearby may become more common. Such families can make it much easier for a single parent to work outside the home, raise children, and perform household tasks. Because remarriage rates are high, however, it remains to be seen whether extended families will become widespread.

A variety of formal laws and informal norms regulate inheritance rights, define the pool of eligible marital partners, and determine whether children will take the surname of the father, the mother, or both. There are also worldwide variations in the types of marriages and residential patterns that characterize families and kinship systems.

■ Types of Marriage

Several types of marriage—including monogamy, polygamy, or a combination—are common in most societies. One anthropologist concluded that only about 20 percent of societies are strictly monogamous. Others permit either polygamy or combinations of polygamy and monogamy (Murdock, 1967).

Monogamy

In **monogamy,** one person is married exclusively to another person. Because divorce and remarriage rates are high in the United States and in many European countries, residents of these countries practice **serial monogamy.** That is, they marry several people, but one at a time—they marry, divorce, remarry, redivorce, and so on.

Polygamy

Polygamy, in which a man or woman has two or more spouses, is subdivided into *polygyny* (one man married to two or more women) and *polyandry* (one woman with two or more husbands). In group marriage, two or more men and two or more women live together and have sexual relations with each other. Polygyny is common in many societies, especially in Africa, South America, and the Mideast. In Saudi Arabia, for example, some wealthy men have as many as 11 wives and 54 children (Dickey and McGinn, 2001). No one knows the actual figures of polygamy worldwide, however, because "accurate censuses of polygyny are generally unavailable" (Hern, 1992: 504).

Although industrial societies forbid polygamy, there are small pockets of polygynous groups. The Mormon Church banned polygamy in the late 1800s. Still, an estimated 300,000 families are headed by fundamentalist men in the Rocky Mountain states and Canada. The men maintain that they practice polygamy according to nineteenth-century Mormon religious beliefs. Marriages often are performed in secret ceremonies, and some girls as young as 11 are married off at the first sign of menstruation (Divoky, 2002; Madigan, 2003).

Wives who have recently escaped from plural families have raised allegations of forced marriage, sexual abuse, pedophilia, and incest (Cart, 2002). Why don't these girls refuse to marry or try to escape? They can't. Among other things, they're typically isolated from outsiders: They live in remote rural areas, and their education is cut off when they're about 10 years old. Their parents support the marriages because elderly men, the patriarchs, have brainwashed them to believe that "This is what the heavenly father wants." In addition, the girls can't run away because there is no place to go and because Utah law enforcement agencies rarely prosecute polygamists (Janofsky, 2003).

Polygynous marriages can be either formal or informal. In a study of marriage forms in Nigeria, Karanja (1987) differentiates between an inside wife and an outside wife. An "inside wife," who marries in a church or civil ceremony, typically subscribes to the Christian ideal of monogamy in marriage. Under native law and custom, however, her husband may also "marry" (no official ceremony is performed) an "outside wife."

The outside wife has regular sexual relations with her "husband," establishes an autonomous residence that the husband pays for, and has children that the man acknowledges as his. Outside wives, however, have limited social recognition and status and much less political and legal recognition. When a well-known Nigerian businessman and politician died at age 60 a few years ago, he had four official wives (because "under Muslim law, a man may have four wives") and more than 40 unofficial wives (Vick, 1998: A9). Some African families that immigrate to Europe continue to live in polygymous families (Randle, 1998).

Some of my students, especially women, become angry when they read about polygynous marriages. They contend that polygyny benefits men at the expense of women because a man has many wives who care for him and his children from birth to death. This may be true, but polygyny is widespread for other reasons. In a study of South Africa, for example, Anderson (2002) concluded that there is often a shortage of men (often because of war), that poor women prefer to marry a rich polygamist than a poor monogamist, that the wives often pool income and cooperative child care, and that the rural wives often contact urban wives when they're looking for jobs. Thus, polygyny is functional because it meets many women's needs.

The very rare practice of polyandry is illustrated by the Todas, a small pastoral tribe that flourished in south India until the late nineteenth century. The Toda woman who married one man became the wife of his brothers—including brothers born after the marriage—and all lived in the same household. When one of the brothers was with the wife, "he placed his cloak and staff outside the hut as a warning to the rest not to disturb him" (Queen et al., 1985: 19). Marital privileges rotated among the brothers, there was no evidence of sexual jealousy, and one of the brothers, usually the oldest, was the legal father of the first two or three children. Another brother could become the legal father of children born later.

According to some anthropologists, polyandry exists in societies where property is difficult to amass. Because there is a limited amount of available land, the kinship group is more likely to survive in harsh environments if more than one husband contributes to food production (Cassidy and Lee, 1989).

▪ Residential Patterns

Families also vary in terms of where they live. In the *patrilocal* residential pattern, newly married couples live with the husband's family. In a *matrilocal* pattern, newly married couples live with the wife's family. A *neolocal* residence is one in which the newly married couple sets up its own residence. Around the world families tend to be extended rather than nuclear, and the most common pattern is residence with the husband's family.

In modern industrial societies, married couples typically establish their own residences. Since the early 1990s, however, the tendency for young married adults to live with the parents of either the wife or husband—or sometimes with the grandparents of one of the partners—has increased. At least half of all families starting out cannot afford a medium-priced house because they don't have the cash for a downpayment and the closing costs (Conley, 1999). Divorced mothers and their children often live with parents or grandparents for economic reasons.

Clearly, there is much diversity in family arrangements both in the United States and around the world. As families change, however, we sometimes get bogged down with idealized images of what a "good" family looks like. Our unrealistic expectations can result in dissatisfaction and anger. Instead of enjoying our families as they are, we might waste a lot of time and energy searching for family relationships that exist only in fairy tales and TV sitcoms.

Myths About Marriage and the Family

Ask yourself the following questions:

- Were families happier in the past than now?
- Is marrying and having children the "natural" thing to do?
- Are "good" families self-sufficient, whereas "bad" families depend on welfare?
- Is the family a bastion of love and support?
- Should all of us strive to be as perfect as possible in our families?

If you answered "yes" to any of these questions, you—like most people in the United States—believe in several myths about marriage and the family. Although most myths are dysfunctional, some can be functional.

Myths Can Be Dysfunctional

Myths can be *dysfunctional* when they result in negative (although often unintended) consequences that disrupt a family. The myth of the perfect family can make us miserable. We may feel there is something wrong with *us* if we do not live up to some ideal scenario. Instead of accepting our current families, we might pressure our children to become what we want them to be or spend a lifetime waiting for our parents or in-laws to accept us. We may become very critical of family members or withdraw emotionally because they don't fit into a mythical mold.

Myths can also divert our attention from widespread social problems that generate family crises. If people blame themselves for the gap they perceive between image and reality, they may not recognize the external forces, such as social policies, that create difficulties on the individual level. For example, if we believe that only bad, sick, or maladjusted people beat their children, we will search for solutions at the individual level, such as counseling, support groups, and therapy. As we will see in later chapters, however, many family crises result from large-scale problems such as racism, poverty, and unemployment.

Myths Can Be Functional

Not all myths are harmful. Some are *functional* because they bring people together and promote social solidarity (Guest, 1988). If myths give us hope that we can have a good marriage and family life, for example, we won't give up at the first sign of problems. In this sense, myths can help us maintain our emotional balance during crises. Myths can also free us from guilt or shame. For instance, "We fell out of love" is a more face-saving explanation for getting a divorce than "I made a stupid mistake" or "I married an alcoholic."

The same myth may be both functional and dysfunctional. A belief in the decline of the family has been functional in generating social policies (such as child-support legislation) that try to keep children of divorced families from sinking into poverty, for example. But this same myth is also dysfunctional if people become unrealistically preoccupied with finding self-fulfillment and happiness.

Myths About the Past

We often hear that in the "good old days" there were fewer problems, people were happier, and families were stronger. Because of the widespread influence of movies and television, many of us cherish romantic notions of the frontier days. These highly unrealistic images of the family have been portrayed in John Wayne films, the antebellum South of *Gone with the Wind*, and the strong, poor, but loving rural family presented in such television shows as *The Waltons* and *Little House on the Prairie* in the 1970s, *Dr. Quinn, Medicine Woman* in the late 1990s, and *7th Heaven* most recently.

Many historians maintain that such golden ages never existed. We glorify them only because we know so little about the past (Coontz, 1992). Even in the 1800s, many families experienced desertion by a parent or out-of-wedlock births (Demos, 1986). Family life in the "good old days" was filled with deprivation, loneliness, and dangers. Families worked very hard and often were decimated by accidents, illness, and disease. Until the mid-1940s, a much shorter life expectancy meant that parental death often led to child placements in extended families, foster care, or orphanages. Thus, the chances of not growing up in an intact family were actually greater in the past than they are now (Walsh, 1993).

People who have the "nostalgia bug" aren't aware of several facts. For example, teenage pregnancy rates were higher in the 1950s than they are today, even though a higher proportion of teen mothers were married (many because of "shotgun marriages"). Until the 1970s, few people ever talked or wrote about child abuse, incest, domestic violence, marital unhappiness, sexual harassment, or gay bashing. Many families lived in silent misery and quiet desperation because these issues, were largely invisible. In addition, parents spend more time with their children today than in "the good old days."

Myths About What Is Natural

Many people have strong opinions about what is "natural" or "unnatural" in marriages and families. Although remaining single is more acceptable today than in the past, there is still a lingering suspicion that something is wrong with a person who doesn't marry.

We sometimes have misgivings about childless marriages or about other committed relationships. We often hear, for instance, that "It's only natural to want to get married and have children" or that "Gays are violating human nature." Other beliefs, also surviving from so-called simpler times, claim that family life is "natural" and that women are "natural" mothers.

The problem with such thinking is that if motherhood is natural, why do many women choose not to have children? If homosexuality is unnatural, how do we explain its existence since time immemorial? If getting married and creating a family are natural, why do millions of men refuse to marry their pregnant partners or abandon their children?

▪ Myths About the Self-Sufficient Family

Some of our most cherished values in the United States idealize individual achievement, self-reliance, and self-sufficiency. The numerous best-selling self-help books on such topics as parenting, combining work and marriage, and having "good sex" also reflect our belief that we should improve ourselves, that we can pull ourselves up by our bootstraps.

Although we have many choices in our personal lives, few families—past or present—have been entirely self-sufficient. Most of us need some kind of help at one time or another. Because of unemployment, underemployment, and recessions, the poverty rate has increased by 40 percent since 1970, and many of the working poor are two-parent families. From time to time, these families need assistance to survive.

The United States has a higher infant mortality rate than many other countries. Among industrialized countries, the United States ranks only twenty-ninth in terms of child well-being, slipping from its twentieth rank in 1995. The plight of black children is even worse. Nationally, black infant mortality rates are more than twice those of whites, largely because of poverty (Kent and Mather, 2002). In our nation's capital, black infant mortality is higher than that in 56 nations, including low-income countries such as Bahamas, Barbados, Dominican Republic, and Oman ("It's Time for New Voices," 2002). Thus, millions of American families are far from self-sufficient in maintaining their children's well-being.

The middle class isn't self-sufficient, either. In the 1950s and 1960s, for example, many middle-class families were able to prosper not because of family savings or individual enterprise but as a result of federal housing loans, education payments, and publicly financed roads that provided suburbanites with inexpensive travel to their jobs in the city (Coontz, 1992).

Currently, poor and rich alike receive Medicare, and the government provides numerous tax cuts for middle-income and affluent families. Even if you're middle class, you or other family members have probably collected unemployment payments after being laid off from a job. In addition, state-based merit scholarships are more likely to subsidize the college costs of rich rather than poor and minority families. Georgia, for example, spends only $5 million per year on merit scholarships for needy students, compared with $40 million for middle- and upper-income families (Heller and Marin, 2002).

■ The Myth of the Family as a Loving Refuge

The family has been described as a "haven in a heartless world" (Lasch, 1977: 8). One of the major functions of the family is to provide love, nurturance, and emotional support. The home can also be one of the most physically and psychologically brutal settings in society. An alarming number of children suffer from physical and sexual abuse from family members, and there is a high rate of violence between married and cohabiting partners.

Many parents experience stress while balancing the demands of work and family responsibilities. Furthermore, concern about crime, drugs, and unemployment has made many parents pessimistic about their children's future. In one national poll—and at the height of an unprecedented economic boom in the late 1990s—33 percent of those surveyed said they expect their children to have a lower quality of life and to be worse off financially than they, the parents, are (Ladd, 1999). The worry that underlies such responses is bound to affect family dynamics.

Sometimes family members are unrealistic about the daily strains that they encounter. For example, if people expect family interactions to always be cheery and pleasant, the level of tension may surge even when routine problems arise. And especially for families with health or economic problems, the home may be loving, but it's hardly a "haven in a heartless world."

■ Myths About the Perfect Marriage, the Perfect Family

Here's how one woman described the clash between marital expectations and reality:

> *Marriage is not what I had assumed it would be. One premarital assumption after another has crashed down on my head. Marriage is like taking an airplane to Florida for a relaxing vacation in January, and when you get off the plane you find you're in the Swiss Alps. There is cold and snow instead of swimming and sunshine. Well, after you buy winter clothes and learn how to ski and learn how to talk a new foreign language, I guess you can have just as good a vacation in the Swiss Alps as you can in Florida. But I can tell you, doctor, it's one hell of a surprise when you get off that marital airplane and find that everything is far different from what one had assumed. (Lederer and Jackson, 1968: 39)*

Even if partners live together and feel they know each other, many couples may find themselves in the Swiss Alps instead of Florida after tying the knot. Numerous marriages dissolve because we cling to myths about conjugal life. After the perfect wedding, the perfect couple must be everything to one another: good providers, fantastic sexual partners, best friends, sympathetic confidantes, stimulating companions, and spiritual soulmates (Rubin, 1985). Are such expectations realistic?

Fables about the perfect family are just as pervasive as those about the perfect marriage. According to historian John Gillis (1996), we all have two families:

one that we live *with* (the way families really are) and another that we live *by* (the way we would like families to be). Gillis maintains that people have been imagining and reimagining family since at least the late Middle Ages because the families we are born and marry into have been too fragile to satisfy most people's need for a sense of continuity, belonging, unity, and rootedness.

Family Values: Three Perspectives on the Changing Family

I introduced this chapter with several definitions of the family. Then we examined the functions of the family, the ways families vary, and some myths about family life. Now we are ready to look at the major theme of this chapter: how the family is changing.

Numerous surveys show that we place a high value on marriage and family. In a recent poll, for example, Americans ranked their family as the most important aspect of life, above health, work, money, and even religion. One national survey found that "almost 8 out of 10 married Americans said they would give their marriage an A grade, with the bulk of the rest saying they would give their marriage a B" (Newport, 1996: 18). There were few Cs, Ds, or Fs. In a recent poll, only 3 percent of the respondents felt that morality and family values were problematic (Walczak et al., 2000). In another study, people cited traffic, urban sprawl, and crime as the biggest problems in their lives. Only 6 percent felt that child and teen issues were a major concern (Knickerbocker, 2000).

Despite these upbeat views, a number of writers worry that the family is falling apart. Quite commonly, journalists and scholars refer to the "vanishing" family, "troubled" marriages, and "appalling" divorce statistics as sure signs that the family is disintegrating. Some claim that our most urgent social problem is the disappearance of many fathers because of divorce or unmarried relationships that break up (Blankenhorn, 1995). Others contend that we have a "marriage problem" because marriage is now a convenient promise that is easily made and just as easily broken (Wilson, 2002).

Who's right? The status of the family continues to spark debate between three schools of thought. One group contends that the family is deteriorating, a second argues that the family is changing but not deteriorating, and a third, smaller group maintains that the family is stronger than ever.

■ The Family Is Deteriorating

More than 100 years ago, the *Boston Quarterly Review* issued a dire warning: "The family, in its old sense, is disappearing from our land, and not only are our institutions threatened, but the very existence of our society is endangered" (cited in Rosen, 1982: 299). In the late 1920s, E. R. Groves (1928), a well-known social scientist, warned that marriages were in "extreme collapse." Some of his explanations for what he called the "marriage crisis" and high divorce rates have a surprisingly modern ring: self-indulgence, too much luxury, extreme independence, financial strain, and incompatible personalities.

Even those who were optimistic a decade ago have become more pessimistic because of recent data on family "decay." Some of these data include high rates of divorce and children born out of wedlock, millions of "latchkey children," an increase in the number of people deciding not to get married, unprecedented numbers of single-parent families, and a decline of parental authority in the home.

Why have these changes occurred? Those who feel the family is in trouble echo Groves, citing such reasons as a lack of individual responsibility, a lack of commitment to the family, and just plain selfishness. Many conservative politicians and influential academics argue that the family is deteriorating because most people put their own needs over family duties (see Benokraitis, 2000, for a discussion of these perspectives). This school of thought claims that many men and women are unwilling to invest their psychological and financial resources in their children or that they give up on marriages too quickly when there are problems (Gallagher, 1996; Popenoe, 1996; Wilson, 2002).

Many of those who believe that the family is deteriorating are headed by *communitarians*, people who are politically more moderate than conservatives on some family issues. For example, they accept the idea that many mothers have to work outside the home for economic reasons. Communitarians claim, however, that because many adults focus almost exclusively on their personal gratification, such traditional family functions as the early care and socialization of children have become a low priority (Glenn, 1996). They contend that there has been a general increase in a sense of entitlement (what people believe they should receive from others) and a decline in a sense of duty (what people believe they should give to others).

The family-decline adherents point out that marriage exists for the sake of the children and not just adults. Simply telling children we love them is not enough. Instead of wasting our money on divorce, the argument goes, we should be investing in children by maintaining a stable marriage:

> A large divorce industry made up of lawyers, investigative accountants; real estate appraisers and salespeople; pension specialists; therapists and psychologists; expert witnesses; and private collectors of child support has sprung up to harvest the fruits of family discord. However necessary their services, these professionals are the recipients of family income that might, in happier circumstances ... [be] invested in children. (Whitehead, 1996: 11)

Many who endorse the "family is deteriorating" perspective blame most of the family's problems on mothers who work outside the home. If mothers stayed at home and took care of their children, these writers maintain, we would have less delinquency, fewer high school dropouts, and more children who are disciplined. Gallagher (1996: 184) argues for example, that if women spent more time finding good provider husbands, they could "devote their talents and education and energy to the rearing of their children, the nurturing of family relationships, and the building of community and neighborhood." The implication is that the deteriorating family could be shored up if fathers were breadwinners and mothers were homemakers.

■The Family Is Changing, Not Deteriorating

In contrast, other scholars argue that the family has not deteriorated as much as we think. Instead, they say, the changes we are experiencing are extensions of long-standing family patterns.

Although more women have entered the labor force since 1970, the mother who works outside the home is not a new phenomenon. Mothers sold dairy products and woven goods during colonial times, took in boarders around the turn of the twentieth century, and held industrial jobs during World War II. The number of married women in the labor force doubled between 1930 and 1980 but *quadrupled* between 1900 and 1904 (Stannard, 1979).

Many family scholars contend that family problems such as desertion, out-of-wedlock birth, and child abuse have *always* existed. Family literature published in the 1930s, for example, included studies that dealt with such issues as divorce, desertion, and family crises due to discord, delinquency, and depression (Broderick, 1988).

Similarly, there have always been single-parent families. The percentage of single-person households has doubled in the last three decades, but this number *tripled* between 1900 and 1950 (Stannard, 1979). Divorce began to be more common in the eighteenth century, parents had less control over their adult married children because there was little land or other property to inherit, and the importance of romantic love increased (Cott, 1976).

There is no question, however, that a greater proportion of people divorce today than in the past and that more early marriages are ending in divorce. As a result, the decision of many singles to postpone marriage until they are older, more mature and have stable careers may often be a sound one.

Families are changing but are also remarkably resilient, despite numerous adversities. They cope with everyday stresses and protect their most vulnerable members: the young, old, ill, or disabled (Patterson, 2002). They overcome financial hardships. They handle everyday conflict and tension as children make a bumpy transition to adolescence and then to early adulthood (Conger and Conger, 2002).

Most poor families have stable and loving relationships despite constant worries and harsh economic environments (Seccombe, 2002). And many gay and lesbian families, despite their rejection by much of "mainstream" society, are also resilient and resourceful in developing successful family relationships (Oswald, 2002). Thus, according to many researchers, there is little empirical evidence that family change is synonymous with family decline.

■The Family Is Stronger Than Ever

Do our nostalgic myths about the past misinterpret the contemporary family as weak and on the decline? Some writers think so, asserting that modern family life is much more loving than in the past. Consider the treatment of women and children in colonial days: If they disobeyed strict male authority, they were often severely punished. And, in contrast to some of our sentimental notions, only a small number of white, middle-class families enjoyed a life that was both gentle and genteel:

> For every nineteenth-century middle-class family that protected its wife and child within the family circle … there was an Irish or a German girl scrubbing floors in that middle-class home, a Welsh boy mining coal to keep the home-baked goodies warm, a black girl doing the family laundry, a black mother and child picking cotton to be made into clothes for the family, and a Jewish or an Italian daughter in a sweatshop making "ladies"' dresses or artificial flowers for the family to purchase. (Coontz, 1992: 11–12)

Some social scientists argue that despite myriad problems, families are happier today than in the past because of the increase in multigenerational relationships. Many people have living grandparents, feel closer to them, and often receive both emotional and economic support from these family members. The recent growth of the older segment of the population has produced four-generation families. On the one hand, more adults in their 60s may be stressed out because they are caring for 80- to 100-year-old parents. On the other hand, more children and grandchildren grow up knowing and enjoying their older relatives.

Families are stronger now than in the past, some claim, because they have more equitable roles at home and are more tolerant of diverse family forms (such as single-parent homes, unmarried couple homes, and families with adopted children). And most Americans believe that marriage is a lifetime commitment that should end only under extreme circumstances, such as domestic violence (Thornton and Young-DeMarco, 2001).

Despite a sharp increase in the number of two-income families, in 1997 children between the ages of 3 and 12 spent, on average, about 3 to 5 more hours a week with their parents than they did in 1981. The time spent together included activities such as reading, playing, conversing, and being in the same room while a parent did household tasks. Thus, contrary to popular belief, children spend more time with parents today than several decades ago, and despite women's greater participation in the labor force (Sandberg and Hofferth, 2001).

Parents often feel guilty about not spending enough time with their children. In reality, what has changed is not the amount of family time, but the pace of family life when both parents work. Parents have to squeeze in household chores between jobs and attending their children's activities, and children often have highly scheduled lives because of numerous school and extracurricular activities (Daly, 2001).

Each of the three schools of thought provides evidence for its position. How, then, can we decide which perspective to believe? Is the family weak, or is it strong? The answer depends largely on how we define, measure, and interpret family "weakness" and family "strength." For better or worse, the family has never been static and continues to change.

🖃 Trends in Changing Families

The family is clearly changing. But how? And why? Demographic transitions, shifts in the racial and ethnic composition of families, and economic transformations have all played a role in these changes.

■ Demographic Changes

Two demographic changes have had especially far-reaching consequences for family life. First, fertility rates have declined. Since the end of the eighteenth century, most American women have been bearing fewer children, having them closer together, and finishing child rearing at an earlier age. Second, the average age of the population has risen from 17 in the mid-1800s to nearly 36 in 2001 (Kinsella and Velkoff, 2001). Both these shifts mean that a larger proportion of the U.S. population now experiences the "empty-nest syndrome"—the departure of grown children from the home—at an earlier age, as well as earlier grandparenthood and prolonged widowhood.

We see other changes in the composition of households as well: a large number of singles and cohabitants, higher rates of marriage and divorce, more one-parent families and working mothers, and a rapid increase in the number of stepfamilies (see *Figure 1.1*). We'll look at these changes briefly now and examine them more closely in later chapters.

Changes in Family and Nonfamily Households

The Census Bureau divides households into two categories: family and nonfamily. A *family household* consists of the two or more people living together who are related through marriage, birth, or adoption. *Nonfamily households* include people who live alone or with nonrelatives (roommates, boarders, or cohabitants). In 2000, 31 percent of all households were nonfamily households, a substantial increase from 19 percent in 1970 (Fields and Casper, 2001).

As *Figure 1.1a* shows, the percentage of married-couple households with children under age 18 declined from 40 percent in 1970 to 24 percent in 2000. The percentage of children under age 18 living in one-parent families has more than doubled during this same period (see "Data Digest"). Part of the increase in one-parent families is due to the surge of births to unmarried women (see *Figure 1.1b*).

Singles and Cohabitants

Singles make up one of the fastest-growing groups. The decrease in household size has resulted in part from fewer children per family, more one-parent families, and greater age segregation, that is, the tendency of young and old people to live separately. The number of cohabitants has also climbed since 1970 (see

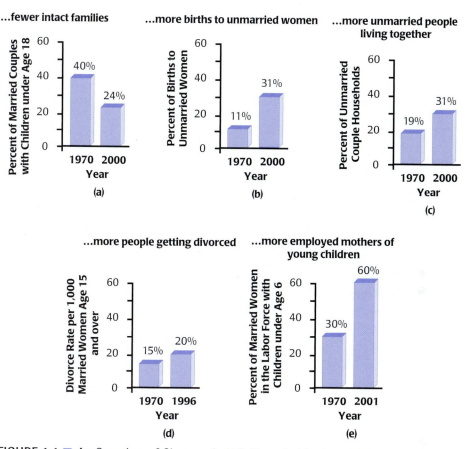

FIGURE 1.1 ▪ *An Overview of Changes in U.S. Households since 1970*
Source: Adapted from Bachu and O'connell, 2001; Fields and Casper, 2001; Labor Force Statistics, stats.bis.gov/news.release/famee.t04.htm (accessed March 1, 2003).

Figure 1.1c) and is expected to grow because societal acceptance of living together is increasing, and many young adults are postponing marriage.

The percentage of people living alone has grown considerably since 1970. For baby-boom women in particular (**baby boomers** are people born in the post–World War II generation between 1946 and 1964), more divorces, increased longevity, and shaky retirement incomes could mean that fewer midlife and older women will have the option of living alone even if this is their preference.

Marriage–Divorce–Remarriage

The number of divorces has increased over the years (see *Figure 1.1d*). Even though divorce rates have reached a plateau and decreased since 2000, one out of every two first marriages is expected to end in divorce (Kreider and Fields, 2002).

Teen marriages and marriages entered into because the woman became pregnant are especially likely to unravel.

Stepfamilies are becoming much more common. About 17 percent of all children live in a stepfamily (Fields, 2001). Whether or not a couple has children seems to have little effect on divorce or remarriage. Women with lower educational levels are more likely to divorce and to remarry than are those with college degrees. This suggests that age and maturation are important factors in lasting marriages.

One-Parent Families

As more adults remain single into their 30s and as divorce rates increase, the number of children living with one parent also increases. The number of one-parent families has almost tripled, from 9 percent in 1960 to nearly 32 percent in 2000 (Fields and Casper, 2001).

The proportion of children living with a never-married parent has also increased, from 4 percent in 1960 to 42 percent in 2000. Of all one-parent families, 83 percent are mother–child families (Fields and Casper, 2001; Hobbs and Stoops, 2002). We'll look at one-parent households in several later chapters.

Employed Mothers

The increased participation of mothers in the labor force has been one of the most important changes in family roles. Two-earner couples with children under age 18 rose from 31 percent in 1976 to 70 percent in 2001 (U.S. Census Bureau, 2002).

About 55 percent of all mothers with children under 1 year of age are in the labor force, down from an all-time high of 59 percent in 1998 (Bachu and O'Connell, 2001). In addition, six out of every ten married women with children under 6 years old are in the labor force (see *Figure 1.1e*). This means that many couples are now coping with domestic and employment responsibilities while raising young children.

■ Racial and Ethnic Changes

What do you call a person who speaks three languages? Multilingual.

What do you call a person who speaks two languages? Bilingual.

What do you call a person who speaks one language? American.

Although, as this joke suggests, many people stereotype (and ridicule) the United States as a single-language and a single-culture society, it's the most multicultural country in the world. Diversity is booming, ethnic groups speak many languages, and foreign-born families live in all states.

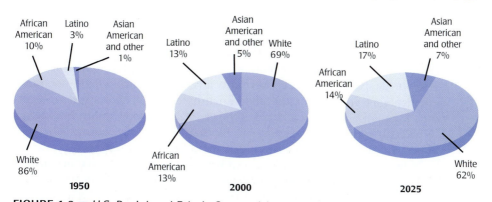

FIGURE 1.2 ■ *U.S. Racial and Ethnic Composition, 1950–2025*
Source: Adapted from U.S. Census Bureau, www.census.gov/population/www.pop-profile/
nat-proj.html (accessed October 24, 1997); U.S. Census Bureau, www.census.gov/population/
cen2000/phc-t08/phc-t-08.pdf (accessed March 4, 2003).

Ethnic Families Are Booming

In 2002, almost 12 percent of the U.S. population was foreign-born, up from
8 percent in 1990. Only one-sixth—about 5 million—are from Europe and
Canada. The other 24 million come from South America, Latin America,
Central America (including Mexico), Asia, and the Caribbean (Schmidley,
2003). Because of huge immigration waves and high birth rates, 1 in 5 people
are either foreign-born or first-generation U.S. residents (Bernstein, 2002). Our
multicultural rainbow includes about 150 distinct ethnic or racial groups among
the almost 285 million people living in the United States today.

By 2025 only 62 percent of the U.S. population will be white, down from
86 percent in 1950 (see *Figure 1.2*). For the first time, in 2003 Latinos edged
past African Americans as the nation's largest minority. The Latino population
is now 37 million, whereas blacks number 36.2 million (Bernstein, 2003). Chinese,
Filipinos, and Japanese still rank as the largest Asian American groups. Since
1990, however, Southeast Asians, Indians, Koreans, Pakistanis, and Bangladeshis
have registered much faster growth. Mexicans, Puerto Ricans, and Cubans are
the largest groups among Latinos, but people from Central and South American
countries—such as El Salvador, Guatemala, Colombia, and Honduras—have
been immigrating in very high numbers.

Ethnic Families Speak Many Languages

Despite the earlier joke about Americans speaking only one language, 18 percent—
almost 47 million people—speak a language other than English at home. The
largest group, 11 percent, is Latinos. Then the number drops to Chinese (0.8 percent); French (0.6 percent); Portuguese, German, and Tagalog (0.5 percent each);
Italian and Vietnamese (0.4 percent each); and myriad other languages such as

Greek, Hebrew, Arabic, Russian, Navajo, Korean, Japanese, and Hindi (*Language Spoken at Home*, 2000).

In some states—especially California, New York, New Jersey, Texas, and Florida—the percentages of people who *don't* speak English are higher than those who *do* speak English. At the county level, for instance, a large proportion of residents speak Spanish rather than English: Hidalgo County, Texas (84 percent); Miami–Dade County, Florida (68 percent); Hudson County, New Jersey (54 percent); Los Angeles County, California; and Bronx County, New York (54 percent each) (*Speaking a Language Other Than English*, 2001).

Nationwide, the Asian-language market includes more than 300 newspapers (92 dailies), 50 radio programs, 75 television shows, and miscellaneous products such as phone directories. By the mid-1990s one Orange County, California, station was broadcasting in Vietnamese 18 hours a day, and another southern California station was entirely Korean-language (Trumbull, 1995). One company publishes a Chinese-language Yellow Pages for New York City (Dortch, 1997).

Where Ethnic Families Live

By 2000, foreign-born groups surpassed the national average of 10 percent in nine states: California (26 percent), New York (20 percent), Florida (18 percent), Hawaii (16 percent), Nevada and New Jersey (15 percent each), Arizona (13 percent), and Massachusetts and Texas (12 percent each) (Schmidley, 2001).

Except for some parts of the Midwest, ethnic families live in all parts of the country but tend to cluster in certain regions. Such clustering reflects job opportunities and established immigrant communities that can help newcomers find housing and jobs. In other cases, past federal government policies have encouraged some communities to accept refugees from Southeast Asia, forced many American Indians to live on reservations, and implemented a variety of exclusionary immigration laws that concentrated some Asian groups to specific geographic areas. Overall,

■ Approximately 53 percent of blacks live in the South, about 10 percent are in the West, and the remaining 37 percent are split evenly between the Midwest and Northeast.

■ More than half of Latinos, many of whom are from Mexico, reside in California and Texas. Nearly 60 percent of recent Latino immigrants in Washington, D.C., identify themselves as Central Americans, and about 31 describe themselves as Salvadorans.

■ A majority of Asians and Pacific Islanders (57 percent) live in just three states: California, New York, and Hawaii.

■ More than 60 percent of Chinese Americans live in California or New York. About two-thirds of Filipinos and Japanese live in California or Hawaii. Asian Indian and Korean families are somewhat less concentrated geographically, although large numbers live in a handful of states that include Illinois, New Jersey, Texas, California, and New York.

- About 48 percent of American Indians, Eskimos, and Aleuts are concentrated in the West. Many (13 percent) live in Oklahoma. The next most likely states of residence include Arizona, California, New Mexico, and Alaska (Benokraitis, 2002).

This brief overview shows that ethnic families are numerous and increasing, speak many languages (though primarily Spanish), and live in practically every state.

Why Are Families Changing?

Clearly, we are seeing changes in the family. These changes reflect both the choices people make (such as choosing to marry later or to divorce) and the constraints that limit those choices (such as economic problems or caring for elderly parents).

To study people's choices, social scientists often take a **micro-level perspective,** focusing on individuals' social interaction in specific settings. To understand the constraints that limit people's options, social scientists use a **macro-level perspective,** focusing on large-scale patterns that characterize society as a whole. Both perspectives and how they interact are crucial in understanding the family.

Micro-Level Influences on the Family

Consider the following scenario: Two students meet in college, fall in love, marry after graduation, find well-paying jobs, and live the good life, feasting on brie and lobster, driving a Corvette, and the like. Then they have an unplanned child. The wife quits her job to take care of the baby, the husband loses his job, and the wife goes to work part time. She has difficulty balancing her multiple roles of mother, wife, and employee. The stress and arguments between the partners increase, and the marriage ends.

When I ask my students what went wrong, most of them take a micro viewpoint and criticize the individuals: "They should have saved some money," "They didn't need a Corvette," "Haven't they heard about contraceptives?" and so on. Almost all my students blame the divorce on the two people involved because they were unrealistic or immature or made "lousy" decisions.

On the one hand, there's much to be said for micro-level perspectives. As you will see throughout this book, some of the biggest societal changes that have had a major impact on families began with the efforts of one person who took a stand on an issue. For example, Mary Beth Whitehead refused to give up her right to see the baby she bore as a surrogate mother. The ensuing court battles created national debates about the ethics of the new reproductive technologies. As a result, many states have instituted surrogacy legislation.

On the other hand, micro explanations should be kept in perspective. Many marriage and family textbooks and pop psychology books stress the importance of individual choices but ignore macro-level variables. Micro analyses are limited. They cannot explain some of the things over which families have very little control. For these broader analyses, we must turn to macro explanations.

■ Macro-Level Influences on the Family

Constraints such as economic forces, technological innovations, popular culture, social movements, and family policies limit our choices. These are broad social issues that require macro-level explanations.

Economic Forces

The Industrial Revolution and urbanization sparked widespread changes that affected the family. By the late eighteenth century, factories replaced the local industries that had employed large numbers of women and children. As families became less self-sufficient and family members worked outside the home, parents' control over their children diminished.

In the latter half of the twentieth century, many corporations moved their companies to developing countries to increase their profits. Such moves resulted in relocations and unemployment for many U.S. workers. These changes created job dissatisfaction, unemployment, and financial distress that disrupted many marital relationships and families.

Many African Americans have been concerned that immigration, another external factor, is diminishing their job opportunities. As you've just read, Latinos and Asians constitute the fastest-growing groups in the United States. A large proportion of African Americans are employed in skilled and semiskilled blue-collar jobs. The influx of new immigrants, who are also competing for such jobs, constitutes a serious economic threat to many working-class blacks and, consequently, to their families.

As the U.S. economy has shifted, millions of low-paying service jobs have replaced higher-paying manufacturing jobs. This has wrought havoc with many families' finances, contributing to the rise in the number of employed mothers. At the other end of the continuum, the high-tech sector requires people to spend more time learning new skills. Learning new skills often means postponing marriage and having children.

Technological Innovations

Advances in medical and other health-related technologies have led to a decline in birth rates and to a longer life. On the one hand, the invention and availability of the birth-control pill in the early 1960s meant that women could prevent unwanted pregnancies, pursue a higher education, and seek long-term jobs. Improved prenatal and postnatal care has also released women from the need to bear six or seven children so that one or two will survive.

On the other hand, because the average man or woman can now expect to live into his or her 80s and beyond, poverty after retirement is more likely. Medical services can eat up savings, and the middle-aged—sometimes called the "sandwich generation"—cope with both raising their own children and helping their aged parents.

Televisions, videocassette recorders (VCRs), digital video discs (DVDs), microwave ovens, and personal computers (PCs) have also affected families positively and negatively. On the negative side, for example, multiple television sets in a home often dilute parental control and supervision of programs that young children watch.

On the positive side, television can enhance children's intellectual development. For example, children aged 2 to 7 who spend a few hours a week watching educational programs such as *Sesame Street, Mister Rogers' Neighborhood, Reading Rainbow, Captain Kangaroo, Mr. Wizard's World,* and *3-2-1 Contact* have higher academic test scores three years later than those who didn't watch such educational programs. Children who watch many hours of entertainment programs and cartoons have lower test scores than those who rarely watch such programs.

The positive effects of educational programming are strongest for children aged 2 and 3. TV may have a greater impact on young children because they are less likely than older children to have formal preschool instruction (Wright et al., 2001). During adolescence, television provides a common source of interest that peers discuss and can share with their parents. Television also provides useful information about other cultures and a variety of work roles.

Some people feel that electronic mail (e-mail) and discussion lists are intrusive because enthusiasts replace close offline relationships with superficial but time-consuming online relationships. College students who spend four to seven hours a day online for nonacademic reasons may earn low grades and experience the risk of dismissal, poorer health because of sleep loss, and greater social isolation. Among other problems, frequent Internet usage decreases participation in extracurricular activities and opportunities to meet new people (Reisberg, 2000). In the general population, people who spend more than ten hours a week on the Internet report a decrease in social activities and less time talking on the phone to friends and family (Nie and Erbring, 2000).

On the other hand, e-mail has encouraged long-distance conversations between parents, children, and relatives that might otherwise not occur because of busy schedules or high telephone costs. Family members who are scattered coast to coast can become more connected by exchanging photos on their own Web pages (including background music and voice commentary), organizing family reunions, tracking down distant relatives, or tracing their ancestral roots (Kanaley, 2000).

Popular Culture

Popular culture—which includes television, pop music, magazines, radio, advertising, sports, hobbies, fads, fashions, and movies—is one of our major sources of information *and* misinformation about our values, roles, and family life. Television is especially influential in transmitting both facts and fictions. According to TV-Free America, a national nonprofit organization, in a 65-year lifetime the average American spends 9 years in front of a TV set (www.tvturnoff.org).

Compared with even five years ago, today there are many programs on black families. Even though Asian and Latino families are huge consumers of prime-time television, they're almost invisible, except for an occasional show such as *George Lopez*. In the music industry, some Latino singers such as Ricky Martin, Marc Anthony, Jennifer Lopez, and Shakira are "hot." Nonetheless, they have nothing to do with family shows. And to my knowledge there isn't a single family program that features Asian or Middle Eastern families.

Social Movements

Over the years, a number of social movements have changed family life. These macro-level movements include the civil rights movement, the women's movement, gay rights movement, and, most recently, a marriage movement.

The *civil rights movement* of the 1960s had a great impact on most U.S. families, black and white. Because of affirmative action legislation, many African Americans and Latinos were able to take advantage of educational and economic opportunities that improved their families' socioeconomic status. As a result, many black and Latino students got into privileged colleges and universities, families received money for small businesses, and a number of bright employees were promoted.

The *women's movements*—in the late 1800s and especially in the 1970s—transformed many women's roles and, consequently, family life. As women gained more rights in law, education, and employment, many became less financially dependent on men and started questioning traditional assumptions about gender roles.

The upside of this is that women—particularly white, middle-class women—enjoyed more personal and professional options and provided their children with less stereotypical female role models. The downside, according to many scholars, is that when women became sexually "liberated," they entered willingly into nonmarital sexual relationships. The result was more out-of-wedlock children who were not supported by their biological fathers.

The *gay rights movement* that began in the 1970s challenged discriminatory laws in such areas as housing, adoption, and employment. Many lesbian women and gay men (as well as sympathetic heterosexuals) feel that the challenges have resulted in very modest changes so far. There has been progress, however. Children with gay or lesbian parents, for example, are less likely to be as stigmatized as they were a decade ago. Many companies now provide benefits to the gay or lesbian partners of employees, a number of adoption agencies assist lesbians and gays who want to become parents, and numerous municipalities or states now recognize civil unions.

People who are alarmed by marital dissolution and the increase in cohabitation rates are joining a burgeoning *marriage movement*. Among other things, the marriage movement seeks to repeal no-fault divorce laws, to reduce the rates and state benefits for out-of-wedlock children, to promote abstinence among young people, to increase funding on marriage-supportive research, and to embrace women's homemaker roles.

In addition, the marriage movement encourages proponents to lobby lawmakers to pass state "covenant marriage" laws requiring couples to take mandatory premarital counseling classes and "marital skills" programs.

Communitarians, a group that you met earlier in this chapter, support the marriage movement and similar organizations. They believe that most current social problems (such as juvenile delinquency, high divorce rates, and high out-of-wedlock birth rates) could be solved by promoting "traditional" family values. These values include enhancing marital stability, reinforcing parental responsibility, reining in children's premature sexualization, and curbing the excessive societywide individualism that endangers many children's well-being (see Elshtain et al., 1993). In contrast, many liberals believe that numerous family problems are due to macro-level forces, such as government policies that subsidize middle-class families but penalize poor and working-class families.

Family Policies

Government policy affects practically every aspect of family life. Thousands of rules and regulations, both civil and criminal—at the local, state, and federal levels—govern domestic matters: laws about when and whom we can marry, how to dissolve a marriage, how children will fare after a divorce, how we treat one another in the home, and even how we dispose of our dead.

Families do not just passively accept policy changes, however. Parents have played critical roles in such major social policy changes as the education of disabled children and joint custody of children after divorce.

A Cross-Cultural and Global Perspective

Why does this textbook include material on U.S. subcultures (American Indians, African Americans, Asian Americans, Middle Eastern Americans, and Latinos) and on cultures in other countries? First, unless you are a full-blooded American Indian, your kin were slaves or immigrants to this country. They contributed their cultural beliefs, and their practices shaped current family institutions. Modern U.S. families are a mosaic of many cultural, religious, ethnic, racial, and socioeconomic groups. A traditional white, middle-class model is not adequate for understanding our marriages and families.

A second reason for this multicultural and cross-cultural approach is that the world is shrinking. Compared with even ten years ago, more people are traveling outside the United States, more students from abroad attend North American colleges and universities, and more exchange programs for students and scholars are offered at all educational levels. In the late twentieth century, the Internet changed our communication processes significantly, shrinking our modern world. As members of the global community, we should be aware of family practices and customs in other cultures.

A third reason for this text's perspective is that U.S. businesses are continuing to recognize the importance of understanding cross-cultural differences. Since the late 1980s, more companies have been requiring their employees to take crash courses about other cultures before they are sent abroad. For example, one of my students who won a job with a Fortune 500 company felt she had gained an edge over some very tough competition because of her knowledge of Portuguese and of Brazil's cultural institutions.

The business sector is not the only one that has learned to appreciate diversity. Many educators believe that multicultural competence is essential to the professional preparation of researchers, faculty, counselors, and therapists who will study and interact with people from many different socioeconomic and national backgrounds in the twenty-first century.

Finally, understanding the customs of other countries challenges our notion that U.S. marriage forms are "natural" or inevitable. According to Hutter (1998: 12), "Americans have been notorious for their lack of understanding and ignorance of other cultures. This is compounded by their gullible ethnocentric belief in the superiority of all things American and not only has made them unaware of how others live and think but also has given them a distorted picture of their own life." Hutter's perspective—and that of this book—is that understanding other people helps us understand ourselves.

CONCLUSION

Families are transforming rather than destroying themselves. Although there have been *changes* in family structures, families of all kinds want caring, supportive, comforting, and enduring relationships. There is nothing inherently better about one type of family form over another. Family structures don't appear by themselves. People create families that meet their needs for love and security.

These greatly expanded *choices* in family structure and function mean that the definition of family no longer reflects the interests of any one social class, gender, or ethnic group. This fluidity generates new questions. Who, for example, will ensure that our children will grow up to be healthy and responsible adults if both parents must work outside the home? Is it possible to pursue personal happiness without sacrificing our obligations to other family members?

Our choices often are limited by *constraints*, especially at the macro level, because of economic and political policies. To deal with changes, choices, and constraints, we need as much information as possible about the family. In the next chapter we will see how scientists conduct research on families, gathering data that make it possible for us to track the trends described in this and other chapters and to make informed decisions about our choices.

SUMMARY

1. Although the nuclear family—composed of husband, wife, and children—is still predominant in U.S. society, the definition of *family* has been challenged to include such less traditional arrangements as single parents, childless couples, foster parents, and siblings sharing a home. Advances in reproductive technology have opened up the possibility of still more varied redefinitions of the family.

2. The family continues to fulfill basic functions such as producing and socializing children, providing family members with emotional support, legitimizing and regulating sexual activity, and placing family members in society.

3. Marriages, families, and kinship systems vary in terms of whether marriages are monogamous or polygamous, whether familial authority is vested in the man or in the woman or both share power, and whether a new family resides with the family of the man or of the woman or creates its own home.

4. The many deep-rooted myths about the family include erroneous beliefs about how the family was in "the good old days," the "naturalness" of marriage and family as human interpersonal and social arrangements, the self-sufficiency of the family, the family as a refuge from outside pressures, and the "perfect family."

5. Social scientists generally agree that the family is changing. They disagree, however, as to whether it is changing in drastic and essentially unhealthy ways, whether it is simply continuing to adapt and adjust to changing circumstances, or whether it is changing in ways that will ultimately make the family stronger.

6. Many changes are occurring in U.S. families: There is more racial and ethnic diversity, membership is more varied than the traditional nuclear family, and there are more single-parent families, stepfamilies, and families in which the mother works outside the home.

7. The reasons for changes in the family can be analyzed on two levels. Micro-level explanations emphasize individual behavior: the choices that people make and the personal and interpersonal factors that influence these choices. Macro-level explanations focus on large-scale patterns that characterize society as a whole and often constrain individual options. Some constraints arise from economic factors, technological advances, the popular culture, social movements, and government policies that affect families.

8. Understanding the family requires an appreciation of racial, gender, ethnic, religious, and cultural diversity, both at home and around the world.

KEY TERMS

marriage
norm
common-law marriage
bigamy
family
fictive kin
nuclear family
incest taboo
endogamy

exogamy
socialization
roles
primary groups
secondary groups
social class
family of orientation
family of procreation
kinship system

extended family
monogamy
serial monogamy
polygamy
baby boomers
micro-level perspective
macro-level perspective

INDEX

NOTES

NOTES

NOTES

NOTES